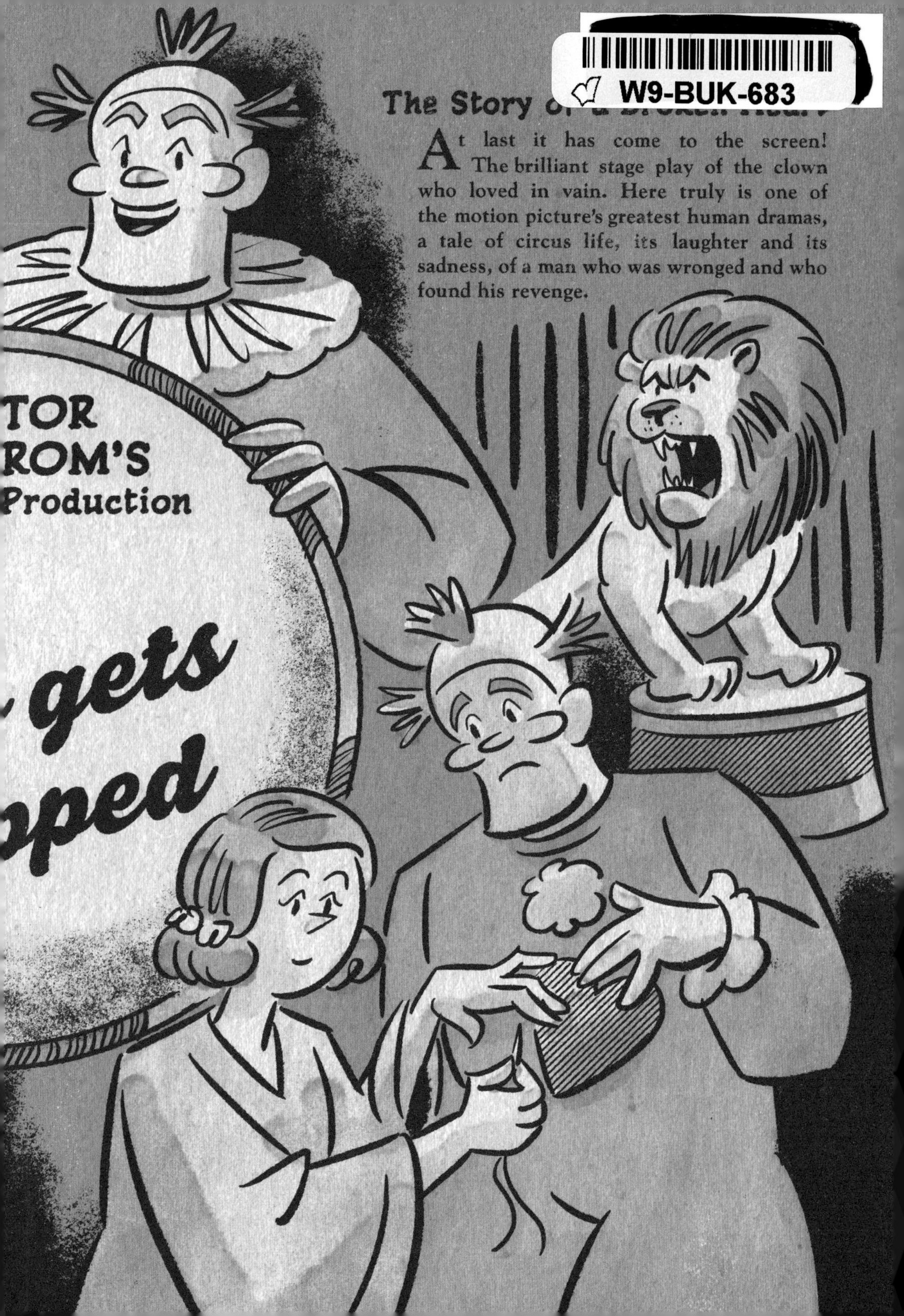
The Story
At last it has come to the screen! The brilliant stage play of the clown who loved in vain. Here truly is one of the motion picture's greatest human dramas, a tale of circus life, its laughter and its sadness, of a man who was wronged and who found his revenge.
Production
gets

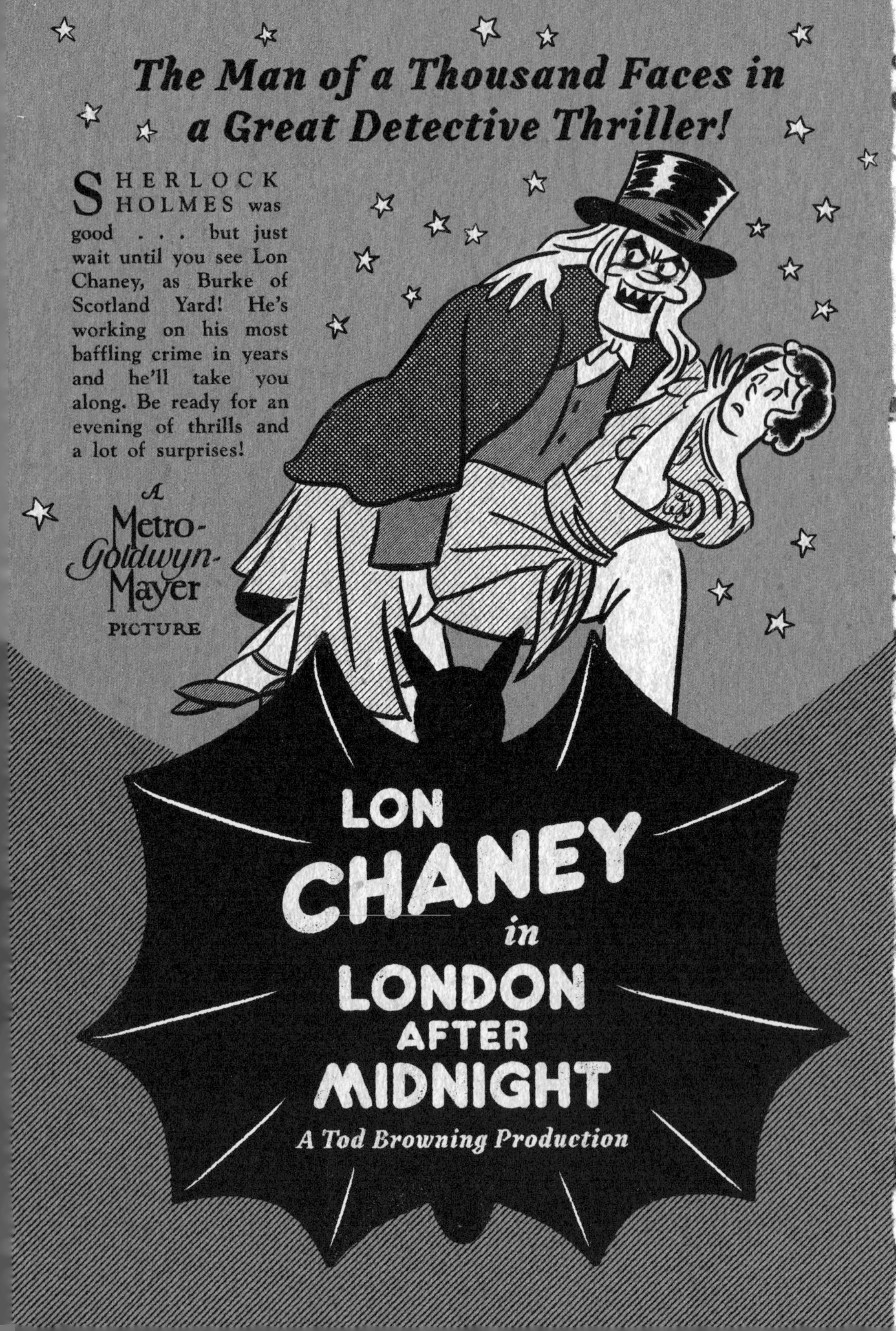
The Man of a Thousand Faces in a Great Detective Thriller!
SHERLOCK HOLMES was good . . . but just wait until you see Lon Chaney, as Burke of Scotland Yard! He's working on his most baffling crime in years and he'll take you along. Be ready for an evening of thrills and a lot of surprises!
A Metro-Goldwyn-Mayer PICTURE
LON CHANEY in LONDON AFTER MIDNIGHT
A Tod Browning Production

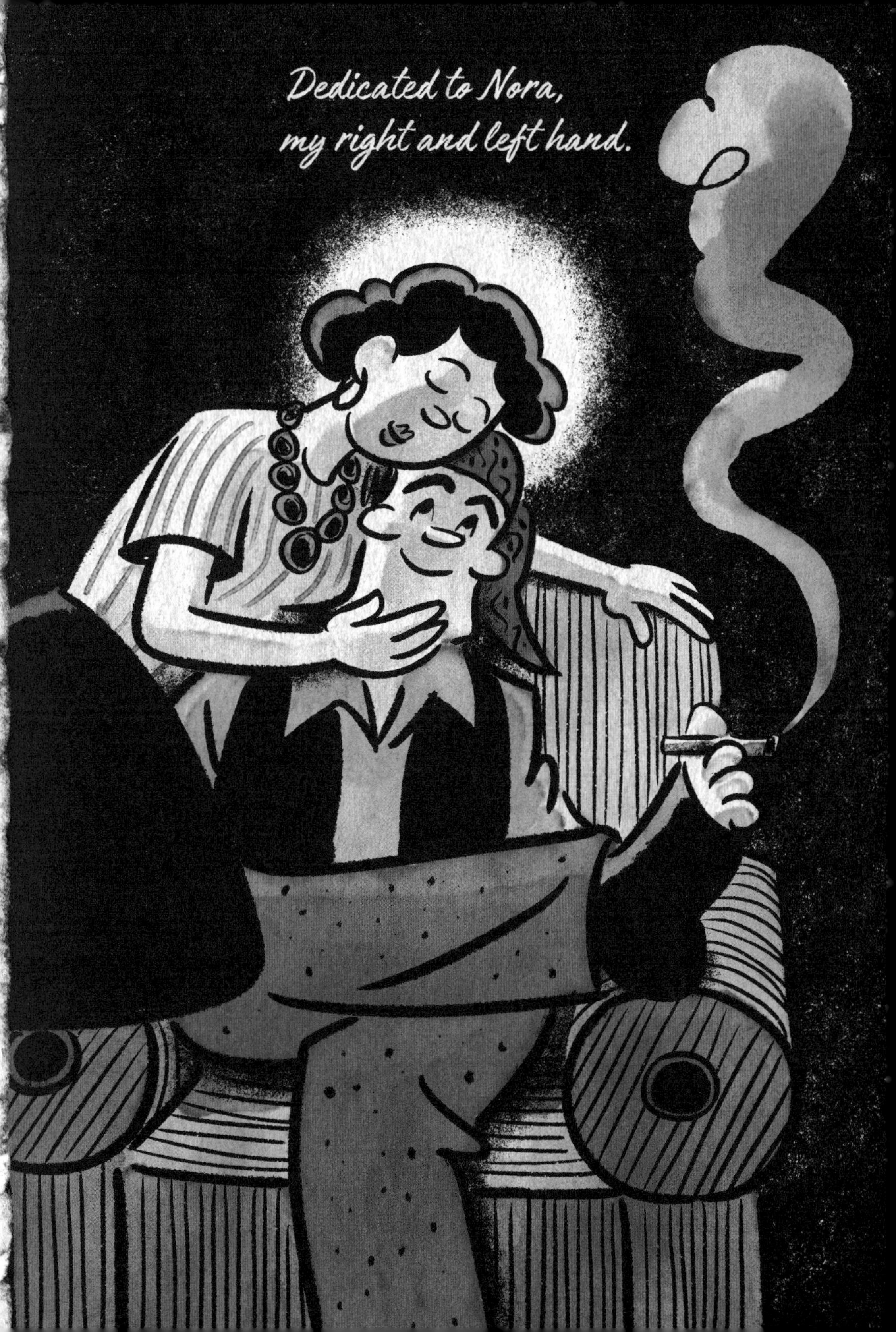
Dedicated to Nora,
my right and left hand.

LON CHANEY

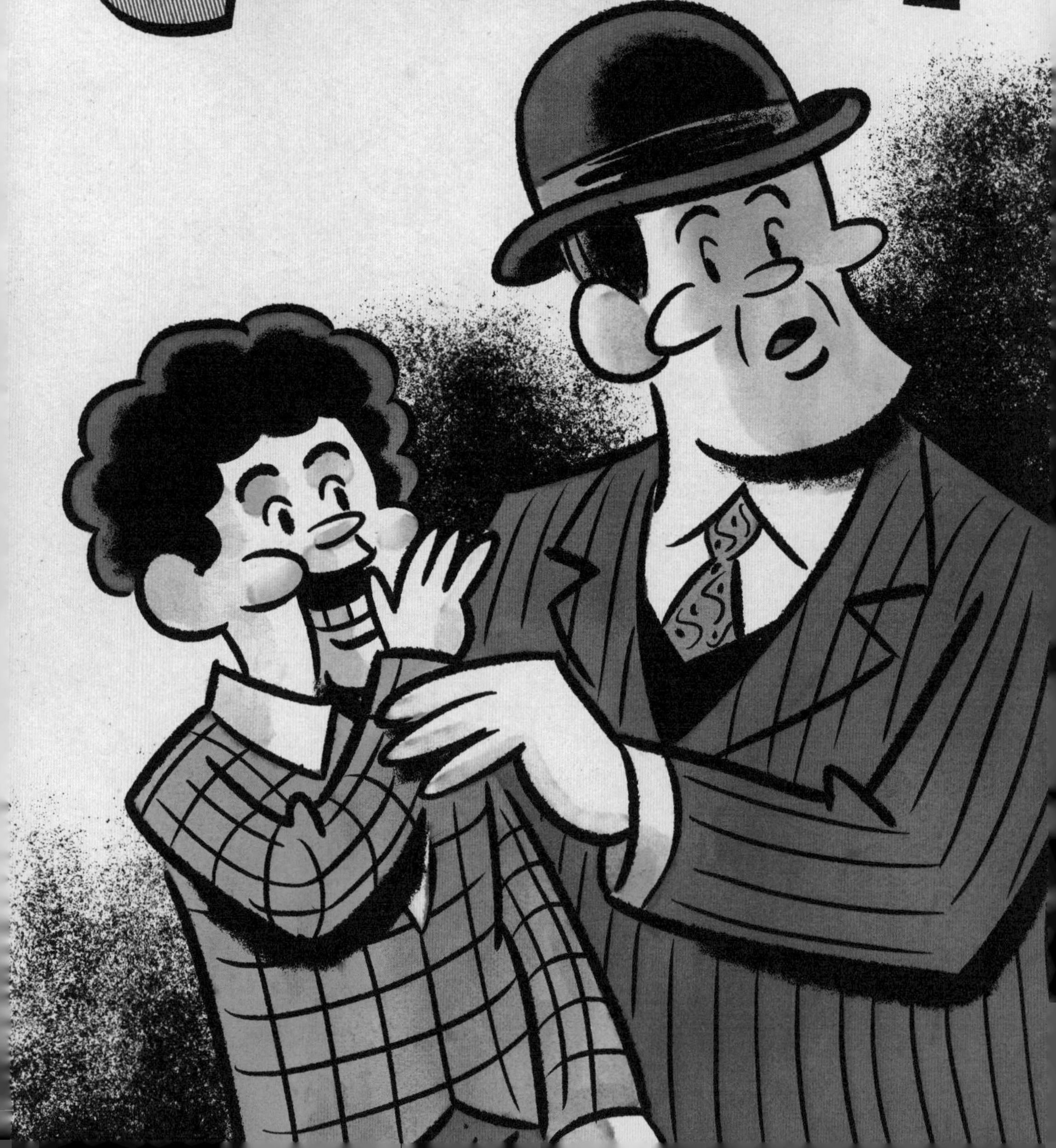

SPEAKS

BY PAT DORIAN

PANTHEON BOOKS
NEW YORK

A NOTE FROM THE AUTHOR

"No one will ever love you!"

THIS IS AN UNSPOKEN FEAR THAT MANY OF US HAVE, AND I THINK IT'S THE REASON WHY LON CHANEY'S FILMS, MADE DURING THE SILENT ERA, REMAIN RELEVANT. CHANEY, KNOWN FOR HIS SENSITIVE PORTRAYAL OF OUTSIDERS, WAS ONE OF CINEMA'S GREATEST ACTORS. AUDIENCES REALLY FELT QUASIMODO'S ANGUISH AS HE WAS SCORNED BY THE MOB. CHANEY PROVED THAT EVEN THE MOST UNLIKABLE CHARACTERS COULD REDEEM THEMSELVES AND WERE DESERVING OF OUR EMPATHY.

"THE MAN OF A THOUSAND FACES" WAS A MAGICIAN WITH MAKEUP LONG BEFORE MAKEUP ARTISTS EXISTED. HIS TALENT AND CREATIVITY MADE HIM AN INTERNATIONAL STAR BY THE 1930S, BUT HE CHOSE TO KEEP HIS PERSONAL LIFE HIDDEN. HE RARELY GAVE INTERVIEWS, PREFERRED NOT TO BE PHOTOGRAPHED WITHOUT MAKEUP, AND HARDLY EVER ATTENDED HOLLYWOOD'S GLAMOROUS EVENTS. PERHAPS THIS WAS A CLEVER STRATEGY TO ENTICE AUDIENCES, BUT IT COULD'VE ALSO BEEN AN ACT OF SELF-PRESERVATION. THIS BOOK IS NOT A HISTORICAL DOCUMENT; AN IMAGINED BIOGRAPHY IS MORE ACCURATE. THE STORY IS INSPIRED BY REAL EVENTS AND DRAWN FROM RESEARCH, BUT EVEN TODAY THE MAJORITY OF CHANEY'S LIFE REMAINS A MYSTERY.

—P.D., NYC, 2020

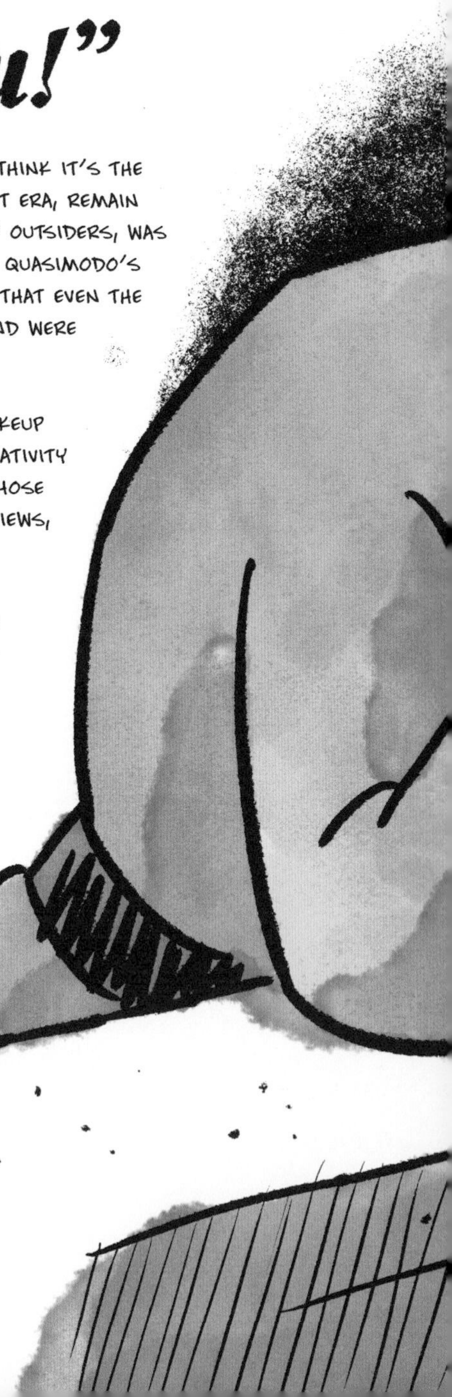

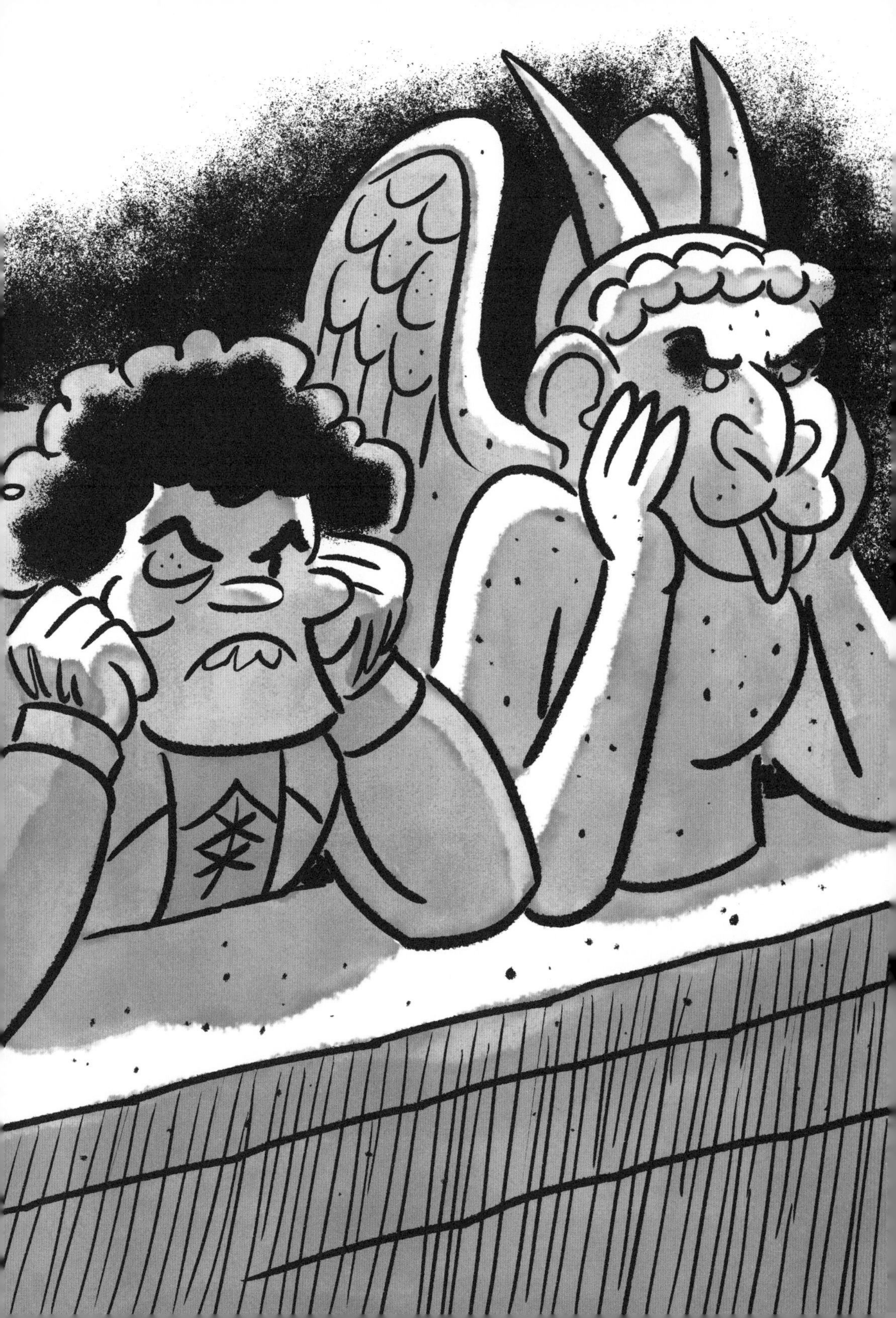

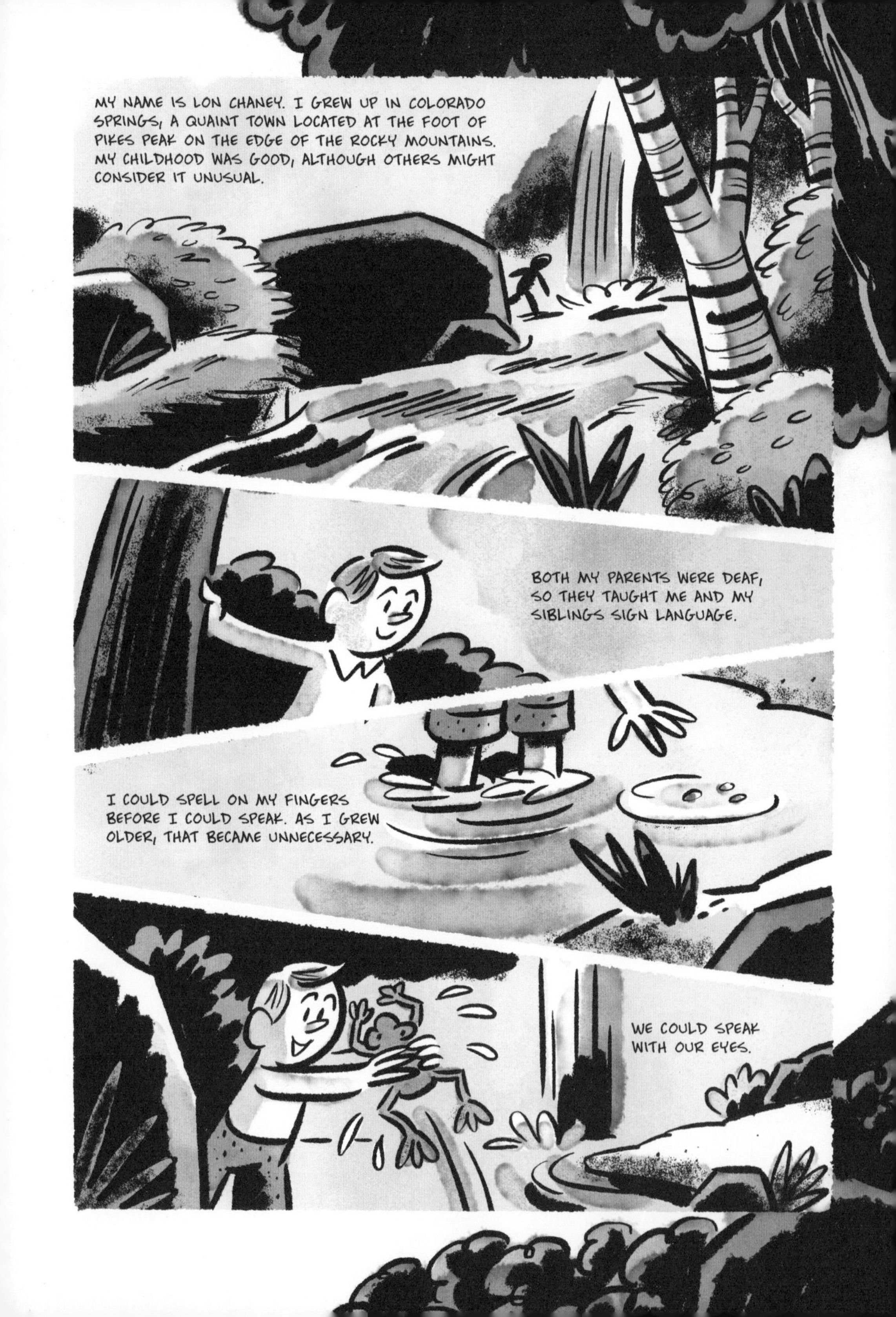
MY NAME IS LON CHANEY. I GREW UP IN COLORADO SPRINGS, A QUAINT TOWN LOCATED AT THE FOOT OF PIKES PEAK ON THE EDGE OF THE ROCKY MOUNTAINS. MY CHILDHOOD WAS GOOD, ALTHOUGH OTHERS MIGHT CONSIDER IT UNUSUAL.
BOTH MY PARENTS WERE DEAF, SO THEY TAUGHT ME AND MY SIBLINGS SIGN LANGUAGE.
I COULD SPELL ON MY FINGERS BEFORE I COULD SPEAK. AS I GREW OLDER, THAT BECAME UNNECESSARY.
WE COULD SPEAK WITH OUR EYES.

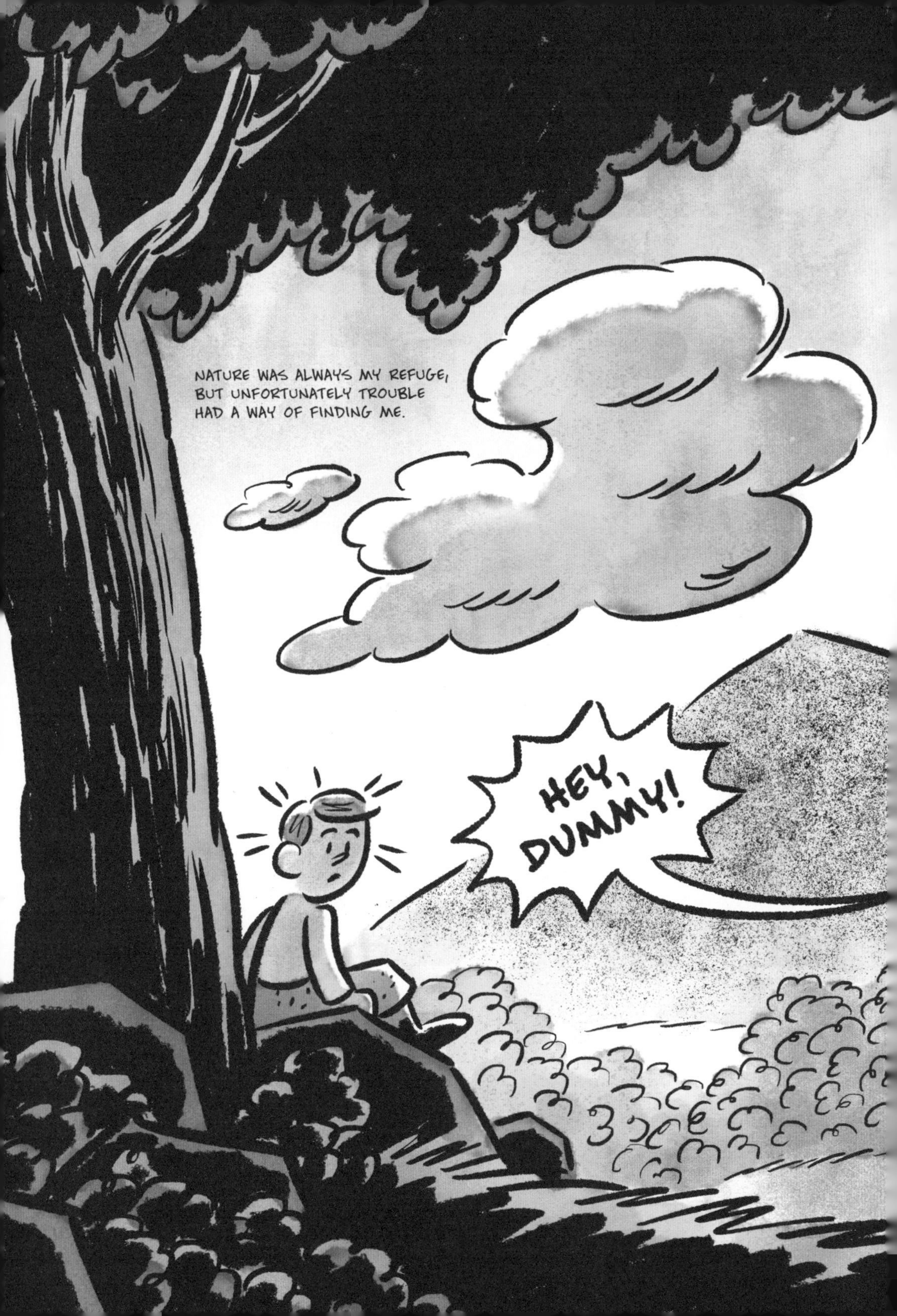
NATURE WAS ALWAYS MY REFUGE, BUT UNFORTUNATELY TROUBLE HAD A WAY OF FINDING ME.
HEY, DUMMY!

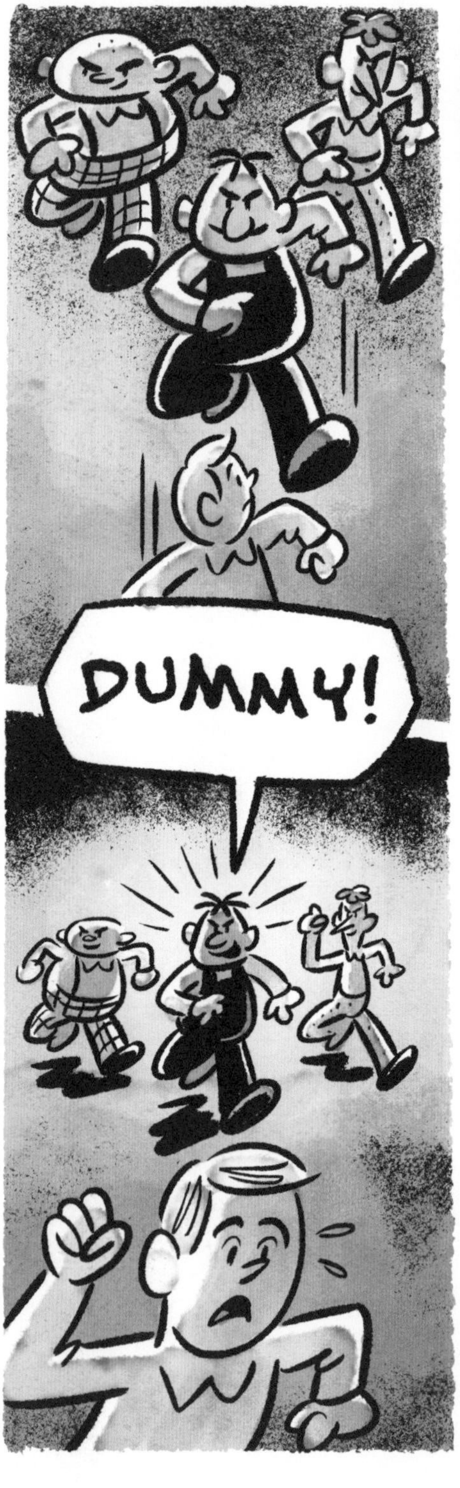
DUMMY!

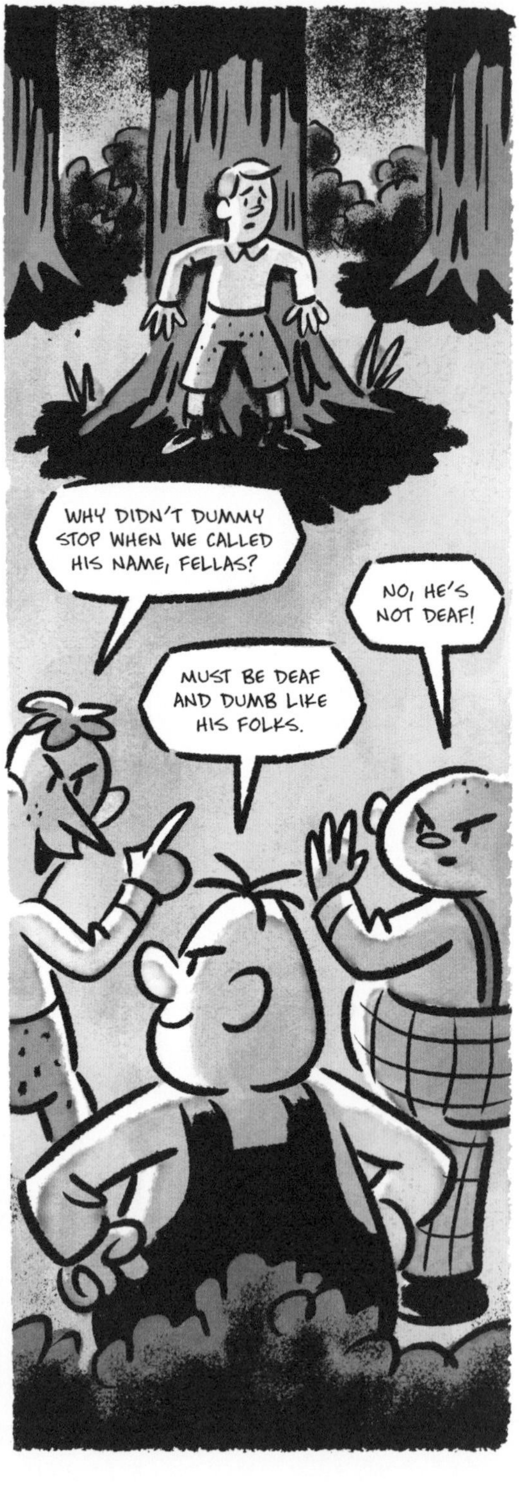
WHY DIDN'T DUMMY STOP WHEN WE CALLED HIS NAME, FELLAS?
MUST BE DEAF AND DUMB LIKE HIS FOLKS.
NO, HE'S NOT DEAF!

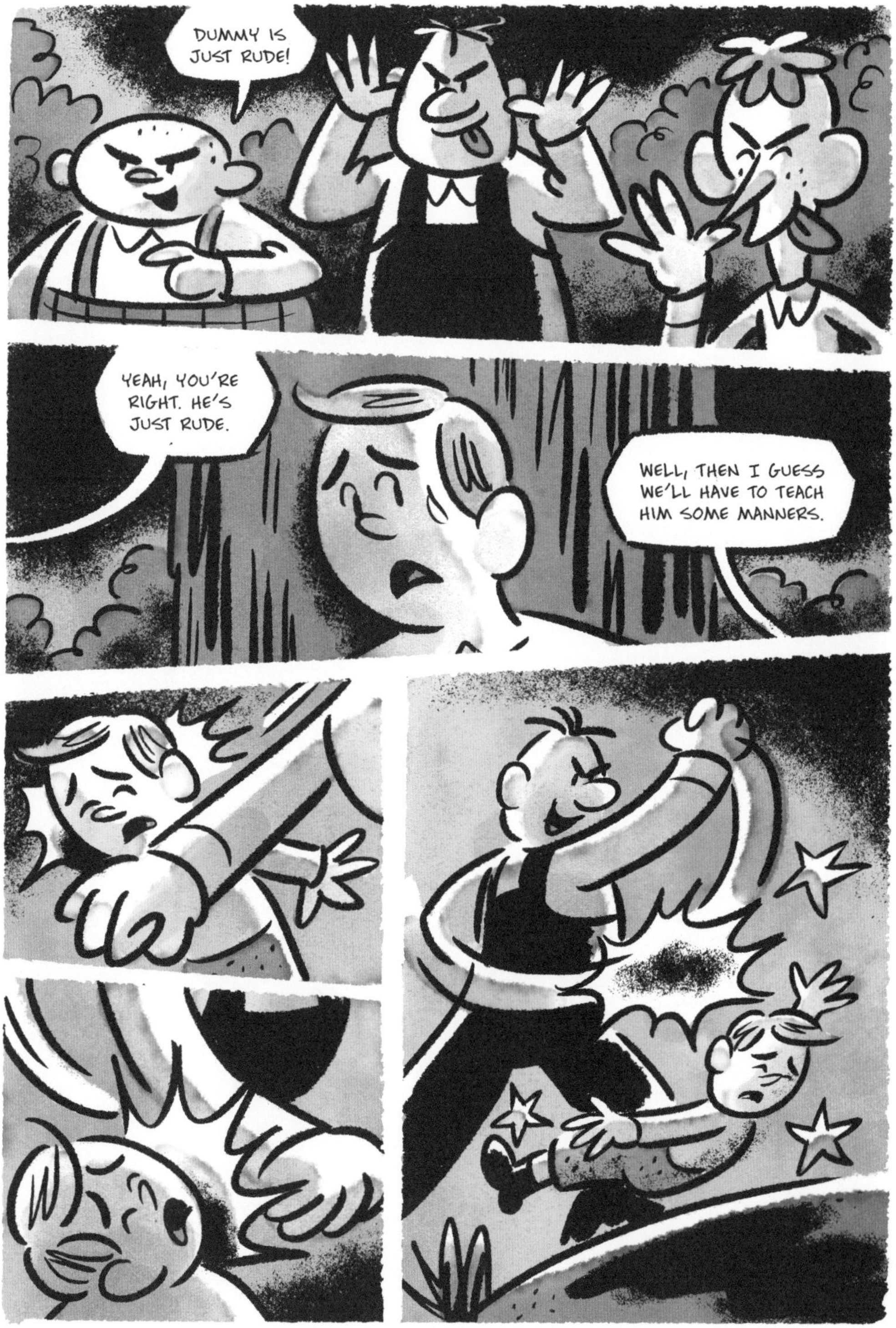
DUMMY IS JUST RUDE!
YEAH, YOU'RE RIGHT. HE'S JUST RUDE.
WELL, THEN I GUESS WE'LL HAVE TO TEACH HIM SOME MANNERS.

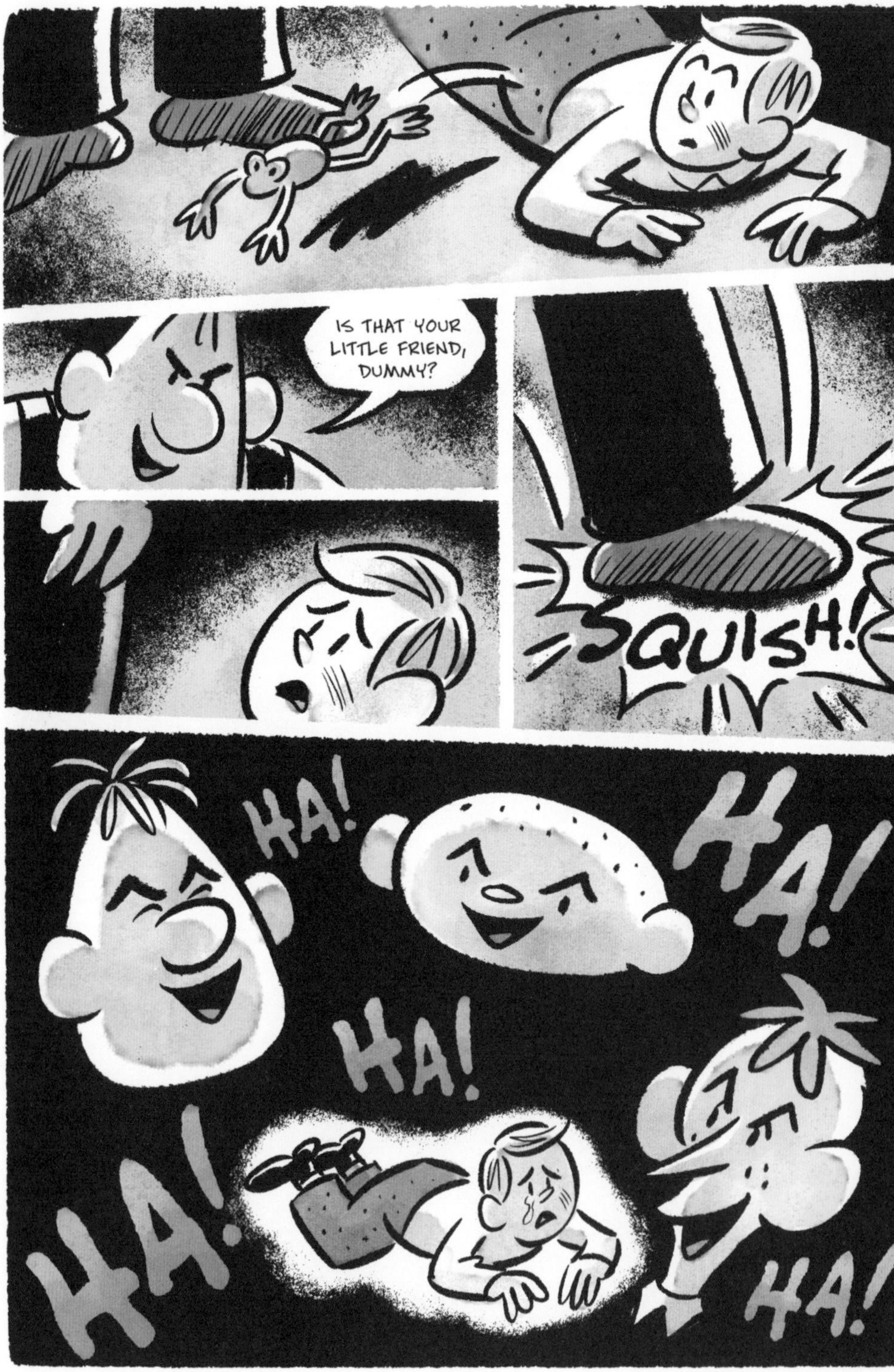
IS THAT YOUR LITTLE FRIEND, DUMMY?
SQUISH!
HA!
HA!
HA!
HA!
HA!

WHEN I WAS IN FOURTH GRADE IT FELL TO ME TO CARE FOR MY BROTHER AND SISTER AND ALSO MY MOM, WHO WAS BEDRIDDEN. BEFORE SHE WAS STRUCK WITH SEVERE RHEUMATOID ARTHRITIS, SHE HAD WORKED AT THE COLORADO SCHOOL FOR THE EDUCATION OF MUTES, FOUNDED BY MY GRANDFATHER. THERE, SHE ALSO DIRECTED PLAYS, WHICH I PERFORMED IN. I DID MY BEST TO KEEP HER SMILING.

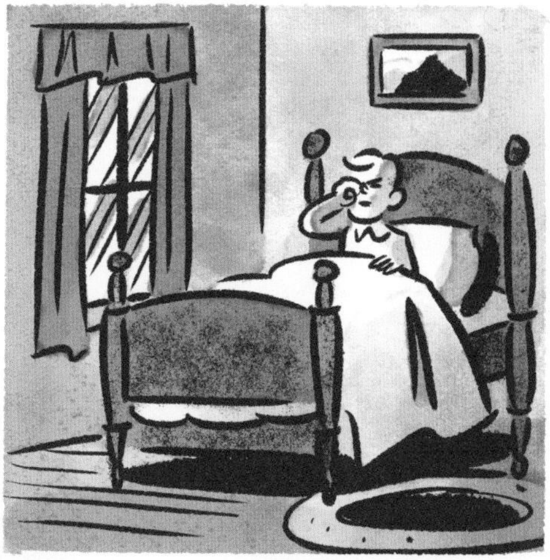

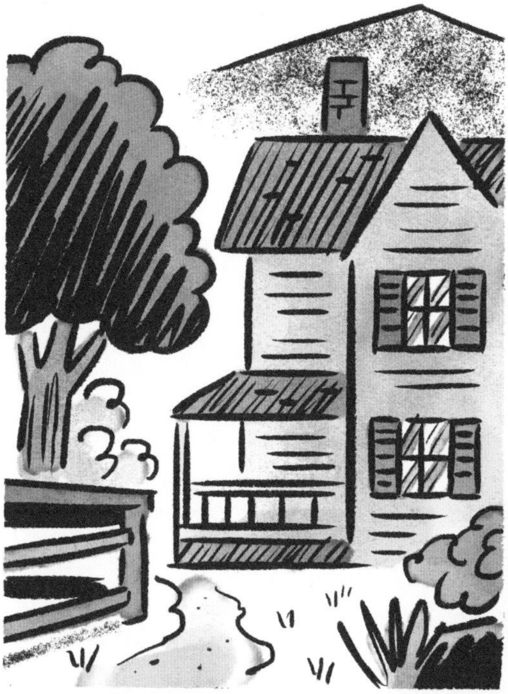

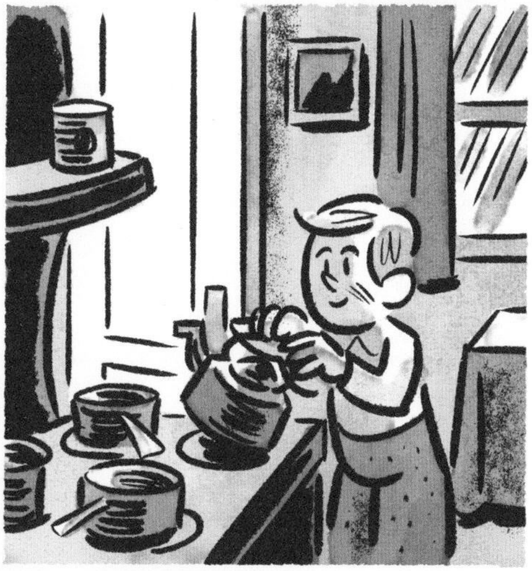

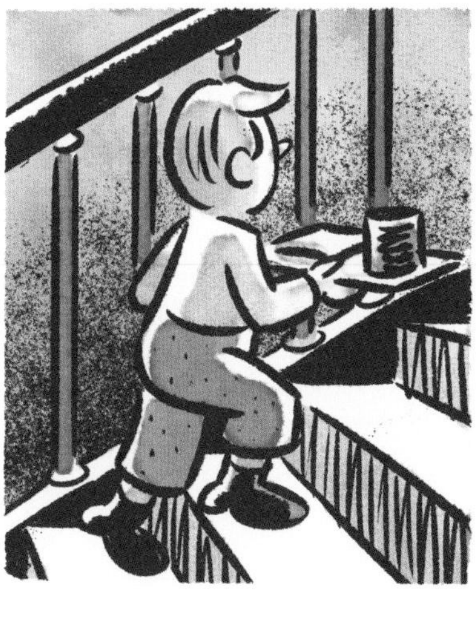

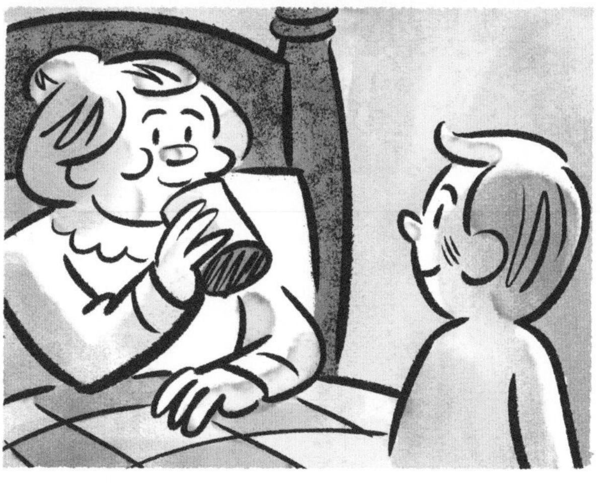

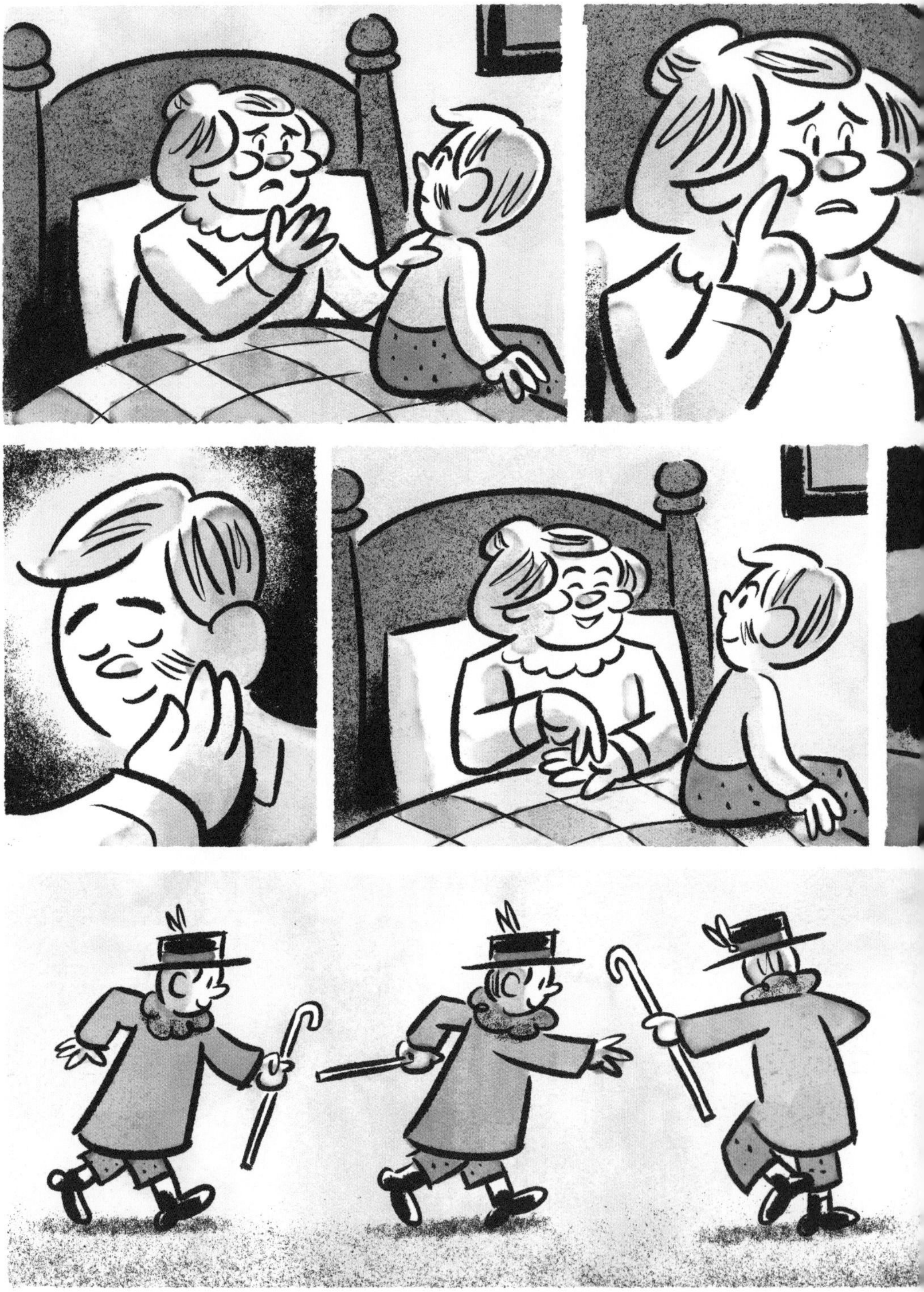

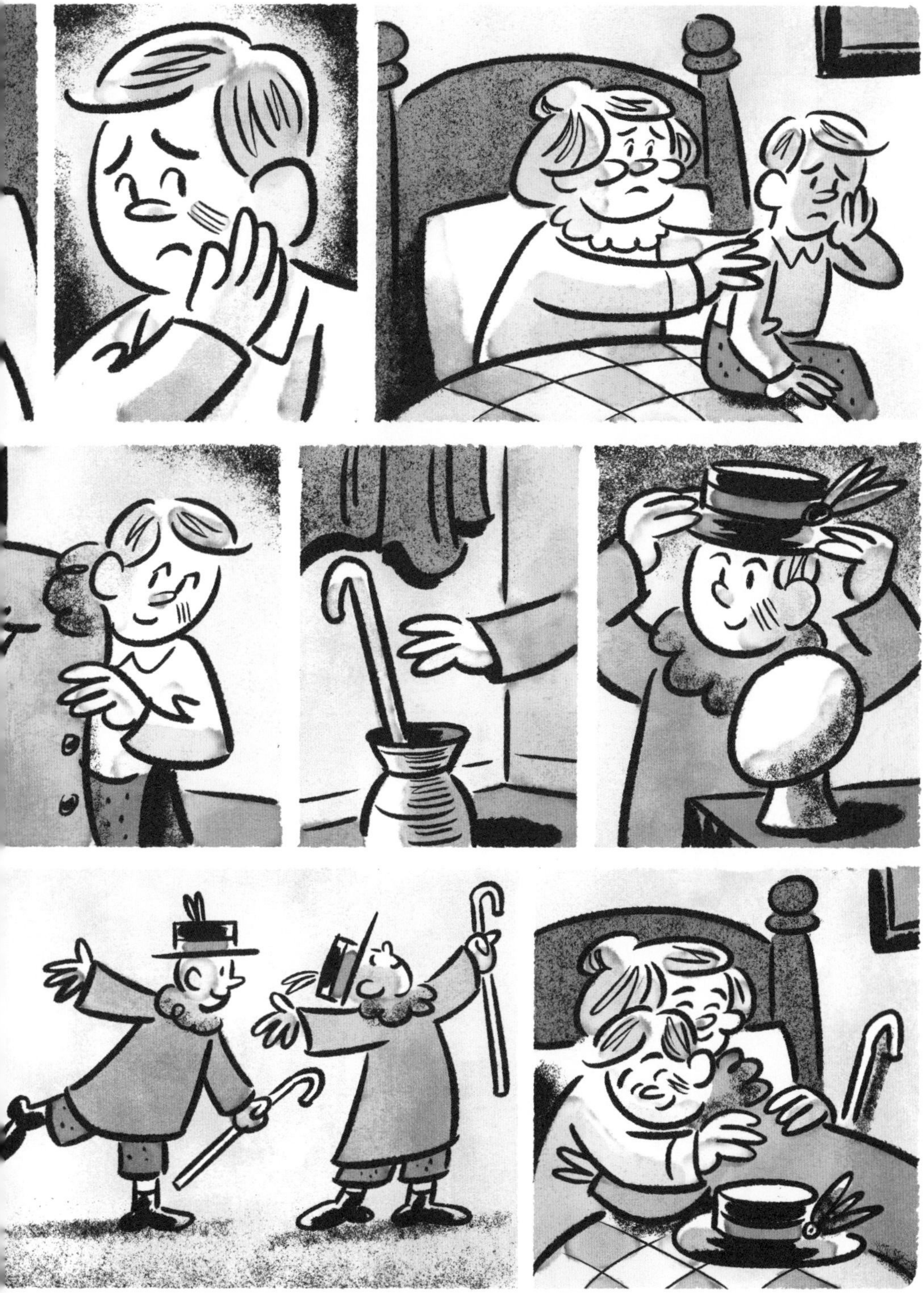

AS I GREW OLDER I CONTINUED TO PERFORM. I WORKED MY WAY UP TO PROP BOY, SCENE SHIFTER, ASSISTANT STAGE DIRECTOR, AND FINALLY STAGE MANAGER. AT TWENTY-ONE, I WENT ON THE ROAD WITH A MUSICAL COMEDY COMPANY. WHILE TRAVELING FROM TOWN TO TOWN, WE PICKED UP A FEW CHORUS GIRLS. ONE OF THOSE CHORUS GIRLS, CLEVA, BECAME MY WIFE. CLEVA'S GOLDEN VOICE MELTED MY HEART. THREE DAYS AFTER WE MET AND WITH THE CONSENT OF HER MOTHER, WE MARRIED.

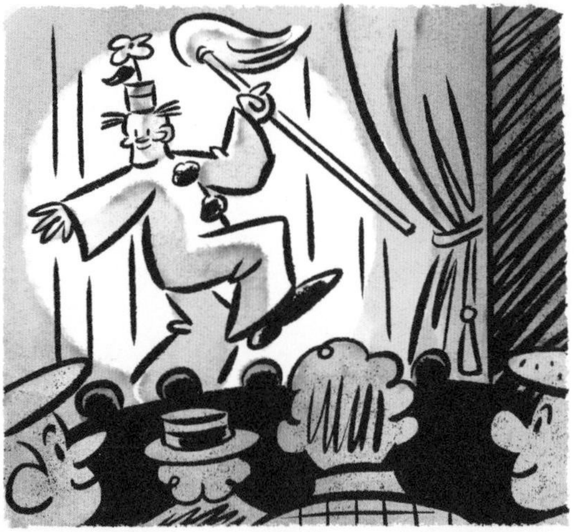

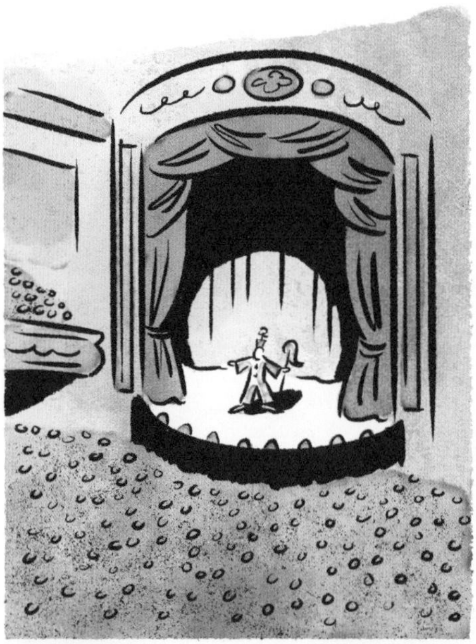

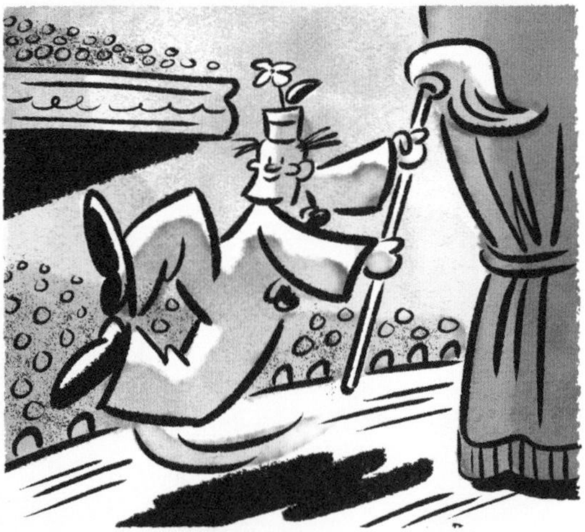

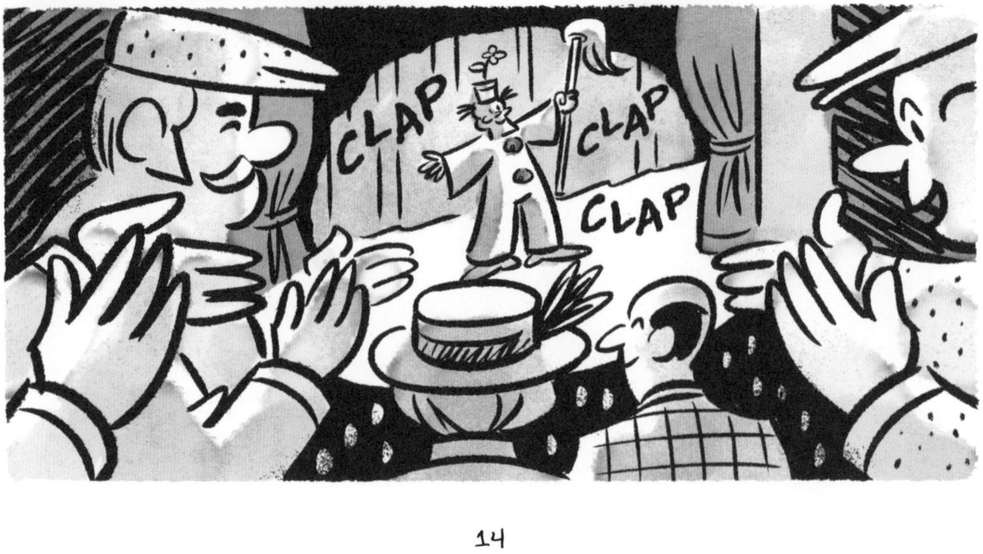
CLAP
CLAP
CLAP

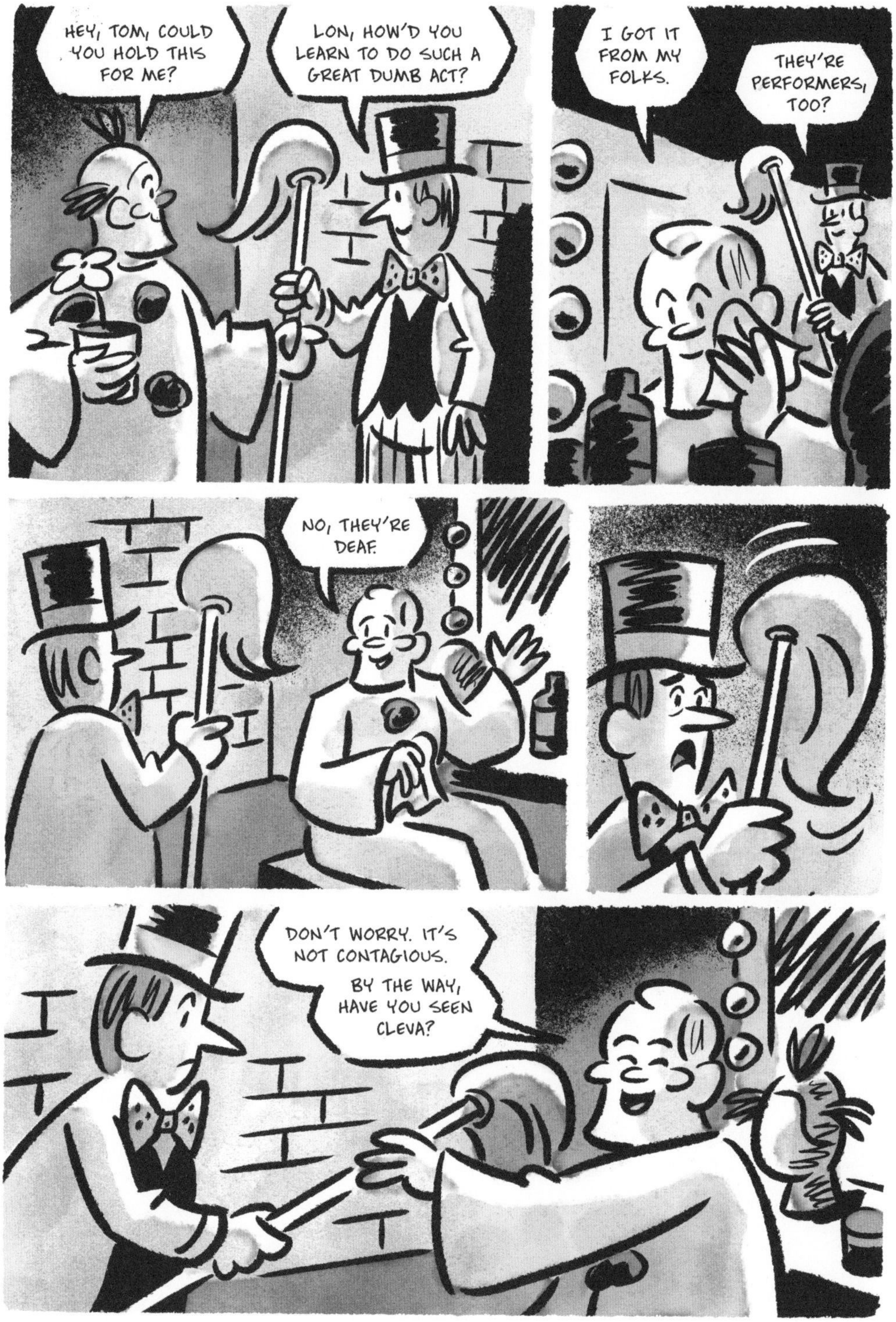
HEY, TOM, COULD YOU HOLD THIS FOR ME?
LON, HOW'D YOU LEARN TO DO SUCH A GREAT DUMB ACT?
I GOT IT FROM MY FOLKS.
THEY'RE PERFORMERS, TOO?
NO, THEY'RE DEAF.
DON'T WORRY. IT'S NOT CONTAGIOUS.
BY THE WAY, HAVE YOU SEEN CLEVA?

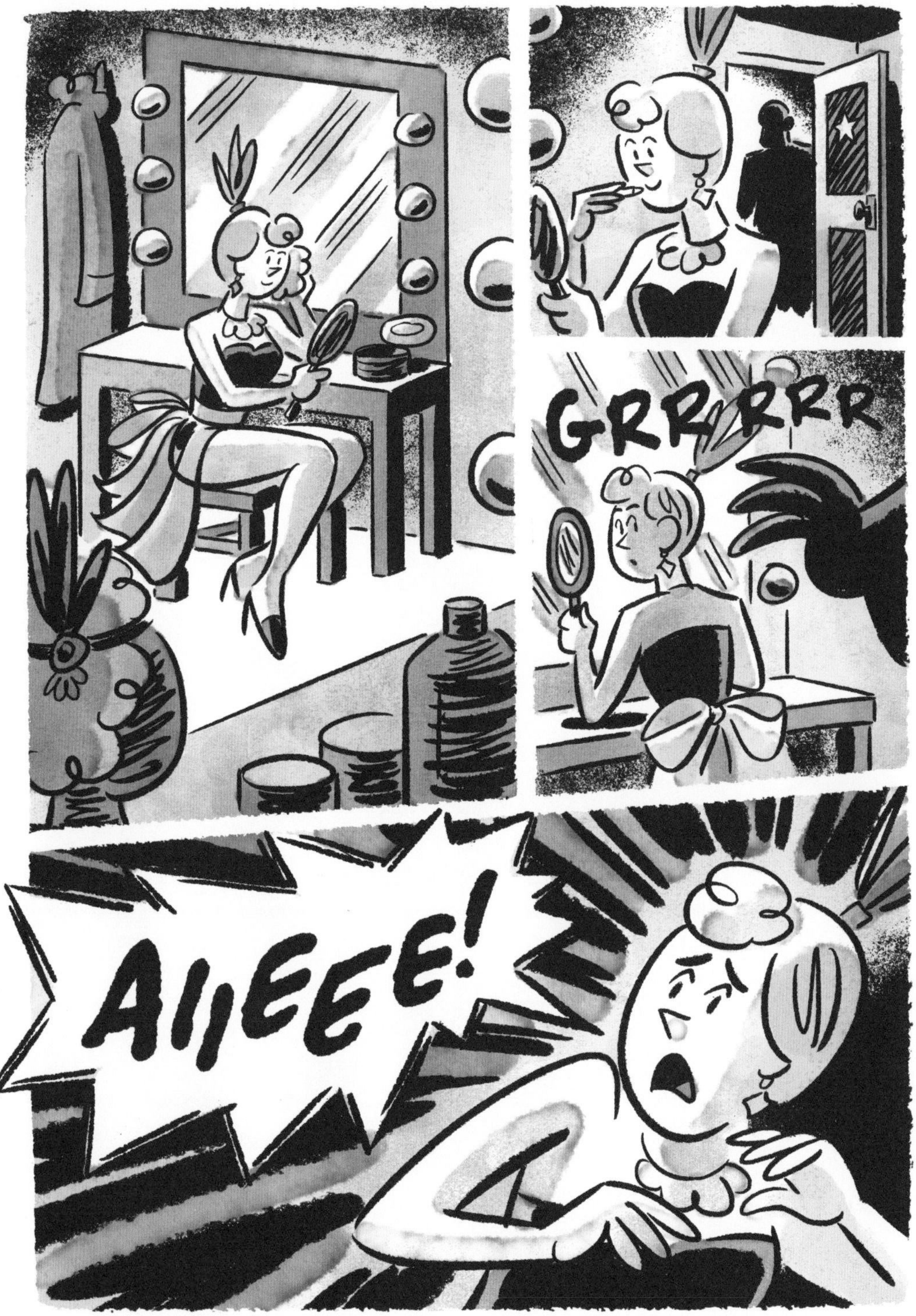
GRRRRRR
AIIEEEE!

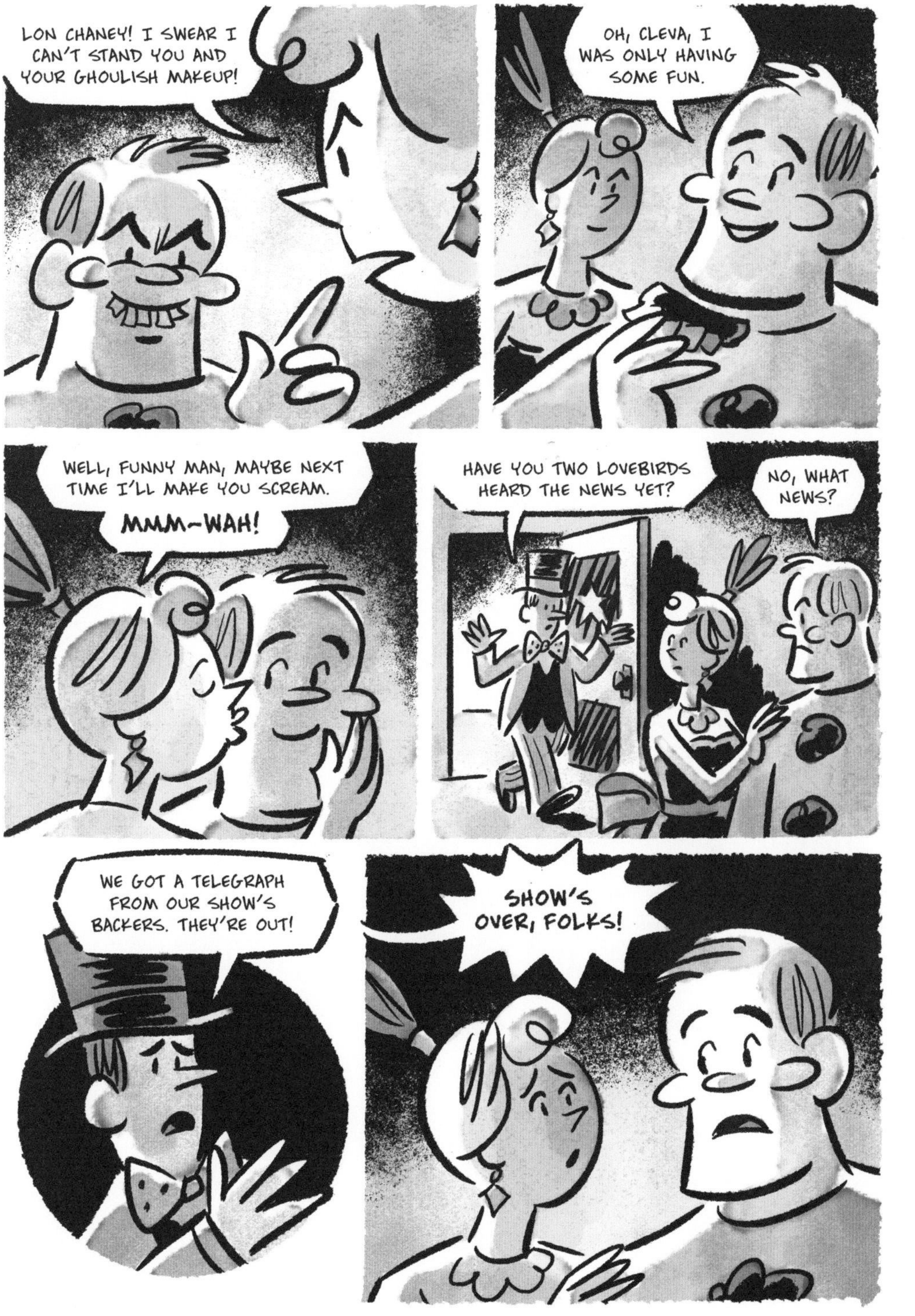
LON CHANEY! I SWEAR I CAN'T STAND YOU AND YOUR GHOULISH MAKEUP!
OH, CLEVA, I WAS ONLY HAVING SOME FUN.
WELL, FUNNY MAN, MAYBE NEXT TIME I'LL MAKE YOU SCREAM.
MMM-WAH!
HAVE YOU TWO LOVEBIRDS HEARD THE NEWS YET?
NO, WHAT NEWS?
WE GOT A TELEGRAPH FROM OUR SHOW'S BACKERS. THEY'RE OUT!
SHOW'S OVER, FOLKS!

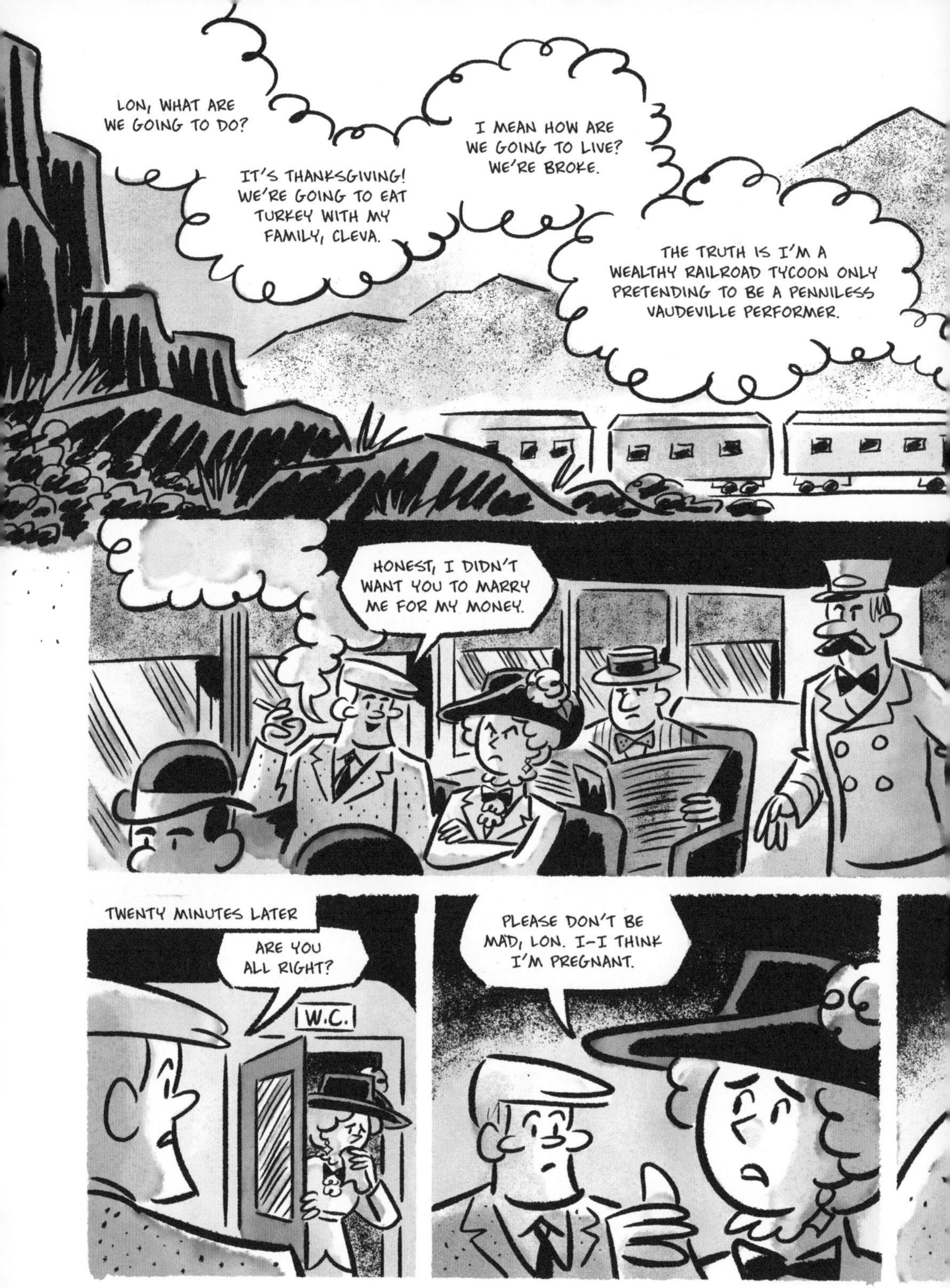

LON, WHAT ARE WE GOING TO DO?
IT'S THANKSGIVING! WE'RE GOING TO EAT TURKEY WITH MY FAMILY, CLEVA.
I MEAN HOW ARE WE GOING TO LIVE? WE'RE BROKE.
THE TRUTH IS I'M A WEALTHY RAILROAD TYCOON ONLY PRETENDING TO BE A PENNILESS VAUDEVILLE PERFORMER.
HONEST, I DIDN'T WANT YOU TO MARRY ME FOR MY MONEY.
TWENTY MINUTES LATER
ARE YOU ALL RIGHT?
W.C.
PLEASE DON'T BE MAD, LON. I-I THINK I'M PREGNANT.

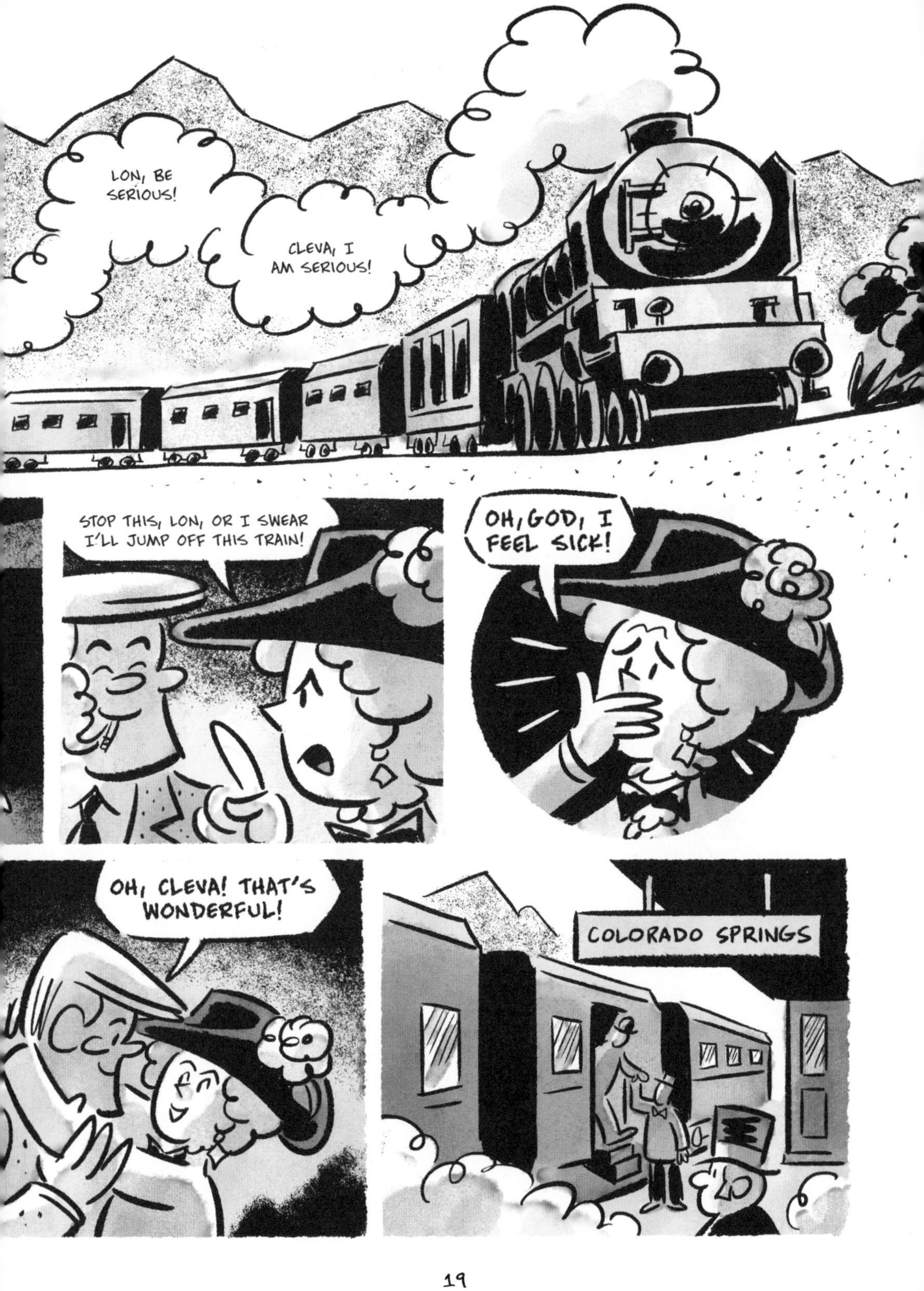
LON, BE SERIOUS!
CLEVA, I AM SERIOUS!
STOP THIS, LON, OR I SWEAR I'LL JUMP OFF THIS TRAIN!
OH, GOD, I FEEL SICK!
OH, CLEVA! THAT'S WONDERFUL!
COLORADO SPRINGS

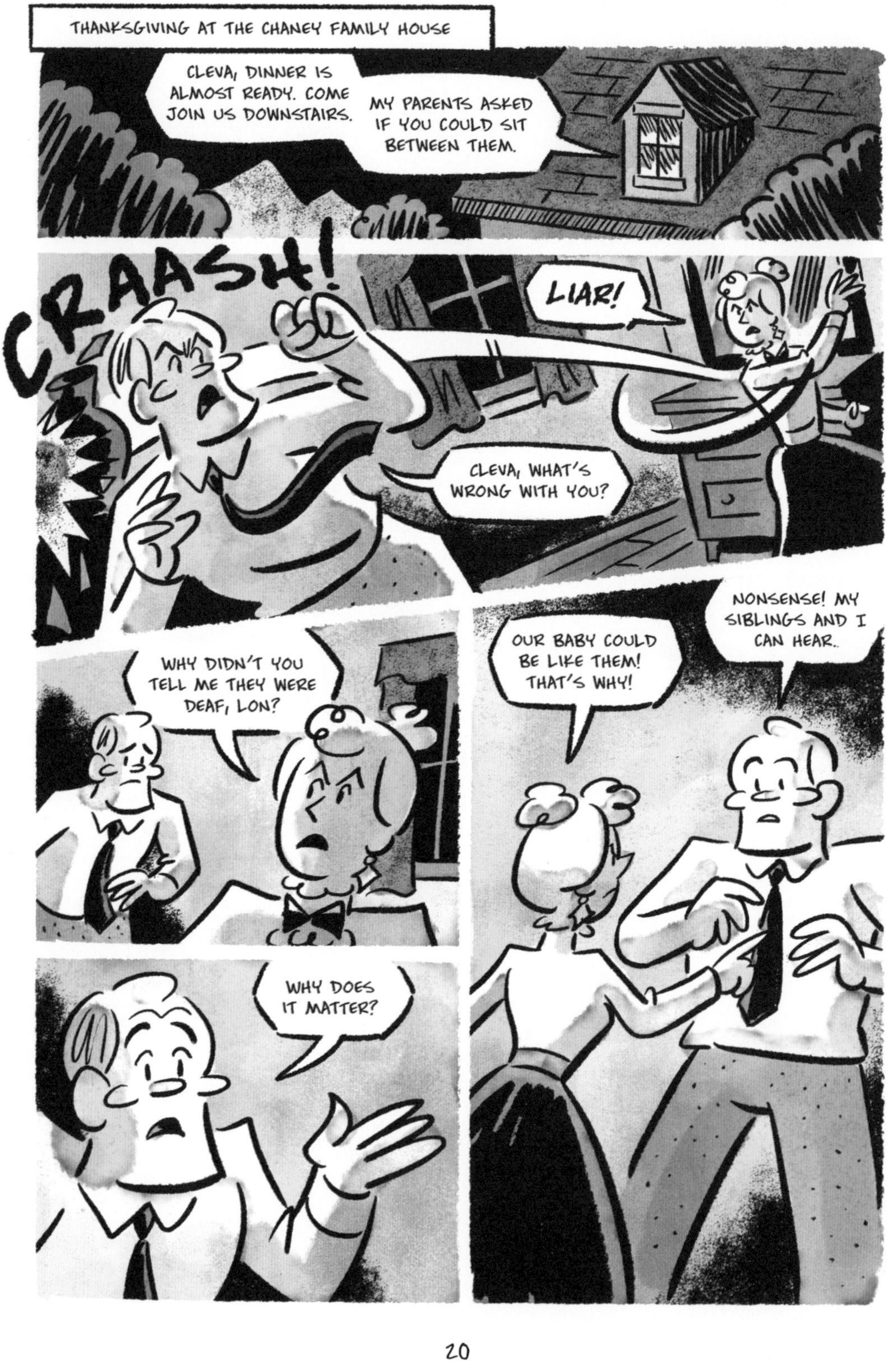
THANKSGIVING AT THE CHANEY FAMILY HOUSE
CLEVA, DINNER IS ALMOST READY. COME JOIN US DOWNSTAIRS.
MY PARENTS ASKED IF YOU COULD SIT BETWEEN THEM.
CRAASH!
LIAR!
CLEVA, WHAT'S WRONG WITH YOU?
WHY DIDN'T YOU TELL ME THEY WERE DEAF, LON?
WHY DOES IT MATTER?
OUR BABY COULD BE LIKE THEM! THAT'S WHY!
NONSENSE! MY SIBLINGS AND I CAN HEAR.

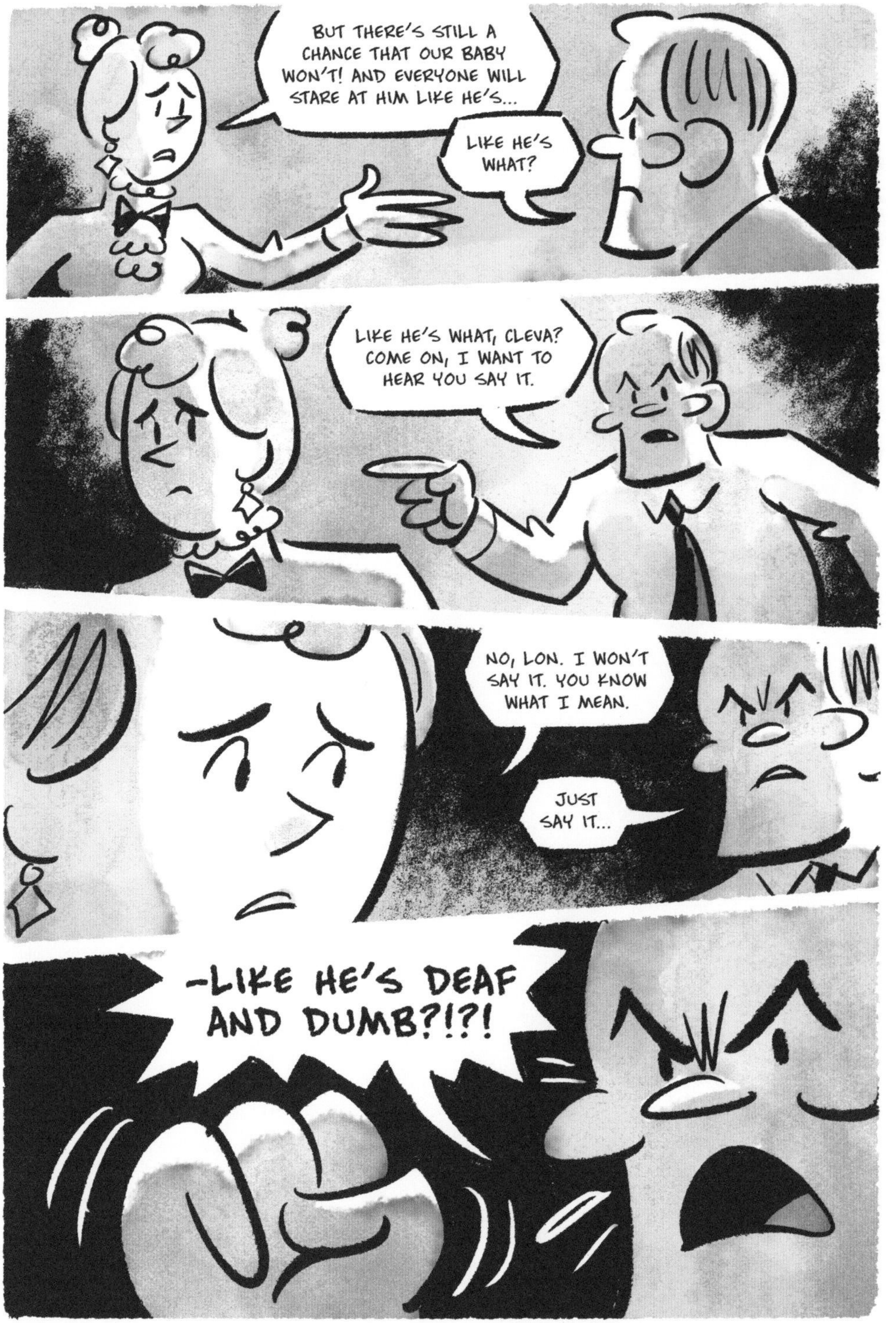
BUT THERE'S STILL A CHANCE THAT OUR BABY WON'T! AND EVERYONE WILL STARE AT HIM LIKE HE'S...
LIKE HE'S WHAT?
LIKE HE'S WHAT, CLEVA? COME ON, I WANT TO HEAR YOU SAY IT.
NO, LON. I WON'T SAY IT. YOU KNOW WHAT I MEAN.
JUST SAY IT...
-LIKE HE'S DEAF AND DUMB?!?!

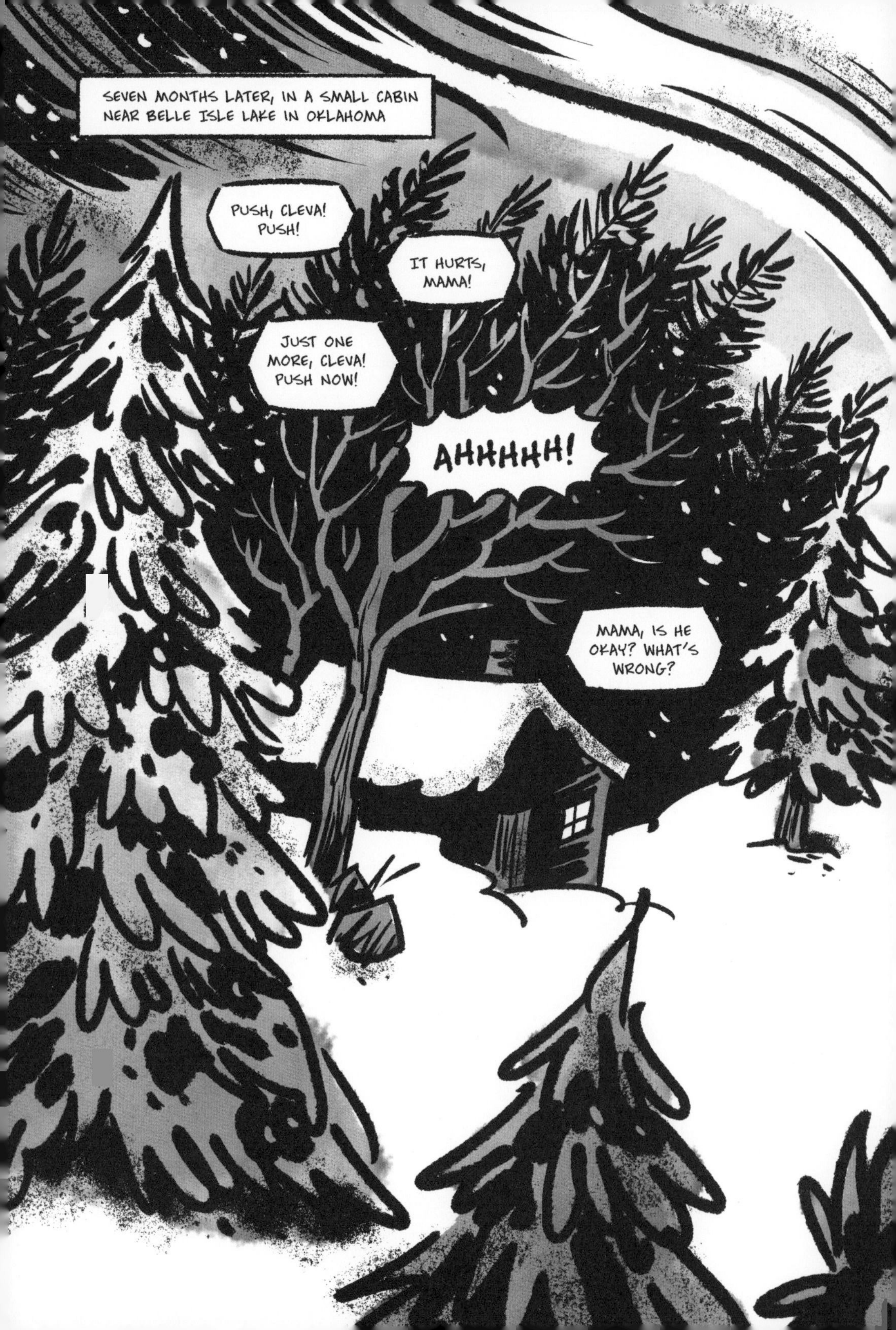
SEVEN MONTHS LATER, IN A SMALL CABIN NEAR BELLE ISLE LAKE IN OKLAHOMA
PUSH, CLEVA! PUSH!
IT HURTS, MAMA!
JUST ONE MORE, CLEVA! PUSH NOW!
AHHHHH!
MAMA, IS HE OKAY? WHAT'S WRONG?

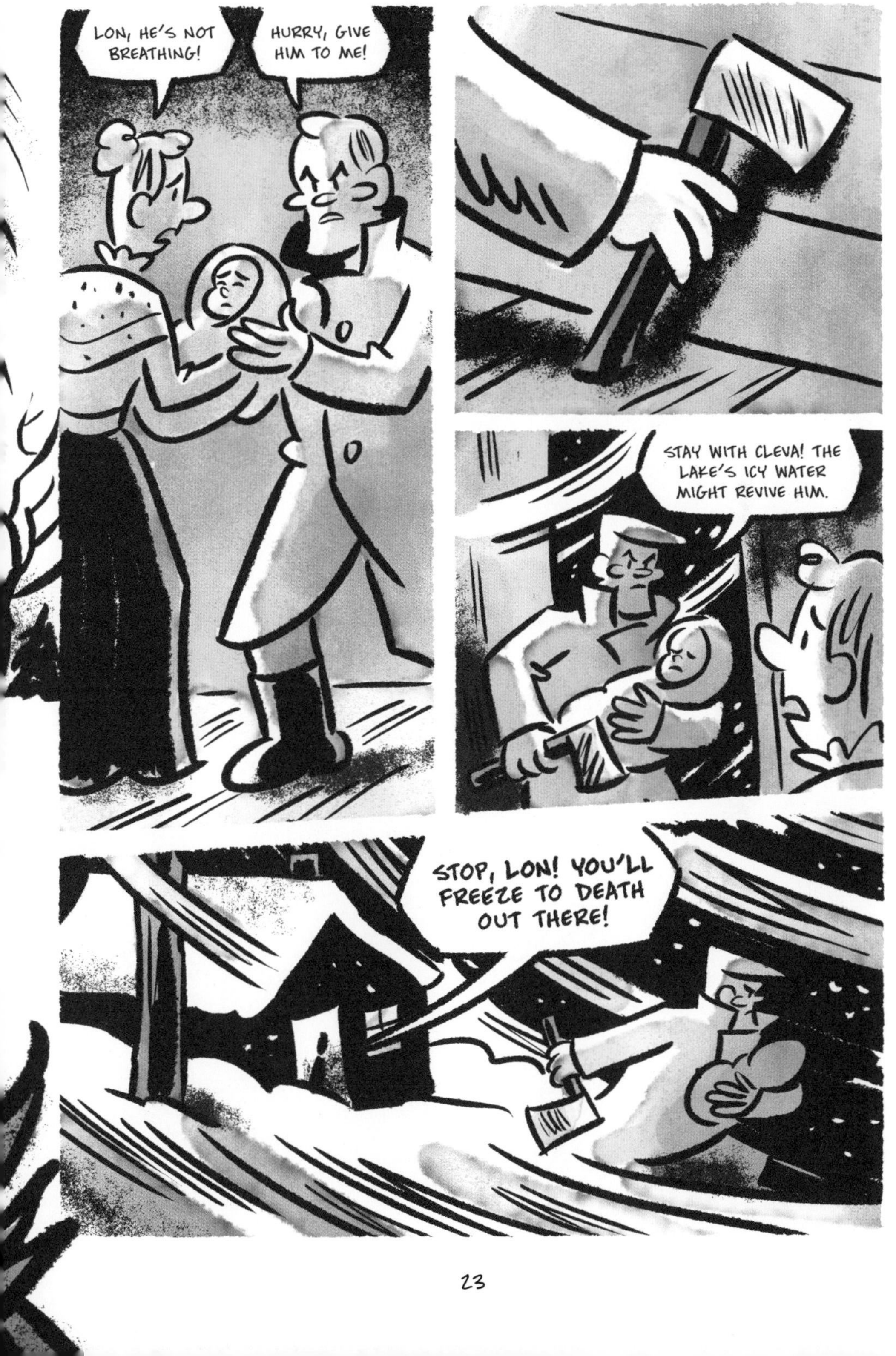
LON, HE'S NOT BREATHING!
HURRY, GIVE HIM TO ME!
STAY WITH CLEVA! THE LAKE'S ICY WATER MIGHT REVIVE HIM.
STOP, LON! YOU'LL FREEZE TO DEATH OUT THERE!

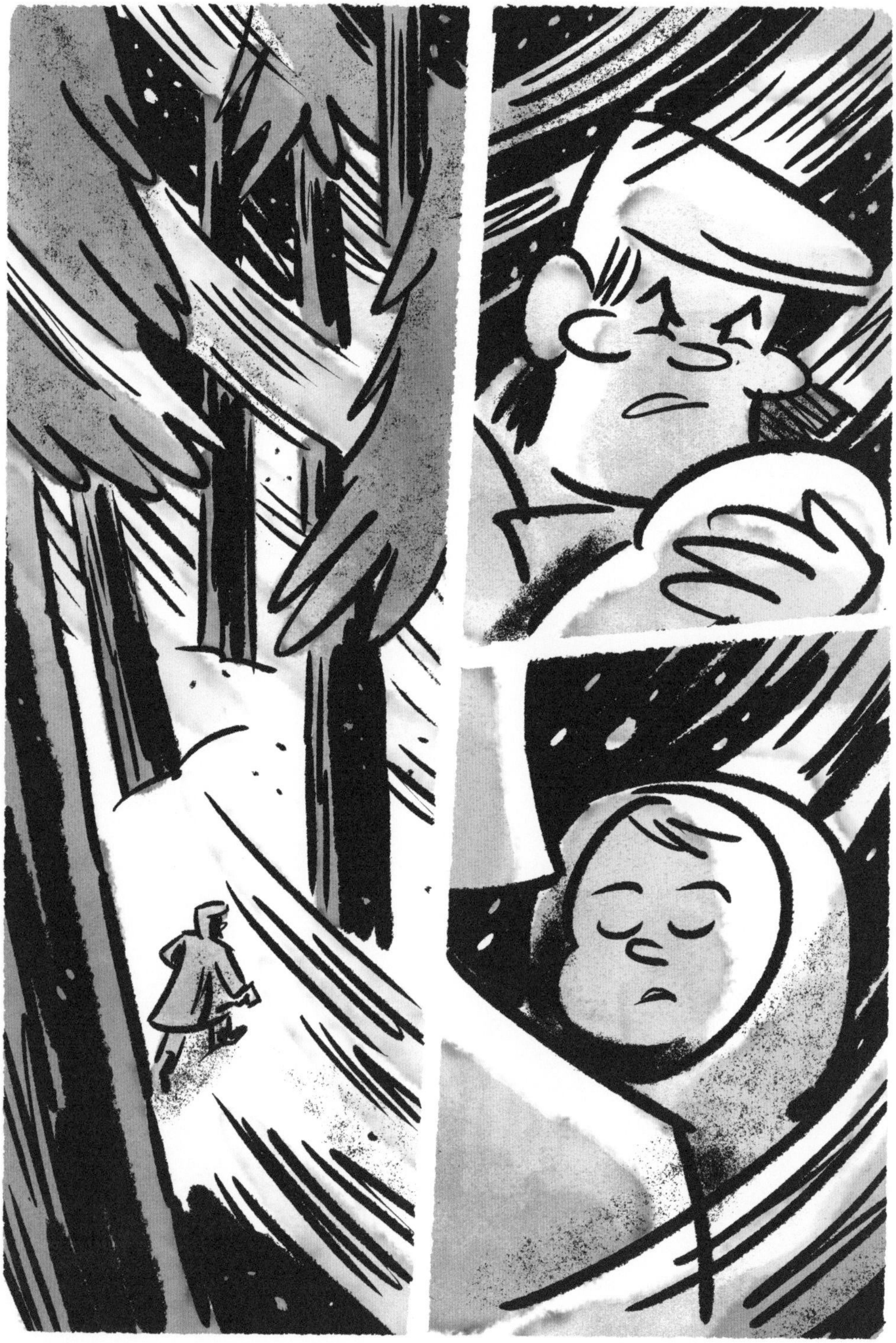

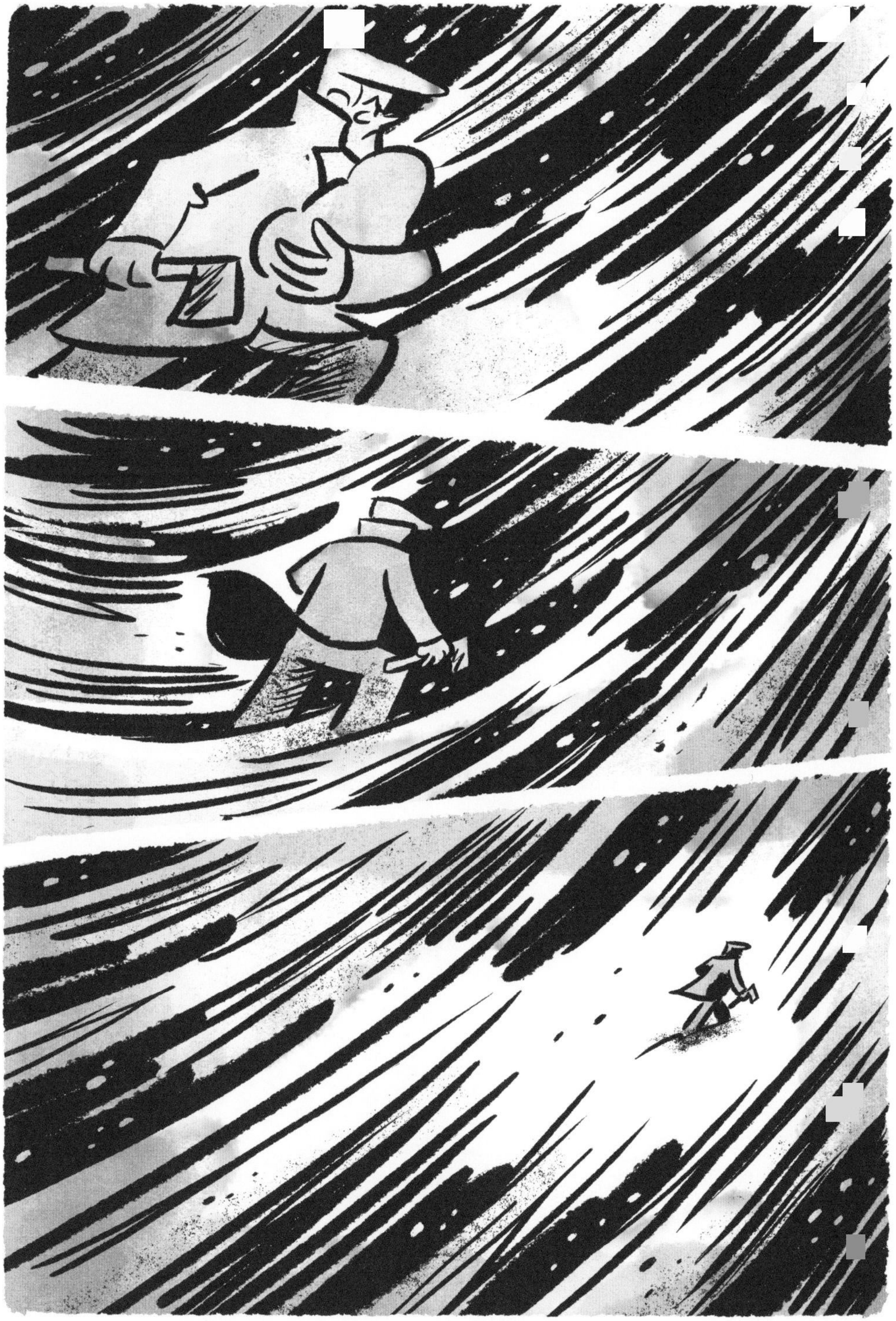

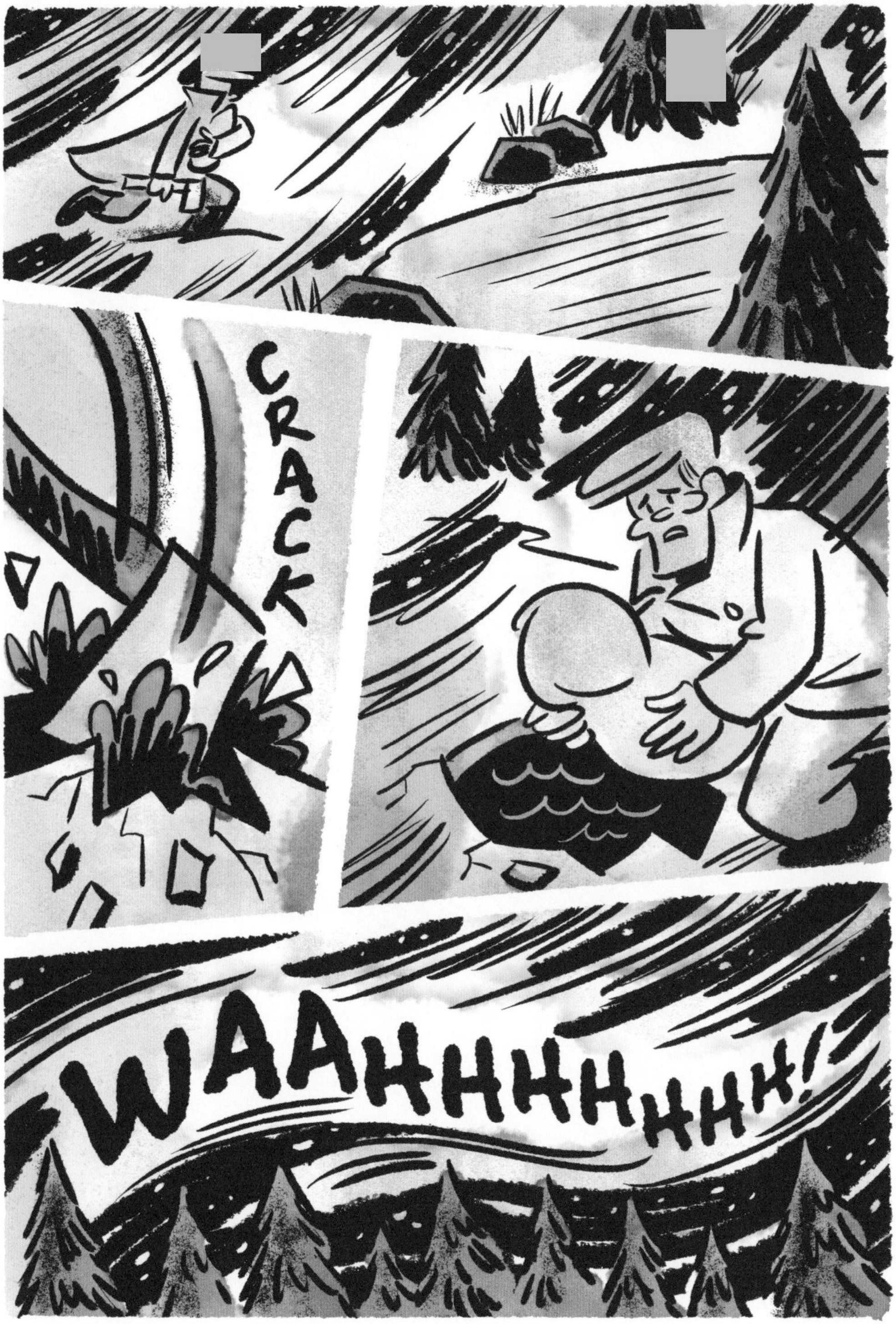
CRACK
WAAHHHHHHHH!

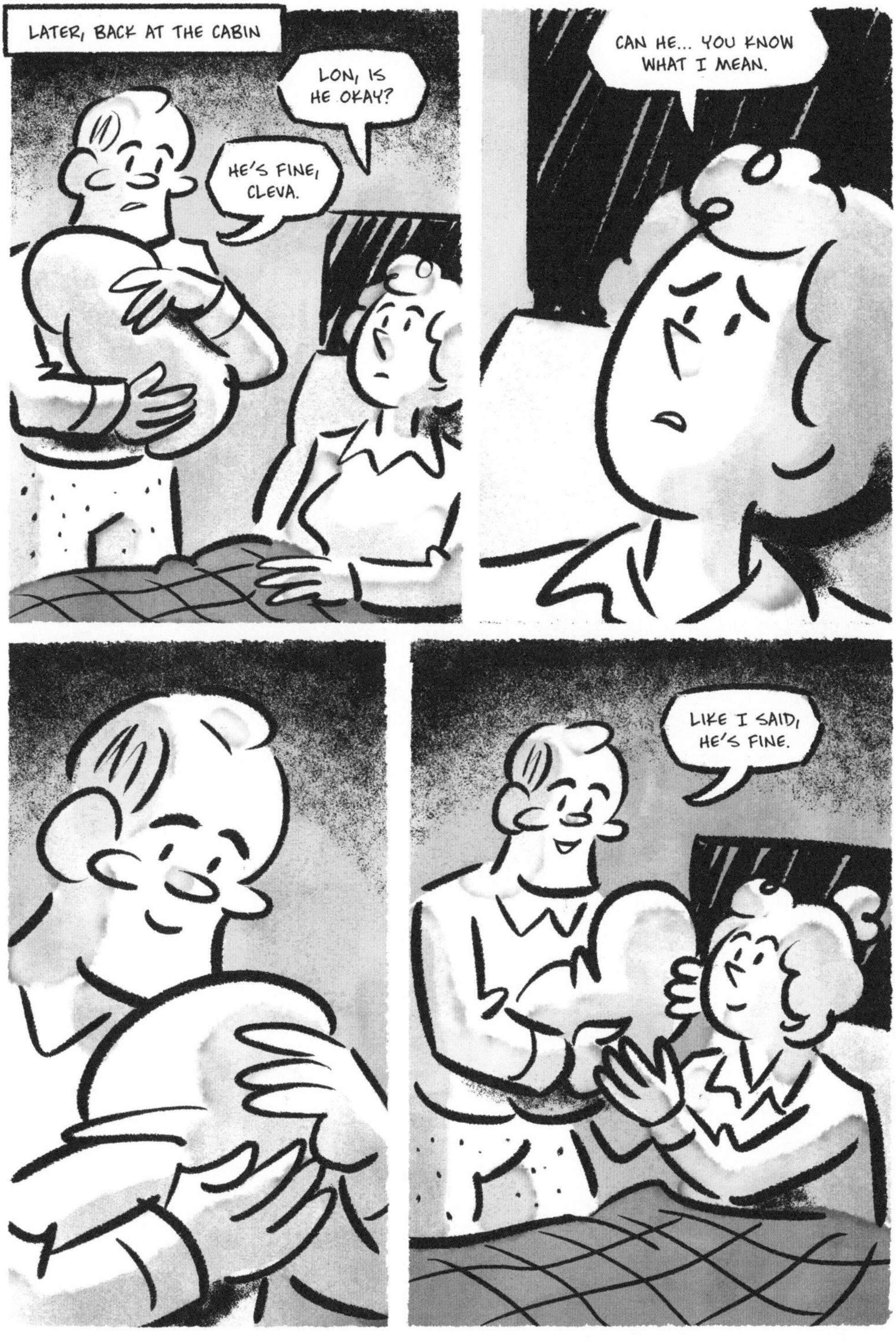
LATER, BACK AT THE CABIN
LON, IS HE OKAY?
HE'S FINE, CLEVA.
CAN HE... YOU KNOW WHAT I MEAN.
LIKE I SAID, HE'S FINE.

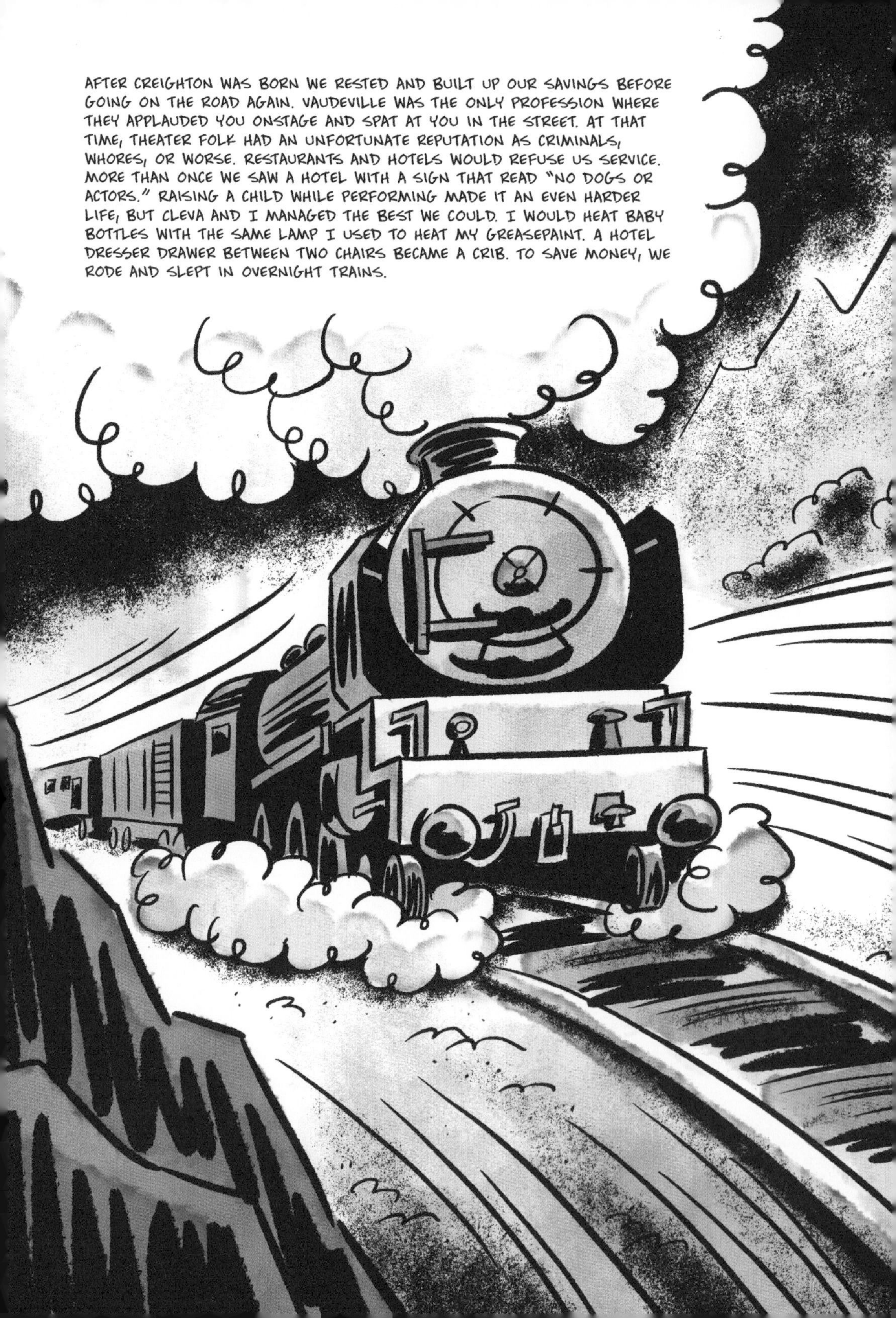
AFTER CREIGHTON WAS BORN WE RESTED AND BUILT UP OUR SAVINGS BEFORE GOING ON THE ROAD AGAIN. VAUDEVILLE WAS THE ONLY PROFESSION WHERE THEY APPLAUDED YOU ONSTAGE AND SPAT AT YOU IN THE STREET. AT THAT TIME, THEATER FOLK HAD AN UNFORTUNATE REPUTATION AS CRIMINALS, WHORES, OR WORSE. RESTAURANTS AND HOTELS WOULD REFUSE US SERVICE. MORE THAN ONCE WE SAW A HOTEL WITH A SIGN THAT READ "NO DOGS OR ACTORS." RAISING A CHILD WHILE PERFORMING MADE IT AN EVEN HARDER LIFE, BUT CLEVA AND I MANAGED THE BEST WE COULD. I WOULD HEAT BABY BOTTLES WITH THE SAME LAMP I USED TO HEAT MY GREASEPAINT. A HOTEL DRESSER DRAWER BETWEEN TWO CHAIRS BECAME A CRIB. TO SAVE MONEY, WE RODE AND SLEPT IN OVERNIGHT TRAINS.

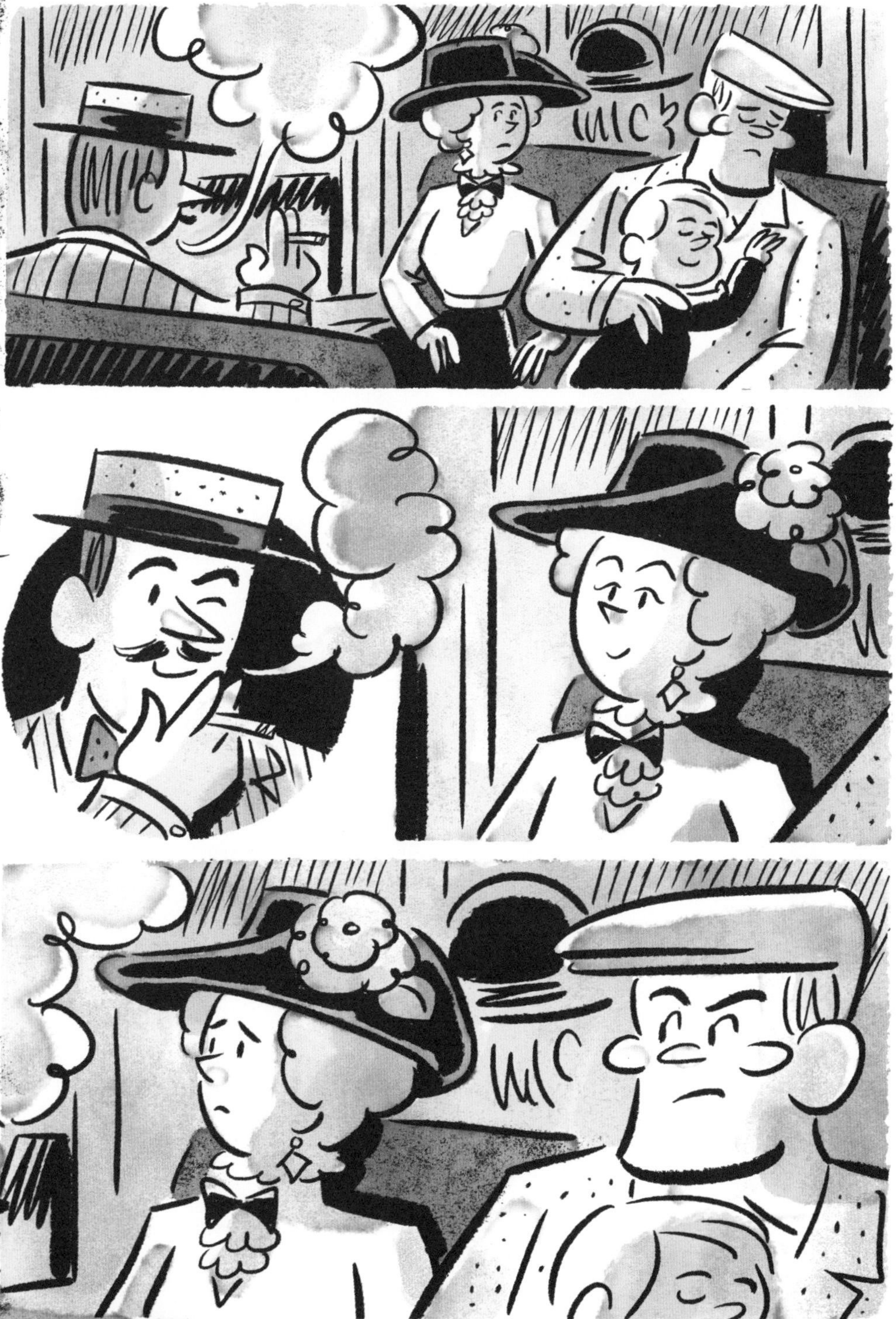

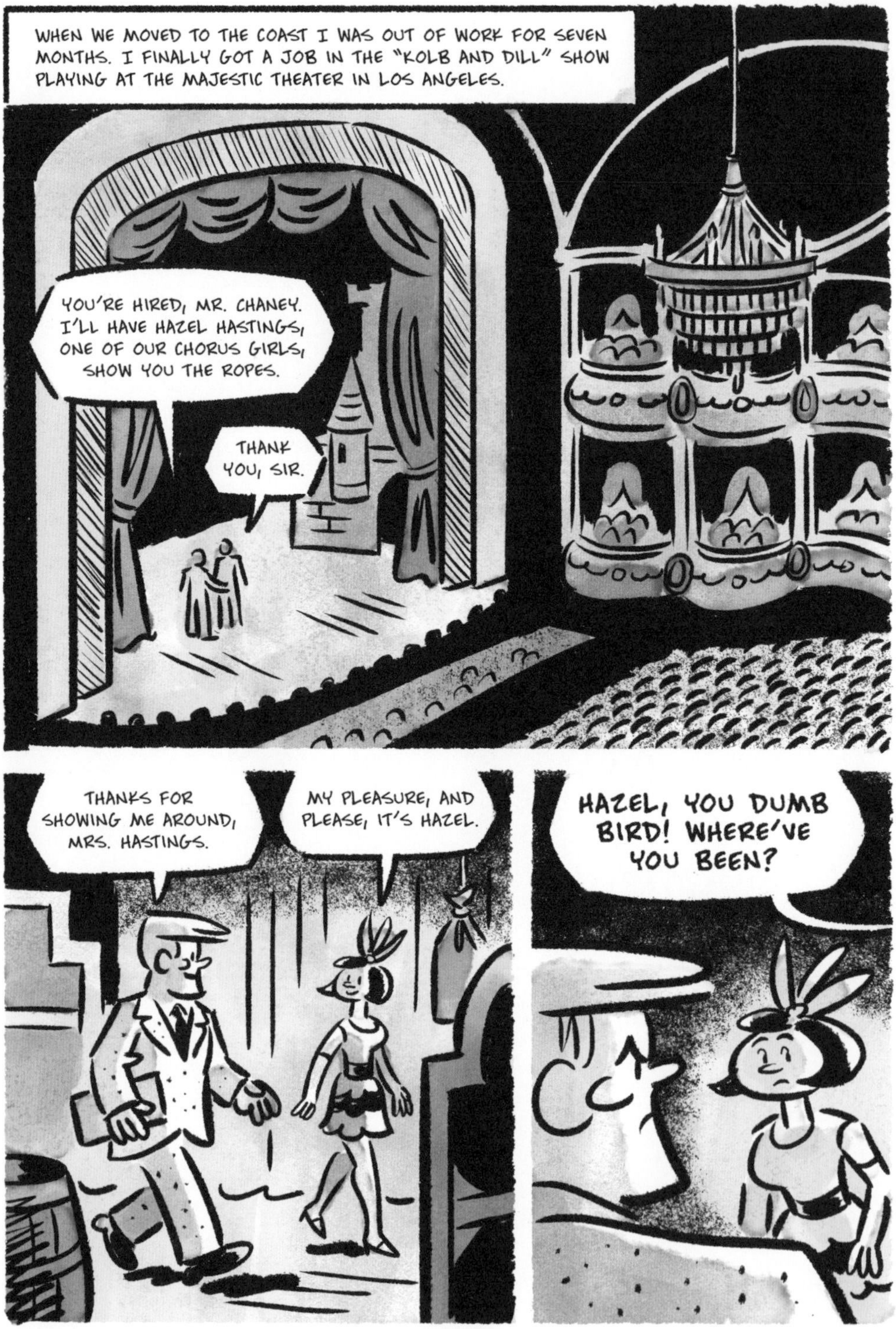
WHEN WE MOVED TO THE COAST I WAS OUT OF WORK FOR SEVEN MONTHS. I FINALLY GOT A JOB IN THE "KOLB AND DILL" SHOW PLAYING AT THE MAJESTIC THEATER IN LOS ANGELES.
YOU'RE HIRED, MR. CHANEY. I'LL HAVE HAZEL HASTINGS, ONE OF OUR CHORUS GIRLS, SHOW YOU THE ROPES.
THANK YOU, SIR.
THANKS FOR SHOWING ME AROUND, MRS. HASTINGS.
MY PLEASURE, AND PLEASE, IT'S HAZEL.
HAZEL, YOU DUMB BIRD! WHERE'VE YOU BEEN?

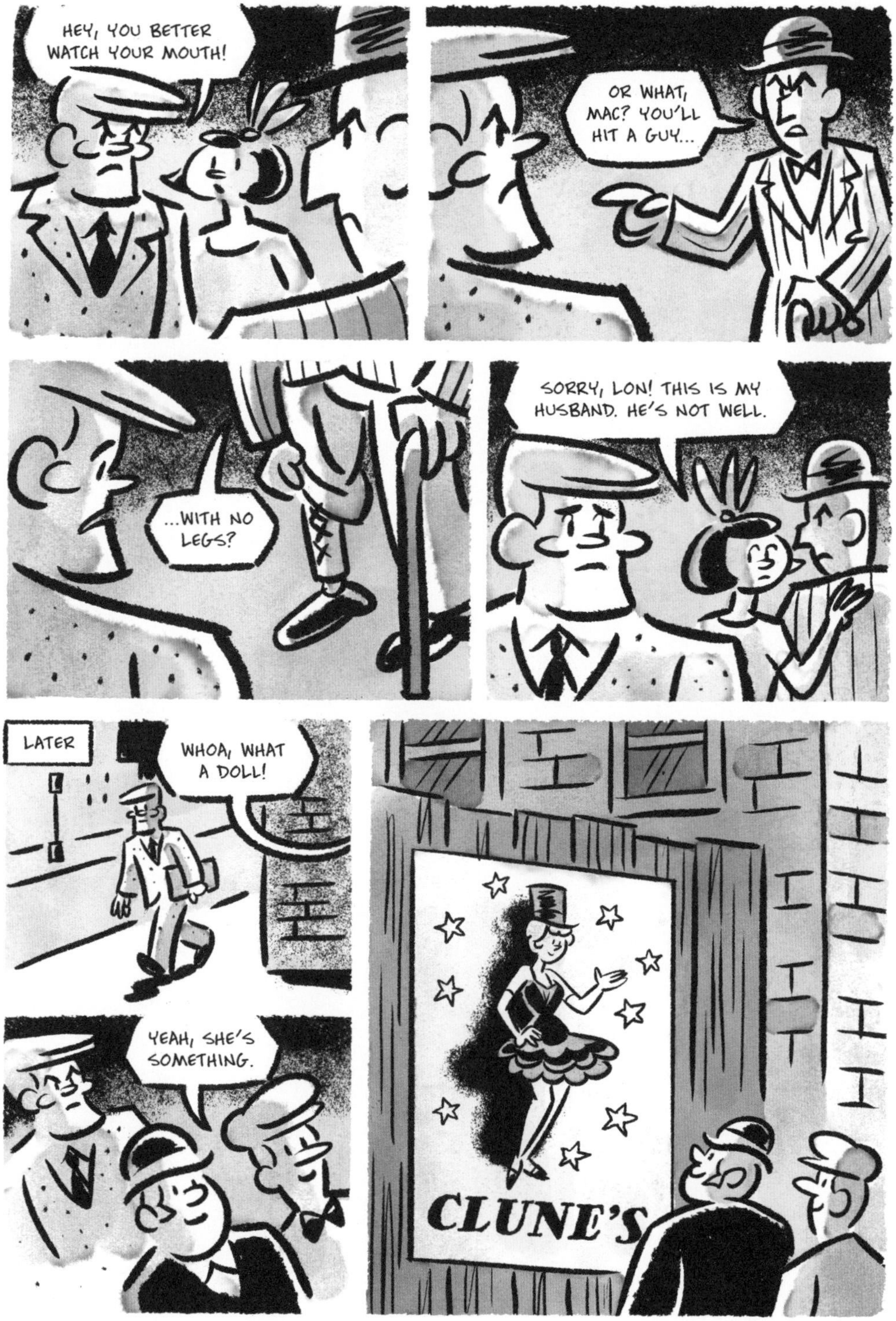
HEY, YOU BETTER WATCH YOUR MOUTH!
OR WHAT, MAC? YOU'LL HIT A GUY...
...WITH NO LEGS?
SORRY, LON! THIS IS MY HUSBAND. HE'S NOT WELL.
LATER
WHOA, WHAT A DOLL!
YEAH, SHE'S SOMETHING.
CLUNE'S

CLEVA BECAME POPULAR IN THE CABARET SHOWS. SHE SANG "CURSE OF AN ACHING HEART." MY OWN HEART ACHED SEEING HER CHUMMING AROUND WITH MALE PATRONS.

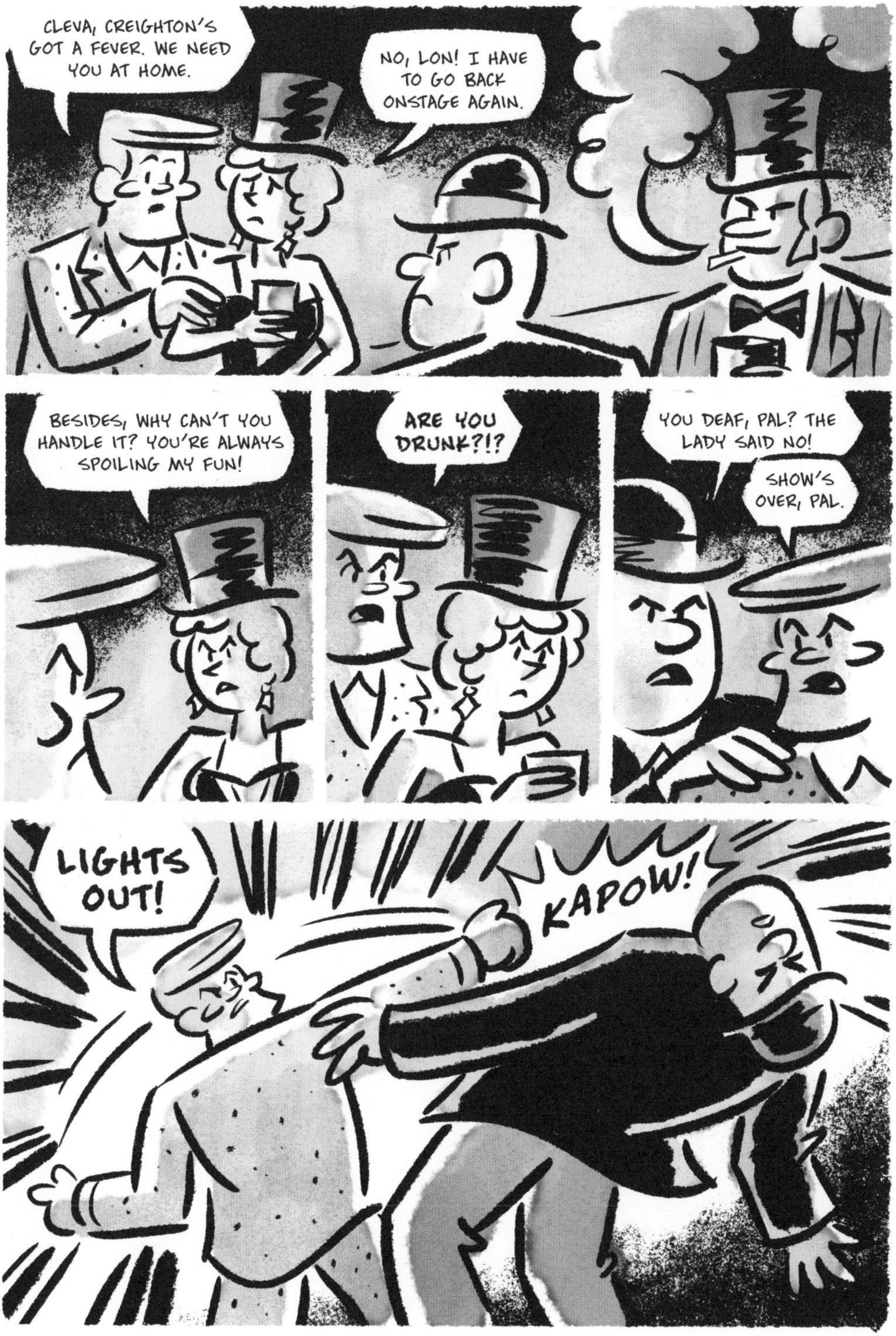
CLEVA, CREIGHTON'S GOT A FEVER. WE NEED YOU AT HOME.
NO, LON! I HAVE TO GO BACK ONSTAGE AGAIN.
BESIDES, WHY CAN'T YOU HANDLE IT? YOU'RE ALWAYS SPOILING MY FUN!
ARE YOU DRUNK?!?
YOU DEAF, PAL? THE LADY SAID NO!
SHOW'S OVER, PAL.
LIGHTS OUT!
KAPOW!

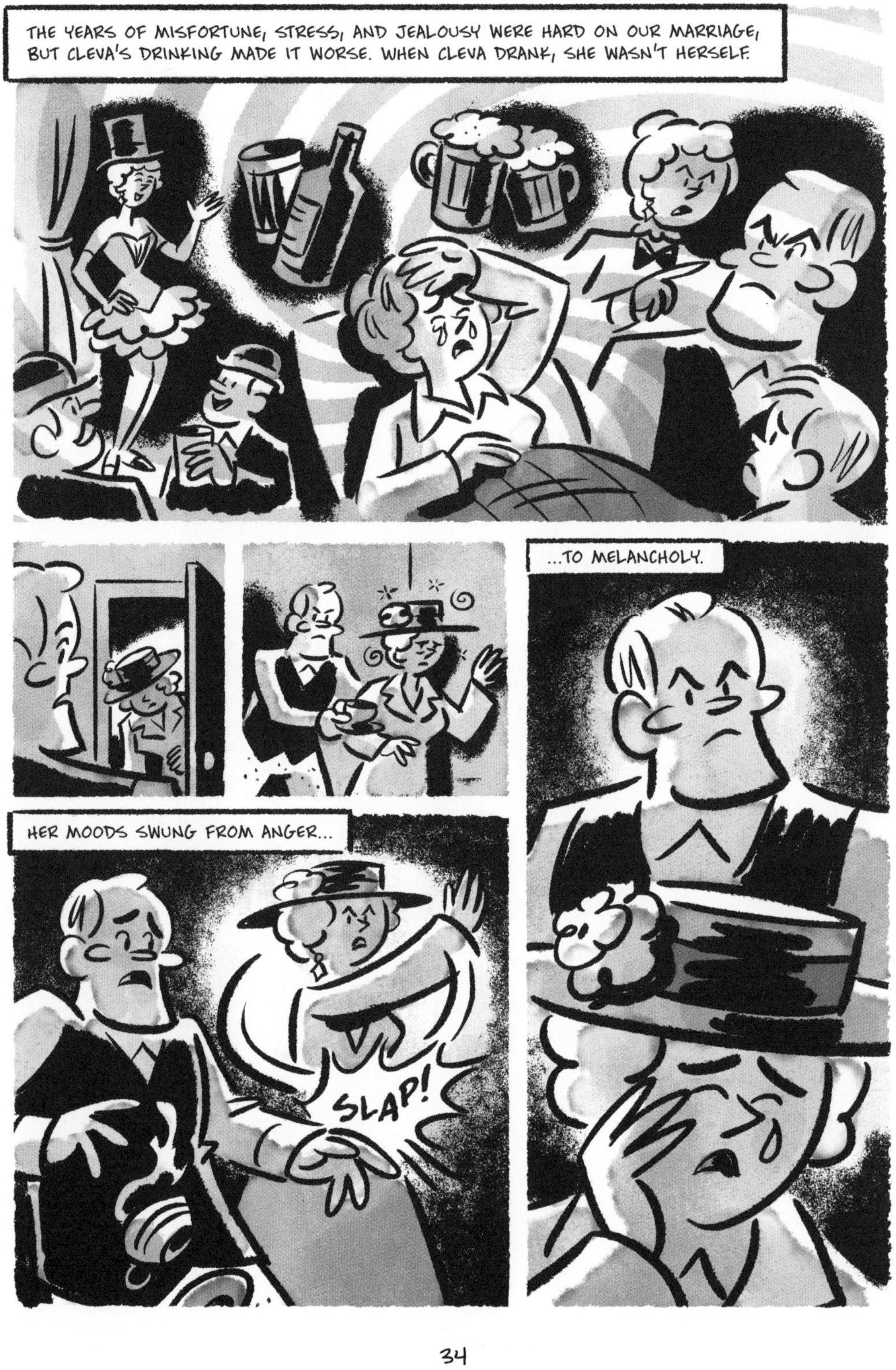
THE YEARS OF MISFORTUNE, STRESS, AND JEALOUSY WERE HARD ON OUR MARRIAGE, BUT CLEVA'S DRINKING MADE IT WORSE. WHEN CLEVA DRANK, SHE WASN'T HERSELF.
HER MOODS SWUNG FROM ANGER...
SLAP!
...TO MELANCHOLY.

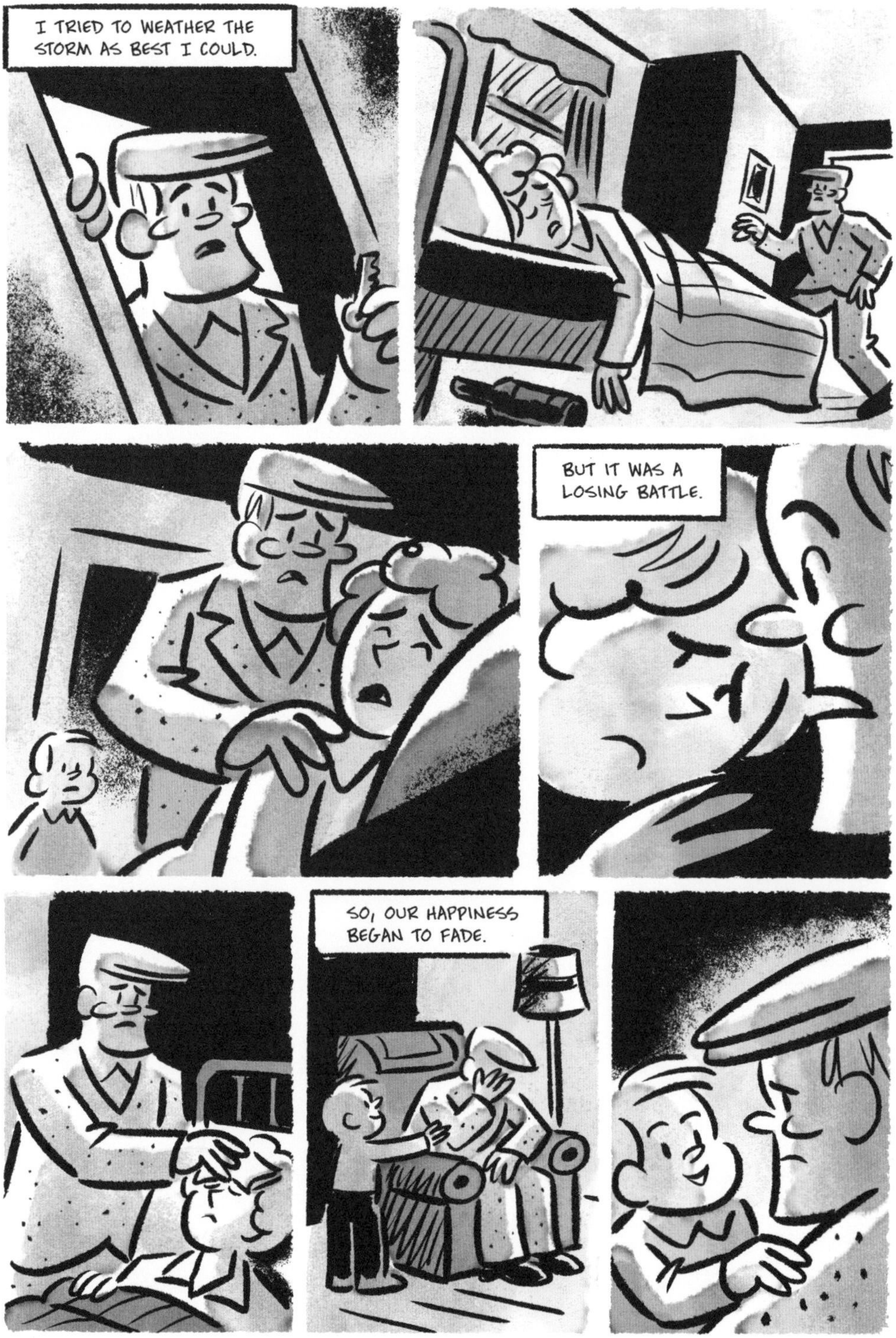
I TRIED TO WEATHER THE STORM AS BEST I COULD.
BUT IT WAS A LOSING BATTLE.
SO, OUR HAPPINESS BEGAN TO FADE.

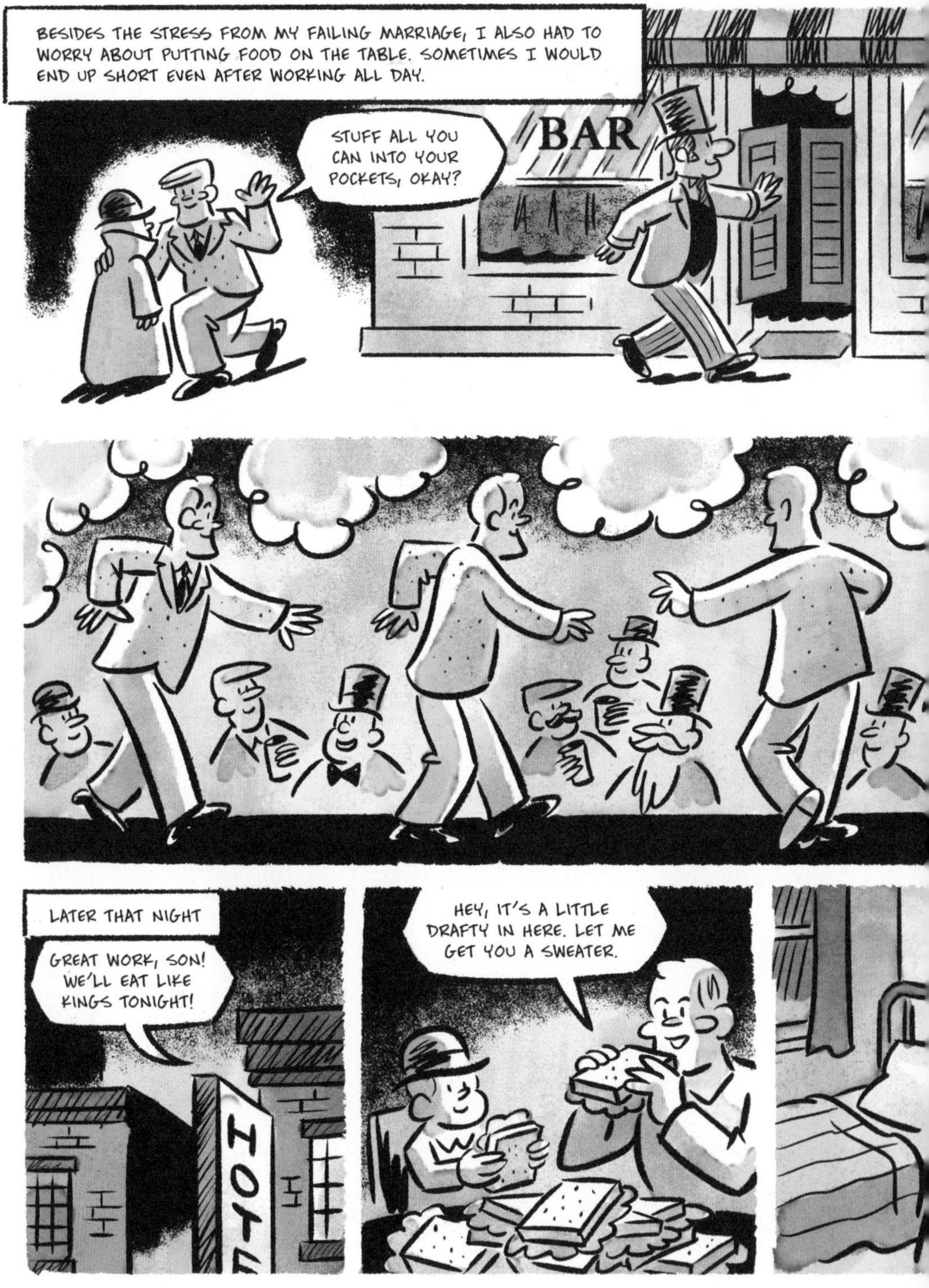
BESIDES THE STRESS FROM MY FAILING MARRIAGE, I ALSO HAD TO WORRY ABOUT PUTTING FOOD ON THE TABLE. SOMETIMES I WOULD END UP SHORT EVEN AFTER WORKING ALL DAY.
STUFF ALL YOU CAN INTO YOUR POCKETS, OKAY?
BAR
LATER THAT NIGHT
GREAT WORK, SON! WE'LL EAT LIKE KINGS TONIGHT!
HOTE
HEY, IT'S A LITTLE DRAFTY IN HERE. LET ME GET YOU A SWEATER.

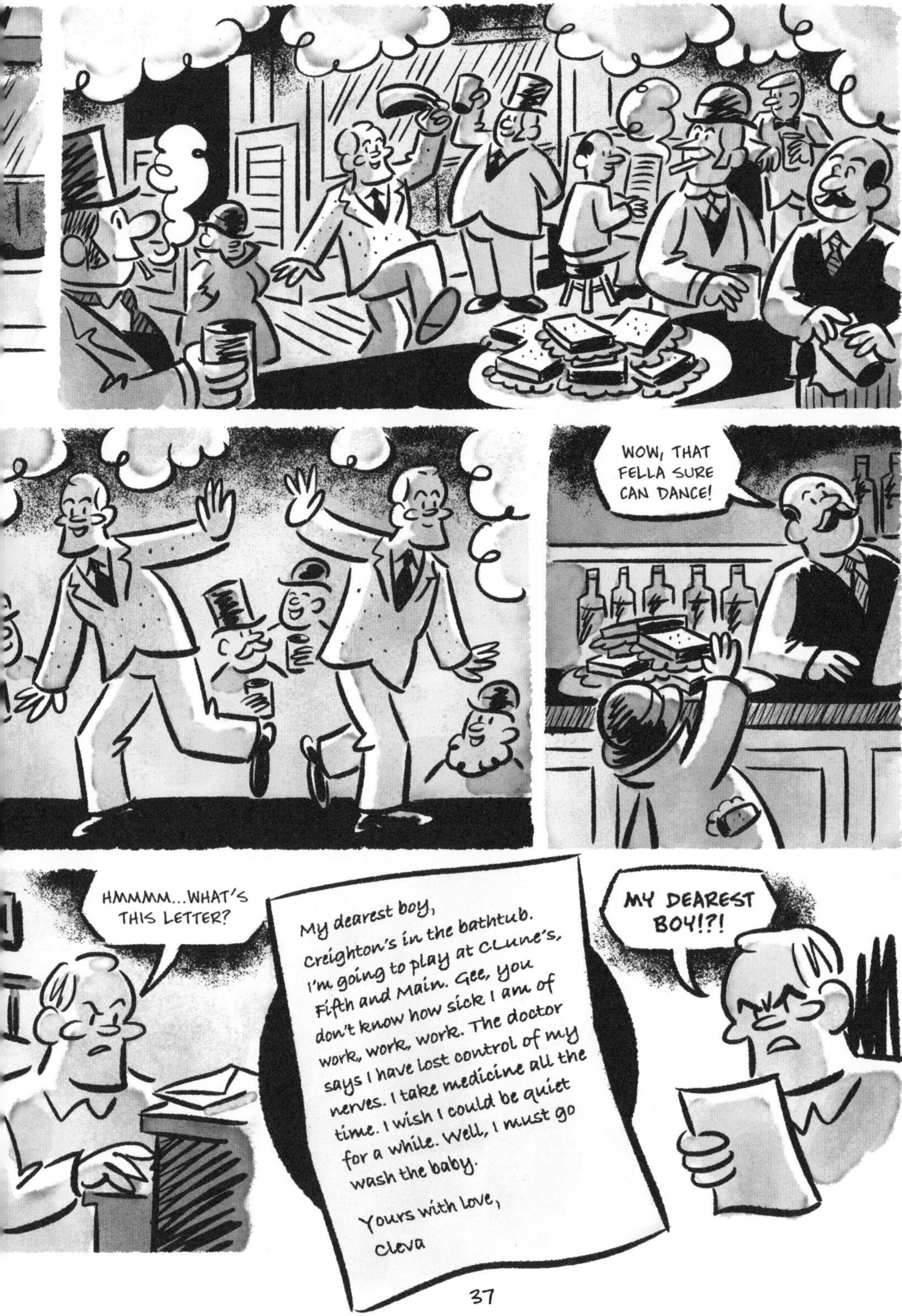
WOW, THAT FELLA SURE CAN DANCE!
HMMMM...WHAT'S THIS LETTER?
My dearest boy,
Creighton's in the bathtub.
I'm going to play at CLune's,
Fifth and Main. Gee, you
don't know how sick I am of
work, work, work. The doctor
says I have lost control of my
nerves. I take medicine all the
time. I wish I could be quiet
for a while. Well, I must go
wash the baby.
Yours with love,
Cleva
MY DEAREST BOY!?!

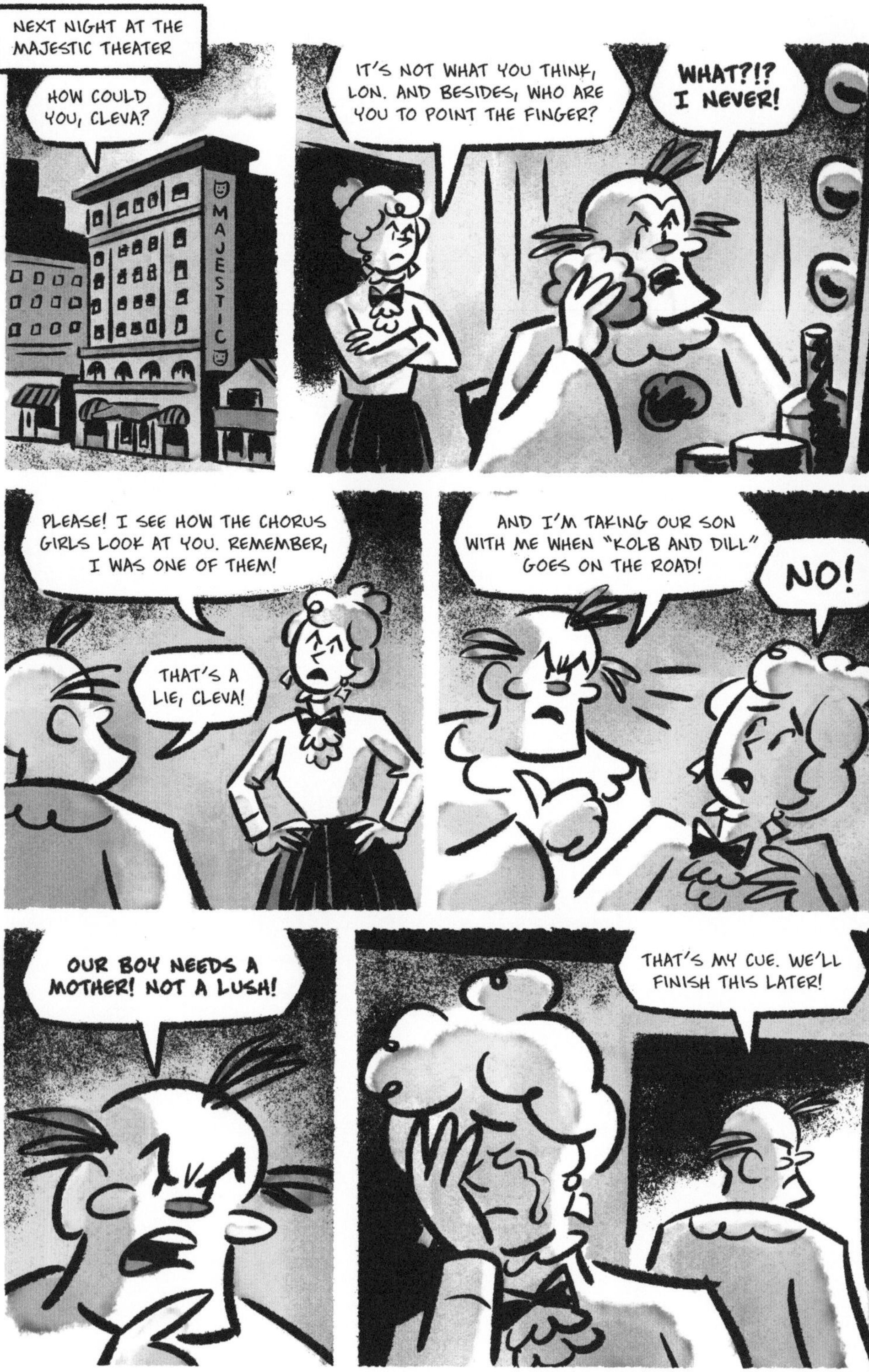
NEXT NIGHT AT THE MAJESTIC THEATER
HOW COULD YOU, CLEVA?
MAJESTIC
IT'S NOT WHAT YOU THINK, LON. AND BESIDES, WHO ARE YOU TO POINT THE FINGER?
WHAT?!? I NEVER!
PLEASE! I SEE HOW THE CHORUS GIRLS LOOK AT YOU. REMEMBER, I WAS ONE OF THEM!
THAT'S A LIE, CLEVA!
AND I'M TAKING OUR SON WITH ME WHEN "KOLB AND DILL" GOES ON THE ROAD!
NO!
OUR BOY NEEDS A MOTHER! NOT A LUSH!
THAT'S MY CUE. WE'LL FINISH THIS LATER!

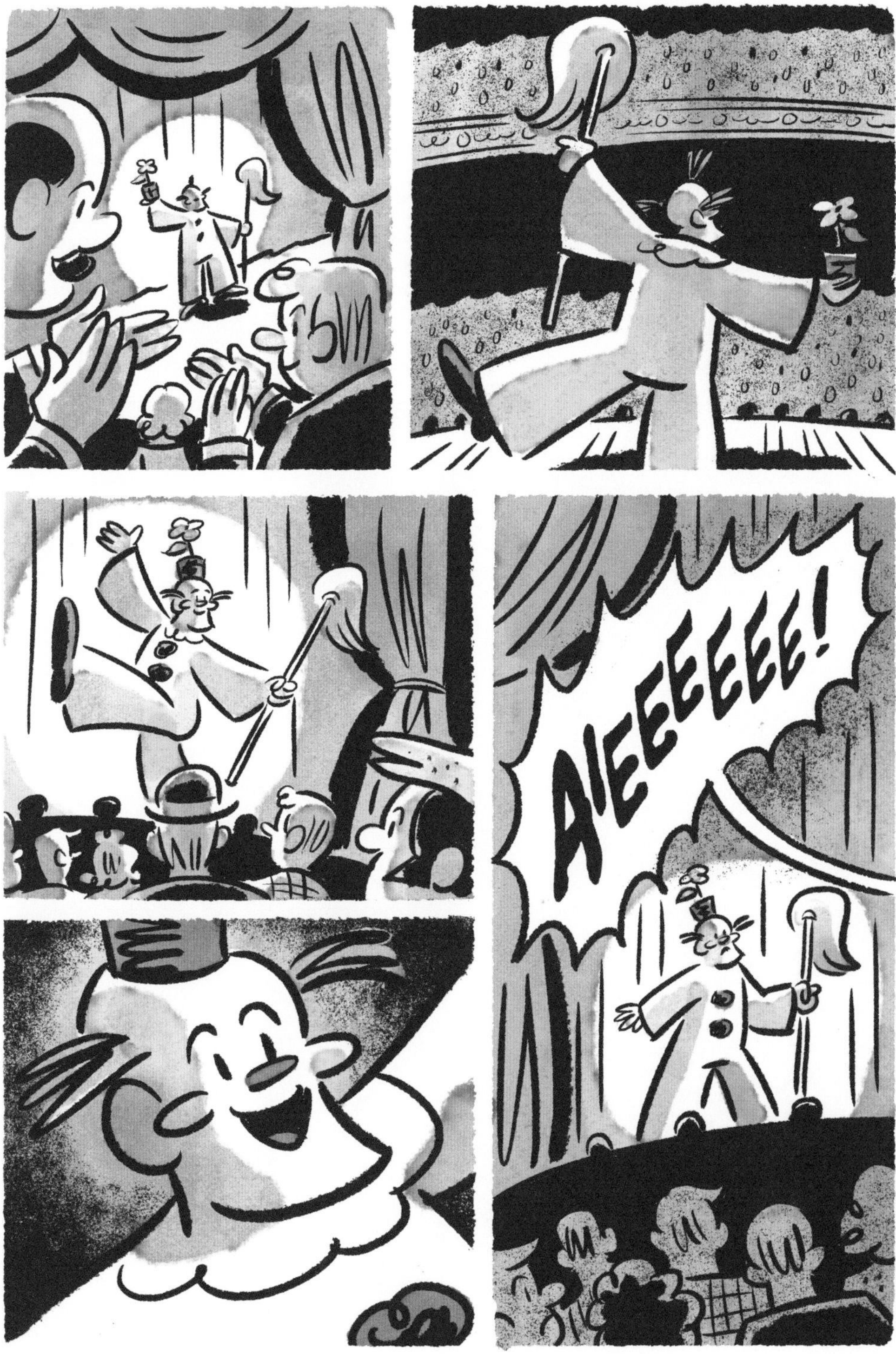
AIEEEEEEE!

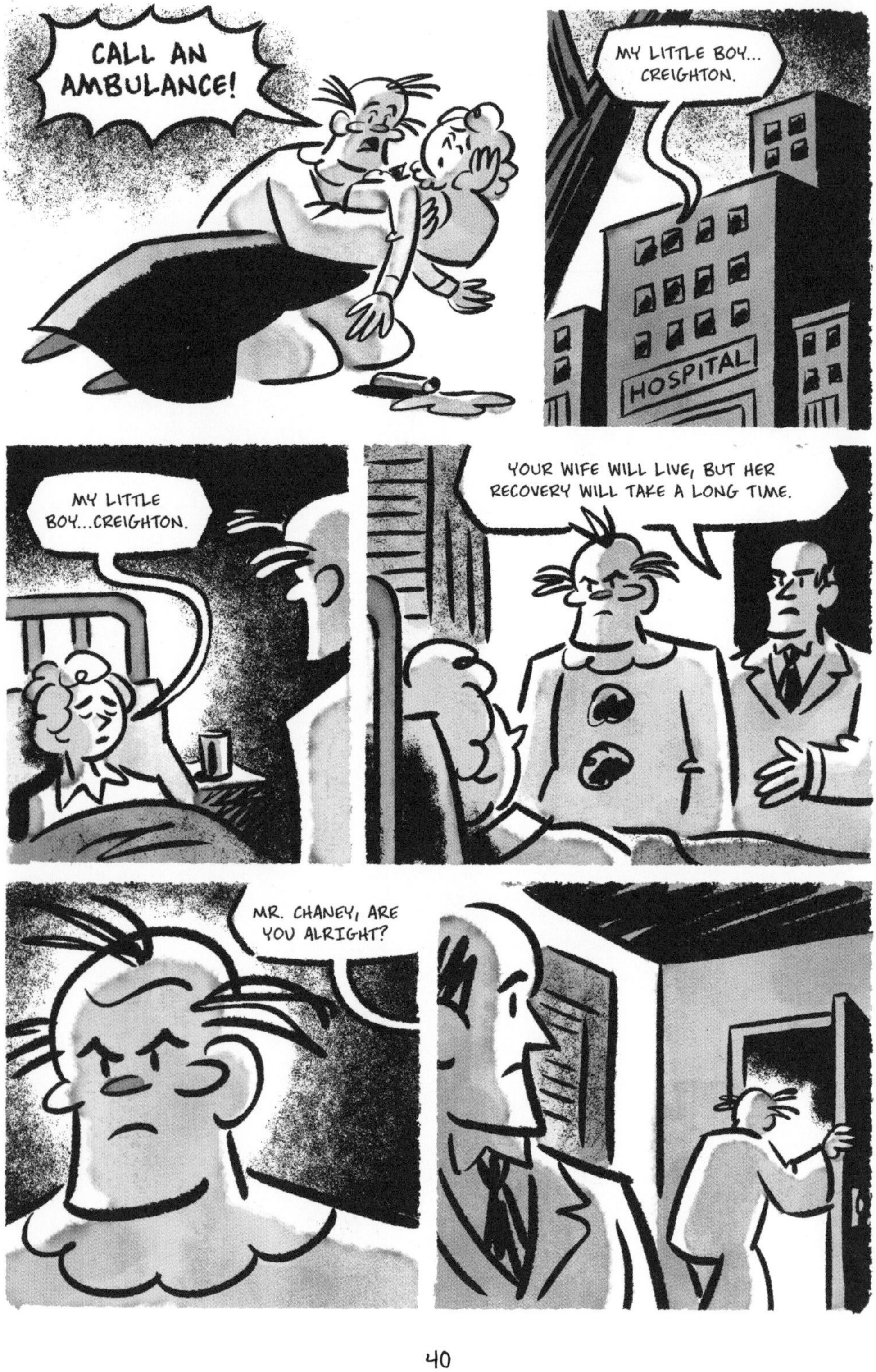
CALL AN AMBULANCE!
MY LITTLE BOY... CREIGHTON.
HOSPITAL
MY LITTLE BOY...CREIGHTON.
YOUR WIFE WILL LIVE, BUT HER RECOVERY WILL TAKE A LONG TIME.
MR. CHANEY, ARE YOU ALRIGHT?

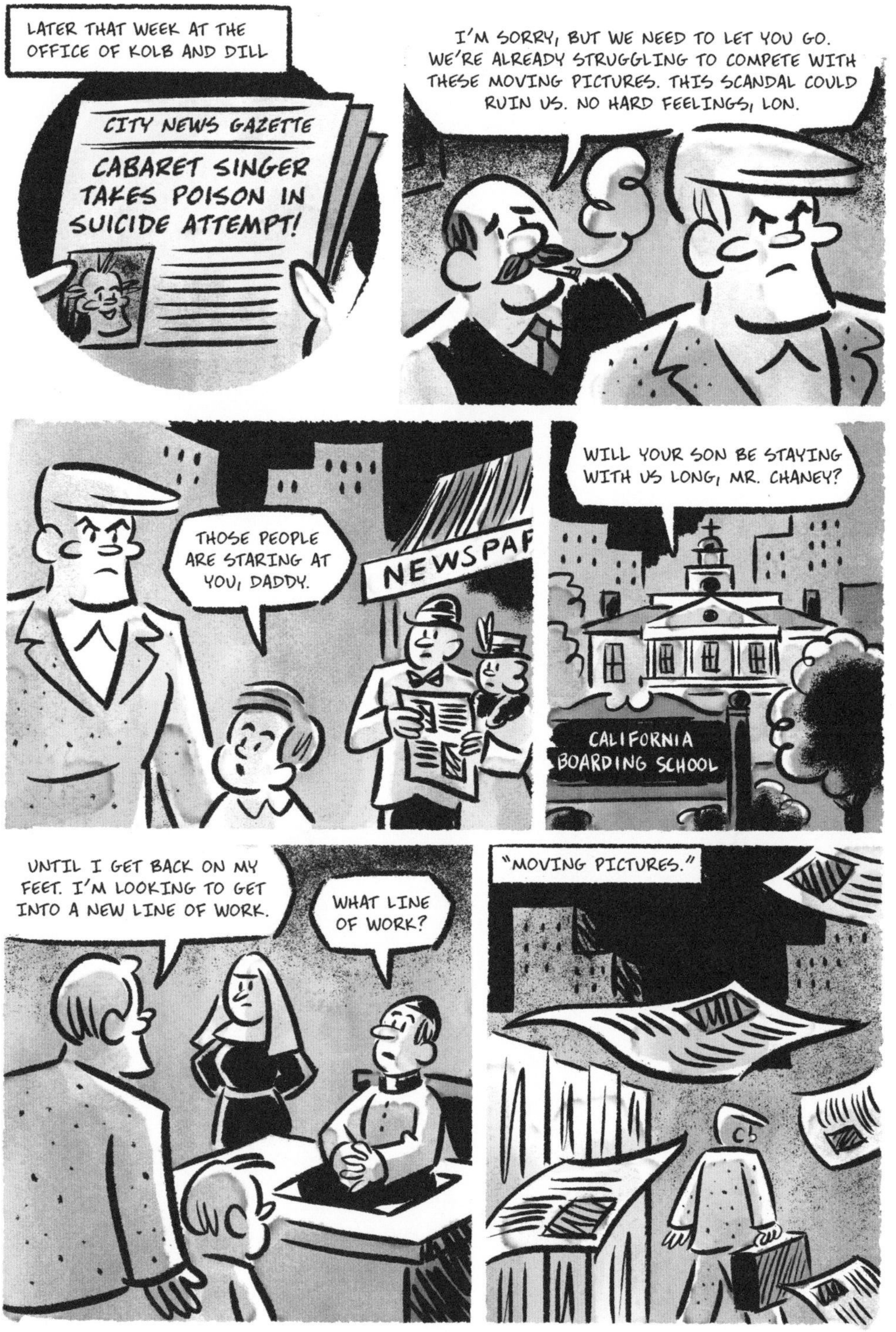
LATER THAT WEEK AT THE OFFICE OF KOLB AND DILL
CITY NEWS GAZETTE
CABARET SINGER TAKES POISON IN SUICIDE ATTEMPT!
I'M SORRY, BUT WE NEED TO LET YOU GO. WE'RE ALREADY STRUGGLING TO COMPETE WITH THESE MOVING PICTURES. THIS SCANDAL COULD RUIN US. NO HARD FEELINGS, LON.
THOSE PEOPLE ARE STARING AT YOU, DADDY.
NEWSPAP
WILL YOUR SON BE STAYING WITH US LONG, MR. CHANEY?
CALIFORNIA BOARDING SCHOOL
UNTIL I GET BACK ON MY FEET. I'M LOOKING TO GET INTO A NEW LINE OF WORK.
WHAT LINE OF WORK?
"MOVING PICTURES."

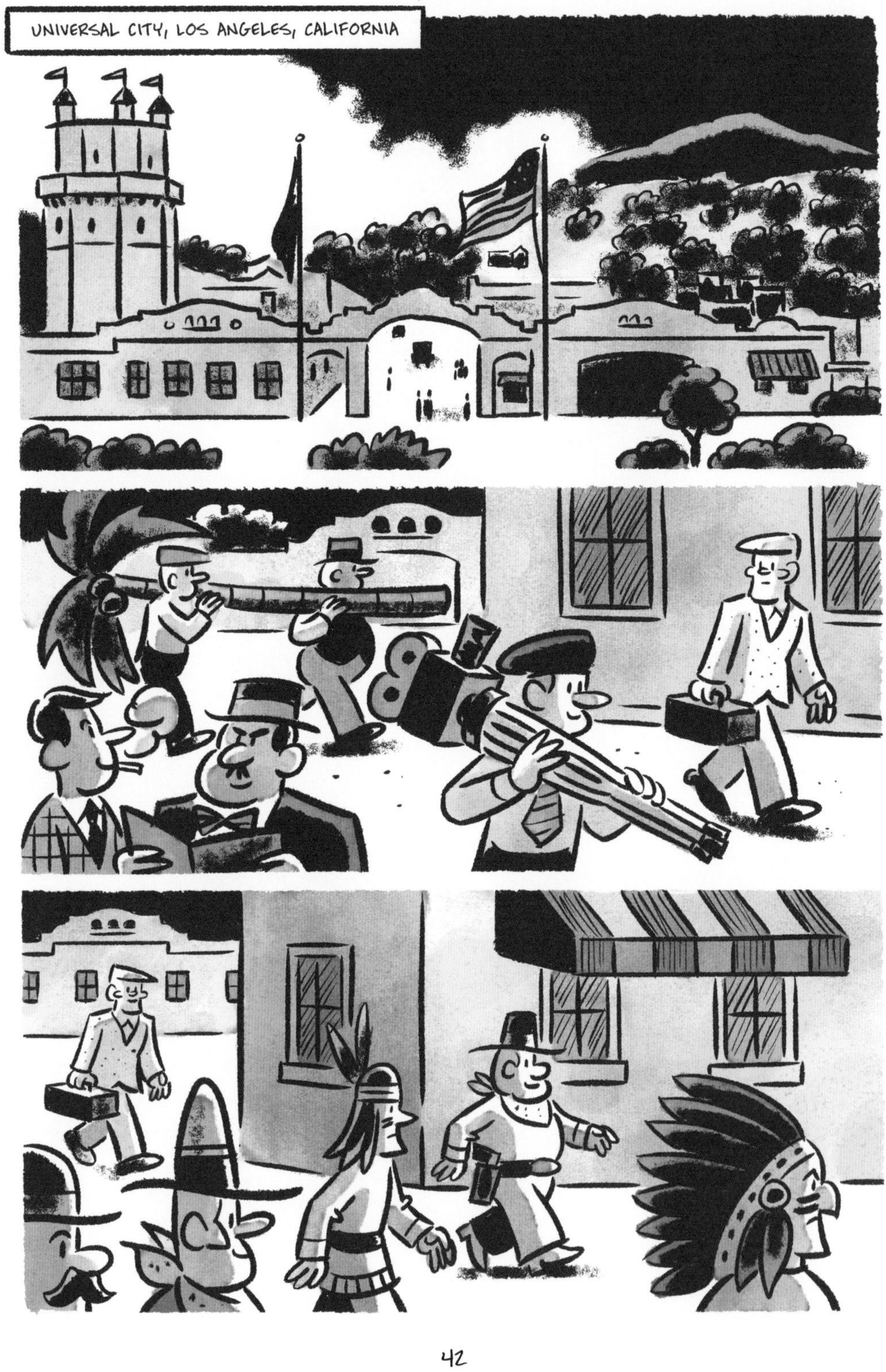
UNIVERSAL CITY, LOS ANGELES, CALIFORNIA

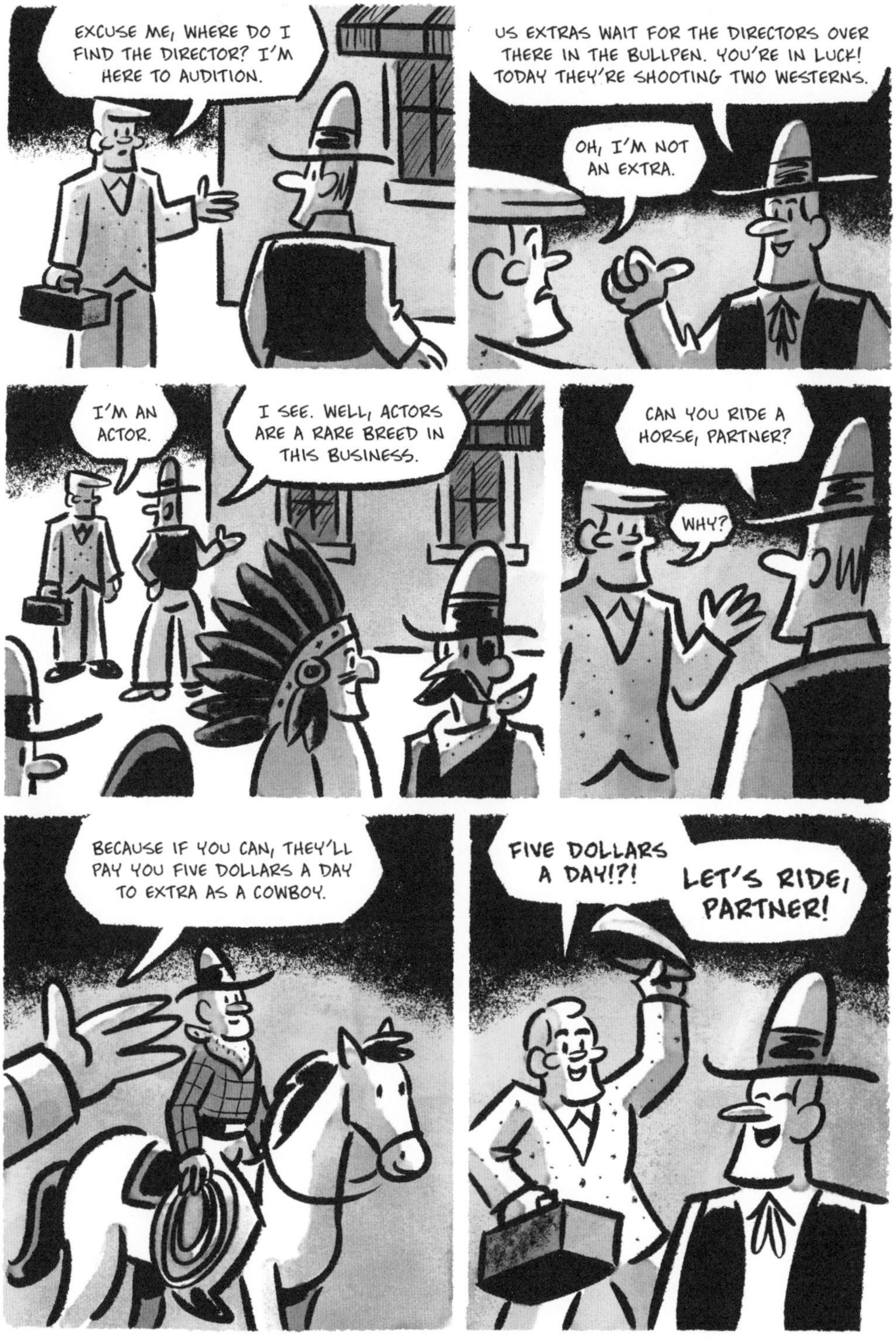
EXCUSE ME, WHERE DO I FIND THE DIRECTOR? I'M HERE TO AUDITION.
US EXTRAS WAIT FOR THE DIRECTORS OVER THERE IN THE BULLPEN. YOU'RE IN LUCK! TODAY THEY'RE SHOOTING TWO WESTERNS.
OH, I'M NOT AN EXTRA.
I'M AN ACTOR.
I SEE. WELL, ACTORS ARE A RARE BREED IN THIS BUSINESS.
CAN YOU RIDE A HORSE, PARTNER?
WHY?
BECAUSE IF YOU CAN, THEY'LL PAY YOU FIVE DOLLARS A DAY TO EXTRA AS A COWBOY.
FIVE DOLLARS A DAY!?!
LET'S RIDE, PARTNER!

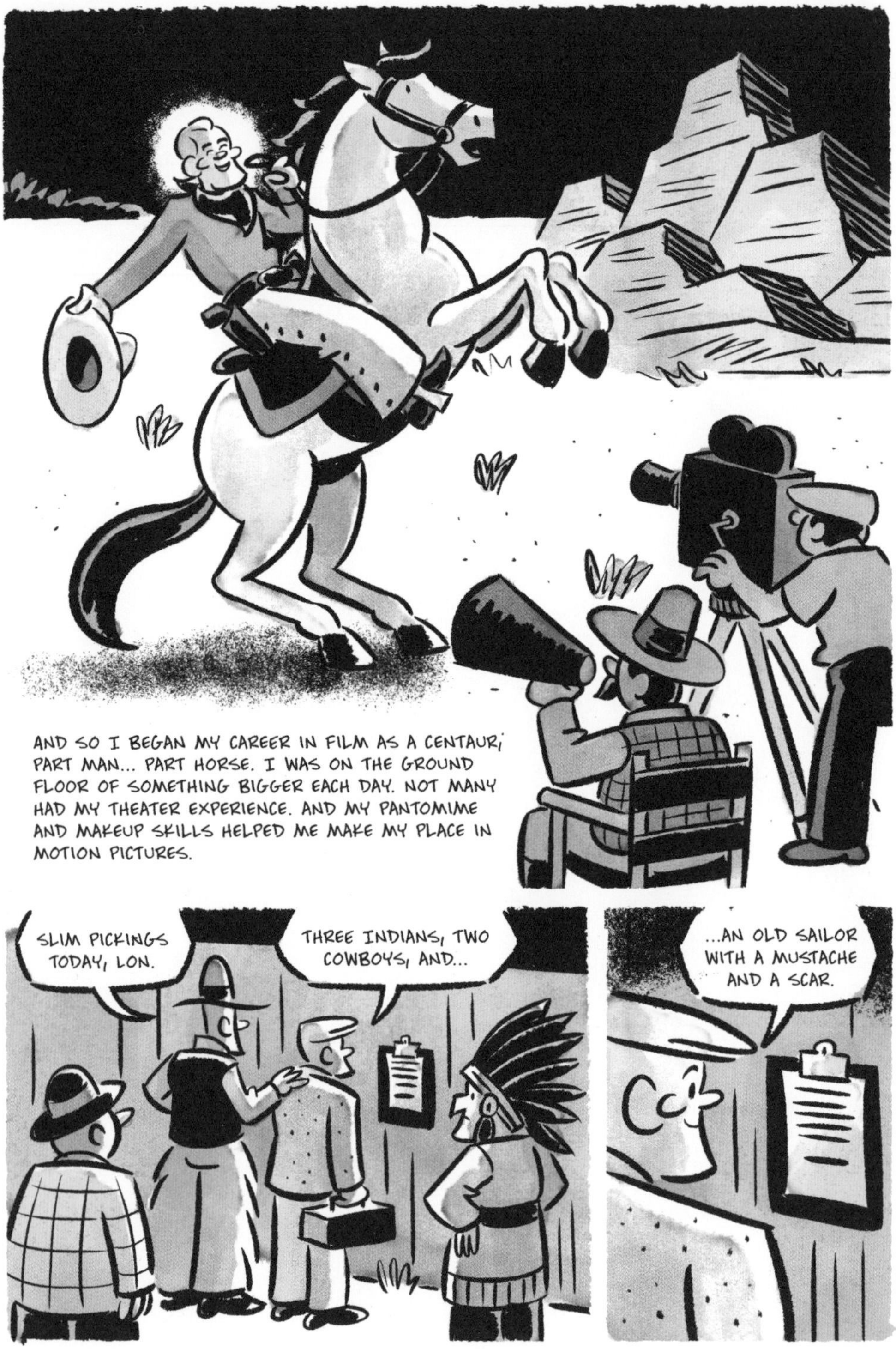
AND SO I BEGAN MY CAREER IN FILM AS A CENTAUR; PART MAN... PART HORSE. I WAS ON THE GROUND FLOOR OF SOMETHING BIGGER EACH DAY. NOT MANY HAD MY THEATER EXPERIENCE. AND MY PANTOMIME AND MAKEUP SKILLS HELPED ME MAKE MY PLACE IN MOTION PICTURES.
SLIM PICKINGS TODAY, LON.
THREE INDIANS, TWO COWBOYS, AND...
...AN OLD SAILOR WITH A MUSTACHE AND A SCAR.

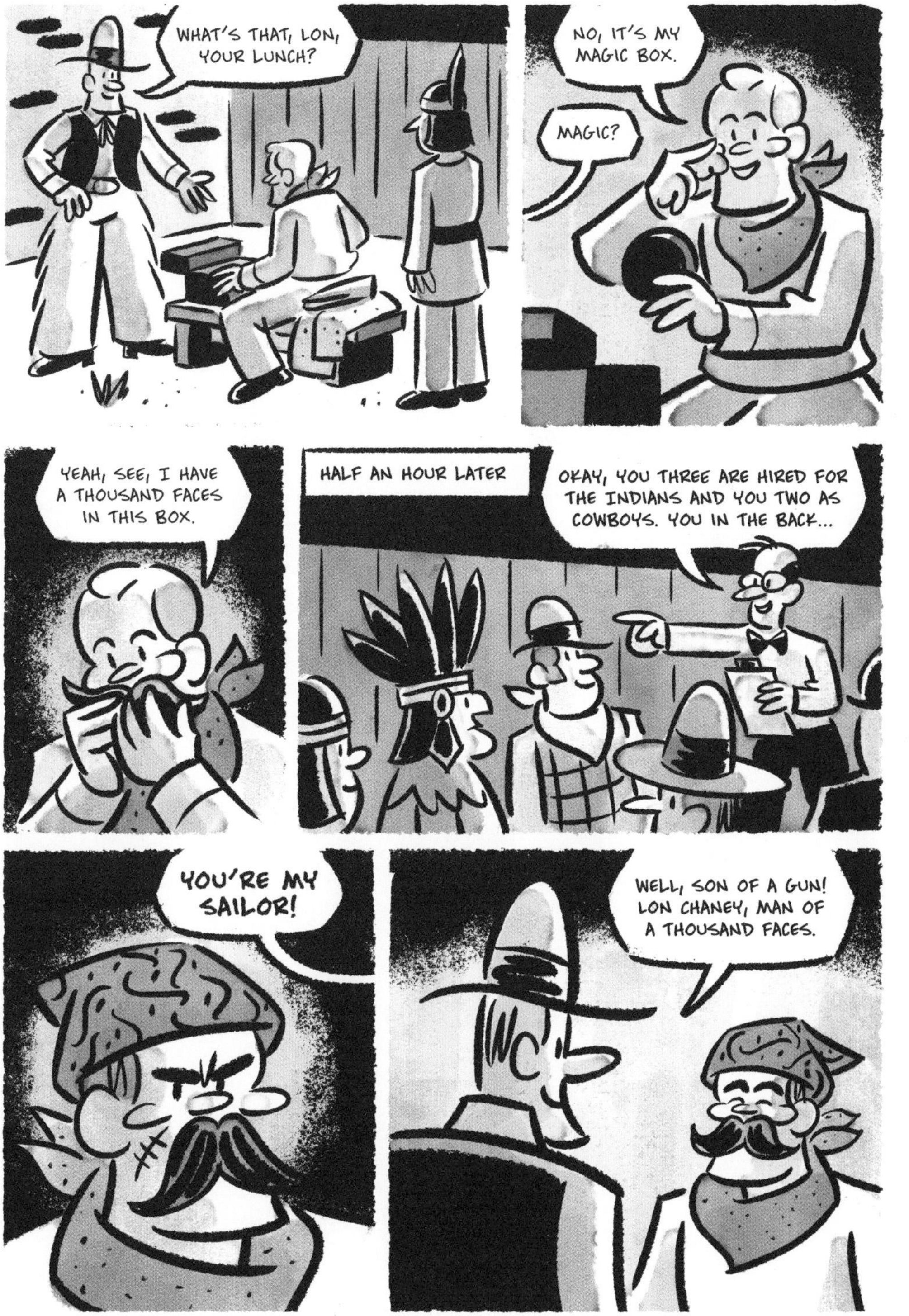
WHAT'S THAT, LON, YOUR LUNCH?
NO, IT'S MY MAGIC BOX.
MAGIC?
YEAH, SEE, I HAVE A THOUSAND FACES IN THIS BOX.
HALF AN HOUR LATER
OKAY, YOU THREE ARE HIRED FOR THE INDIANS AND YOU TWO AS COWBOYS. YOU IN THE BACK...
YOU'RE MY SAILOR!
WELL, SON OF A GUN! LON CHANEY, MAN OF A THOUSAND FACES.

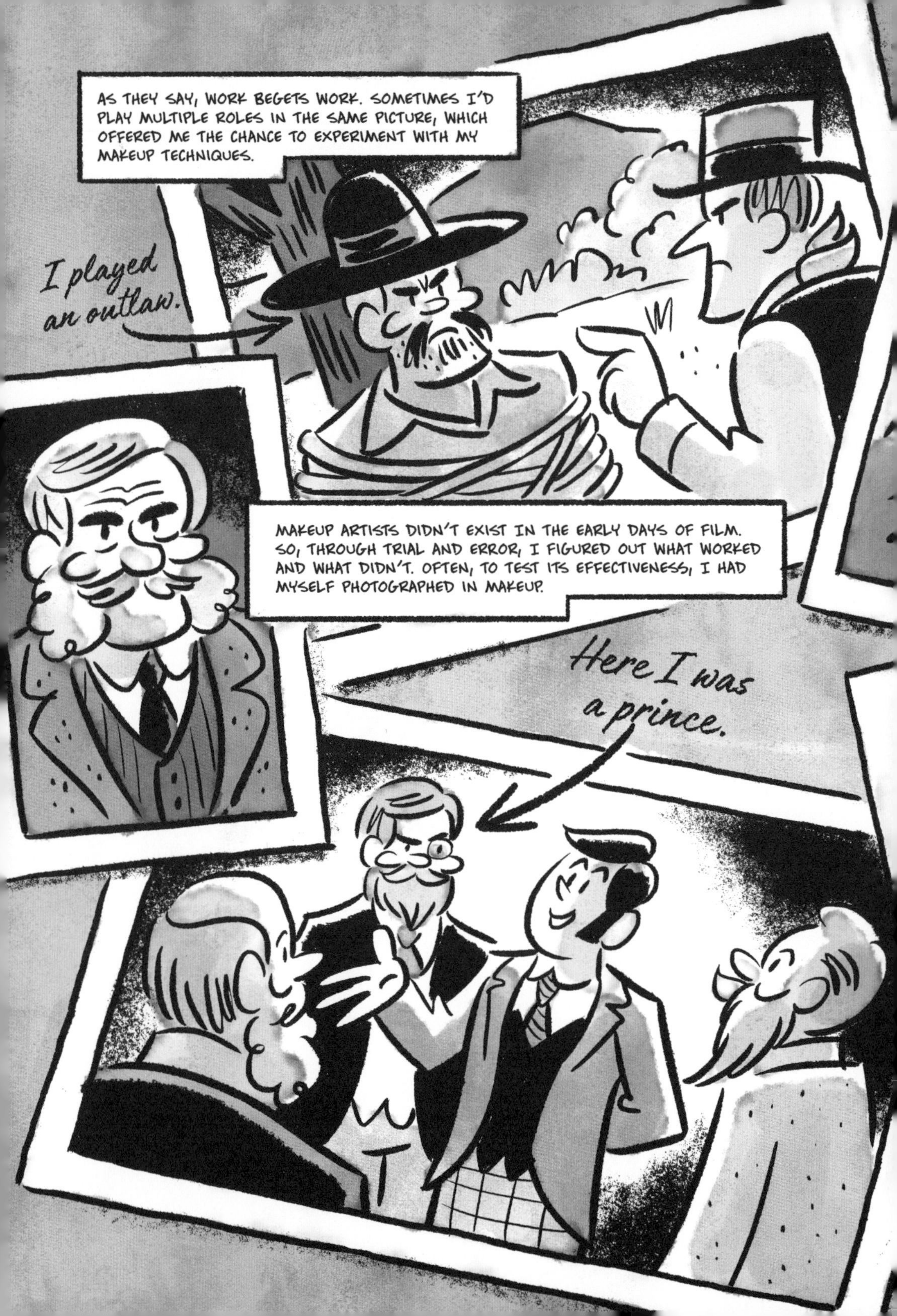
AS THEY SAY, WORK BEGETS WORK. SOMETIMES I'D PLAY MULTIPLE ROLES IN THE SAME PICTURE, WHICH OFFERED ME THE CHANCE TO EXPERIMENT WITH MY MAKEUP TECHNIQUES.
I played an outlaw.
MAKEUP ARTISTS DIDN'T EXIST IN THE EARLY DAYS OF FILM. SO, THROUGH TRIAL AND ERROR, I FIGURED OUT WHAT WORKED AND WHAT DIDN'T. OFTEN, TO TEST ITS EFFECTIVENESS, I HAD MYSELF PHOTOGRAPHED IN MAKEUP.
Here I was a prince.

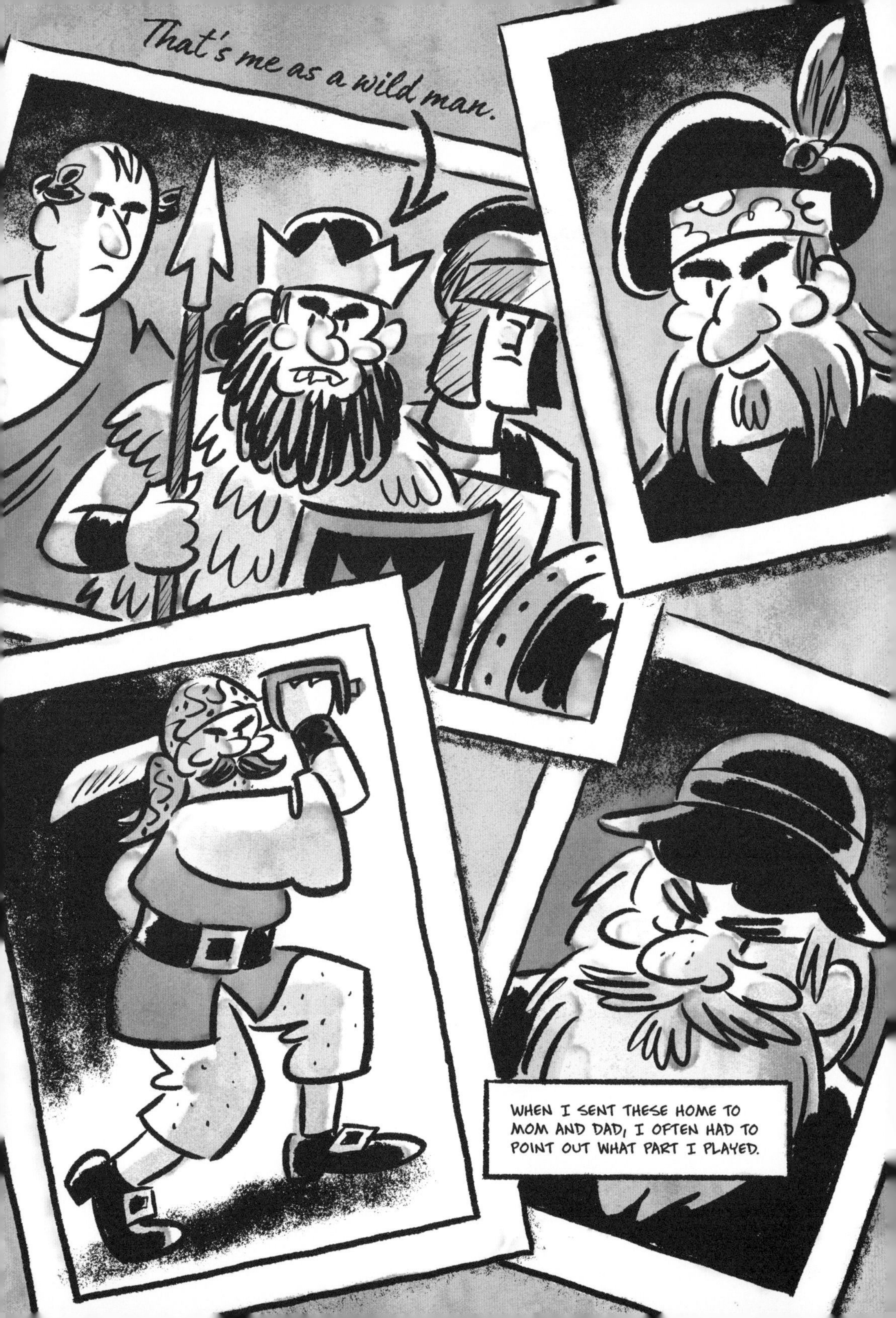

That's me as a wild man.
WHEN I SENT THESE HOME TO MOM AND DAD, I OFTEN HAD TO POINT OUT WHAT PART I PLAYED.

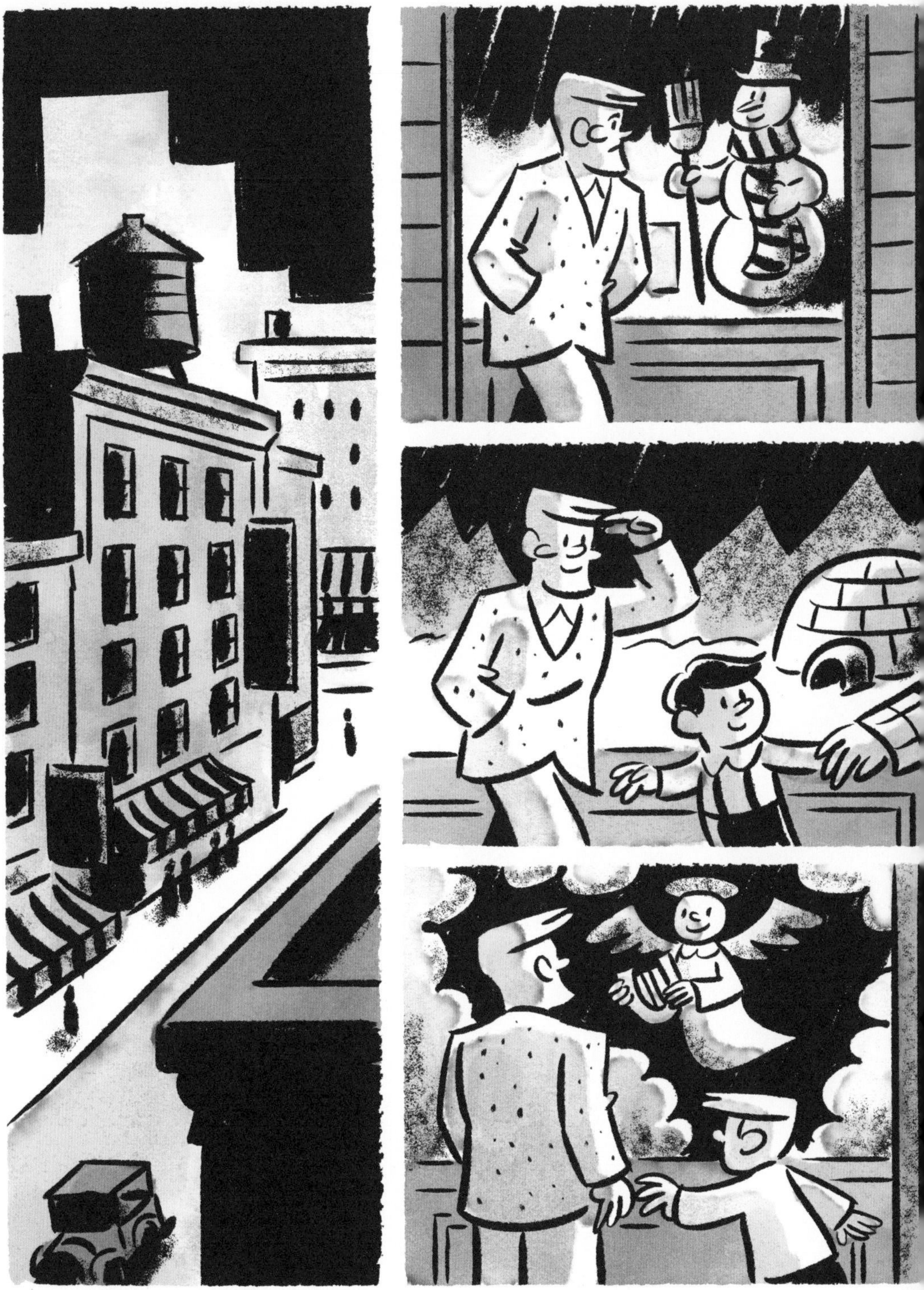

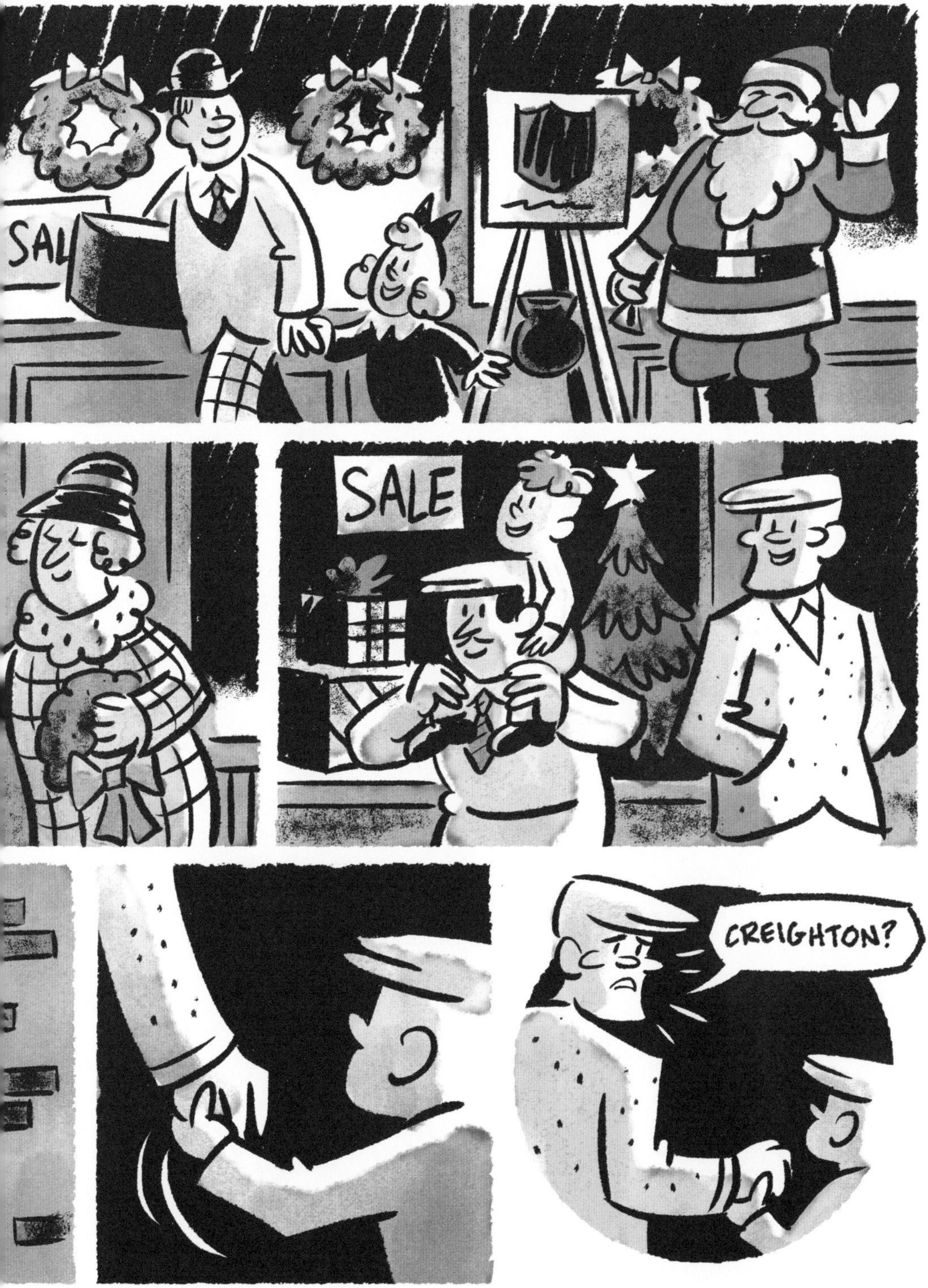
SAL
SALE
CREIGHTON?

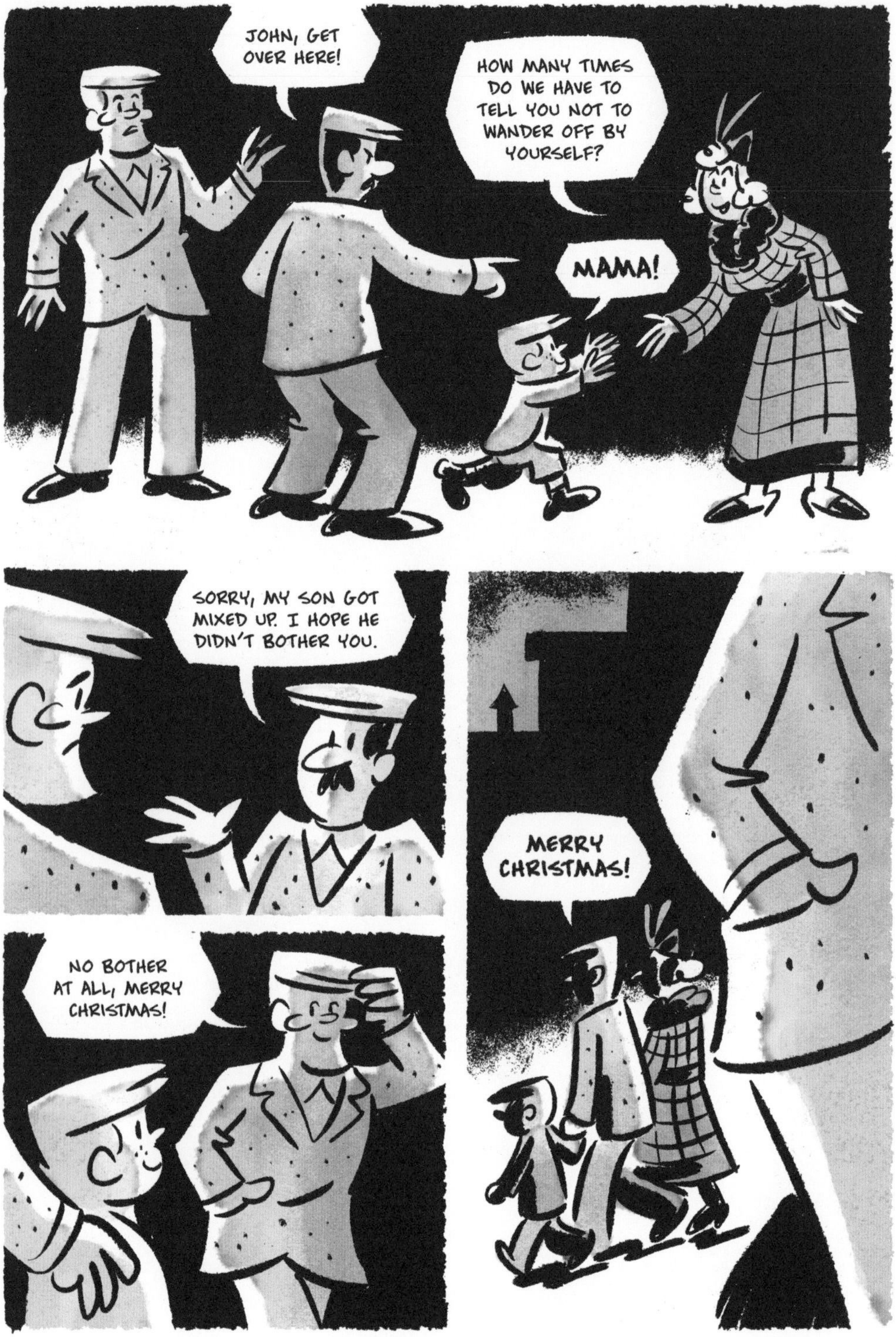
JOHN, GET OVER HERE!
HOW MANY TIMES DO WE HAVE TO TELL YOU NOT TO WANDER OFF BY YOURSELF?
MAMA!
SORRY, MY SON GOT MIXED UP. I HOPE HE DIDN'T BOTHER YOU.
NO BOTHER AT ALL, MERRY CHRISTMAS!
MERRY CHRISTMAS!

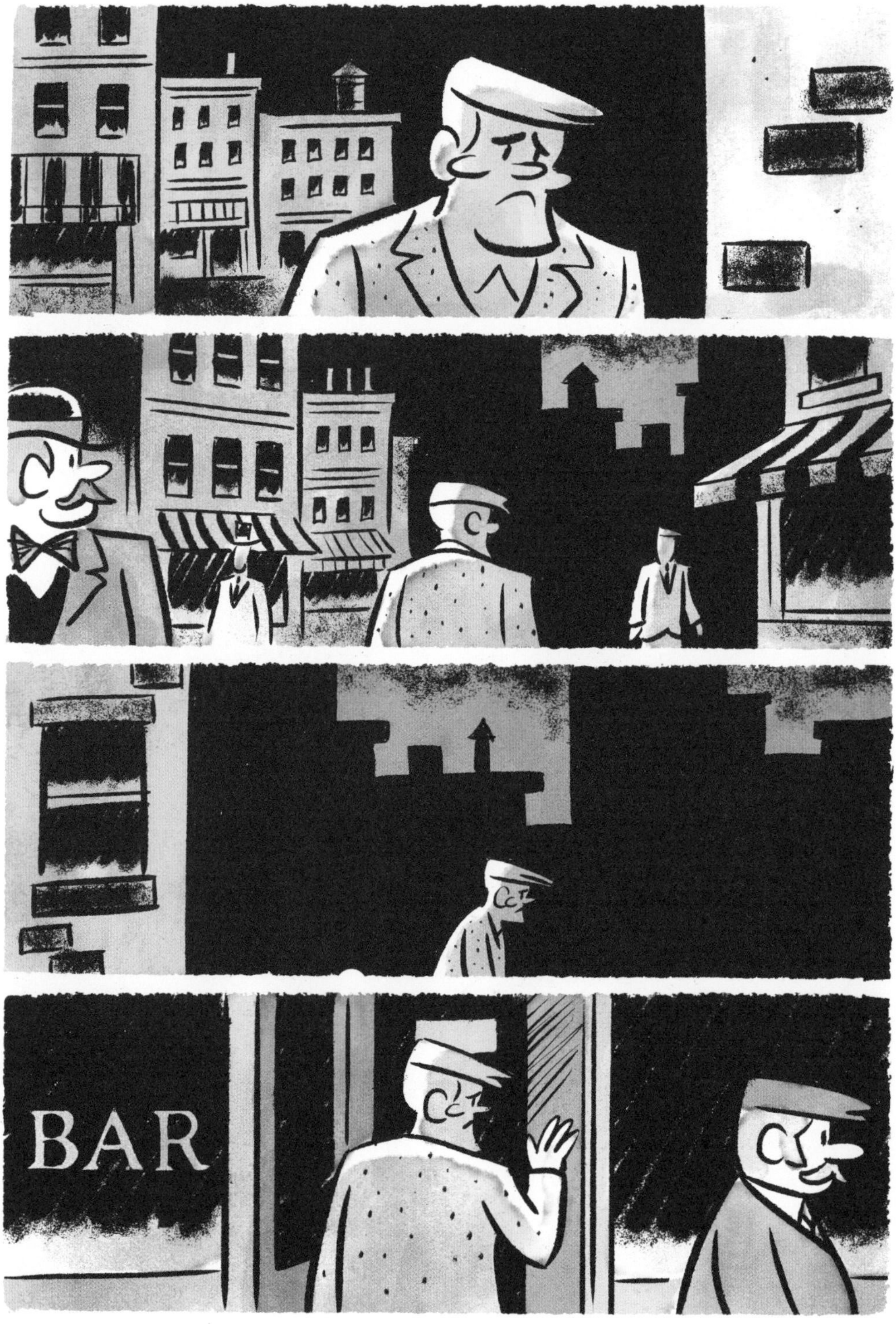
BAR

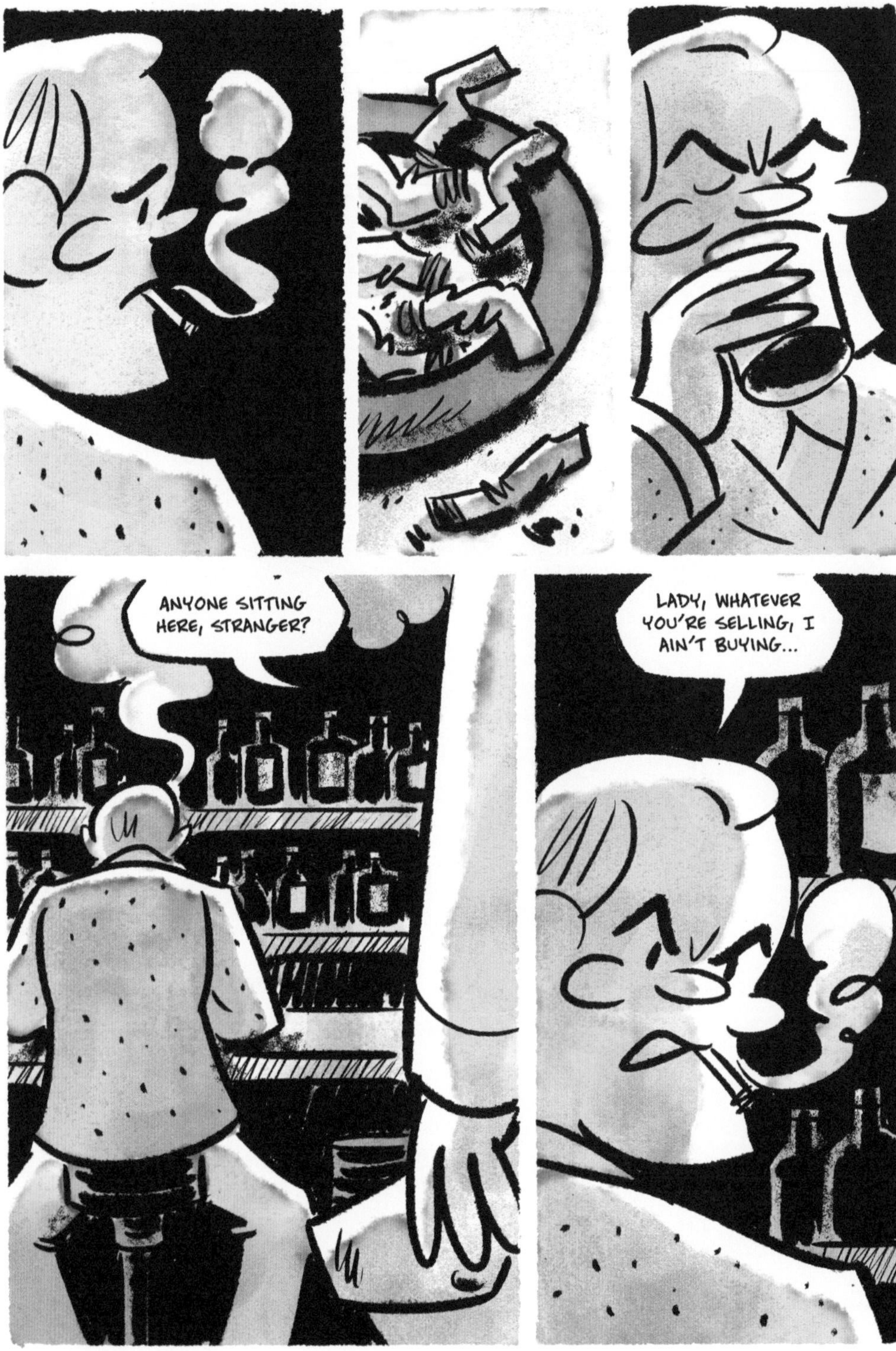
ANYONE SITTING HERE, STRANGER?
LADY, WHATEVER YOU'RE SELLING, I AIN'T BUYING...

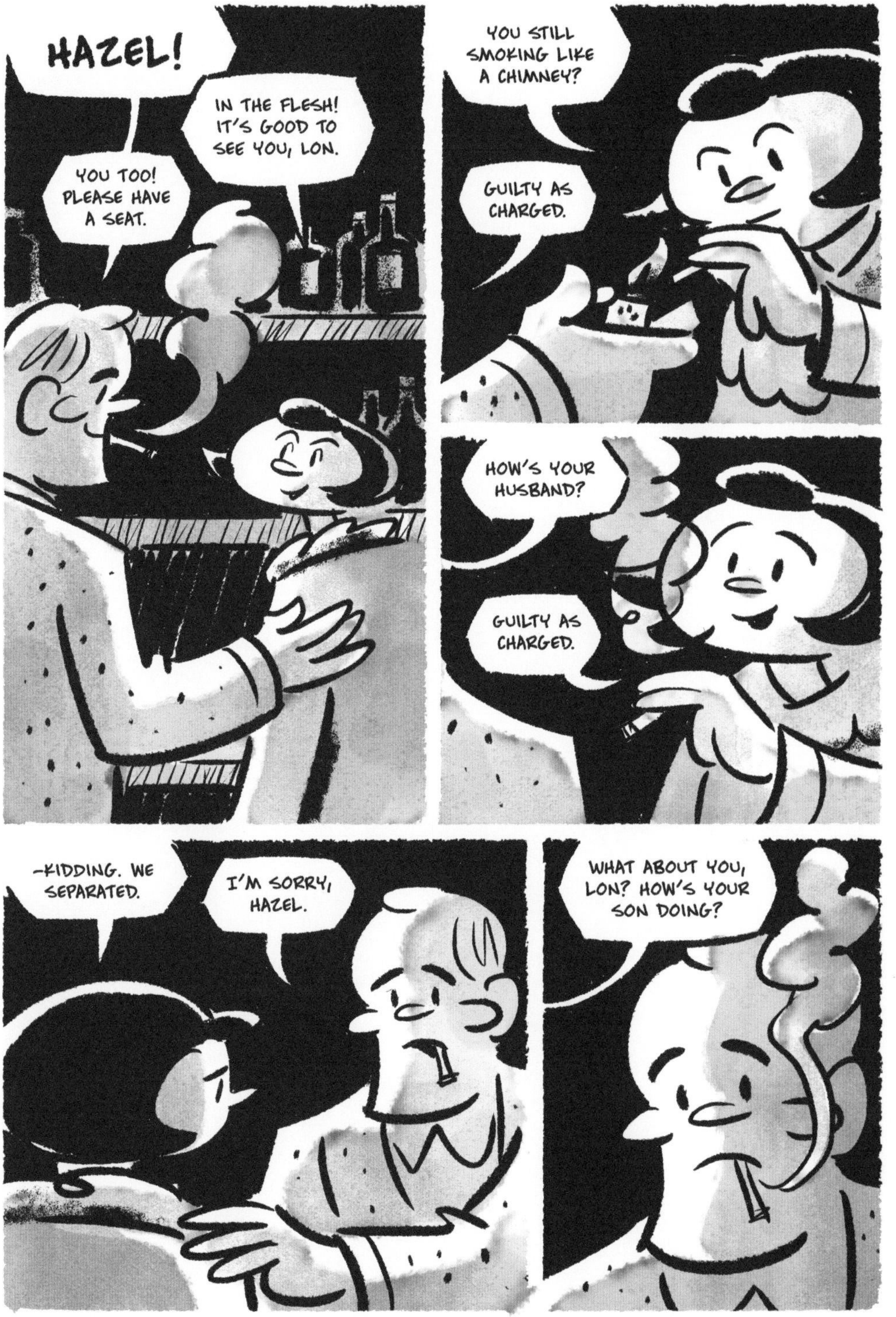
HAZEL!
IN THE FLESH! IT'S GOOD TO SEE YOU, LON.
YOU TOO! PLEASE HAVE A SEAT.
YOU STILL SMOKING LIKE A CHIMNEY?
GUILTY AS CHARGED.
HOW'S YOUR HUSBAND?
GUILTY AS CHARGED.
-KIDDING. WE SEPARATED.
I'M SORRY, HAZEL.
WHAT ABOUT YOU, LON? HOW'S YOUR SON DOING?

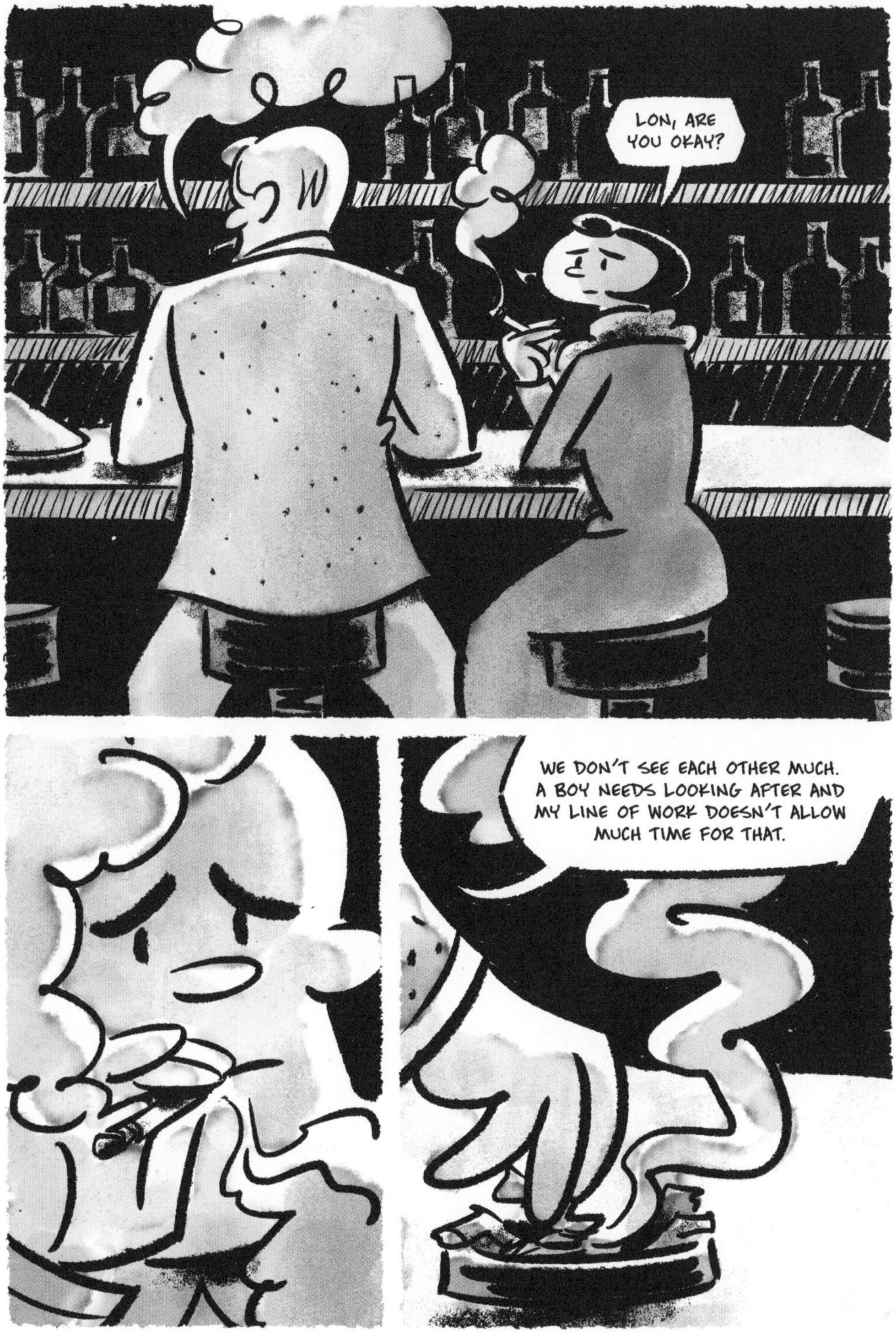
LON, ARE YOU OKAY?
WE DON'T SEE EACH OTHER MUCH. A BOY NEEDS LOOKING AFTER AND MY LINE OF WORK DOESN'T ALLOW MUCH TIME FOR THAT.

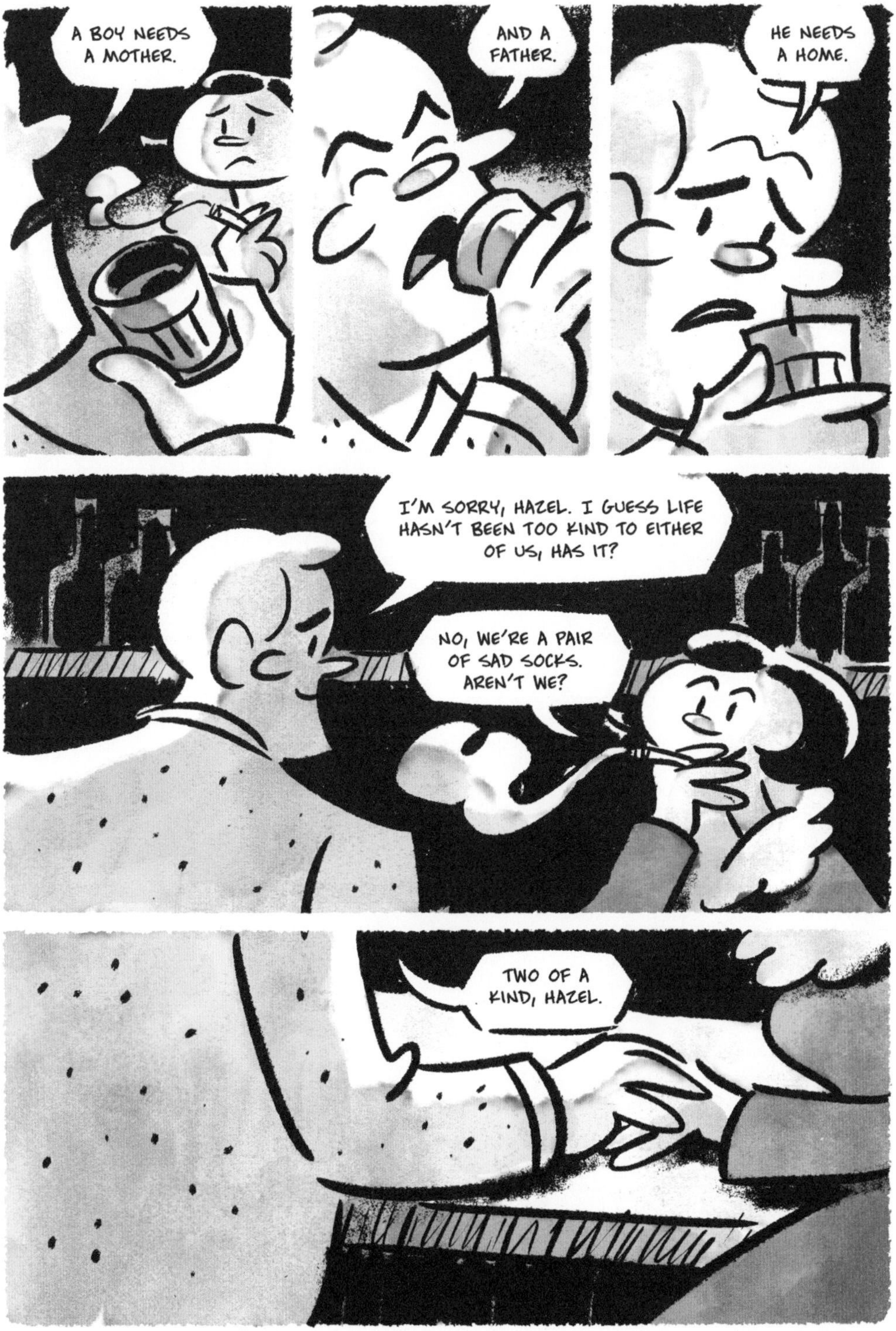
A BOY NEEDS A MOTHER.
AND A FATHER.
HE NEEDS A HOME.
I'M SORRY, HAZEL. I GUESS LIFE HASN'T BEEN TOO KIND TO EITHER OF US, HAS IT?
NO, WE'RE A PAIR OF SAD SOCKS. AREN'T WE?
TWO OF A KIND, HAZEL.

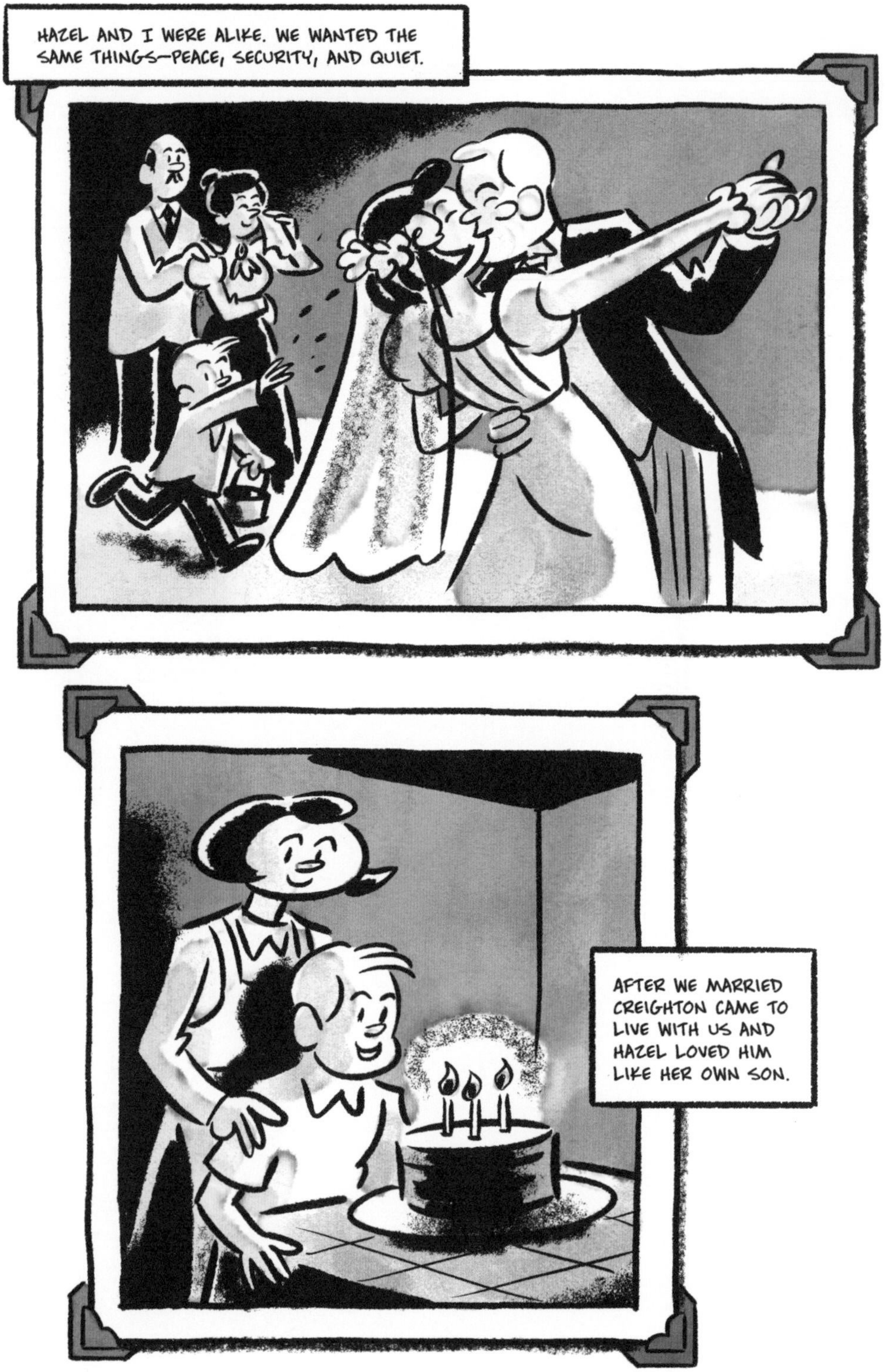
HAZEL AND I WERE ALIKE. WE WANTED THE SAME THINGS—PEACE, SECURITY, AND QUIET.
AFTER WE MARRIED CREIGHTON CAME TO LIVE WITH US AND HAZEL LOVED HIM LIKE HER OWN SON.

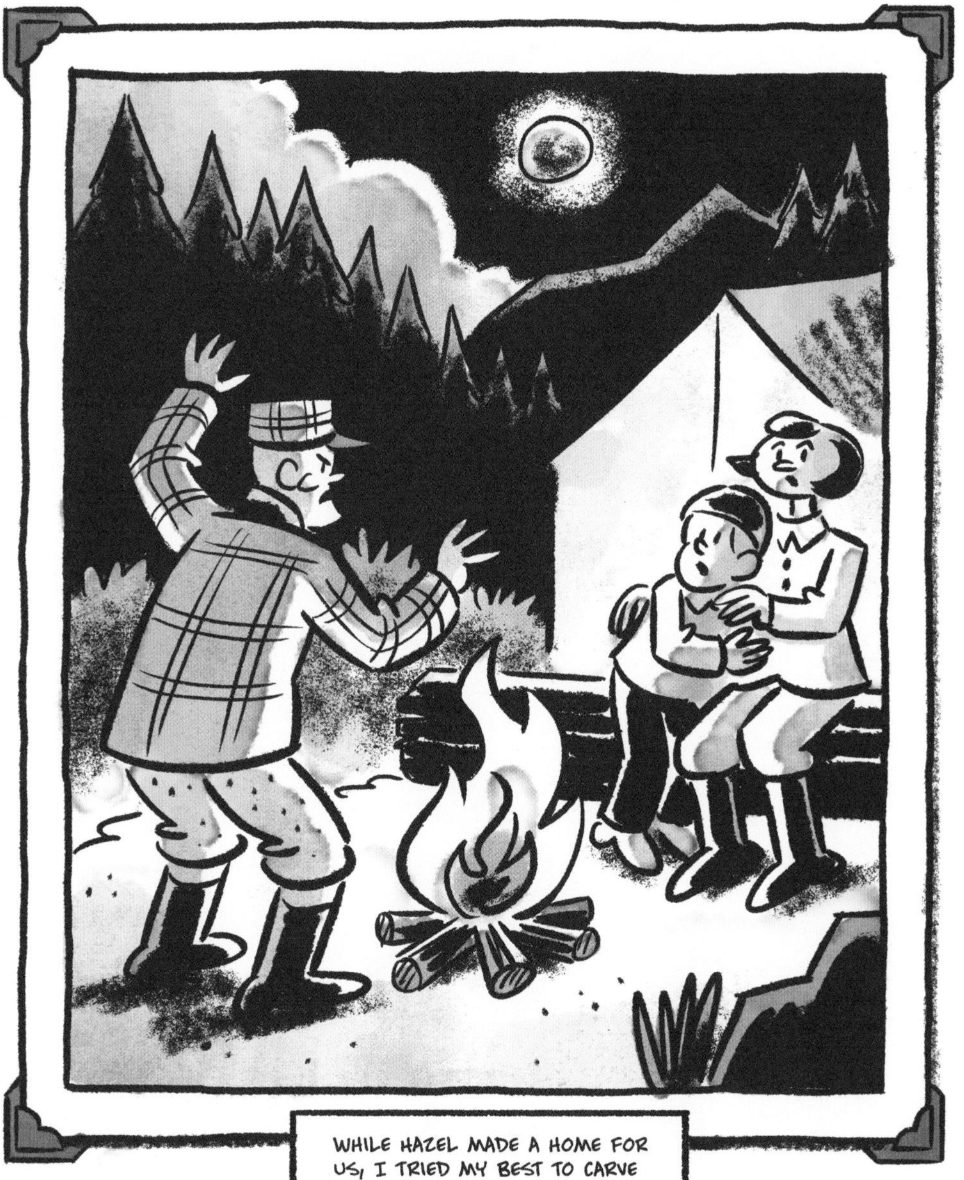

WHILE HAZEL MADE A HOME FOR US, I TRIED MY BEST TO CARVE OUT A NICHE IN PICTURES.

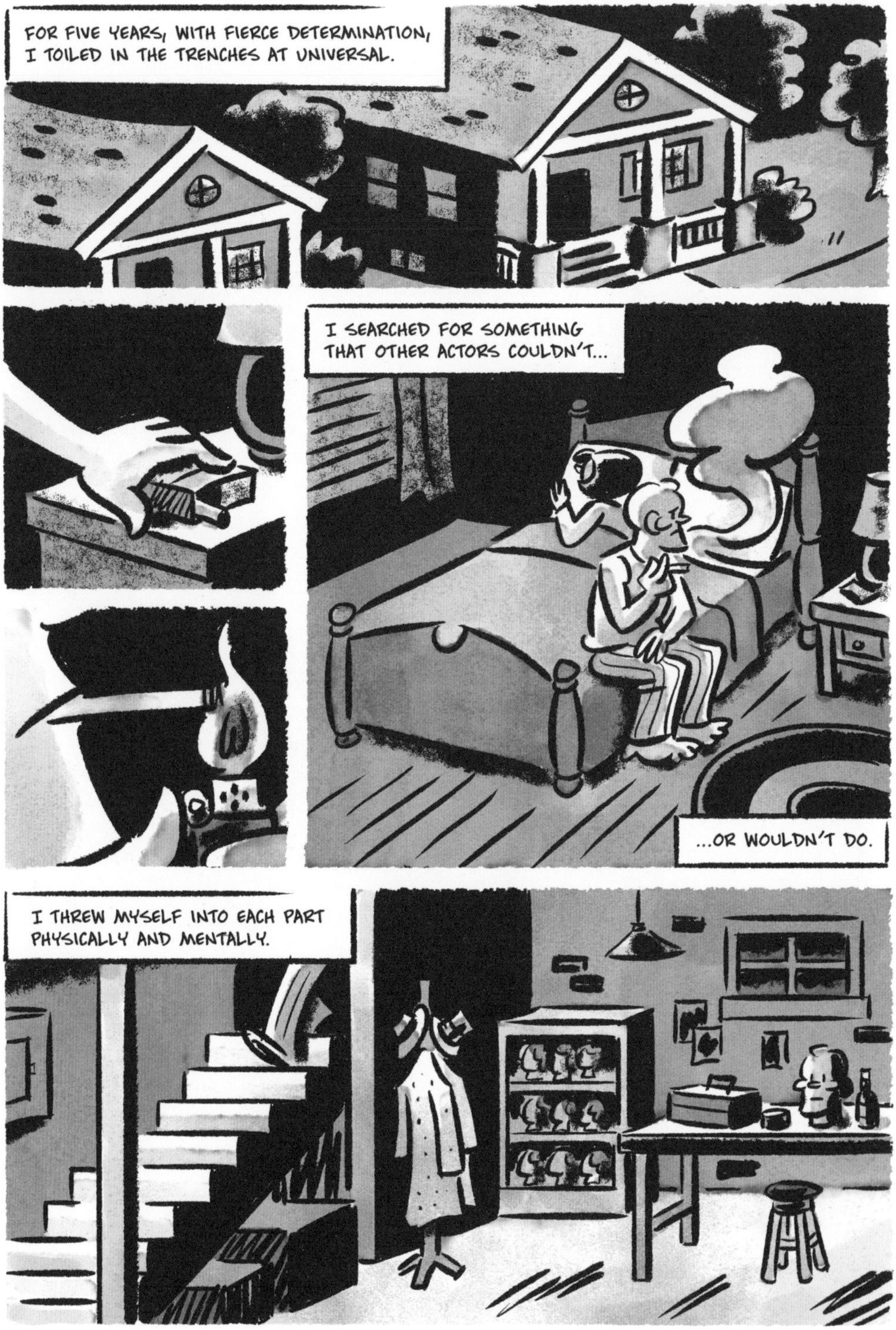
FOR FIVE YEARS, WITH FIERCE DETERMINATION, I TOILED IN THE TRENCHES AT UNIVERSAL.
I SEARCHED FOR SOMETHING THAT OTHER ACTORS COULDN'T...
...OR WOULDN'T DO.
I THREW MYSELF INTO EACH PART PHYSICALLY AND MENTALLY.

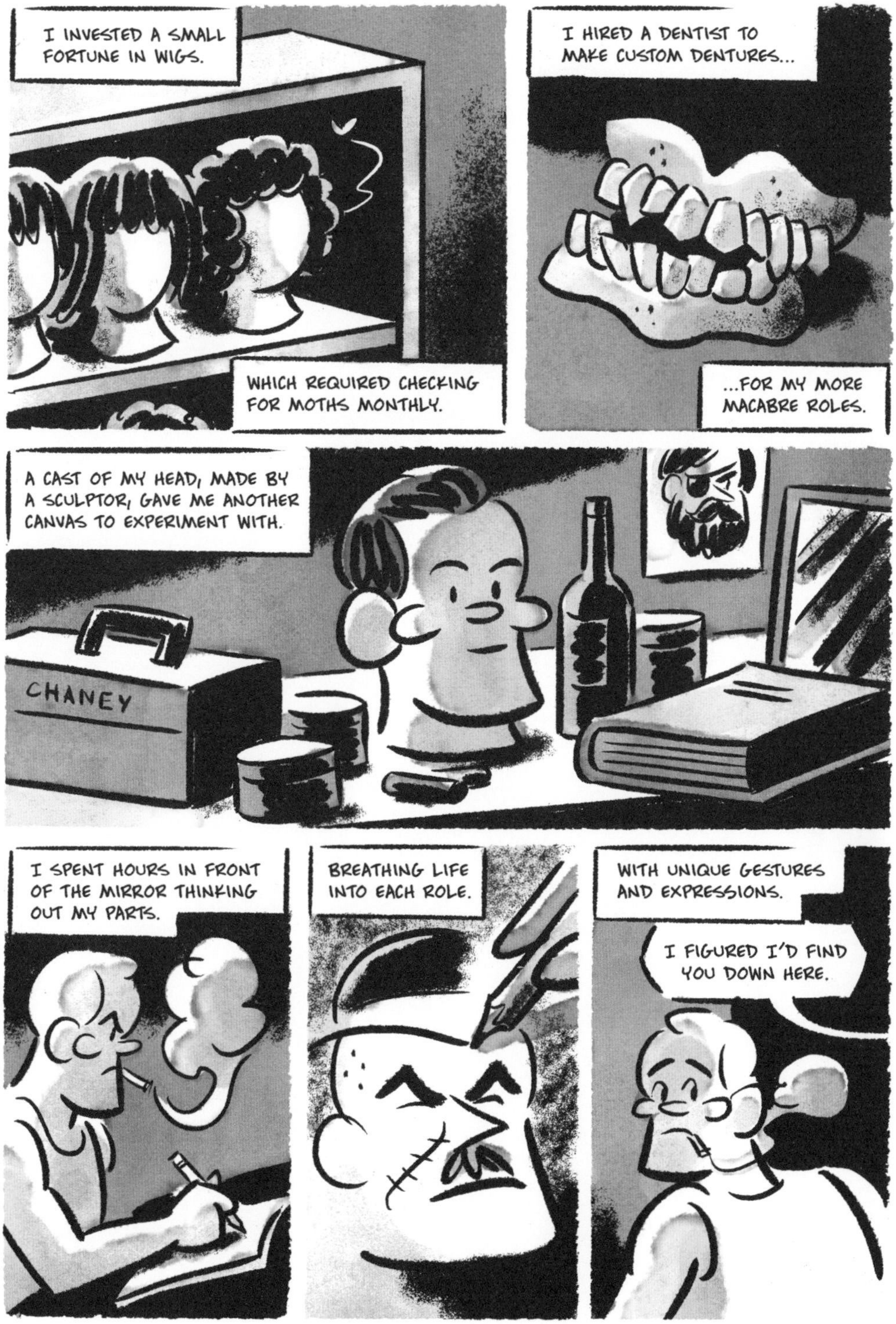

I INVESTED A SMALL FORTUNE IN WIGS.
WHICH REQUIRED CHECKING FOR MOTHS MONTHLY.
I HIRED A DENTIST TO MAKE CUSTOM DENTURES...
...FOR MY MORE MACABRE ROLES.
A CAST OF MY HEAD, MADE BY A SCULPTOR, GAVE ME ANOTHER CANVAS TO EXPERIMENT WITH.
CHANEY
I SPENT HOURS IN FRONT OF THE MIRROR THINKING OUT MY PARTS.
BREATHING LIFE INTO EACH ROLE.
WITH UNIQUE GESTURES AND EXPRESSIONS.
I FIGURED I'D FIND YOU DOWN HERE.

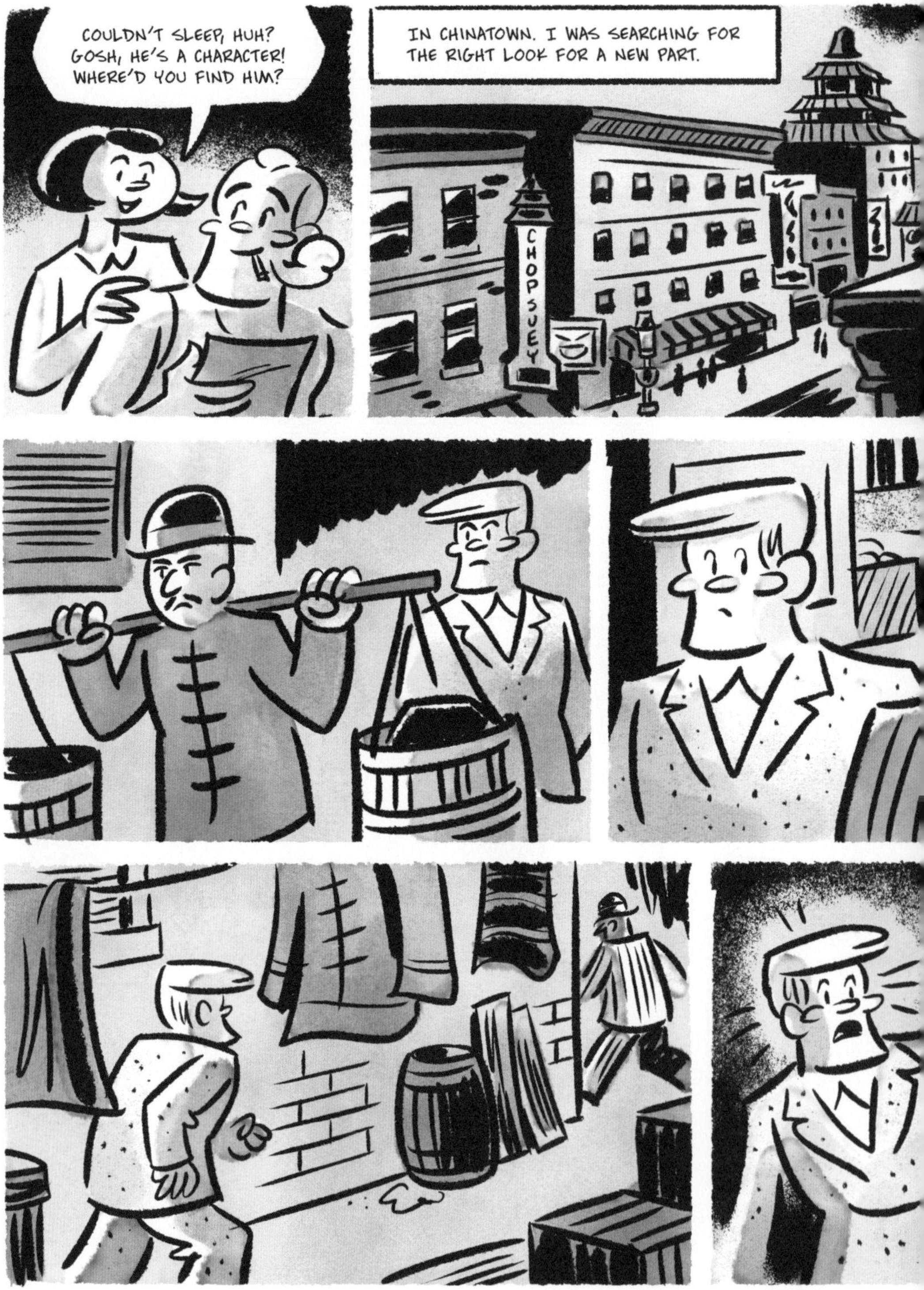
COULDN'T SLEEP, HUH? GOSH, HE'S A CHARACTER! WHERE'D YOU FIND HIM?
IN CHINATOWN. I WAS SEARCHING FOR THE RIGHT LOOK FOR A NEW PART.
CHOP SUEY

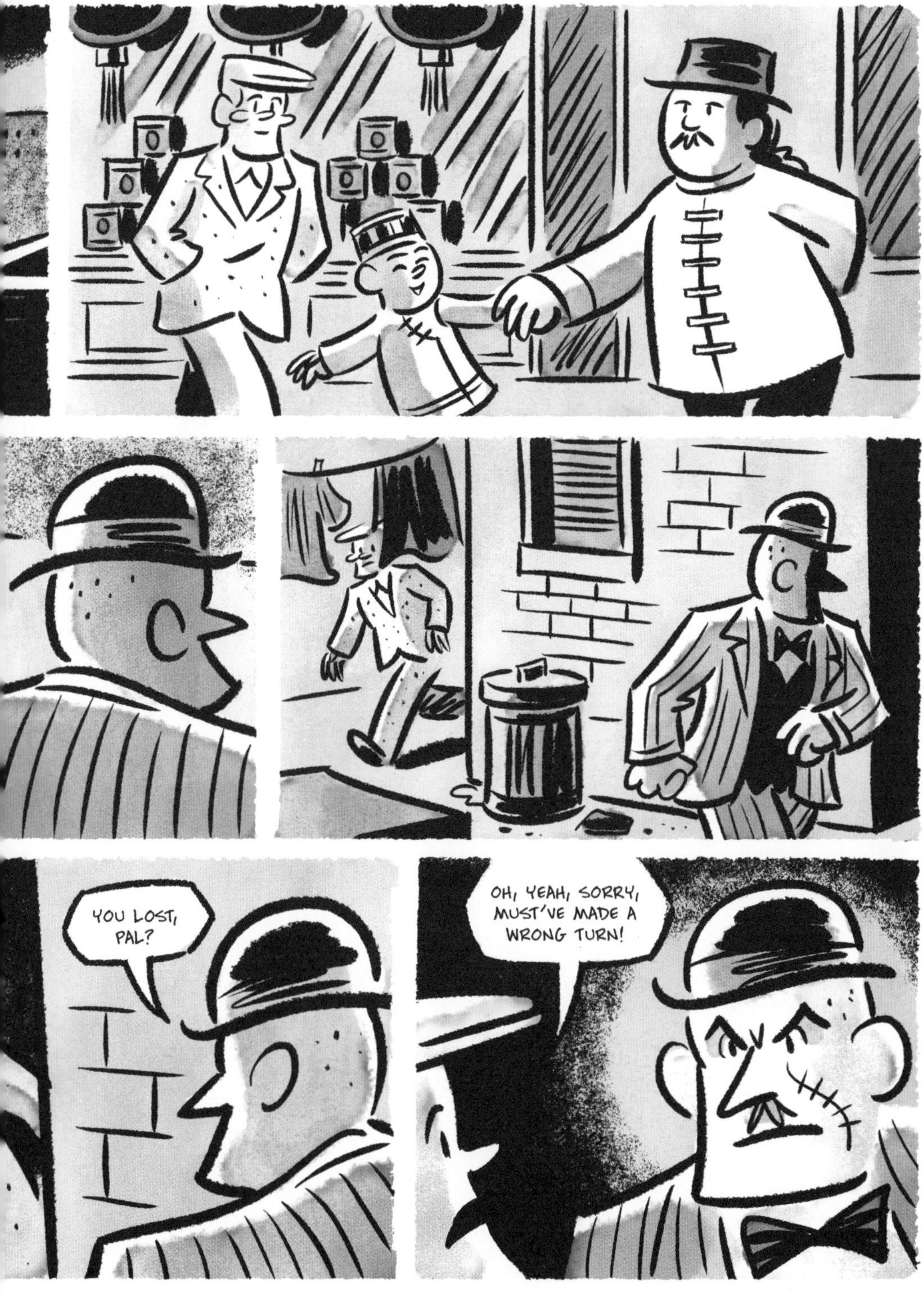

YOU LOST, PAL?
OH, YEAH, SORRY, MUST'VE MADE A WRONG TURN!

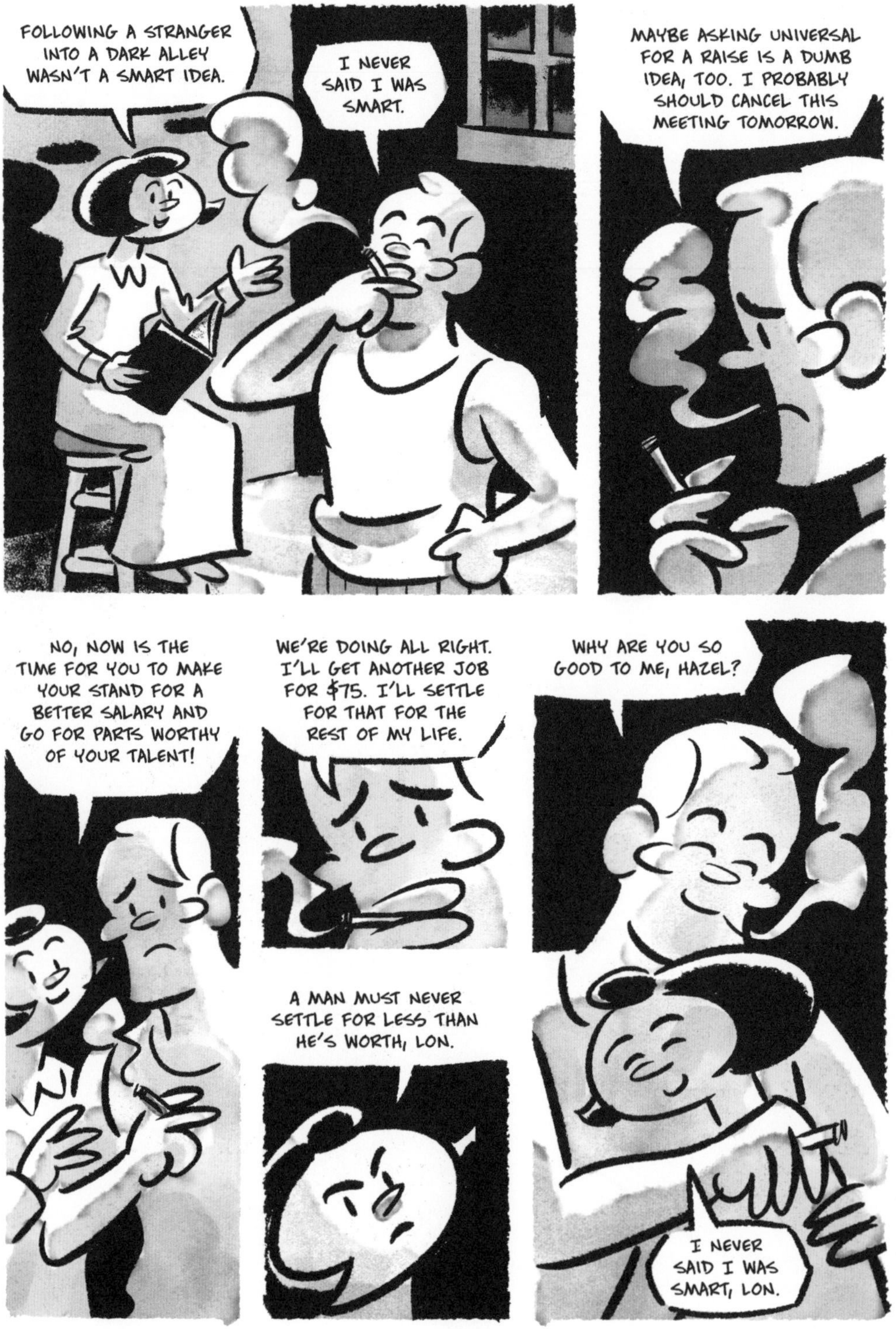
FOLLOWING A STRANGER INTO A DARK ALLEY WASN'T A SMART IDEA.
I NEVER SAID I WAS SMART.
MAYBE ASKING UNIVERSAL FOR A RAISE IS A DUMB IDEA, TOO. I PROBABLY SHOULD CANCEL THIS MEETING TOMORROW.
NO, NOW IS THE TIME FOR YOU TO MAKE YOUR STAND FOR A BETTER SALARY AND GO FOR PARTS WORTHY OF YOUR TALENT!
WE'RE DOING ALL RIGHT. I'LL GET ANOTHER JOB FOR $75. I'LL SETTLE FOR THAT FOR THE REST OF MY LIFE.
A MAN MUST NEVER SETTLE FOR LESS THAN HE'S WORTH, LON.
WHY ARE YOU SO GOOD TO ME, HAZEL?
I NEVER SAID I WAS SMART, LON.

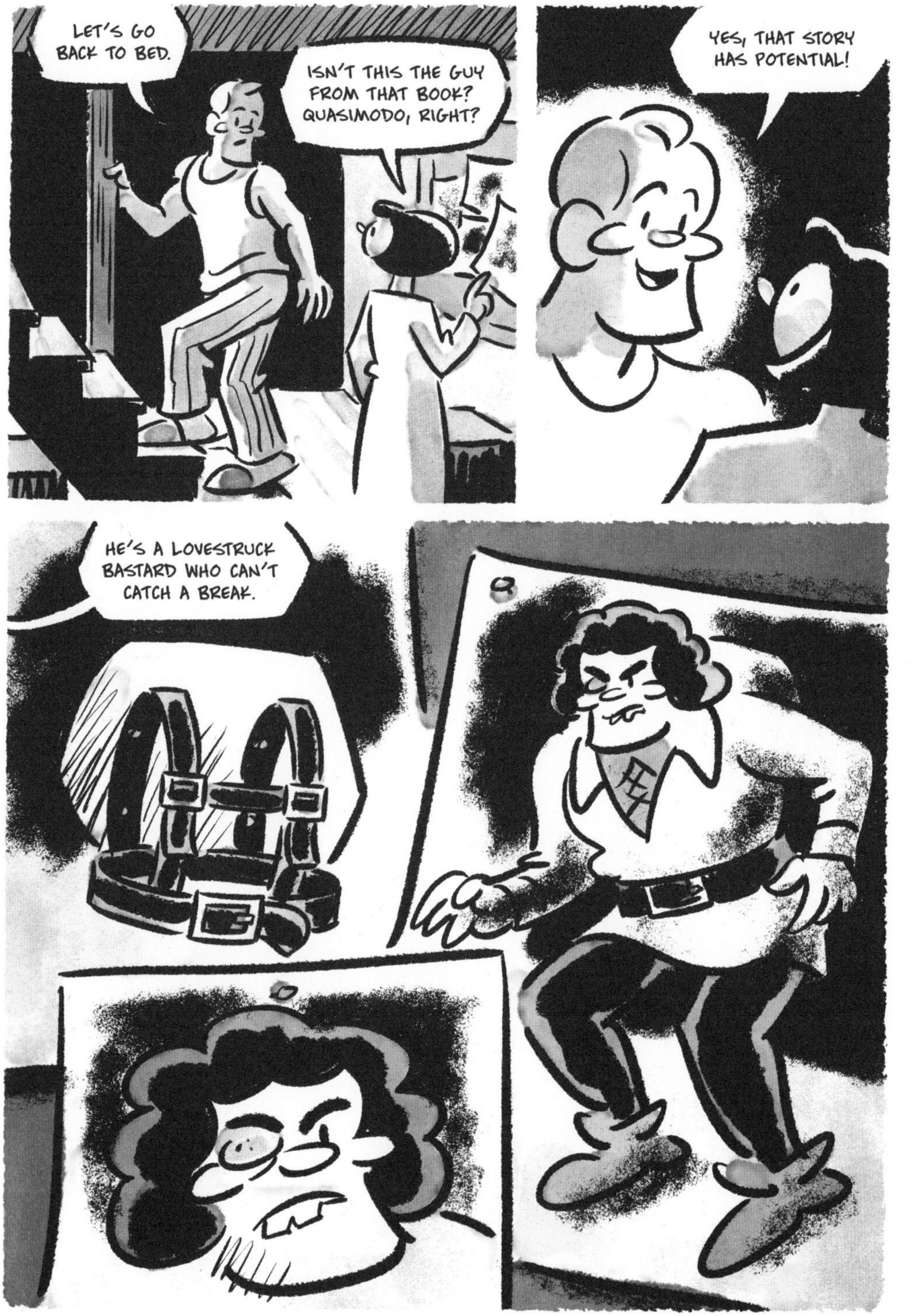
LET'S GO BACK TO BED.
ISN'T THIS THE GUY FROM THAT BOOK? QUASIMODO, RIGHT?
YES, THAT STORY HAS POTENTIAL!
HE'S A LOVESTRUCK BASTARD WHO CAN'T CATCH A BREAK.

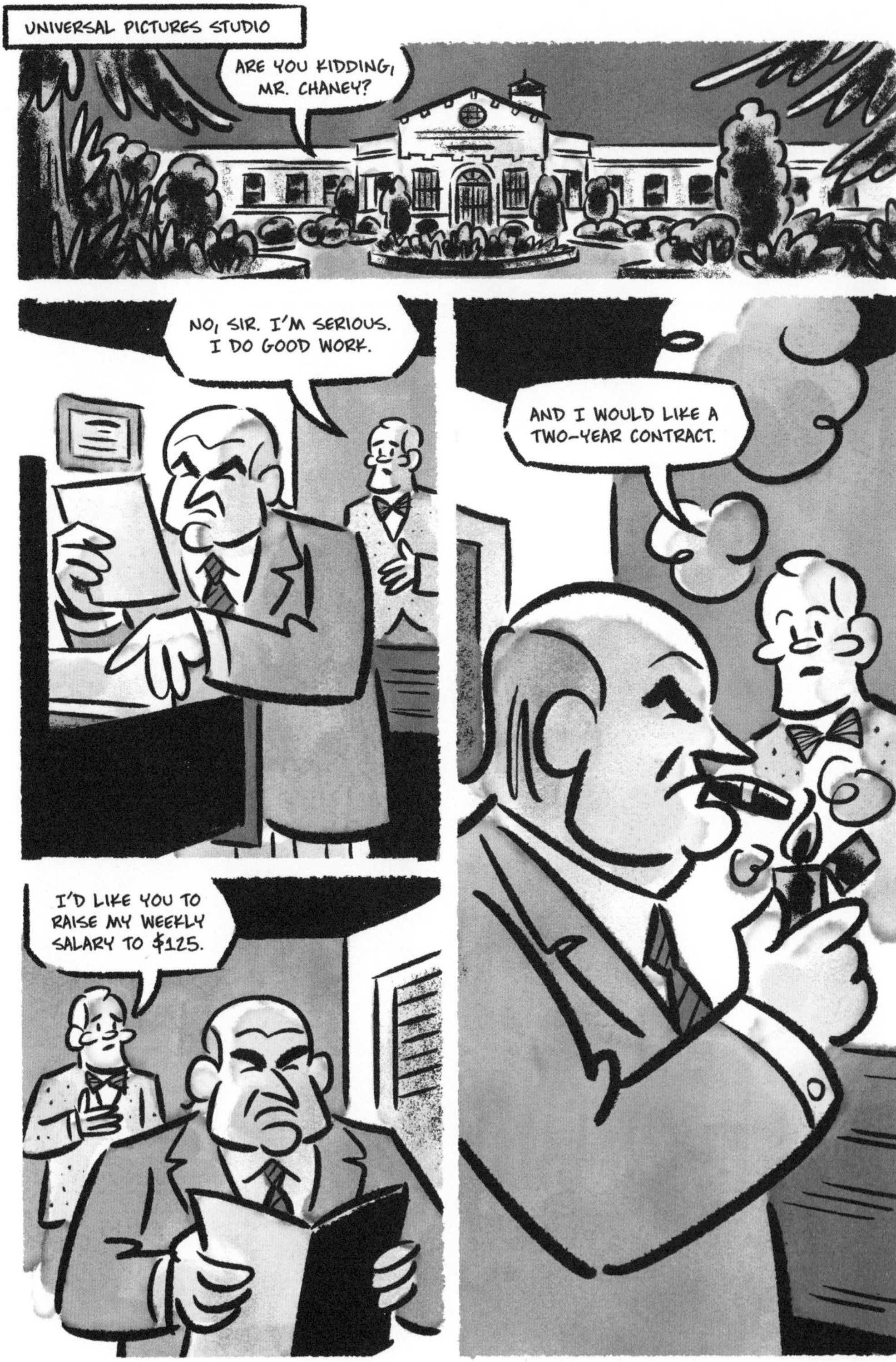
UNIVERSAL PICTURES STUDIO
ARE YOU KIDDING, MR. CHANEY?
NO, SIR. I'M SERIOUS. I DO GOOD WORK.
I'D LIKE YOU TO RAISE MY WEEKLY SALARY TO $125.
AND I WOULD LIKE A TWO-YEAR CONTRACT.

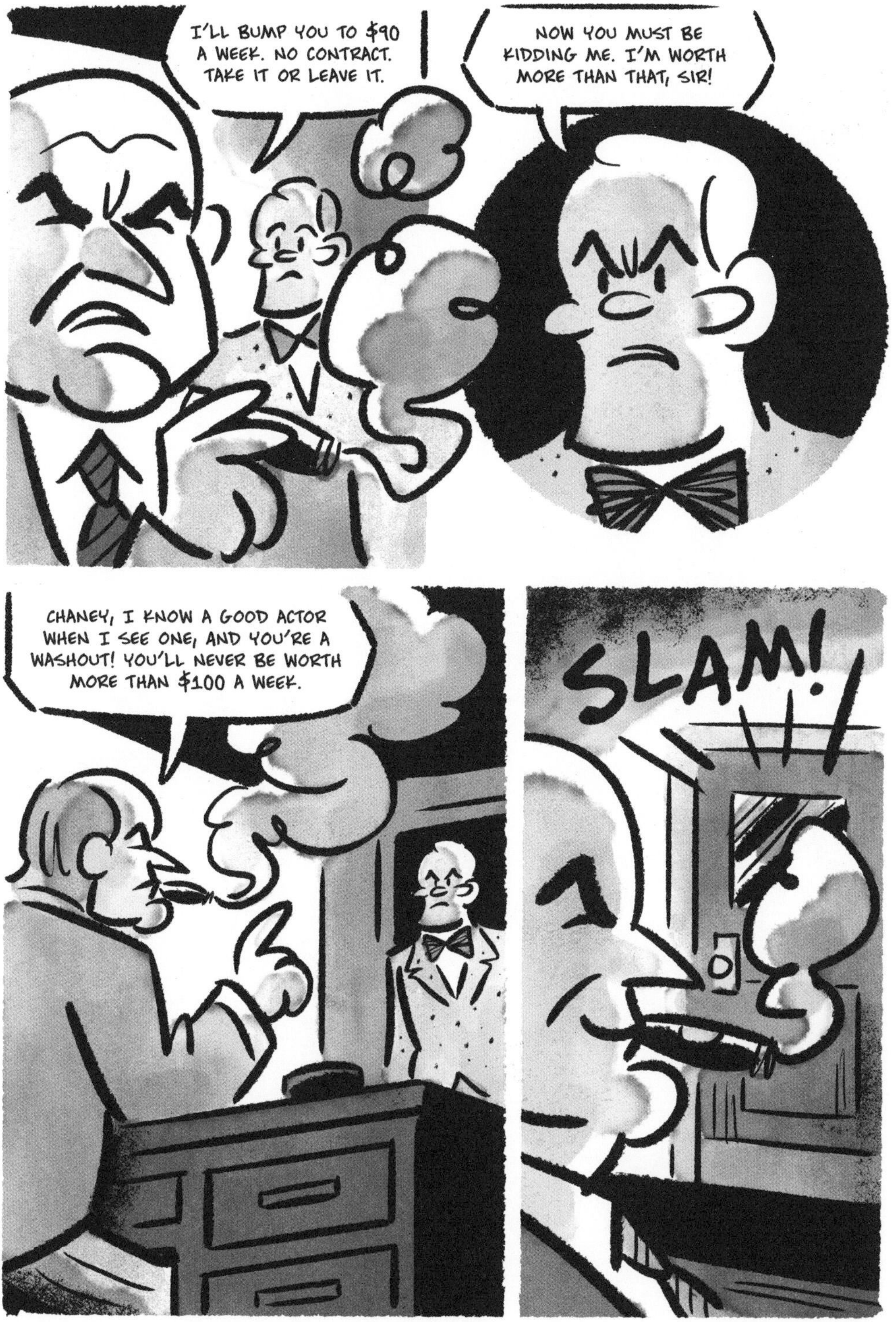
I'LL BUMP YOU TO $90 A WEEK. NO CONTRACT. TAKE IT OR LEAVE IT.
NOW YOU MUST BE KIDDING ME. I'M WORTH MORE THAN THAT, SIR!
CHANEY, I KNOW A GOOD ACTOR WHEN I SEE ONE, AND YOU'RE A WASHOUT! YOU'LL NEVER BE WORTH MORE THAN $100 A WEEK.
SLAM!

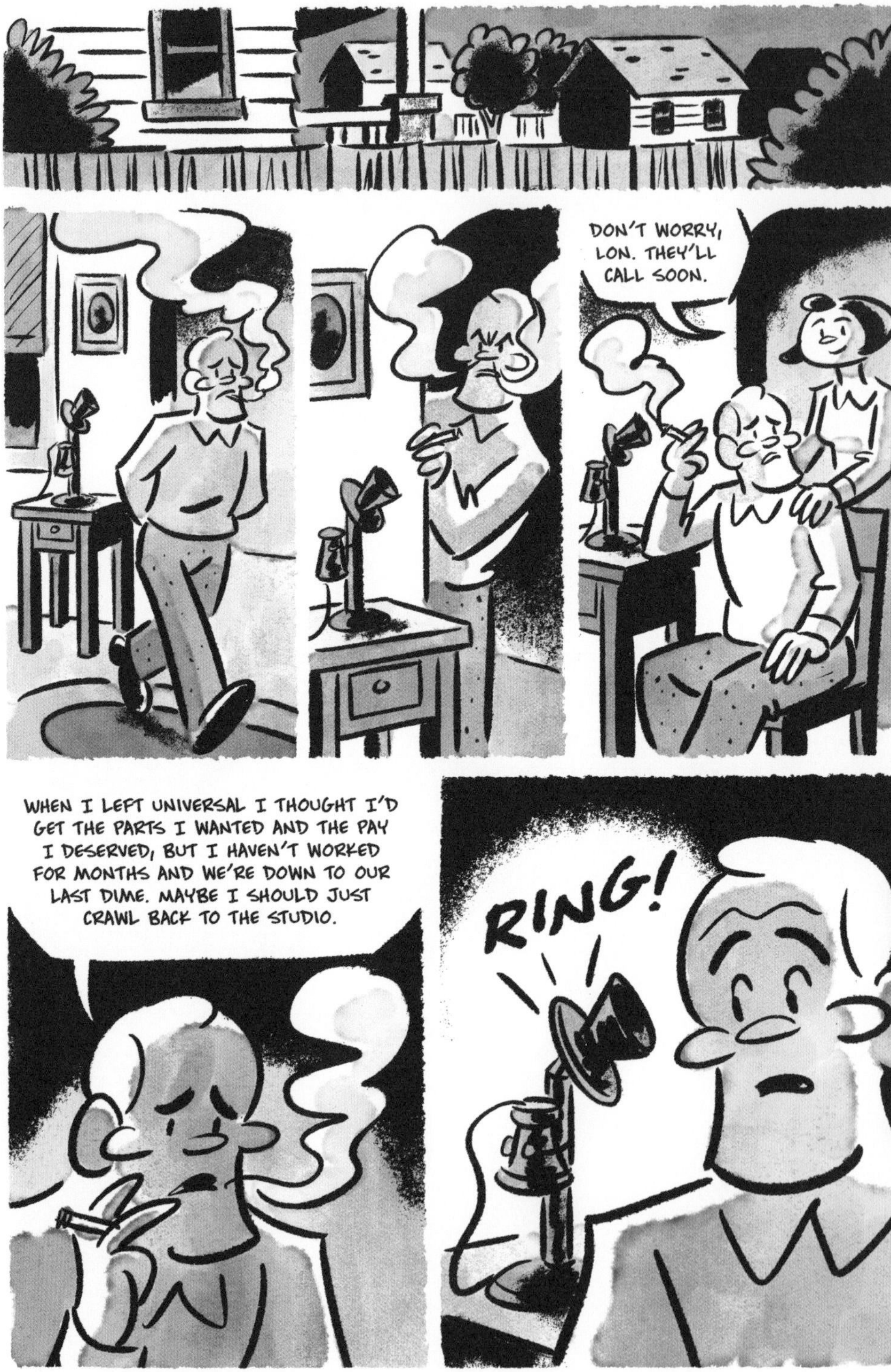
DON'T WORRY, LON. THEY'LL CALL SOON.
WHEN I LEFT UNIVERSAL I THOUGHT I'D GET THE PARTS I WANTED AND THE PAY I DESERVED, BUT I HAVEN'T WORKED FOR MONTHS AND WE'RE DOWN TO OUR LAST DIME. MAYBE I SHOULD JUST CRAWL BACK TO THE STUDIO.
RING!

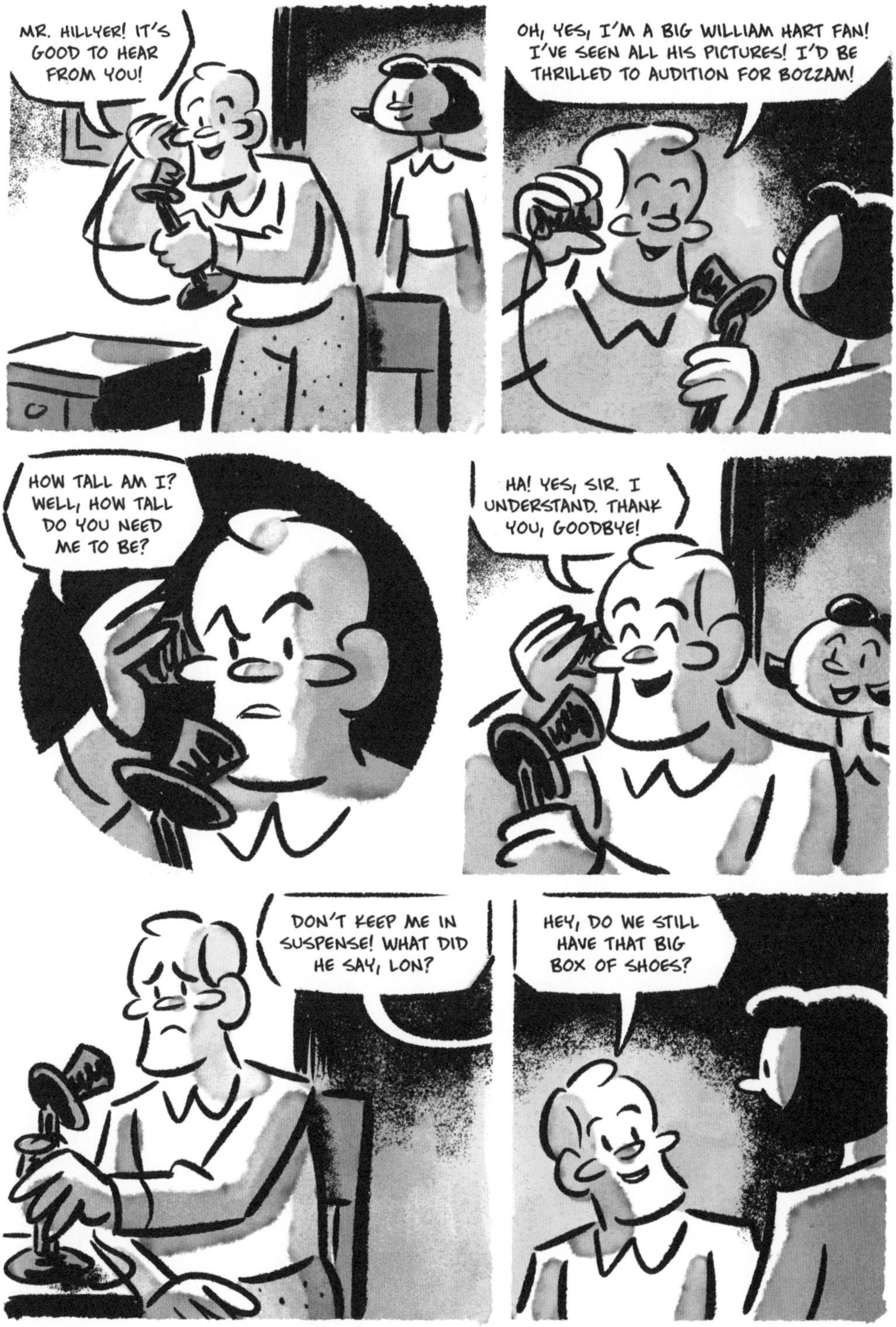
MR. HILLYER! IT'S GOOD TO HEAR FROM YOU!
OH, YES, I'M A BIG WILLIAM HART FAN! I'VE SEEN ALL HIS PICTURES! I'D BE THRILLED TO AUDITION FOR BOZZAM!
HOW TALL AM I? WELL, HOW TALL DO YOU NEED ME TO BE?
HA! YES, SIR. I UNDERSTAND. THANK YOU, GOODBYE!
DON'T KEEP ME IN SUSPENSE! WHAT DID HE SAY, LON?
HEY, DO WE STILL HAVE THAT BIG BOX OF SHOES?

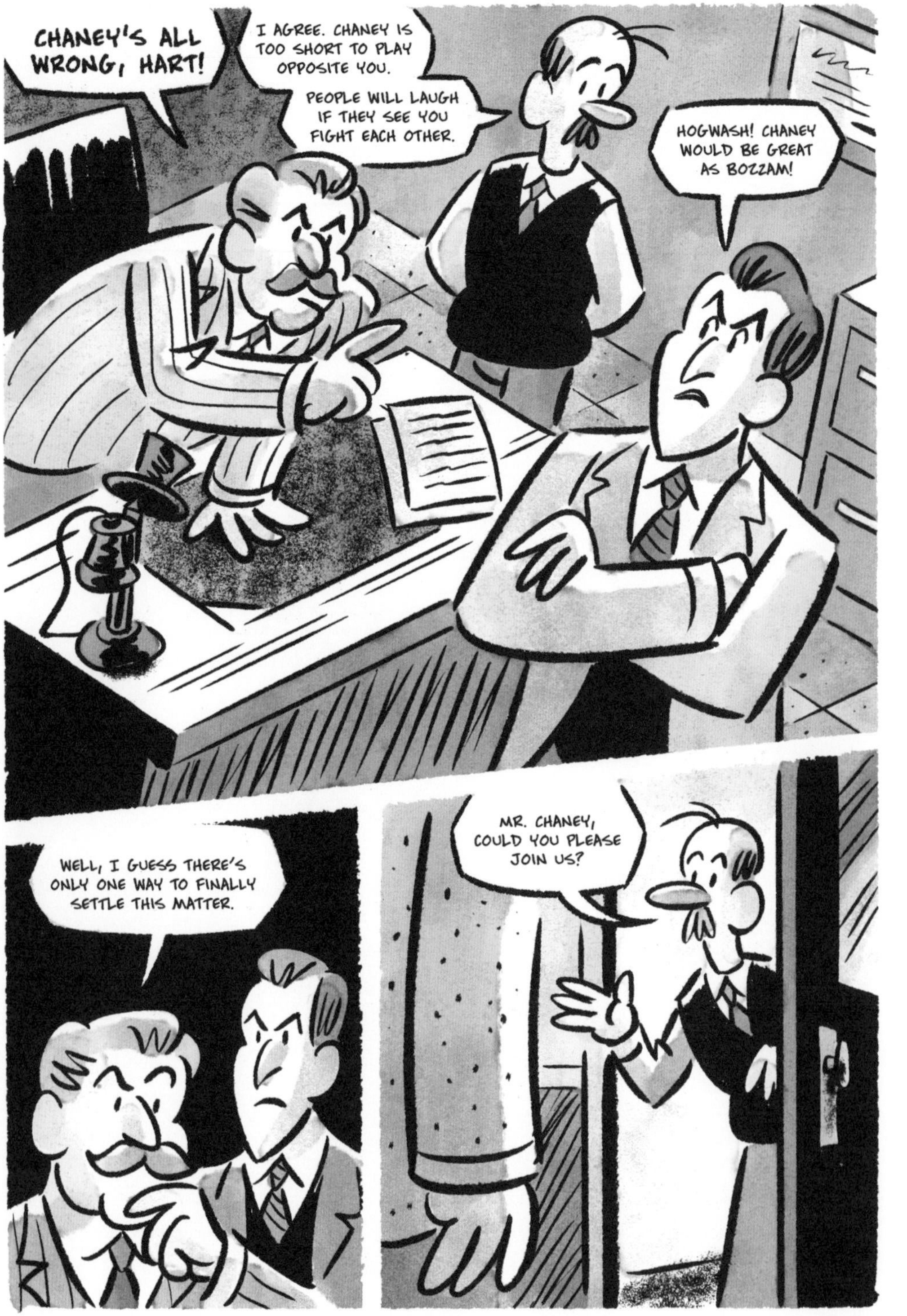
CHANEY'S ALL WRONG, HART!
I AGREE. CHANEY IS TOO SHORT TO PLAY OPPOSITE YOU.
PEOPLE WILL LAUGH IF THEY SEE YOU FIGHT EACH OTHER.
HOGWASH! CHANEY WOULD BE GREAT AS BOZZAM!
WELL, I GUESS THERE'S ONLY ONE WAY TO FINALLY SETTLE THIS MATTER.
MR. CHANEY, COULD YOU PLEASE JOIN US?

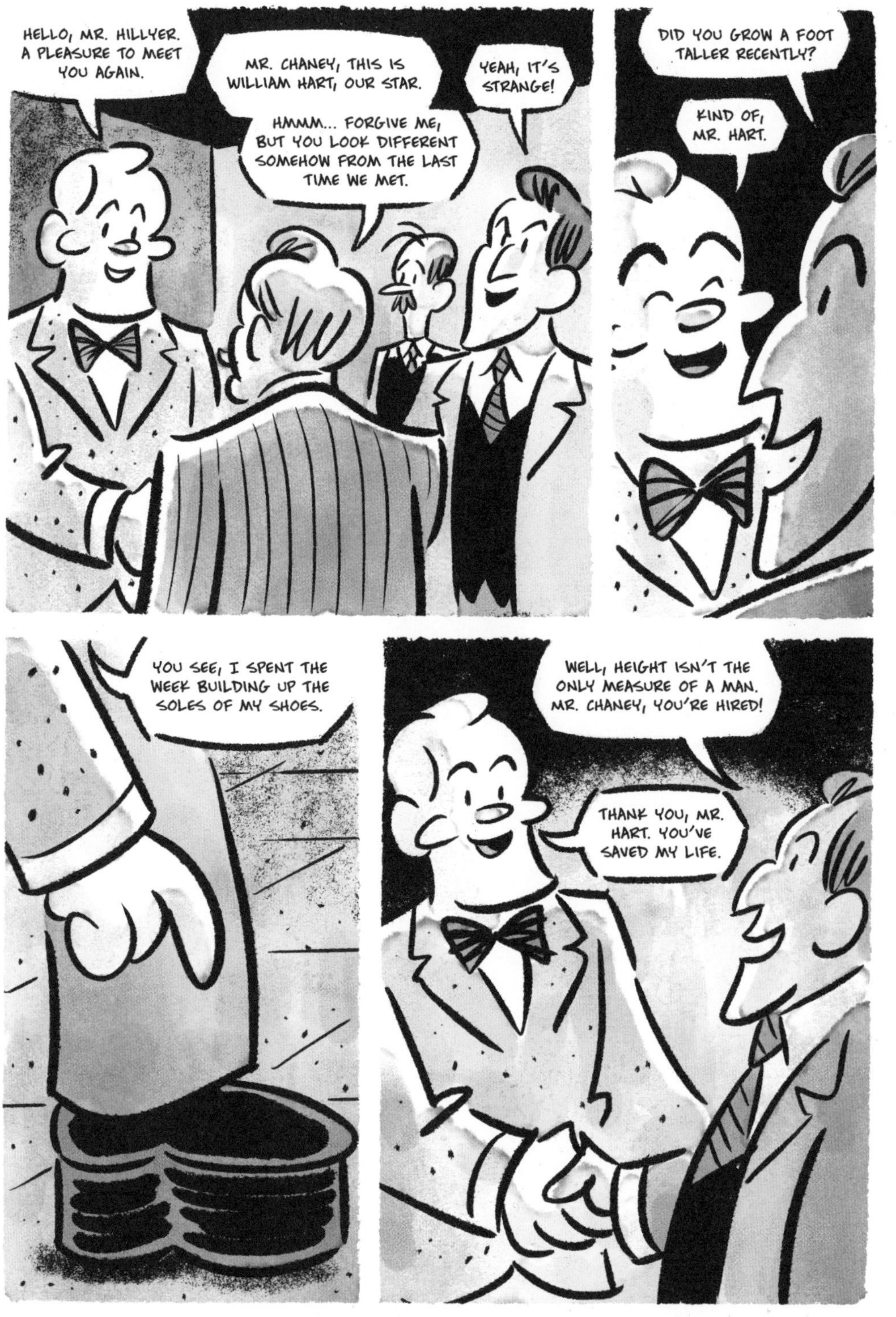
HELLO, MR. HILLYER. A PLEASURE TO MEET YOU AGAIN.
MR. CHANEY, THIS IS WILLIAM HART, OUR STAR.
YEAH, IT'S STRANGE!
HMMM... FORGIVE ME, BUT YOU LOOK DIFFERENT SOMEHOW FROM THE LAST TIME WE MET.
DID YOU GROW A FOOT TALLER RECENTLY?
KIND OF, MR. HART.
YOU SEE, I SPENT THE WEEK BUILDING UP THE SOLES OF MY SHOES.
WELL, HEIGHT ISN'T THE ONLY MEASURE OF A MAN. MR. CHANEY, YOU'RE HIRED!
THANK YOU, MR. HART. YOU'VE SAVED MY LIFE.

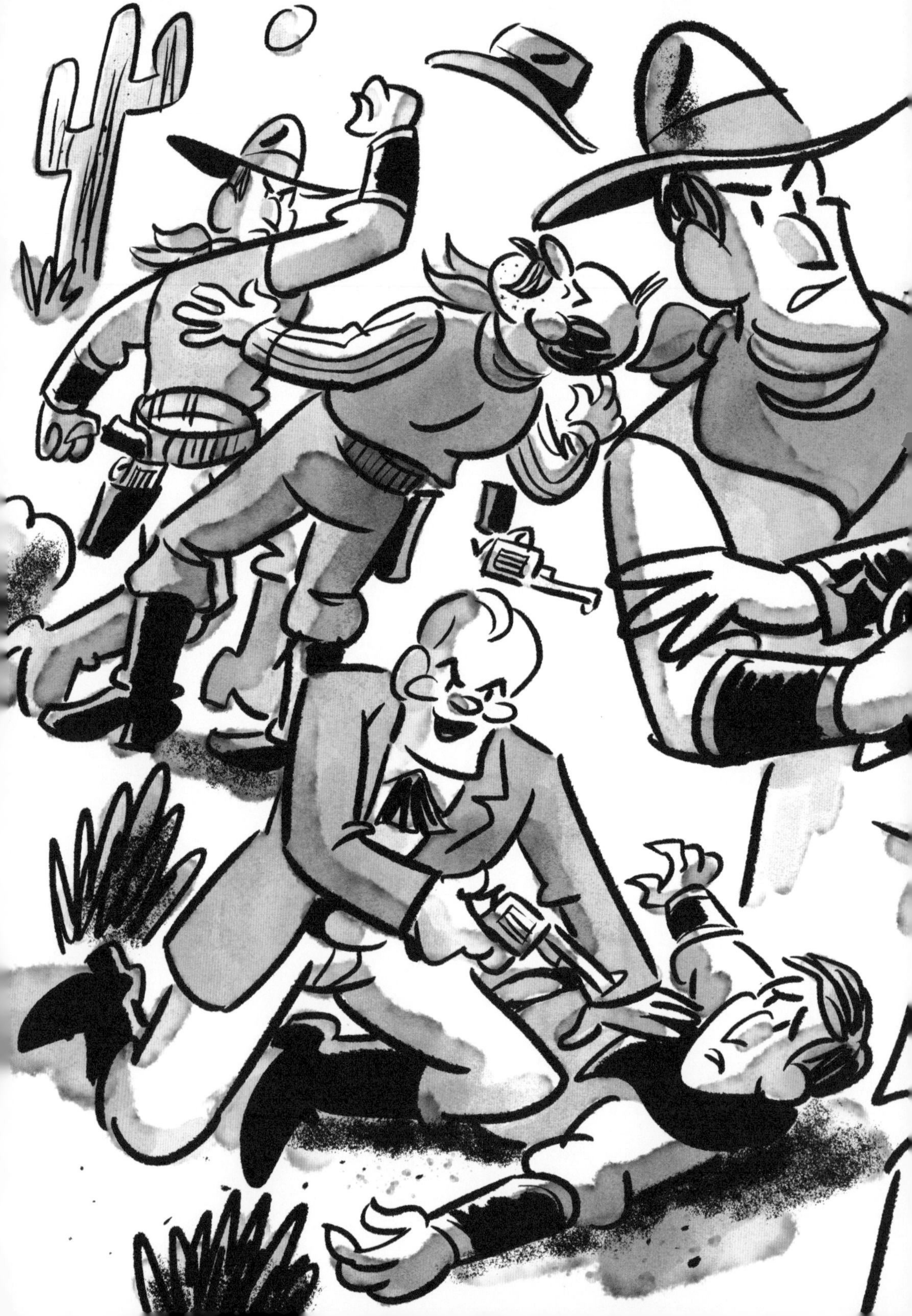

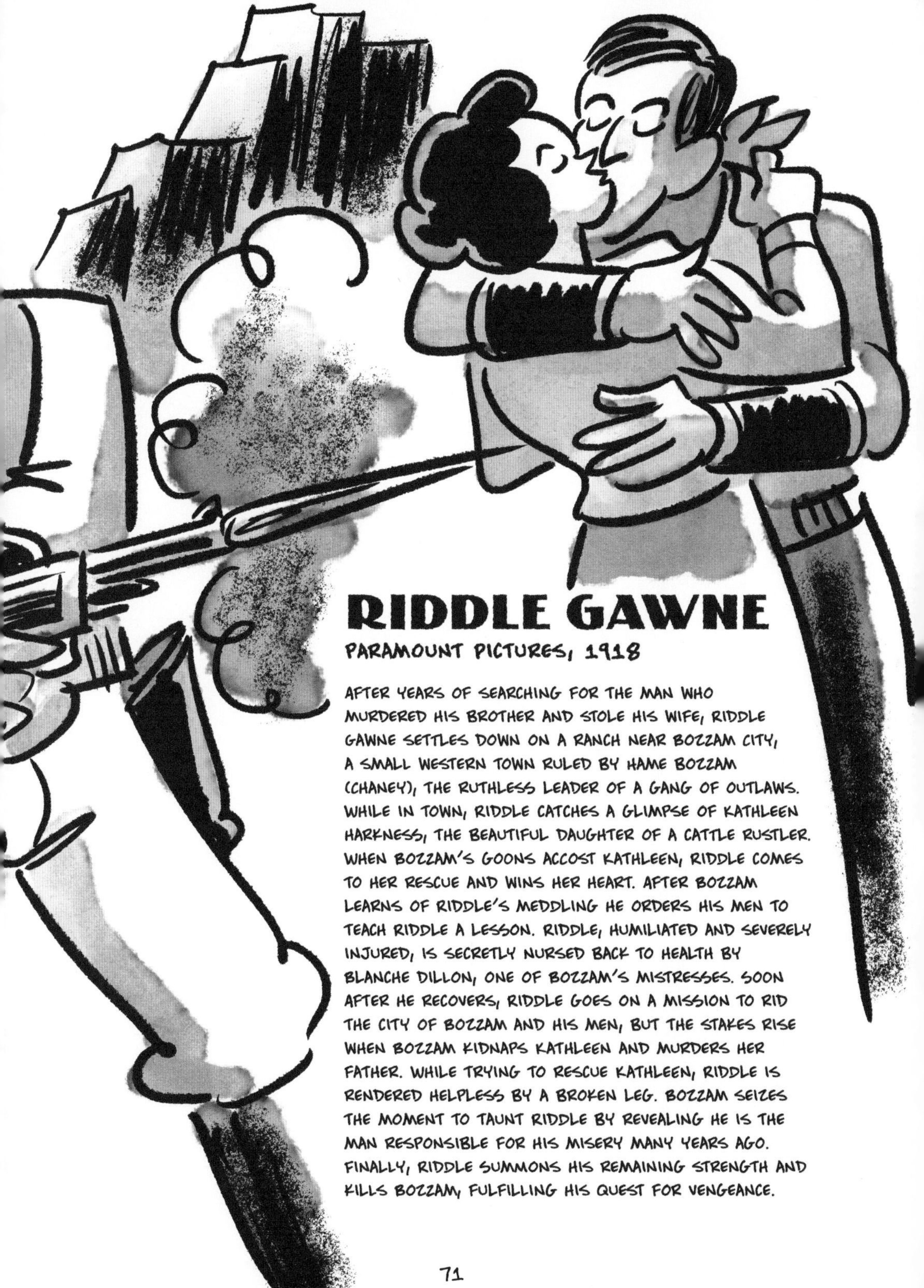

RIDDLE GAWNE

PARAMOUNT PICTURES, 1918

AFTER YEARS OF SEARCHING FOR THE MAN WHO MURDERED HIS BROTHER AND STOLE HIS WIFE, RIDDLE GAWNE SETTLES DOWN ON A RANCH NEAR BOZZAM CITY, A SMALL WESTERN TOWN RULED BY HAME BOZZAM (CHANEY), THE RUTHLESS LEADER OF A GANG OF OUTLAWS. WHILE IN TOWN, RIDDLE CATCHES A GLIMPSE OF KATHLEEN HARKNESS, THE BEAUTIFUL DAUGHTER OF A CATTLE RUSTLER. WHEN BOZZAM'S GOONS ACCOST KATHLEEN, RIDDLE COMES TO HER RESCUE AND WINS HER HEART. AFTER BOZZAM LEARNS OF RIDDLE'S MEDDLING HE ORDERS HIS MEN TO TEACH RIDDLE A LESSON. RIDDLE, HUMILIATED AND SEVERELY INJURED, IS SECRETLY NURSED BACK TO HEALTH BY BLANCHE DILLON, ONE OF BOZZAM'S MISTRESSES. SOON AFTER HE RECOVERS, RIDDLE GOES ON A MISSION TO RID THE CITY OF BOZZAM AND HIS MEN, BUT THE STAKES RISE WHEN BOZZAM KIDNAPS KATHLEEN AND MURDERS HER FATHER. WHILE TRYING TO RESCUE KATHLEEN, RIDDLE IS RENDERED HELPLESS BY A BROKEN LEG. BOZZAM SEIZES THE MOMENT TO TAUNT RIDDLE BY REVEALING HE IS THE MAN RESPONSIBLE FOR HIS MISERY MANY YEARS AGO. FINALLY, RIDDLE SUMMONS HIS REMAINING STRENGTH AND KILLS BOZZAM, FULFILLING HIS QUEST FOR VENGEANCE.

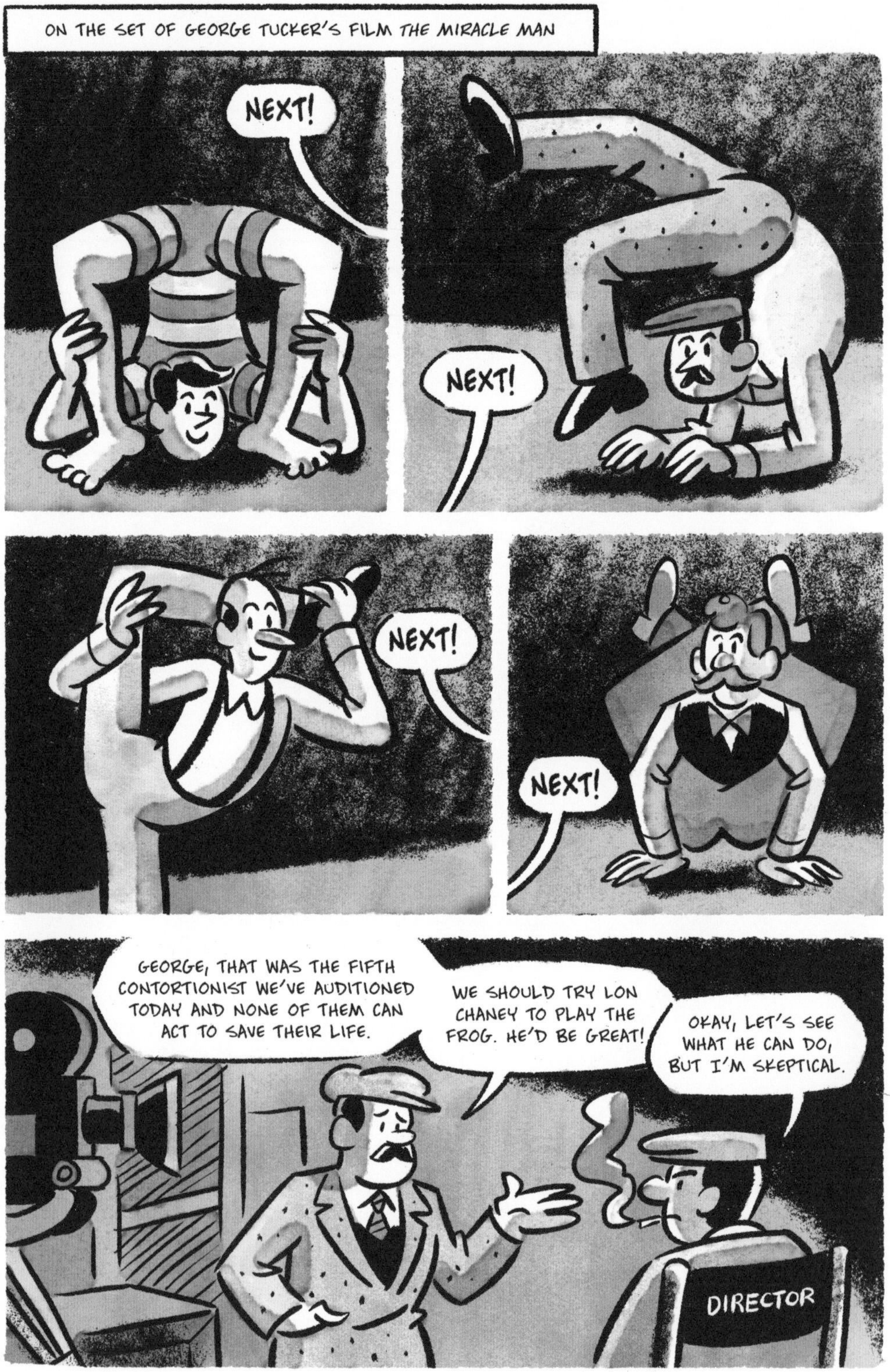
ON THE SET OF GEORGE TUCKER'S FILM THE MIRACLE MAN
NEXT!
NEXT!
NEXT!
NEXT!
GEORGE, THAT WAS THE FIFTH CONTORTIONIST WE'VE AUDITIONED TODAY AND NONE OF THEM CAN ACT TO SAVE THEIR LIFE.
WE SHOULD TRY LON CHANEY TO PLAY THE FROG. HE'D BE GREAT!
OKAY, LET'S SEE WHAT HE CAN DO, BUT I'M SKEPTICAL.
DIRECTOR

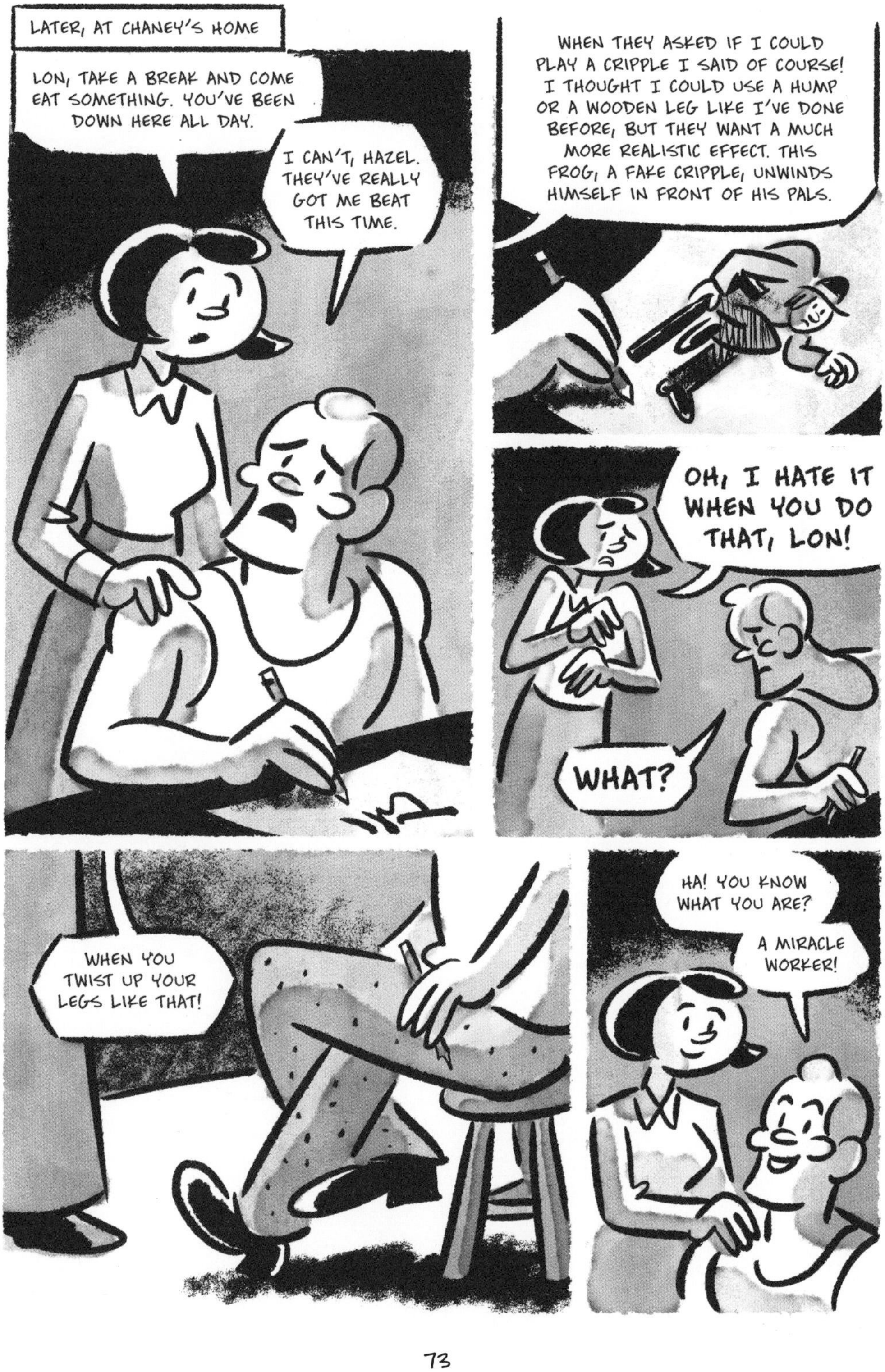
LATER, AT CHANEY'S HOME
LON, TAKE A BREAK AND COME EAT SOMETHING. YOU'VE BEEN DOWN HERE ALL DAY.
I CAN'T, HAZEL. THEY'VE REALLY GOT ME BEAT THIS TIME.
WHEN THEY ASKED IF I COULD PLAY A CRIPPLE I SAID OF COURSE! I THOUGHT I COULD USE A HUMP OR A WOODEN LEG LIKE I'VE DONE BEFORE, BUT THEY WANT A MUCH MORE REALISTIC EFFECT. THIS FROG, A FAKE CRIPPLE, UNWINDS HIMSELF IN FRONT OF HIS PALS.
OH, I HATE IT WHEN YOU DO THAT, LON!
WHAT?
WHEN YOU TWIST UP YOUR LEGS LIKE THAT!
HA! YOU KNOW WHAT YOU ARE?
A MIRACLE WORKER!

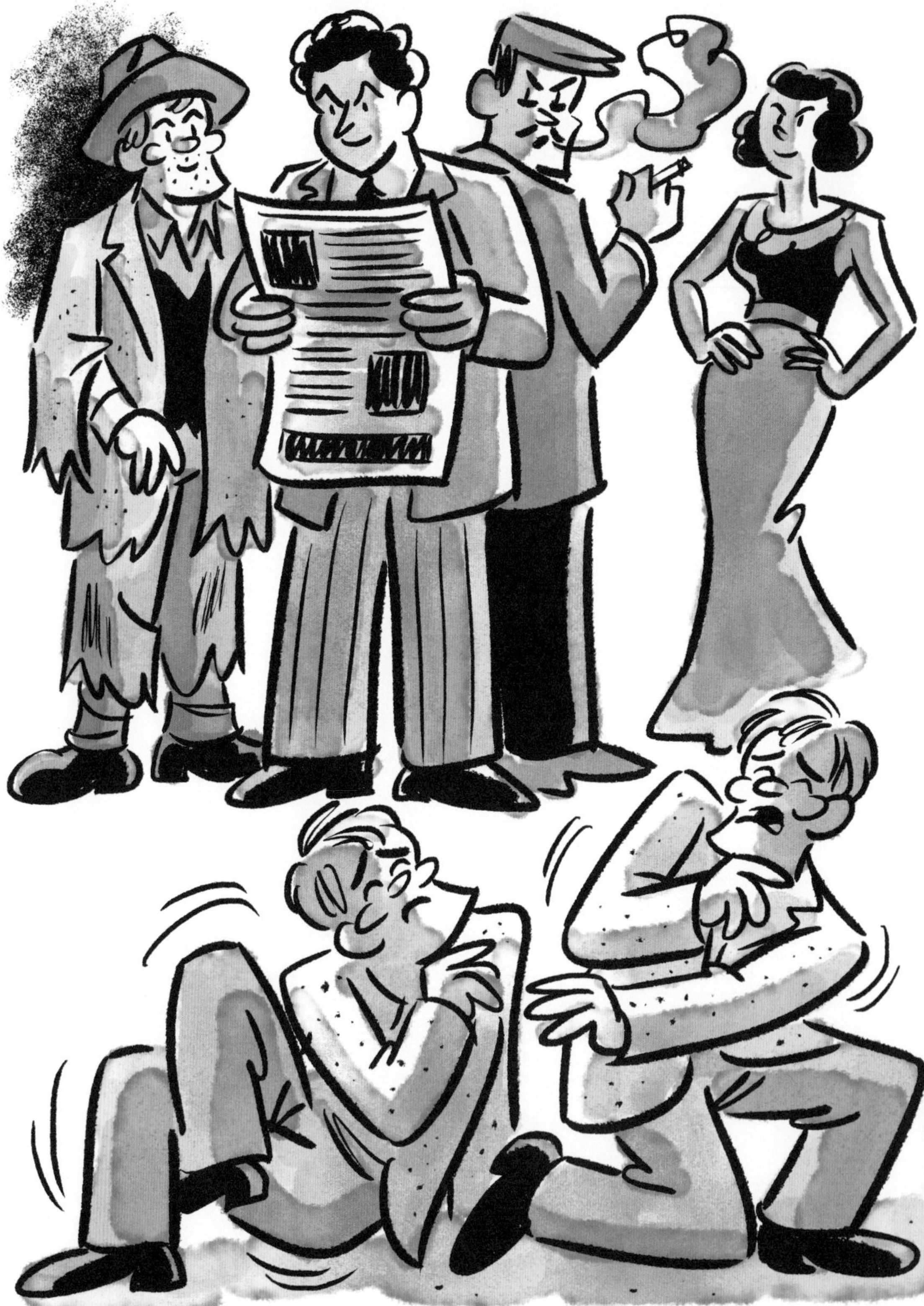

The Miracle Man

PARAMOUNT PICTURES, 1919

FOUR CROOKS COME UP WITH A FAITH-HEALING SCAM AFTER READING ABOUT A PATRIARCH CAPABLE OF WORKING MIRACLES. DURING A PUBLIC GATHERING, THE FROG (CHANEY), A CONTORTIONIST, POSES AS DISABLED AND PRETENDS TO BE HEALED BY THE PATRIARCH. PEOPLE CHEER AS THE FROG'S MANGLED LIMBS BEGIN TO STRAIGHTEN. THEN THE CROWD WITNESSES A REAL MIRACLE AS A DISABLED BOY IS CURED BECAUSE OF HIS DEEP FAITH IN THE PATRIARCH'S POWER. THE PATRIARCH ALSO LATER EFFECTS A CHANGE IN THE BAND OF CRIMINALS. ONE BY ONE, THEY DISBAND, EACH CHOOSING TO GO STRAIGHT.

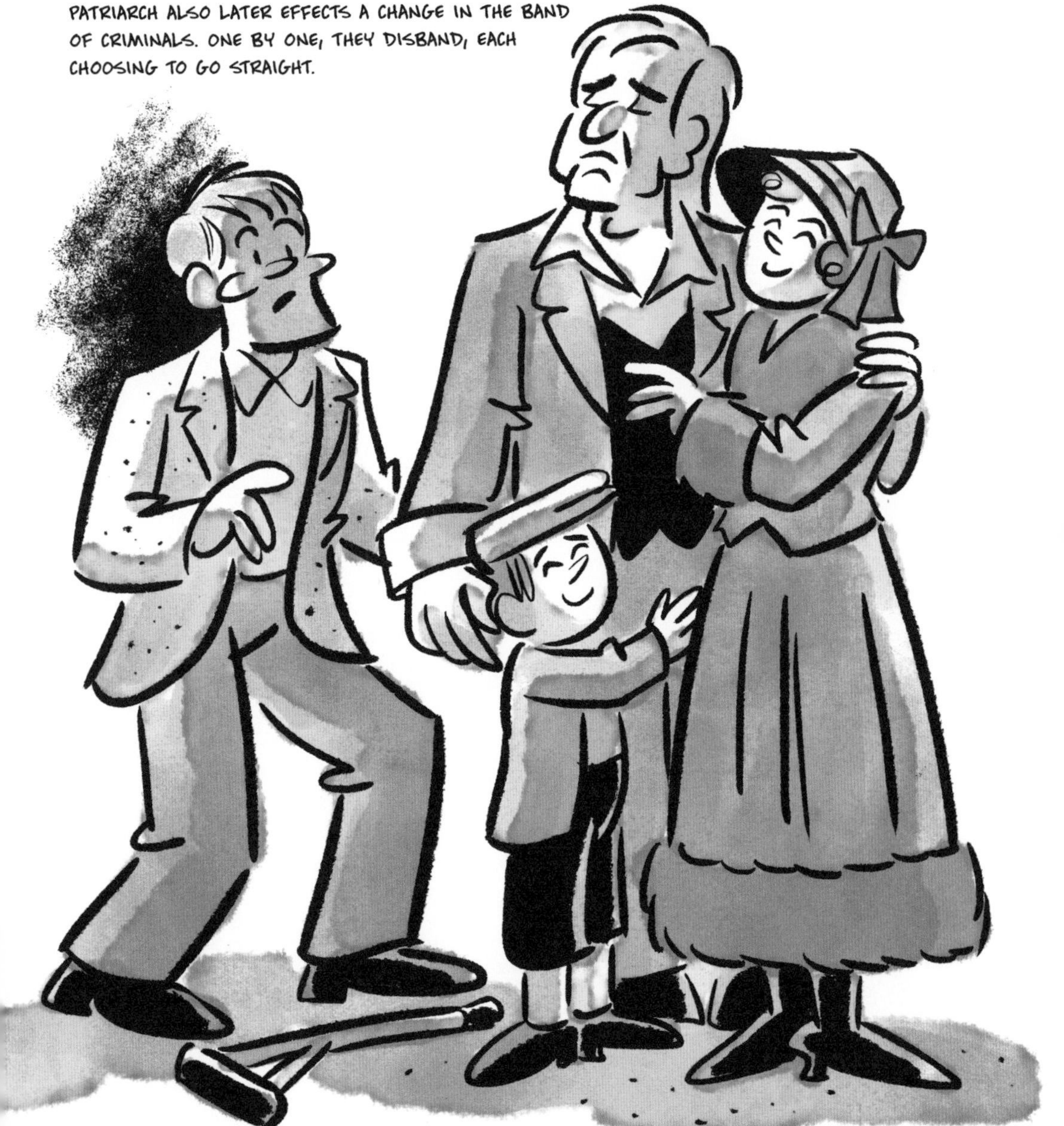

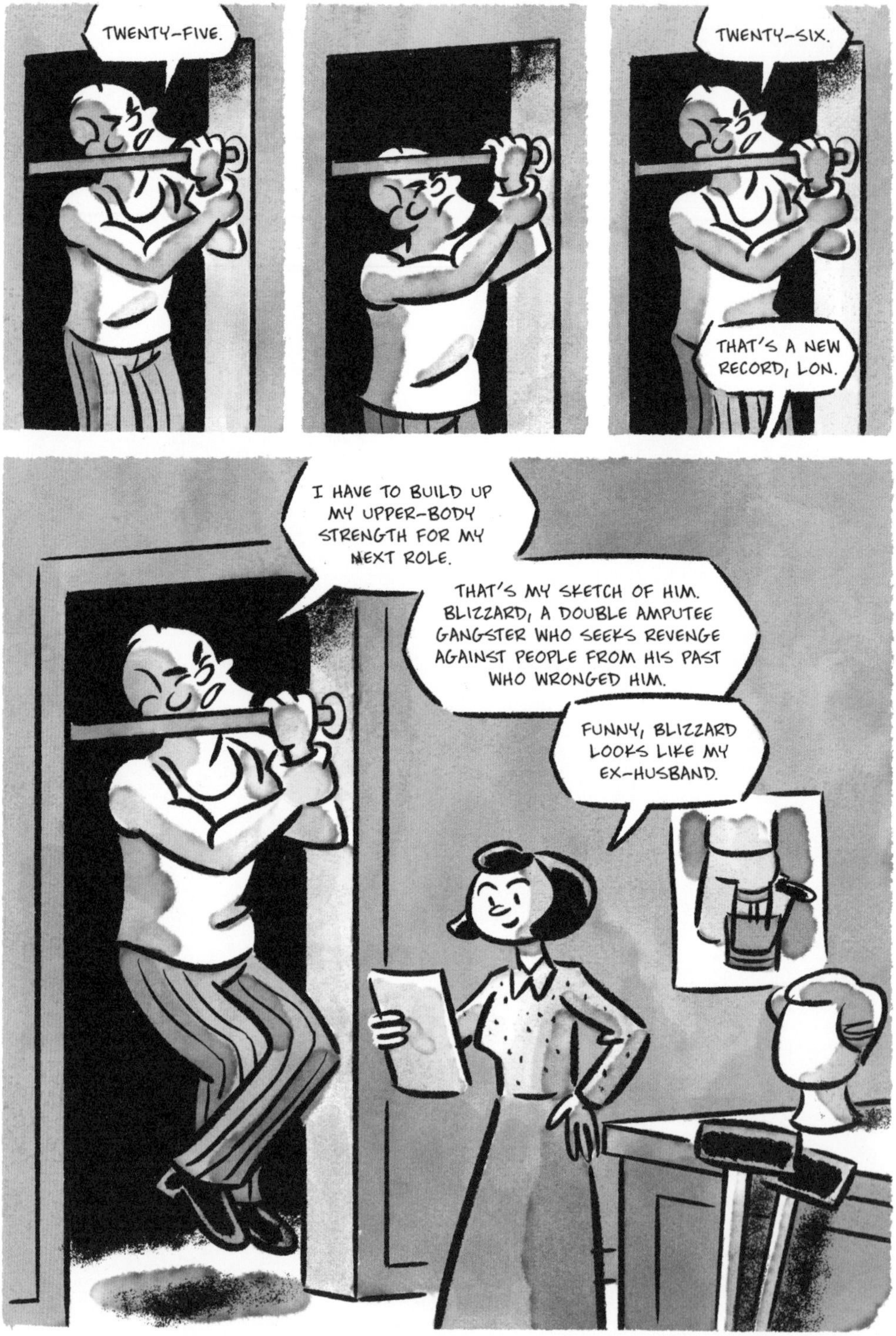
TWENTY-FIVE.
TWENTY-SIX.
THAT'S A NEW RECORD, LON.
I HAVE TO BUILD UP MY UPPER-BODY STRENGTH FOR MY NEXT ROLE.
THAT'S MY SKETCH OF HIM. BLIZZARD, A DOUBLE AMPUTEE GANGSTER WHO SEEKS REVENGE AGAINST PEOPLE FROM HIS PAST WHO WRONGED HIM.
FUNNY, BLIZZARD LOOKS LIKE MY EX-HUSBAND.

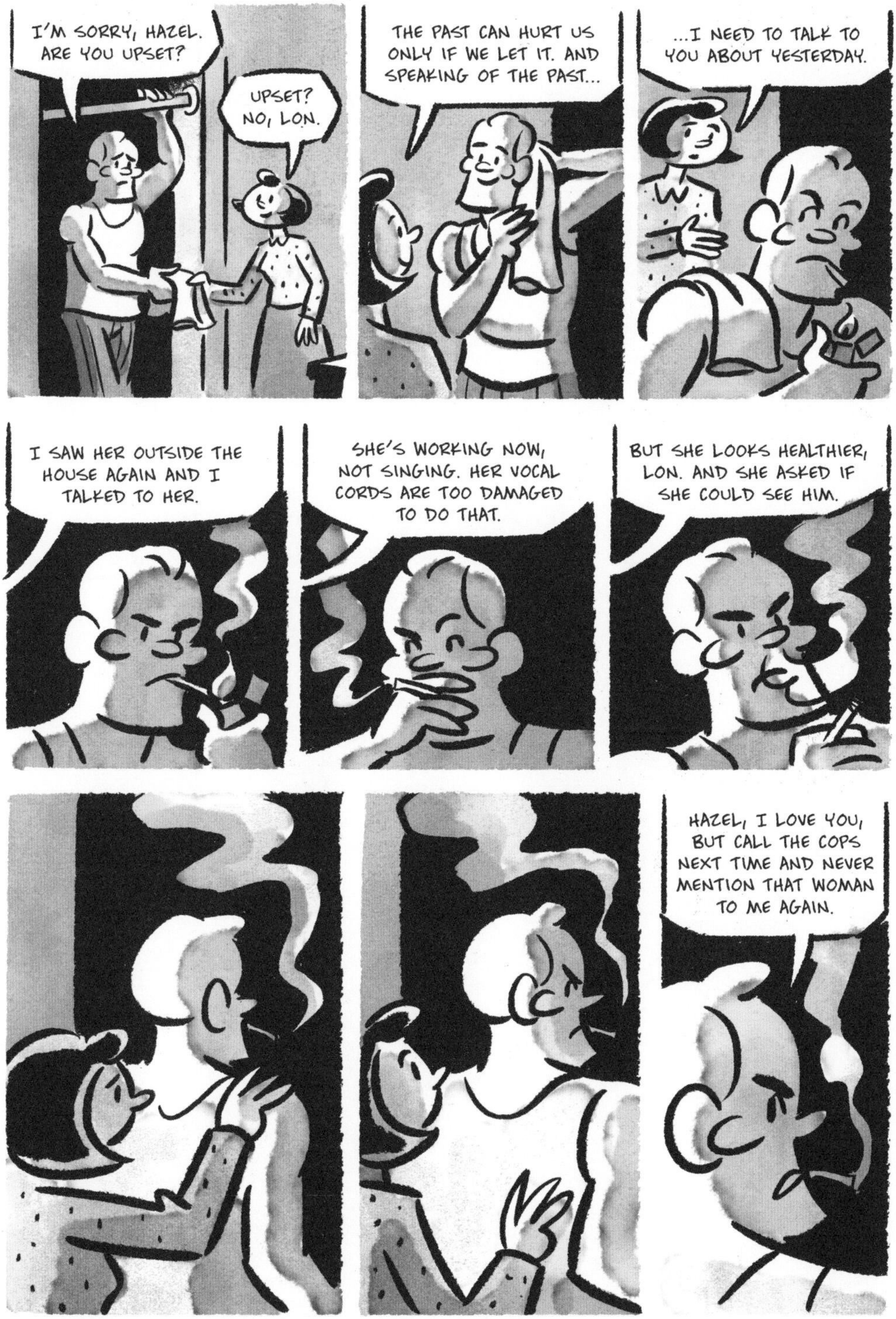
I'M SORRY, HAZEL. ARE YOU UPSET?
UPSET? NO, LON.
THE PAST CAN HURT US ONLY IF WE LET IT. AND SPEAKING OF THE PAST...
...I NEED TO TALK TO YOU ABOUT YESTERDAY.
I SAW HER OUTSIDE THE HOUSE AGAIN AND I TALKED TO HER.
SHE'S WORKING NOW, NOT SINGING. HER VOCAL CORDS ARE TOO DAMAGED TO DO THAT.
BUT SHE LOOKS HEALTHIER, LON. AND SHE ASKED IF SHE COULD SEE HIM.
HAZEL, I LOVE YOU, BUT CALL THE COPS NEXT TIME AND NEVER MENTION THAT WOMAN TO ME AGAIN.

The Penalty

GOLDWYN PICTURES, 1920

THE YOUNG AND INEXPERIENCED DR. FERRIS TREATS A BOY WHO HAS BEEN INJURED IN A TERRIBLE CAR ACCIDENT. TO SAVE THE BOY'S LIFE, FERRIS AMPUTATES BOTH OF HIS LEGS, BUT WHEN A SENIOR COLLEAGUE EXAMINES THE PATIENT HE LEARNS A TERRIBLE MISTAKE HAS BEEN MADE. FERRIS BELIEVES HE'S RUINED UNTIL HIS COLLEAGUE OFFERS TO COVER FOR HIM.

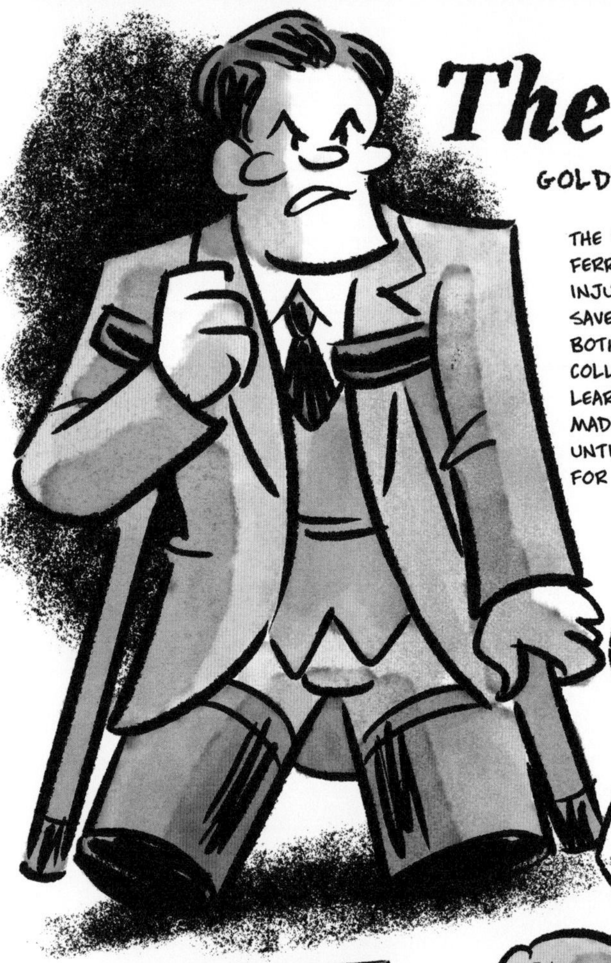

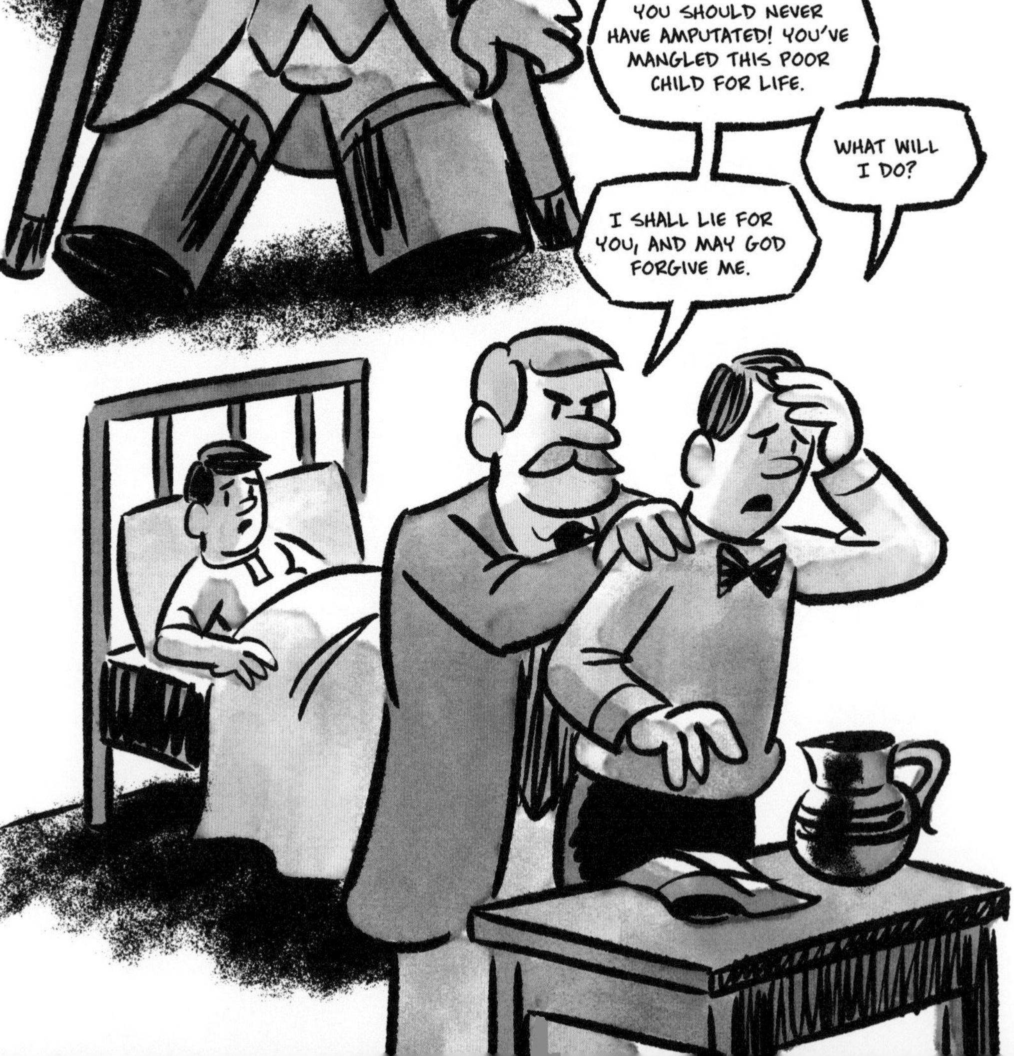
YOU SHOULD NEVER HAVE AMPUTATED! YOU'VE MANGLED THIS POOR CHILD FOR LIFE.
WHAT WILL I DO?
I SHALL LIE FOR YOU, AND MAY GOD FORGIVE ME.

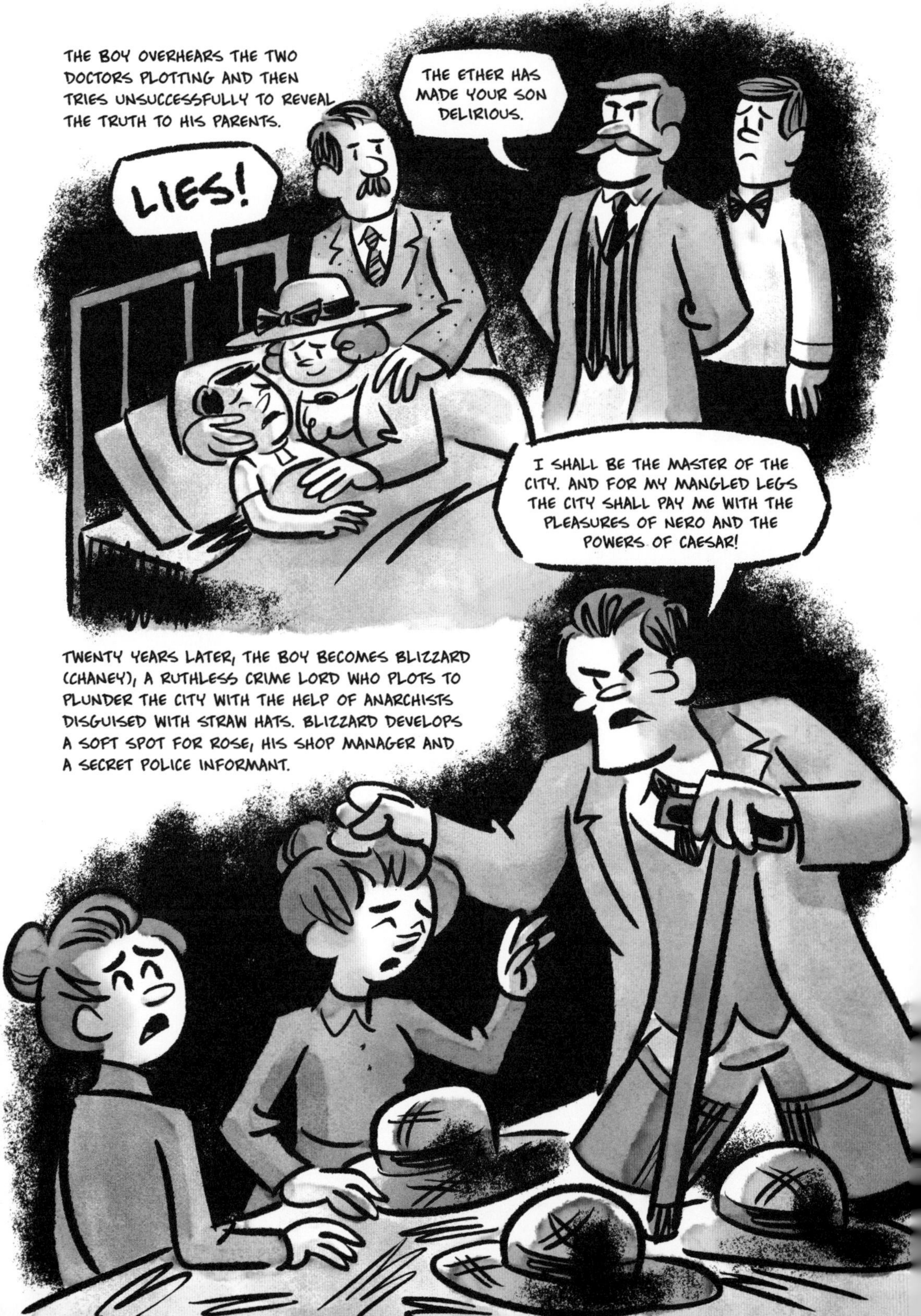
THE BOY OVERHEARS THE TWO DOCTORS PLOTTING AND THEN TRIES UNSUCCESSFULLY TO REVEAL THE TRUTH TO HIS PARENTS.
LIES!
THE ETHER HAS MADE YOUR SON DELIRIOUS.
TWENTY YEARS LATER, THE BOY BECOMES BLIZZARD (CHANEY), A RUTHLESS CRIME LORD WHO PLOTS TO PLUNDER THE CITY WITH THE HELP OF ANARCHISTS DISGUISED WITH STRAW HATS. BLIZZARD DEVELOPS A SOFT SPOT FOR ROSE, HIS SHOP MANAGER AND A SECRET POLICE INFORMANT.
I SHALL BE THE MASTER OF THE CITY. AND FOR MY MANGLED LEGS THE CITY SHALL PAY ME WITH THE PLEASURES OF NERO AND THE POWERS OF CAESAR!

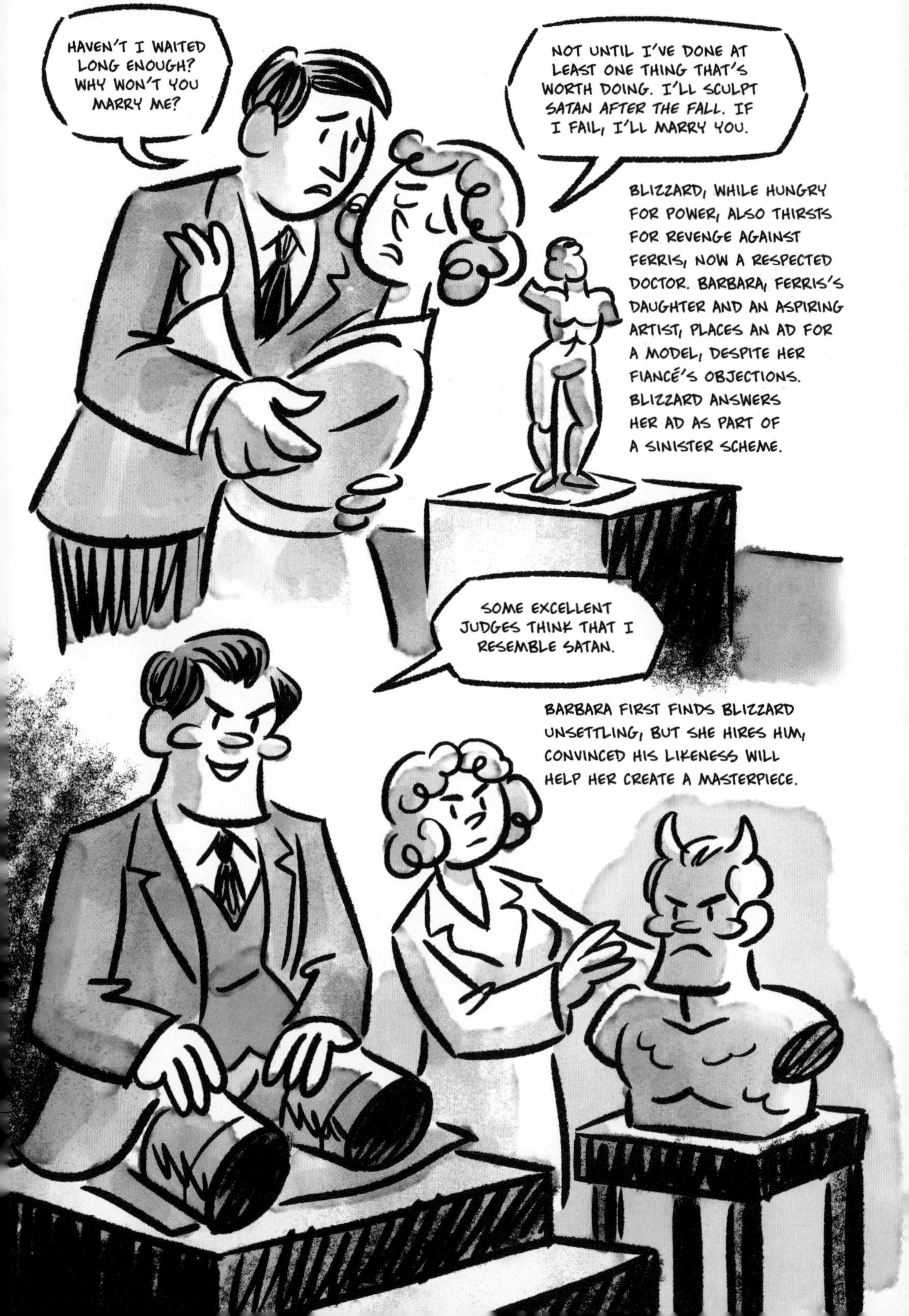
HAVEN'T I WAITED LONG ENOUGH? WHY WON'T YOU MARRY ME?
NOT UNTIL I'VE DONE AT LEAST ONE THING THAT'S WORTH DOING. I'LL SCULPT SATAN AFTER THE FALL. IF I FAIL, I'LL MARRY YOU.
BLIZZARD, WHILE HUNGRY FOR POWER, ALSO THIRSTS FOR REVENGE AGAINST FERRIS, NOW A RESPECTED DOCTOR. BARBARA, FERRIS'S DAUGHTER AND AN ASPIRING ARTIST, PLACES AN AD FOR A MODEL, DESPITE HER FIANCÉ'S OBJECTIONS. BLIZZARD ANSWERS HER AD AS PART OF A SINISTER SCHEME.
SOME EXCELLENT JUDGES THINK THAT I RESEMBLE SATAN.
BARBARA FIRST FINDS BLIZZARD UNSETTLING, BUT SHE HIRES HIM, CONVINCED HIS LIKENESS WILL HELP HER CREATE A MASTERPIECE.

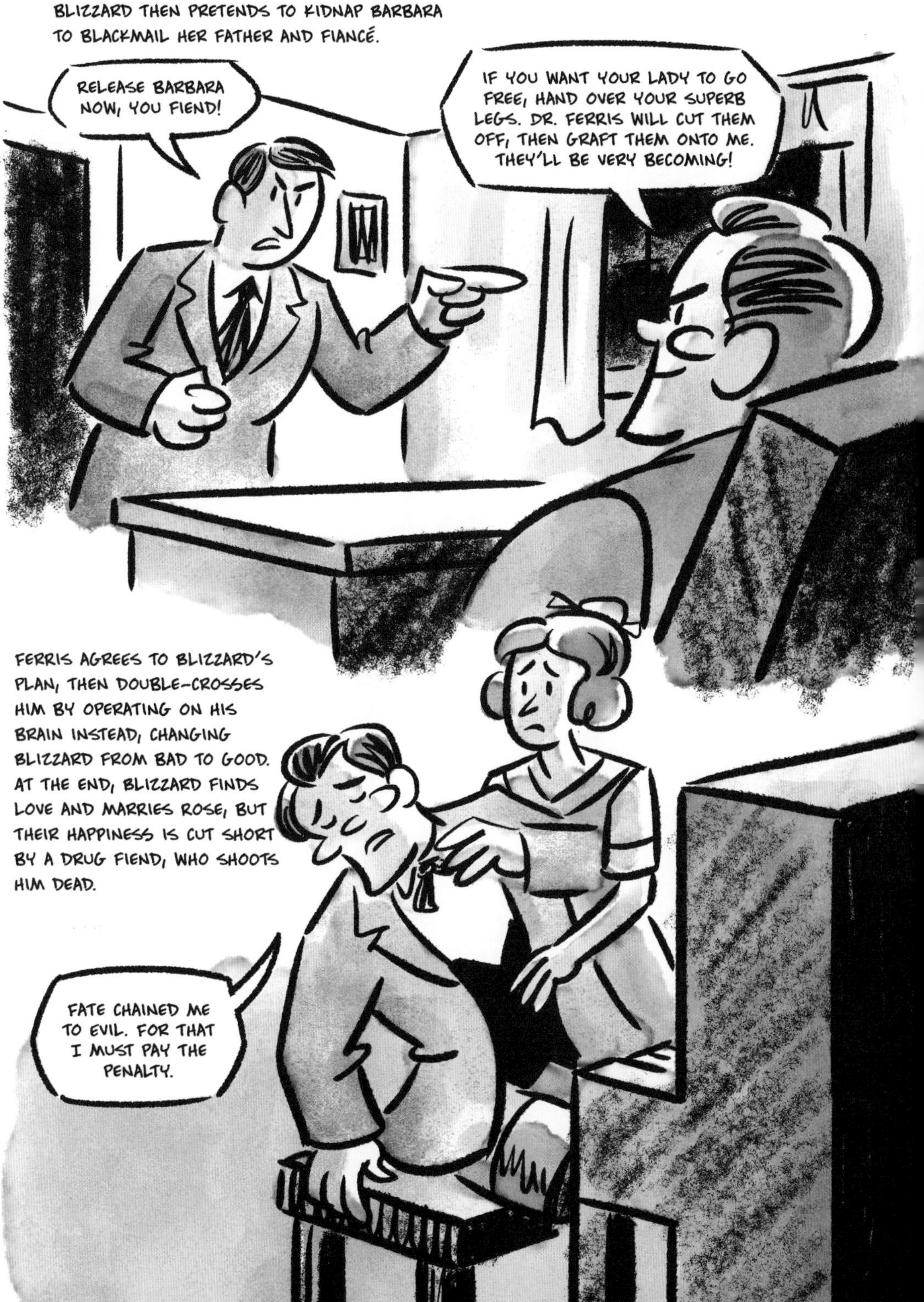
BLIZZARD THEN PRETENDS TO KIDNAP BARBARA TO BLACKMAIL HER FATHER AND FIANCÉ.
RELEASE BARBARA NOW, YOU FIEND!
IF YOU WANT YOUR LADY TO GO FREE, HAND OVER YOUR SUPERB LEGS. DR. FERRIS WILL CUT THEM OFF, THEN GRAFT THEM ONTO ME. THEY'LL BE VERY BECOMING!
FERRIS AGREES TO BLIZZARD'S PLAN, THEN DOUBLE-CROSSES HIM BY OPERATING ON HIS BRAIN INSTEAD, CHANGING BLIZZARD FROM BAD TO GOOD. AT THE END, BLIZZARD FINDS LOVE AND MARRIES ROSE, BUT THEIR HAPPINESS IS CUT SHORT BY A DRUG FIEND, WHO SHOOTS HIM DEAD.
FATE CHAINED ME TO EVIL. FOR THAT I MUST PAY THE PENALTY.

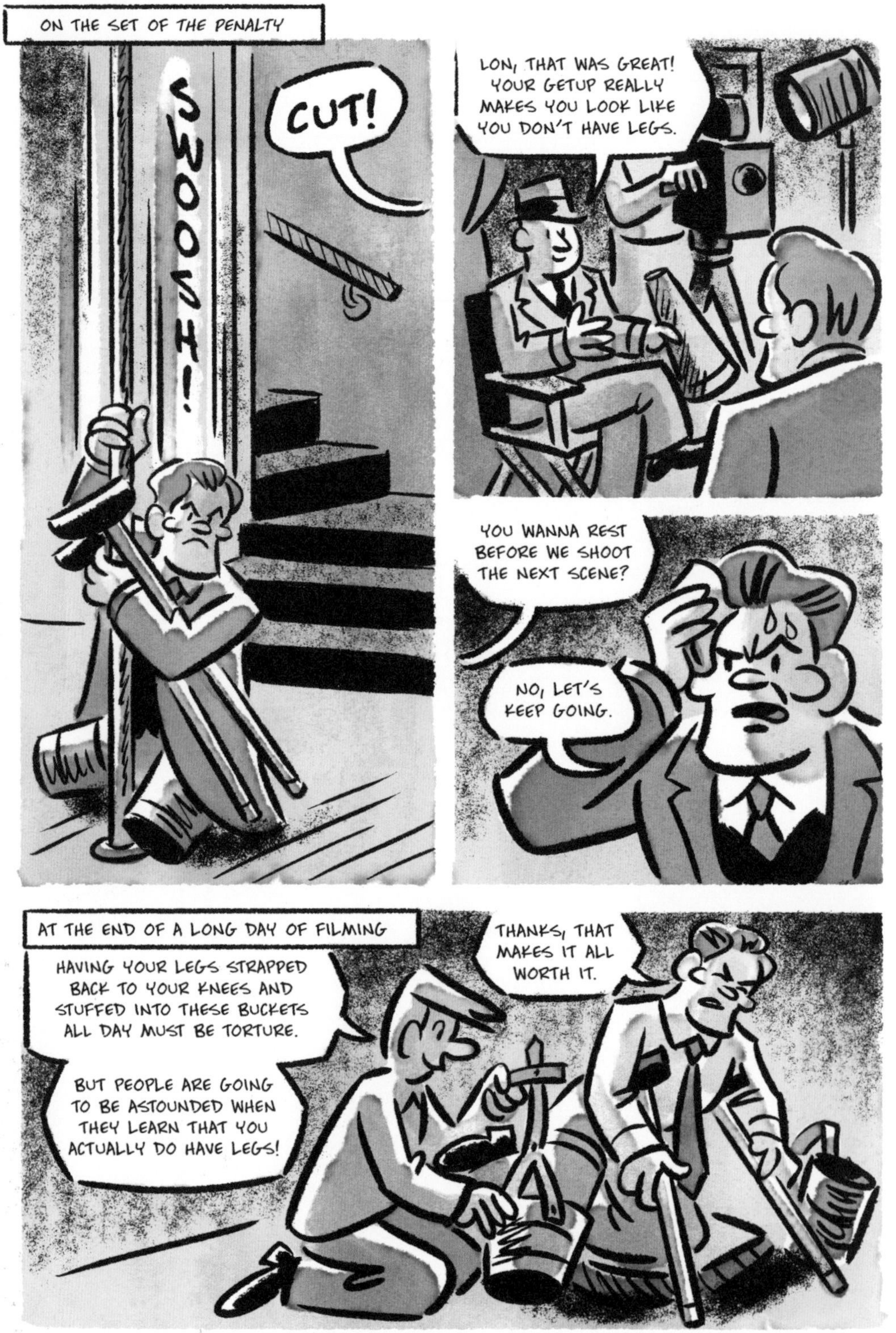
ON THE SET OF THE PENALTY
SWOOSH!
CUT!
LON, THAT WAS GREAT! YOUR GETUP REALLY MAKES YOU LOOK LIKE YOU DON'T HAVE LEGS.
YOU WANNA REST BEFORE WE SHOOT THE NEXT SCENE?
NO, LET'S KEEP GOING.
AT THE END OF A LONG DAY OF FILMING
HAVING YOUR LEGS STRAPPED BACK TO YOUR KNEES AND STUFFED INTO THESE BUCKETS ALL DAY MUST BE TORTURE.
BUT PEOPLE ARE GOING TO BE ASTOUNDED WHEN THEY LEARN THAT YOU ACTUALLY DO HAVE LEGS!
THANKS, THAT MAKES IT ALL WORTH IT.

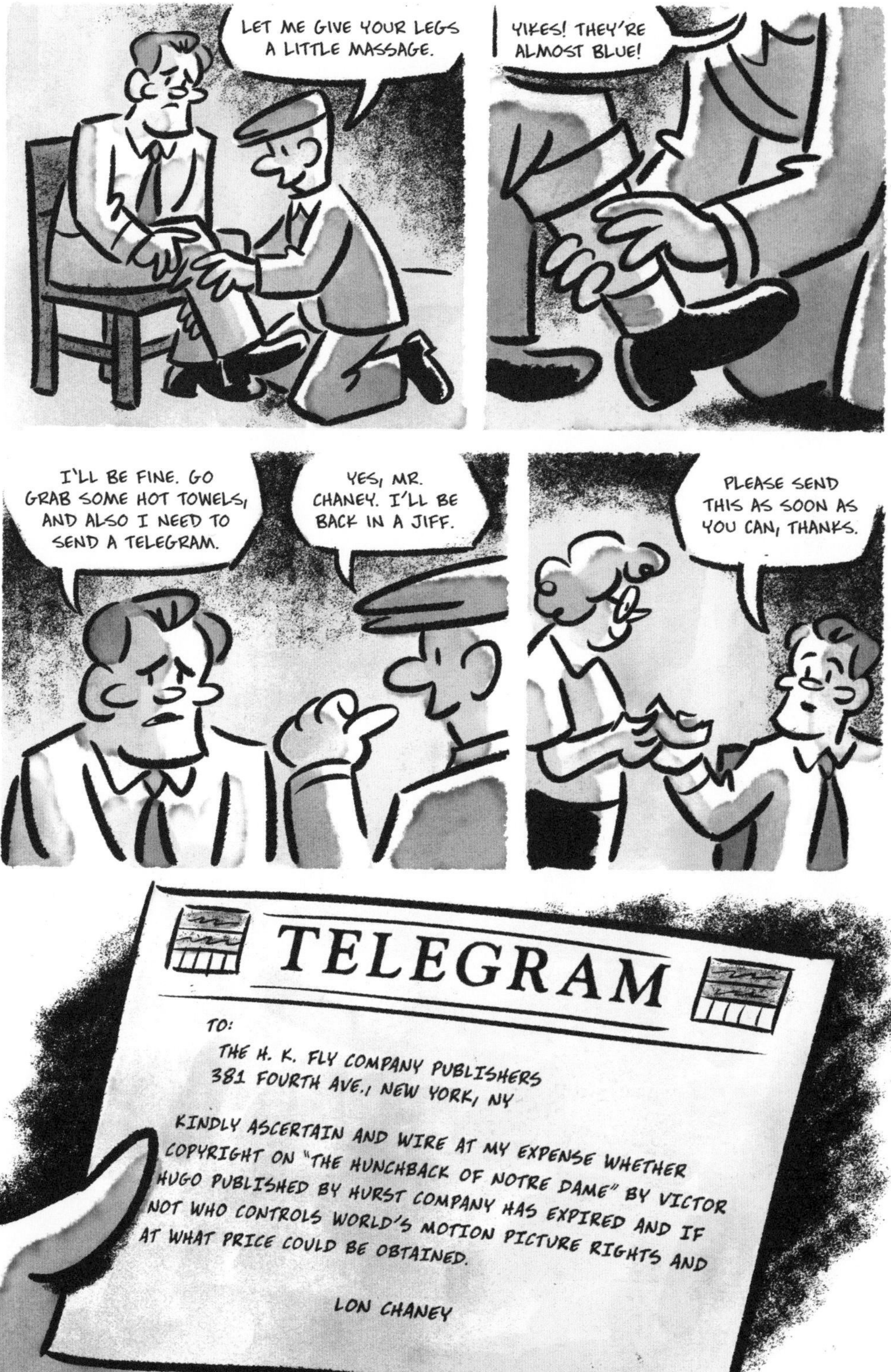
LET ME GIVE YOUR LEGS A LITTLE MASSAGE.
YIKES! THEY'RE ALMOST BLUE!
I'LL BE FINE. GO GRAB SOME HOT TOWELS, AND ALSO I NEED TO SEND A TELEGRAM.
YES, MR. CHANEY. I'LL BE BACK IN A JIFF.
PLEASE SEND THIS AS SOON AS YOU CAN, THANKS.
TELEGRAM
TO:
THE H. K. FLY COMPANY PUBLISHERS
381 FOURTH AVE., NEW YORK, NY
KINDLY ASCERTAIN AND WIRE AT MY EXPENSE WHETHER COPYRIGHT ON "THE HUNCHBACK OF NOTRE DAME" BY VICTOR HUGO PUBLISHED BY HURST COMPANY HAS EXPIRED AND IF NOT WHO CONTROLS WORLD'S MOTION PICTURE RIGHTS AND AT WHAT PRICE COULD BE OBTAINED.
LON CHANEY

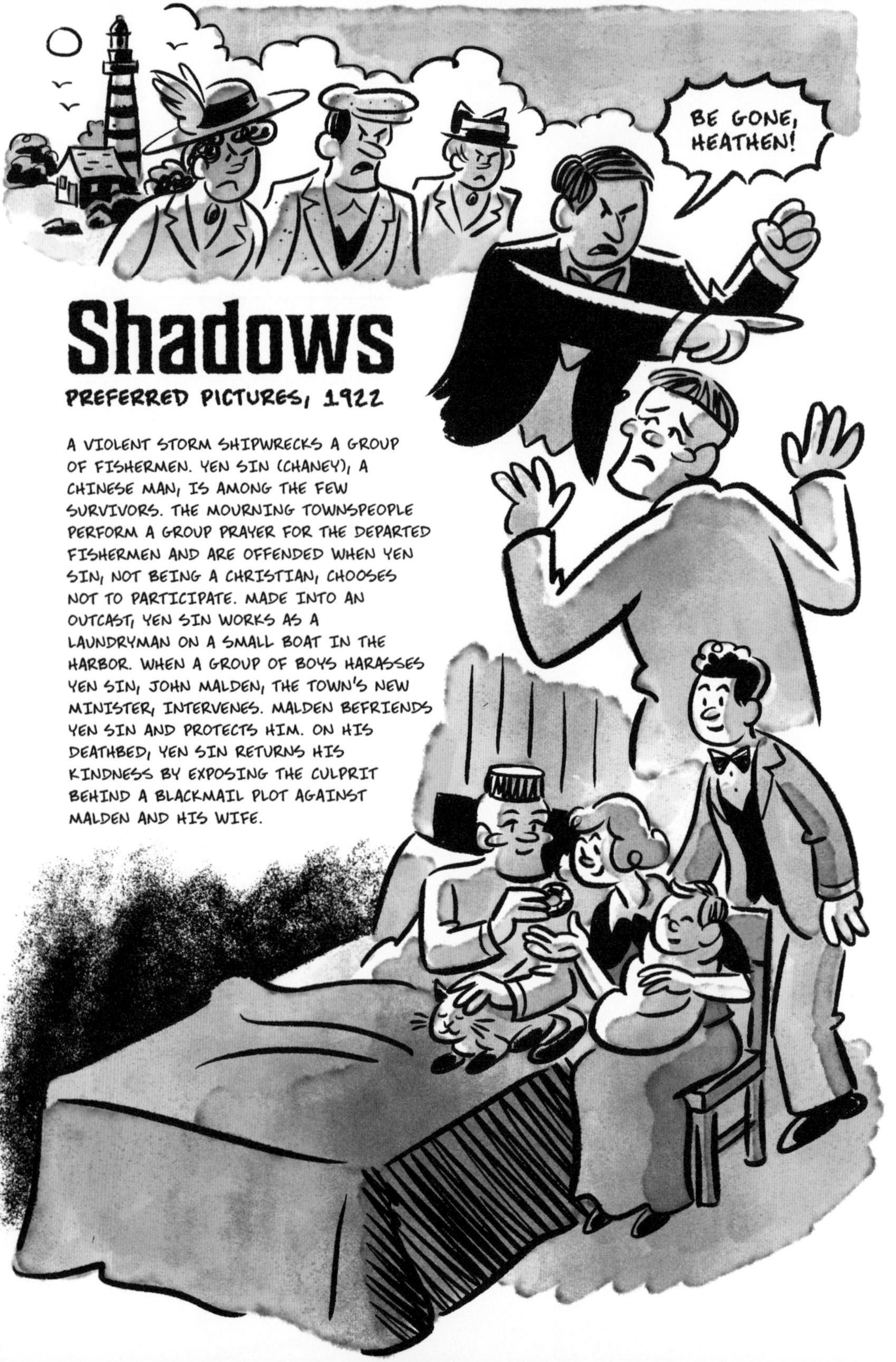
BE GONE, HEATHEN!

Shadows

PREFERRED PICTURES, 1922

A VIOLENT STORM SHIPWRECKS A GROUP OF FISHERMEN. YEN SIN (CHANEY), A CHINESE MAN, IS AMONG THE FEW SURVIVORS. THE MOURNING TOWNSPEOPLE PERFORM A GROUP PRAYER FOR THE DEPARTED FISHERMEN AND ARE OFFENDED WHEN YEN SIN, NOT BEING A CHRISTIAN, CHOOSES NOT TO PARTICIPATE. MADE INTO AN OUTCAST, YEN SIN WORKS AS A LAUNDRYMAN ON A SMALL BOAT IN THE HARBOR. WHEN A GROUP OF BOYS HARASSES YEN SIN, JOHN MALDEN, THE TOWN'S NEW MINISTER, INTERVENES. MALDEN BEFRIENDS YEN SIN AND PROTECTS HIM. ON HIS DEATHBED, YEN SIN RETURNS HIS KINDNESS BY EXPOSING THE CULPRIT BEHIND A BLACKMAIL PLOT AGAINST MALDEN AND HIS WIFE.

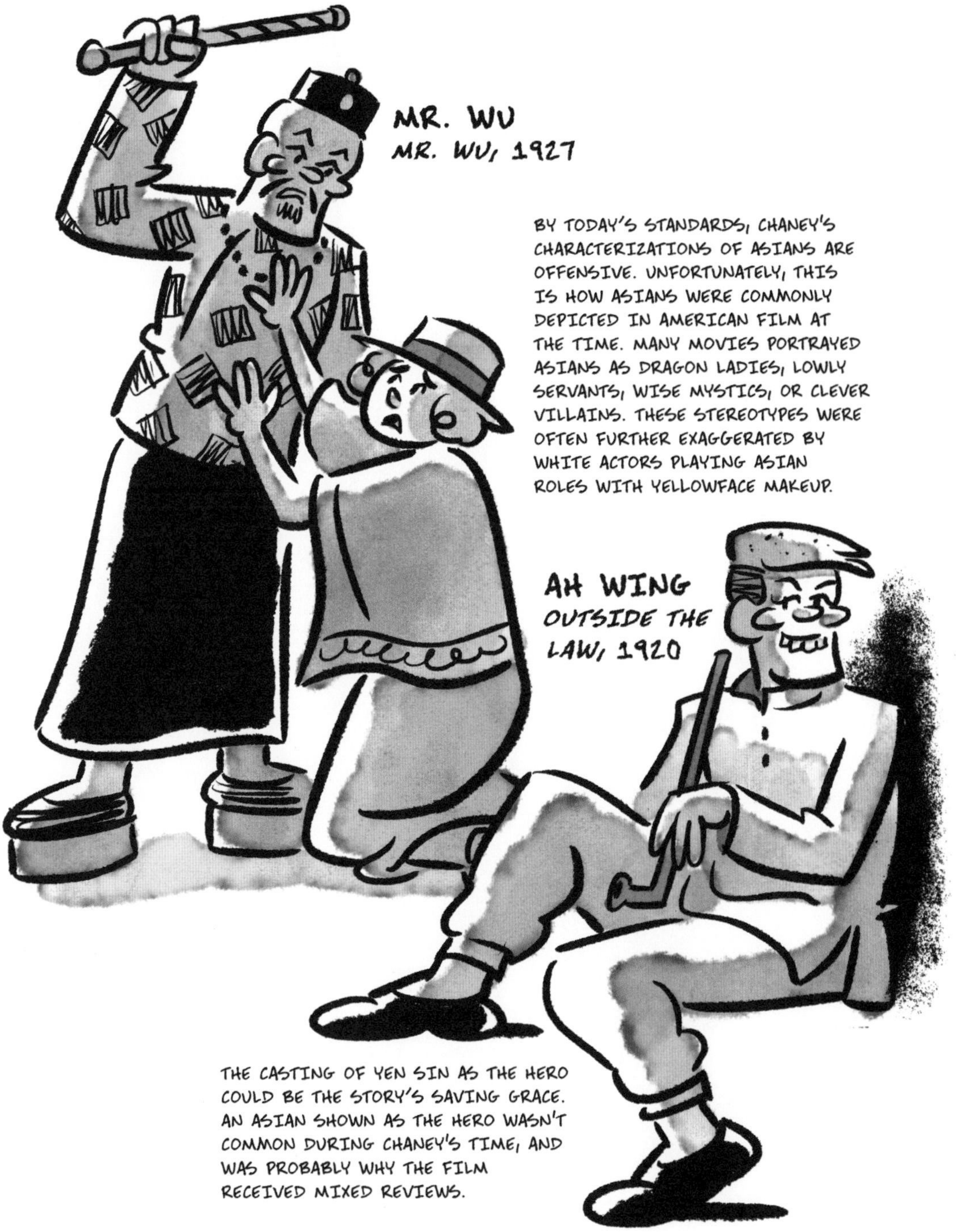
MR. WU
MR. WU, 1927
AH WING
OUTSIDE THE LAW, 1920

BY TODAY'S STANDARDS, CHANEY'S CHARACTERIZATIONS OF ASIANS ARE OFFENSIVE. UNFORTUNATELY, THIS IS HOW ASIANS WERE COMMONLY DEPICTED IN AMERICAN FILM AT THE TIME. MANY MOVIES PORTRAYED ASIANS AS DRAGON LADIES, LOWLY SERVANTS, WISE MYSTICS, OR CLEVER VILLAINS. THESE STEREOTYPES WERE OFTEN FURTHER EXAGGERATED BY WHITE ACTORS PLAYING ASIAN ROLES WITH YELLOWFACE MAKEUP.

THE CASTING OF YEN SIN AS THE HERO COULD BE THE STORY'S SAVING GRACE. AN ASIAN SHOWN AS THE HERO WASN'T COMMON DURING CHANEY'S TIME, AND WAS PROBABLY WHY THE FILM RECEIVED MIXED REVIEWS.

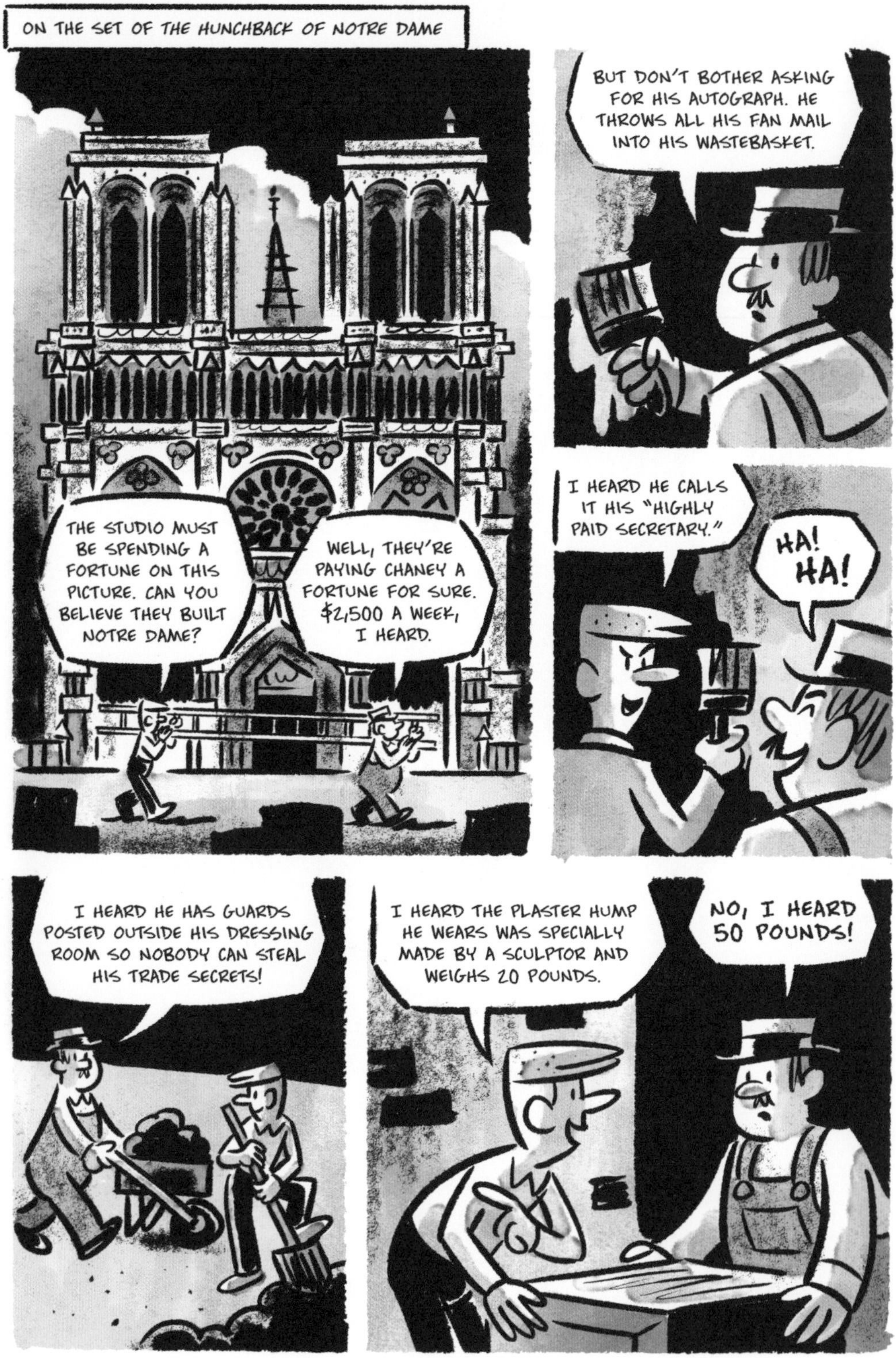
ON THE SET OF THE HUNCHBACK OF NOTRE DAME
THE STUDIO MUST BE SPENDING A FORTUNE ON THIS PICTURE. CAN YOU BELIEVE THEY BUILT NOTRE DAME?
WELL, THEY'RE PAYING CHANEY A FORTUNE FOR SURE. $2,500 A WEEK, I HEARD.
BUT DON'T BOTHER ASKING FOR HIS AUTOGRAPH. HE THROWS ALL HIS FAN MAIL INTO HIS WASTEBASKET.
I HEARD HE CALLS IT HIS "HIGHLY PAID SECRETARY."
HA! HA!
I HEARD HE HAS GUARDS POSTED OUTSIDE HIS DRESSING ROOM SO NOBODY CAN STEAL HIS TRADE SECRETS!
I HEARD THE PLASTER HUMP HE WEARS WAS SPECIALLY MADE BY A SCULPTOR AND WEIGHS 20 POUNDS.
NO, I HEARD 50 POUNDS!

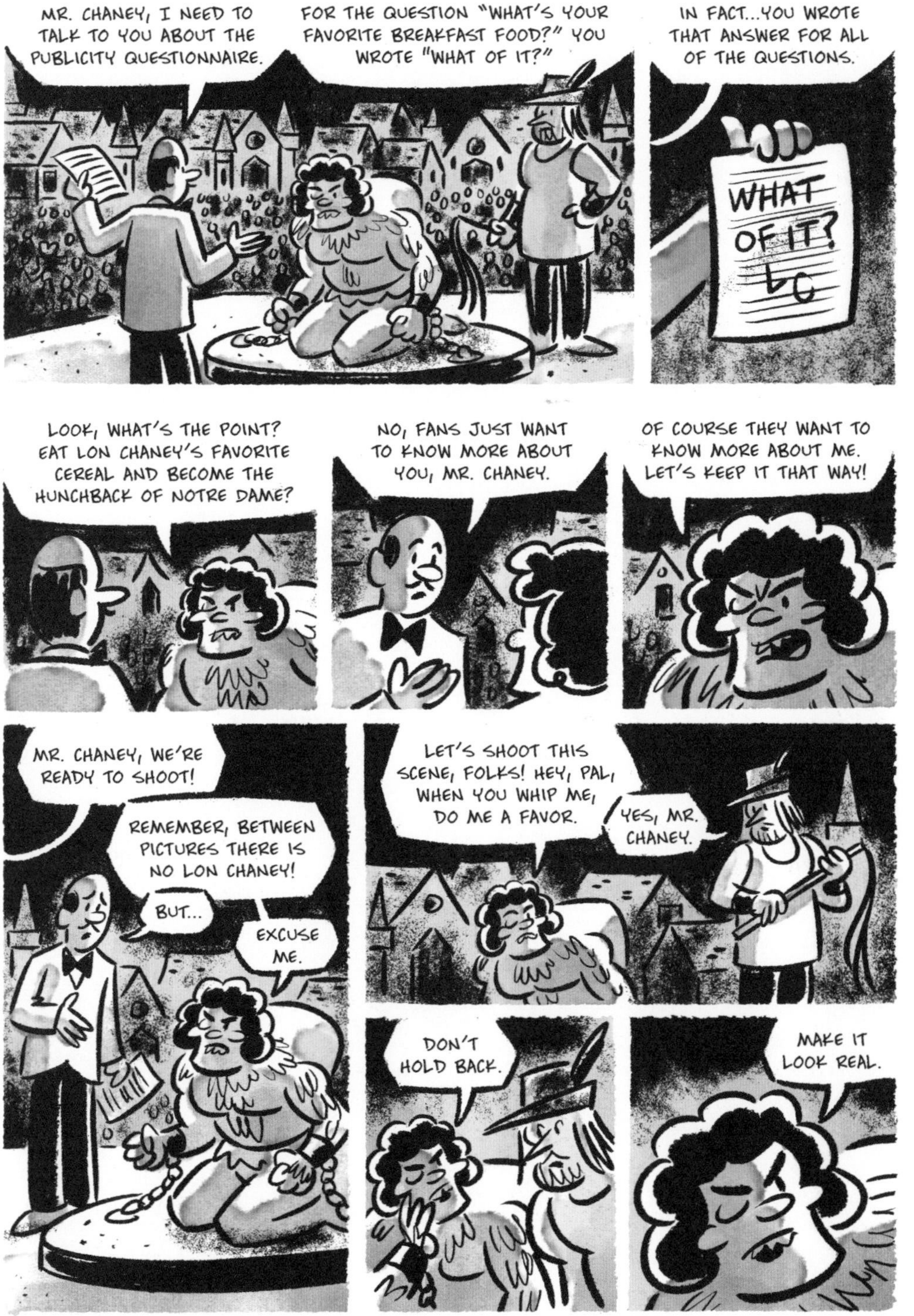
MR. CHANEY, I NEED TO TALK TO YOU ABOUT THE PUBLICITY QUESTIONNAIRE.
FOR THE QUESTION "WHAT'S YOUR FAVORITE BREAKFAST FOOD?" YOU WROTE "WHAT OF IT?"
IN FACT...YOU WROTE THAT ANSWER FOR ALL OF THE QUESTIONS.
WHAT OF IT?
LC
LOOK, WHAT'S THE POINT? EAT LON CHANEY'S FAVORITE CEREAL AND BECOME THE HUNCHBACK OF NOTRE DAME?
NO, FANS JUST WANT TO KNOW MORE ABOUT YOU, MR. CHANEY.
OF COURSE THEY WANT TO KNOW MORE ABOUT ME. LET'S KEEP IT THAT WAY!
MR. CHANEY, WE'RE READY TO SHOOT!
REMEMBER, BETWEEN PICTURES THERE IS NO LON CHANEY!
BUT...
EXCUSE ME.
LET'S SHOOT THIS SCENE, FOLKS! HEY, PAL, WHEN YOU WHIP ME, DO ME A FAVOR.
YES, MR. CHANEY.
DON'T HOLD BACK.
MAKE IT LOOK REAL.

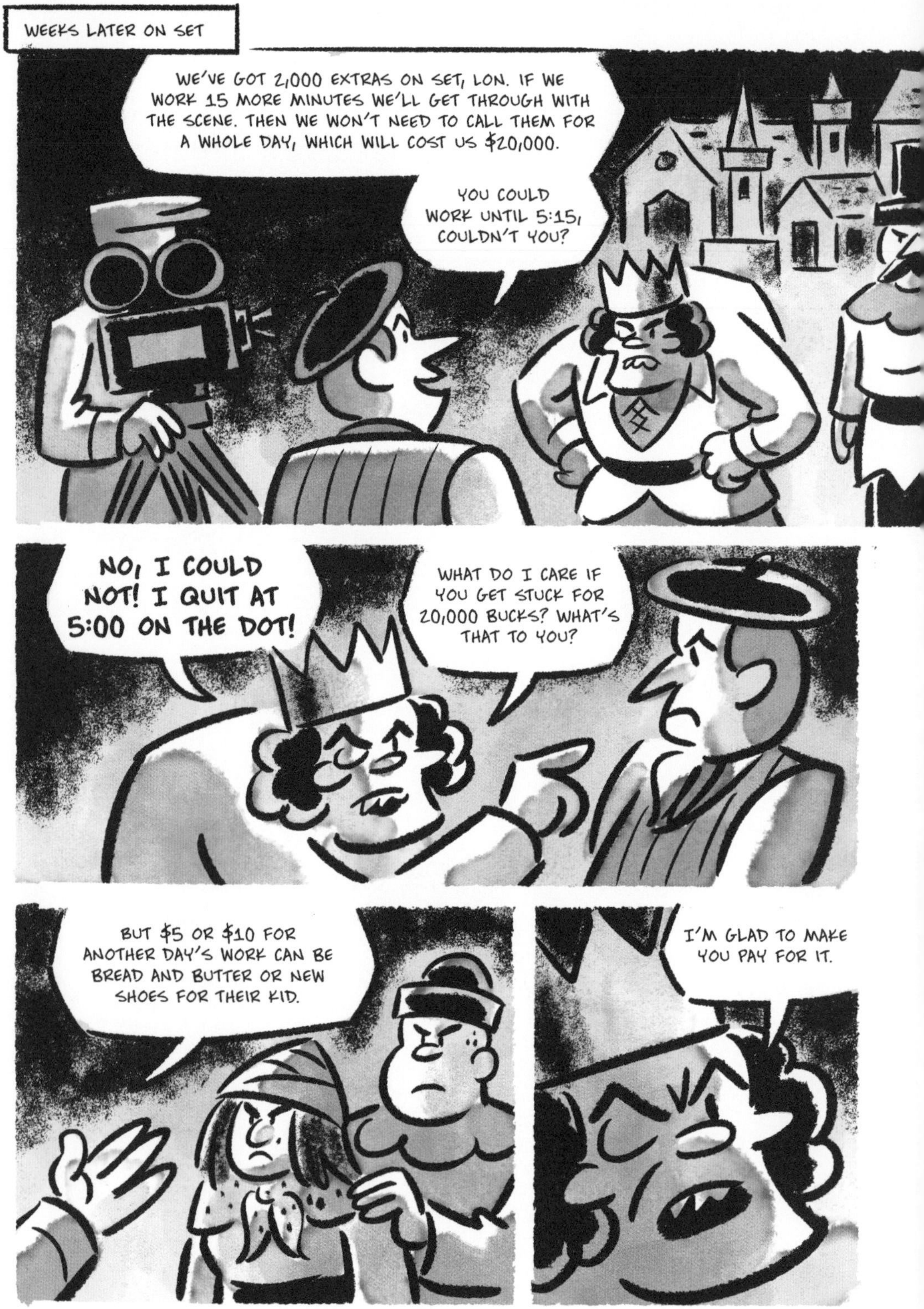
WEEKS LATER ON SET
WE'VE GOT 2,000 EXTRAS ON SET, LON. IF WE WORK 15 MORE MINUTES WE'LL GET THROUGH WITH THE SCENE. THEN WE WON'T NEED TO CALL THEM FOR A WHOLE DAY, WHICH WILL COST US $20,000.
YOU COULD WORK UNTIL 5:15, COULDN'T YOU?
NO, I COULD NOT! I QUIT AT 5:00 ON THE DOT!
WHAT DO I CARE IF YOU GET STUCK FOR 20,000 BUCKS? WHAT'S THAT TO YOU?
BUT $5 OR $10 FOR ANOTHER DAY'S WORK CAN BE BREAD AND BUTTER OR NEW SHOES FOR THEIR KID.
I'M GLAD TO MAKE YOU PAY FOR IT.

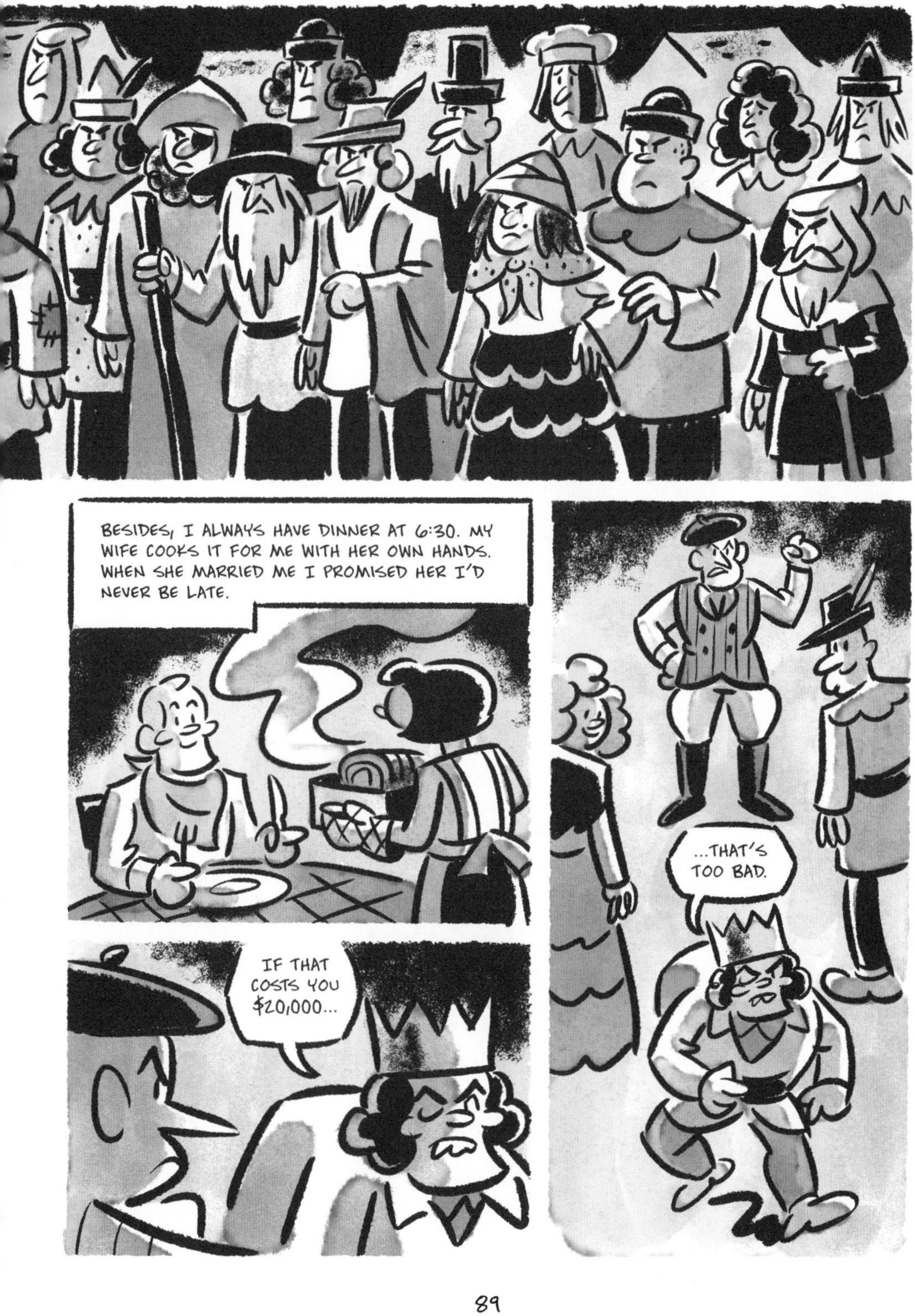
BESIDES, I ALWAYS HAVE DINNER AT 6:30. MY WIFE COOKS IT FOR ME WITH HER OWN HANDS. WHEN SHE MARRIED ME I PROMISED HER I'D NEVER BE LATE.
IF THAT COSTS YOU $20,000...
...THAT'S TOO BAD.

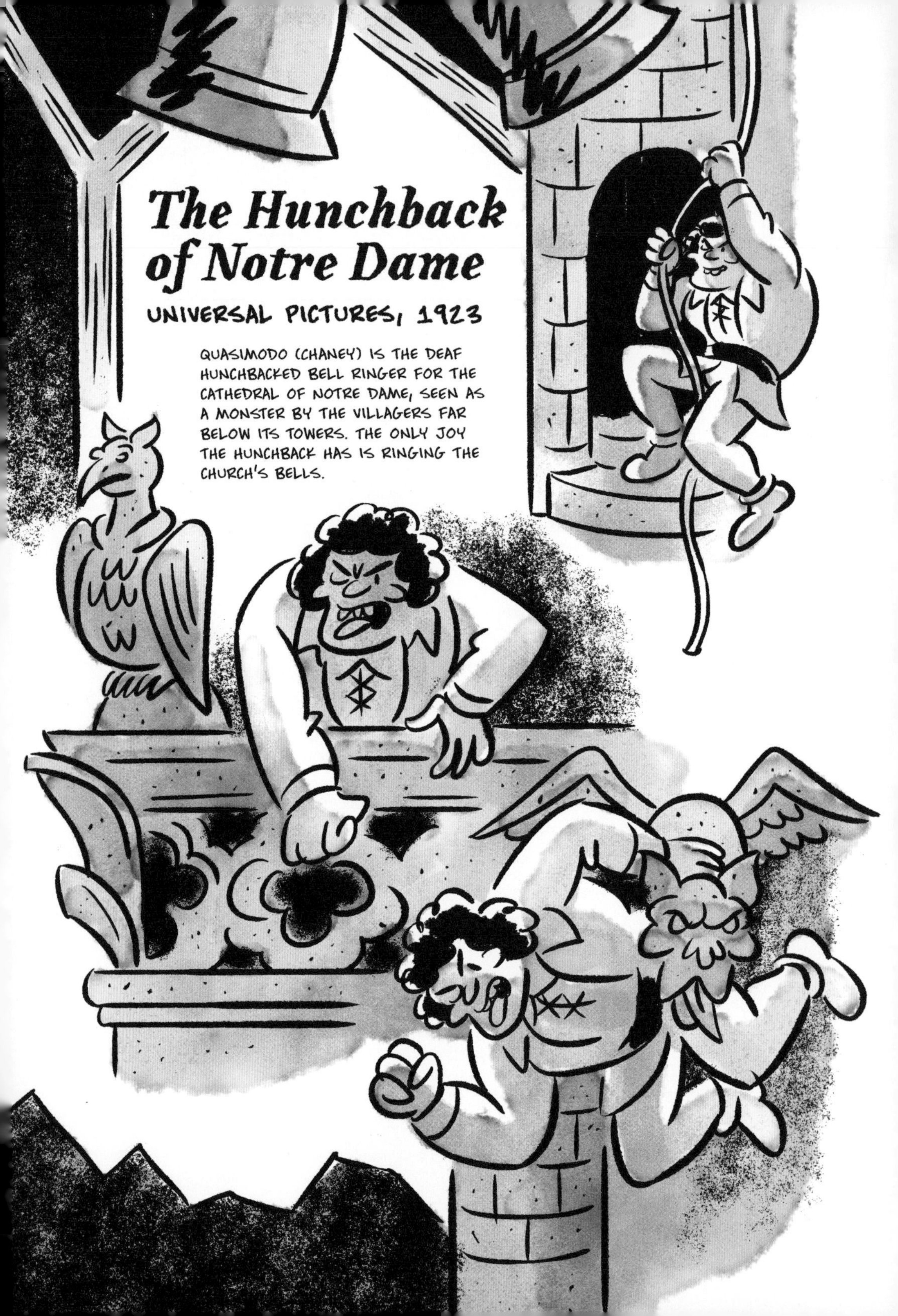

The Hunchback of Notre Dame

UNIVERSAL PICTURES, 1923

QUASIMODO (CHANEY) IS THE DEAF HUNCHBACKED BELL RINGER FOR THE CATHEDRAL OF NOTRE DAME, SEEN AS A MONSTER BY THE VILLAGERS FAR BELOW ITS TOWERS. THE ONLY JOY THE HUNCHBACK HAS IS RINGING THE CHURCH'S BELLS.

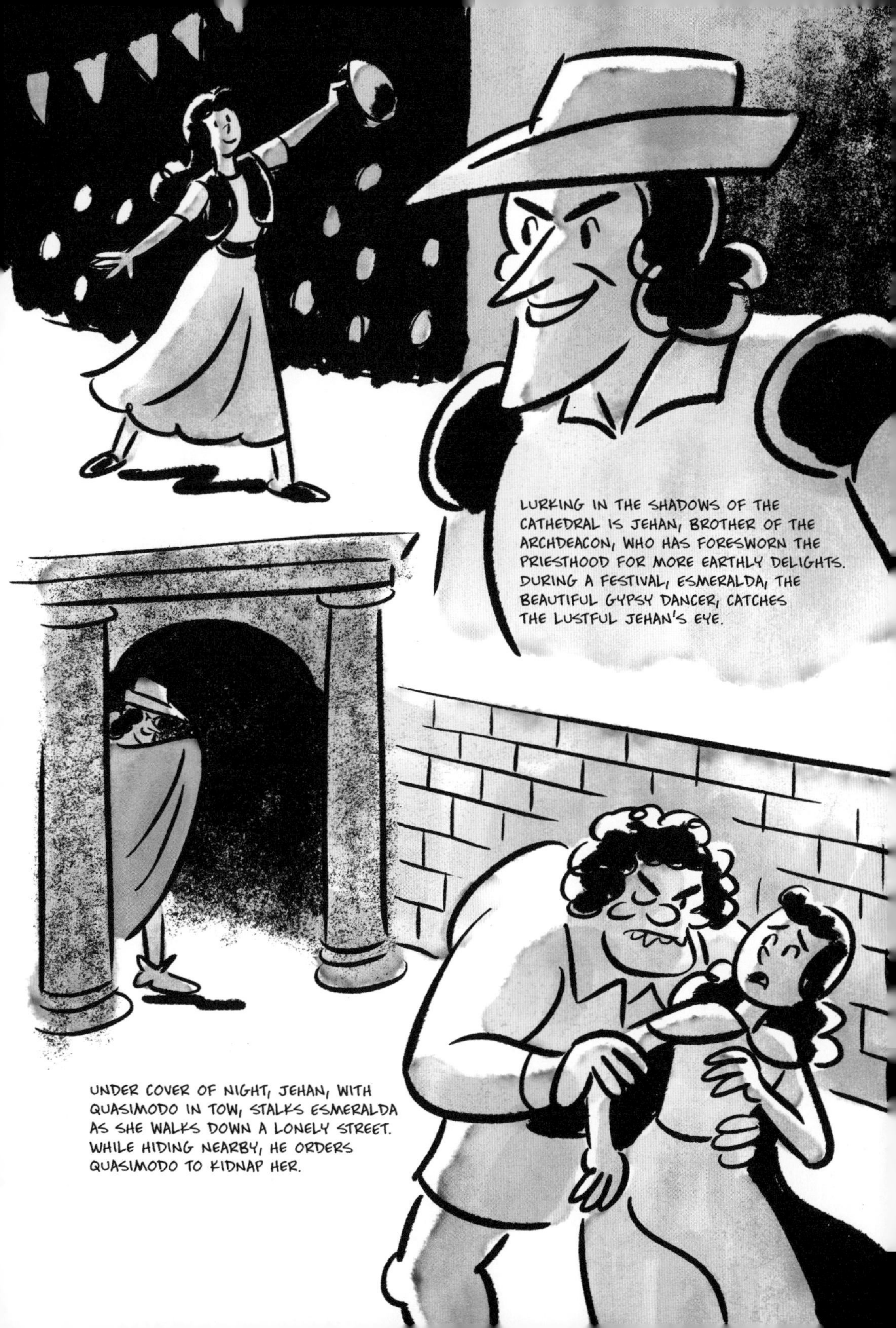
LURKING IN THE SHADOWS OF THE CATHEDRAL IS JEHAN, BROTHER OF THE ARCHDEACON, WHO HAS FORESWORN THE PRIESTHOOD FOR MORE EARTHLY DELIGHTS. DURING A FESTIVAL, ESMERALDA, THE BEAUTIFUL GYPSY DANCER, CATCHES THE LUSTFUL JEHAN'S EYE.
UNDER COVER OF NIGHT, JEHAN, WITH QUASIMODO IN TOW, STALKS ESMERALDA AS SHE WALKS DOWN A LONELY STREET. WHILE HIDING NEARBY, HE ORDERS QUASIMODO TO KIDNAP HER.

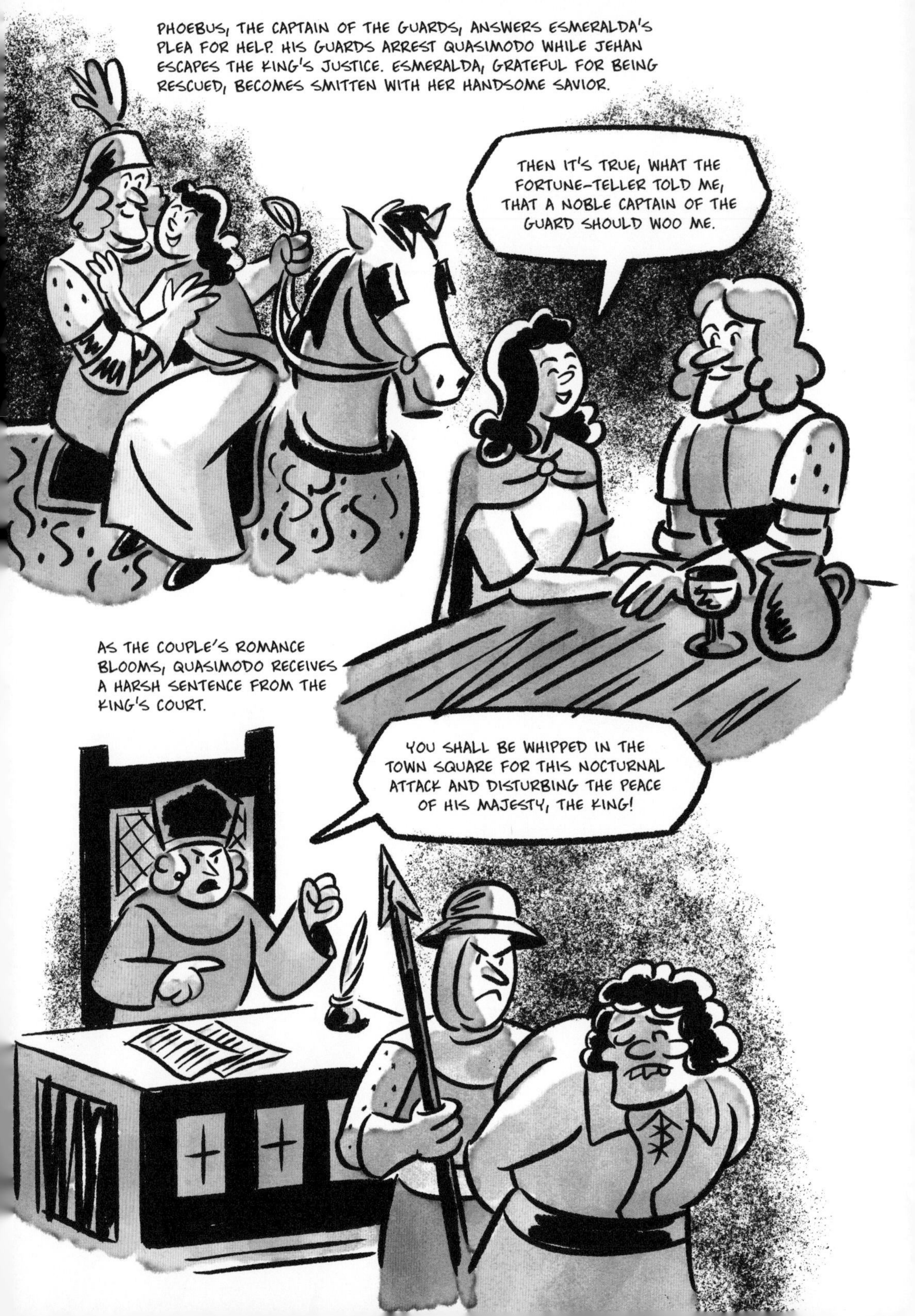
PHOEBUS, THE CAPTAIN OF THE GUARDS, ANSWERS ESMERALDA'S PLEA FOR HELP. HIS GUARDS ARREST QUASIMODO WHILE JEHAN ESCAPES THE KING'S JUSTICE. ESMERALDA, GRATEFUL FOR BEING RESCUED, BECOMES SMITTEN WITH HER HANDSOME SAVIOR.
THEN IT'S TRUE, WHAT THE FORTUNE-TELLER TOLD ME, THAT A NOBLE CAPTAIN OF THE GUARD SHOULD WOO ME.
AS THE COUPLE'S ROMANCE BLOOMS, QUASIMODO RECEIVES A HARSH SENTENCE FROM THE KING'S COURT.
YOU SHALL BE WHIPPED IN THE TOWN SQUARE FOR THIS NOCTURNAL ATTACK AND DISTURBING THE PEACE OF HIS MAJESTY, THE KING!

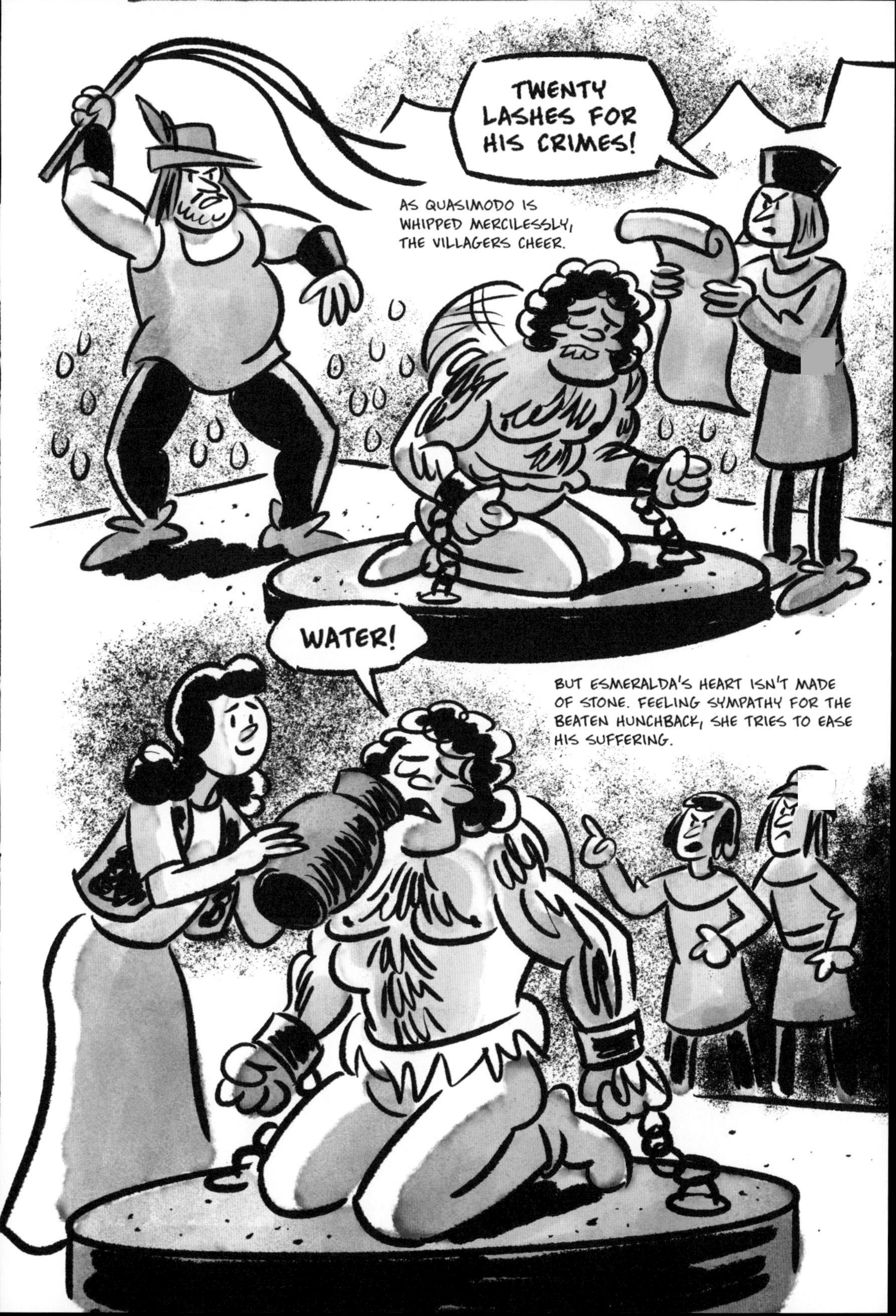
TWENTY LASHES FOR HIS CRIMES!
AS QUASIMODO IS WHIPPED MERCILESSLY, THE VILLAGERS CHEER.
WATER!
BUT ESMERALDA'S HEART ISN'T MADE OF STONE. FEELING SYMPATHY FOR THE BEATEN HUNCHBACK, SHE TRIES TO EASE HIS SUFFERING.

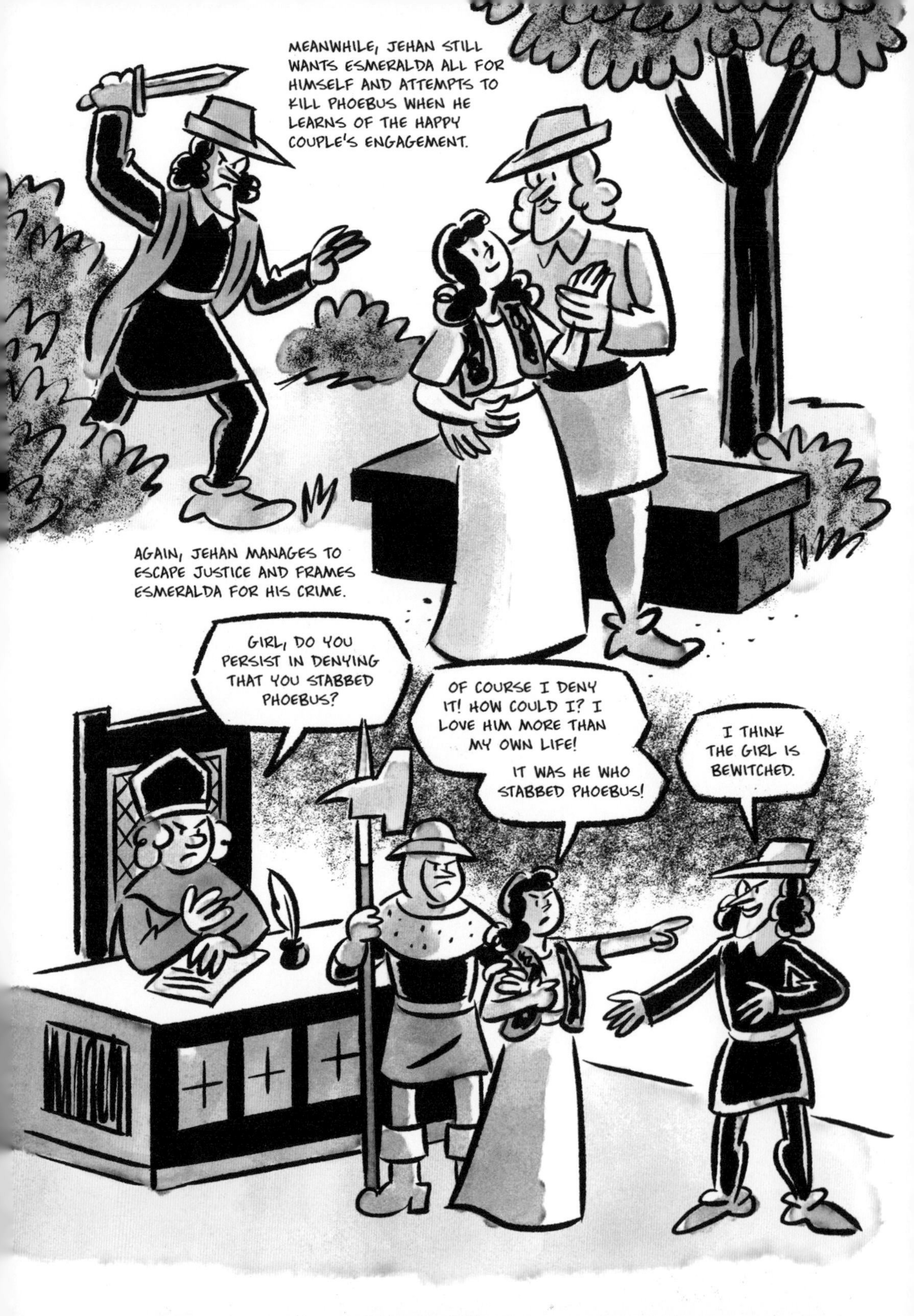
MEANWHILE, JEHAN STILL WANTS ESMERALDA ALL FOR HIMSELF AND ATTEMPTS TO KILL PHOEBUS WHEN HE LEARNS OF THE HAPPY COUPLE'S ENGAGEMENT.
AGAIN, JEHAN MANAGES TO ESCAPE JUSTICE AND FRAMES ESMERALDA FOR HIS CRIME.
GIRL, DO YOU PERSIST IN DENYING THAT YOU STABBED PHOEBUS?
OF COURSE I DENY IT! HOW COULD I? I LOVE HIM MORE THAN MY OWN LIFE!
IT WAS HE WHO STABBED PHOEBUS!
I THINK THE GIRL IS BEWITCHED.

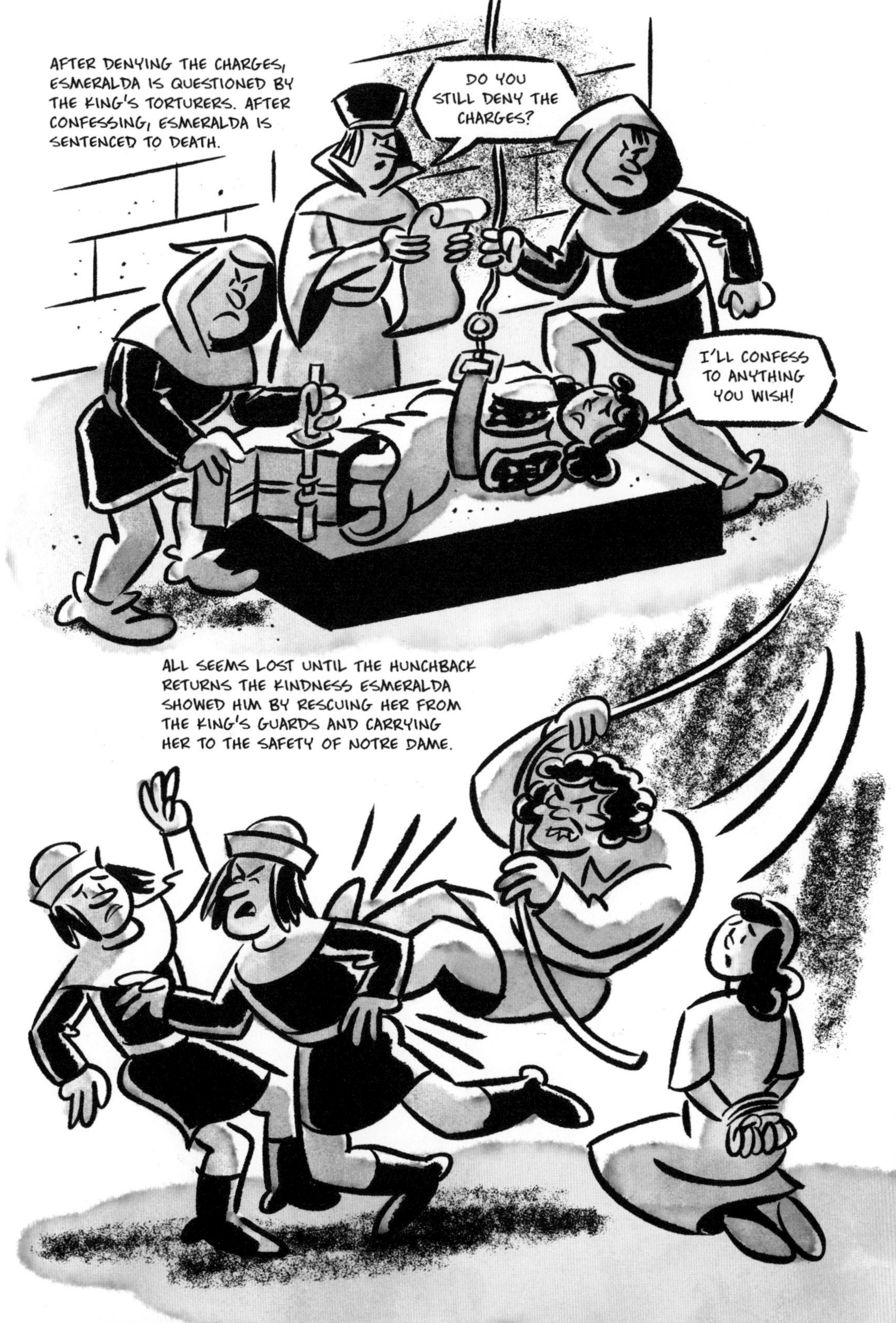
AFTER DENYING THE CHARGES, ESMERALDA IS QUESTIONED BY THE KING'S TORTURERS. AFTER CONFESSING, ESMERALDA IS SENTENCED TO DEATH.
DO YOU STILL DENY THE CHARGES?
I'LL CONFESS TO ANYTHING YOU WISH!
ALL SEEMS LOST UNTIL THE HUNCHBACK RETURNS THE KINDNESS ESMERALDA SHOWED HIM BY RESCUING HER FROM THE KING'S GUARDS AND CARRYING HER TO THE SAFETY OF NOTRE DAME.

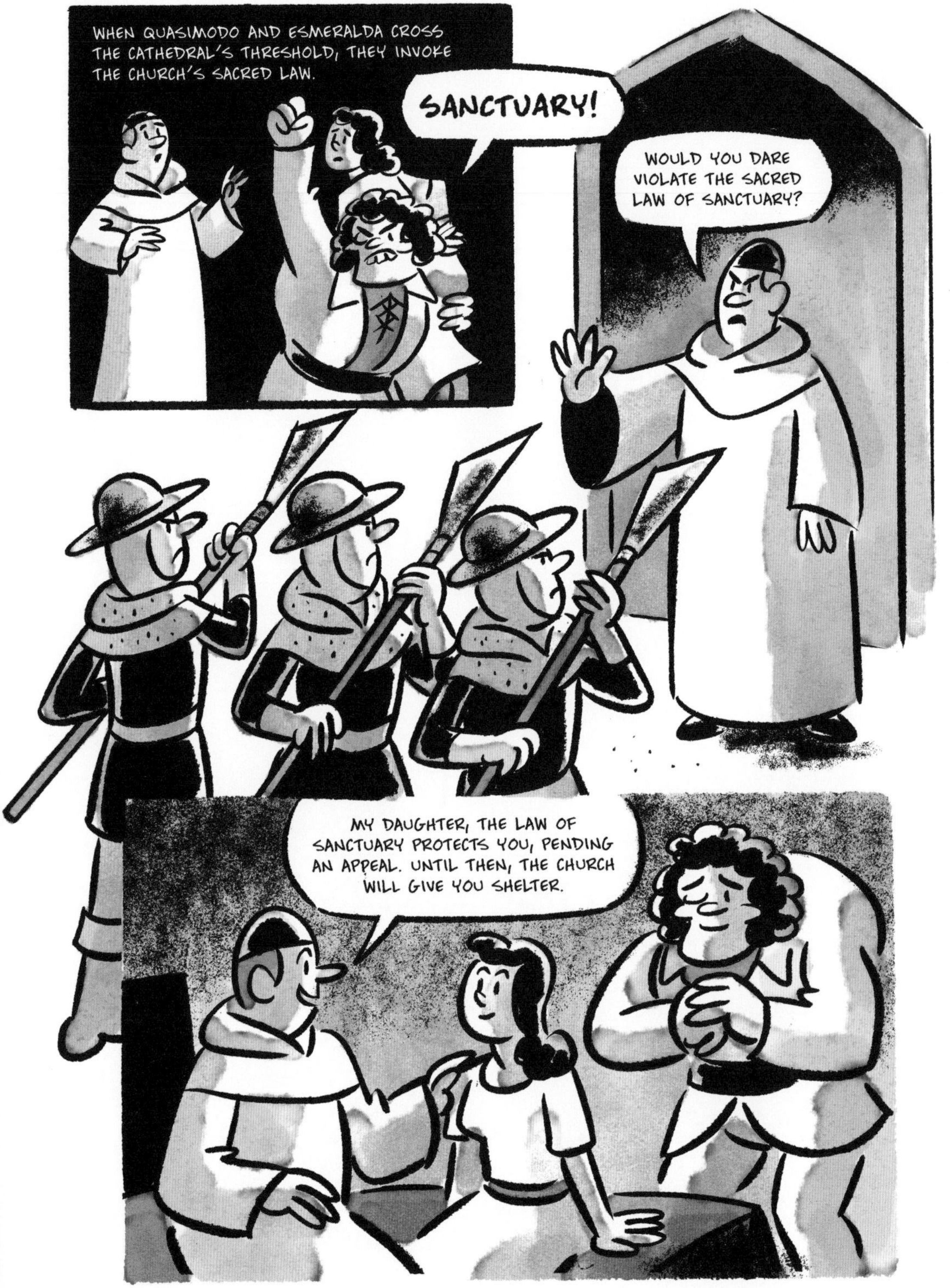
WHEN QUASIMODO AND ESMERALDA CROSS THE CATHEDRAL'S THRESHOLD, THEY INVOKE THE CHURCH'S SACRED LAW.
SANCTUARY!
WOULD YOU DARE VIOLATE THE SACRED LAW OF SANCTUARY?
MY DAUGHTER, THE LAW OF SANCTUARY PROTECTS YOU, PENDING AN APPEAL. UNTIL THEN, THE CHURCH WILL GIVE YOU SHELTER.

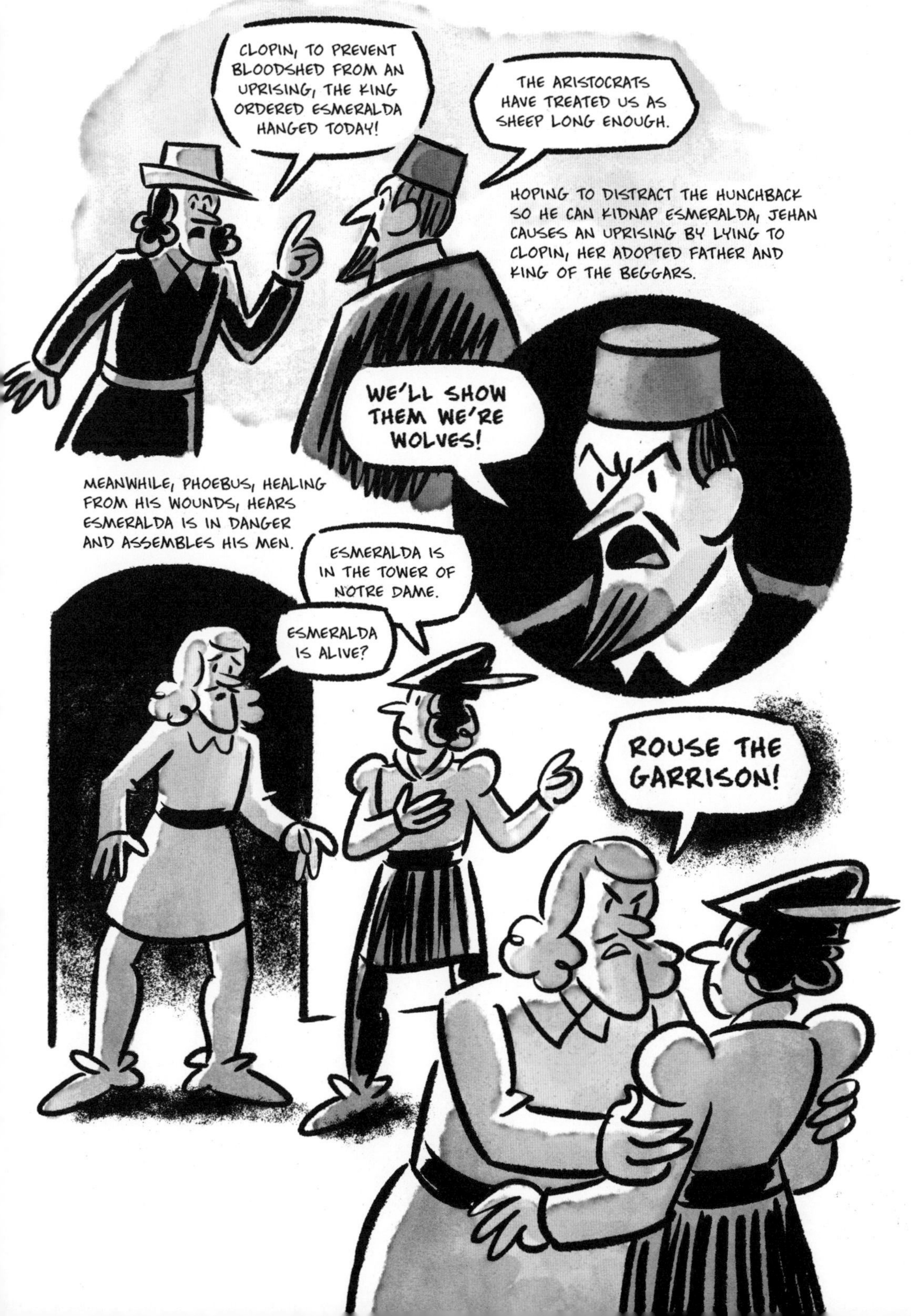
CLOPIN, TO PREVENT BLOODSHED FROM AN UPRISING, THE KING ORDERED ESMERALDA HANGED TODAY!
THE ARISTOCRATS HAVE TREATED US AS SHEEP LONG ENOUGH.
HOPING TO DISTRACT THE HUNCHBACK SO HE CAN KIDNAP ESMERALDA, JEHAN CAUSES AN UPRISING BY LYING TO CLOPIN, HER ADOPTED FATHER AND KING OF THE BEGGARS.
WE'LL SHOW THEM WE'RE WOLVES!
MEANWHILE, PHOEBUS, HEALING FROM HIS WOUNDS, HEARS ESMERALDA IS IN DANGER AND ASSEMBLES HIS MEN.
ESMERALDA IS IN THE TOWER OF NOTRE DAME.
ESMERALDA IS ALIVE?
ROUSE THE GARRISON!

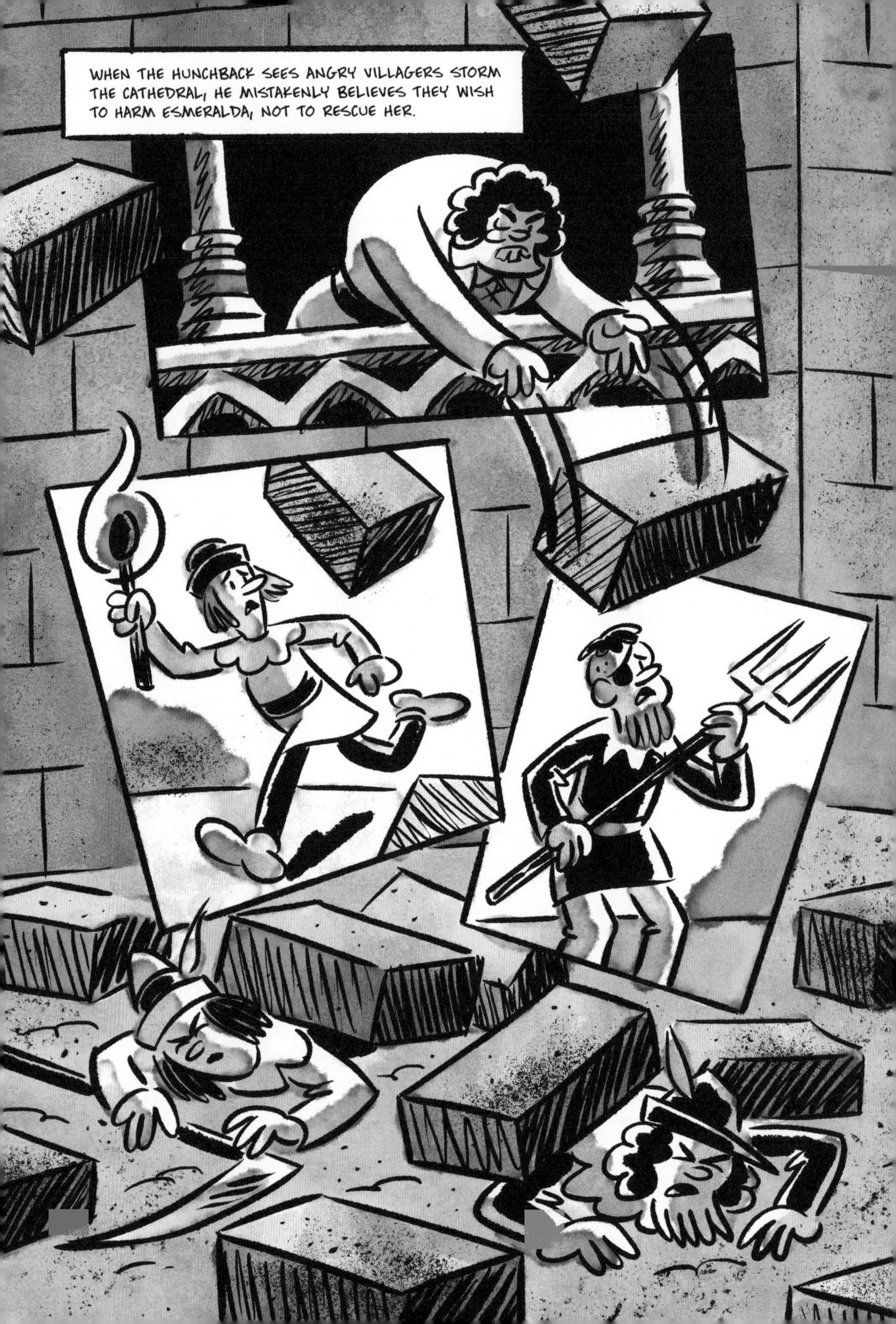
WHEN THE HUNCHBACK SEES ANGRY VILLAGERS STORM THE CATHEDRAL, HE MISTAKENLY BELIEVES THEY WISH TO HARM ESMERALDA, NOT TO RESCUE HER.

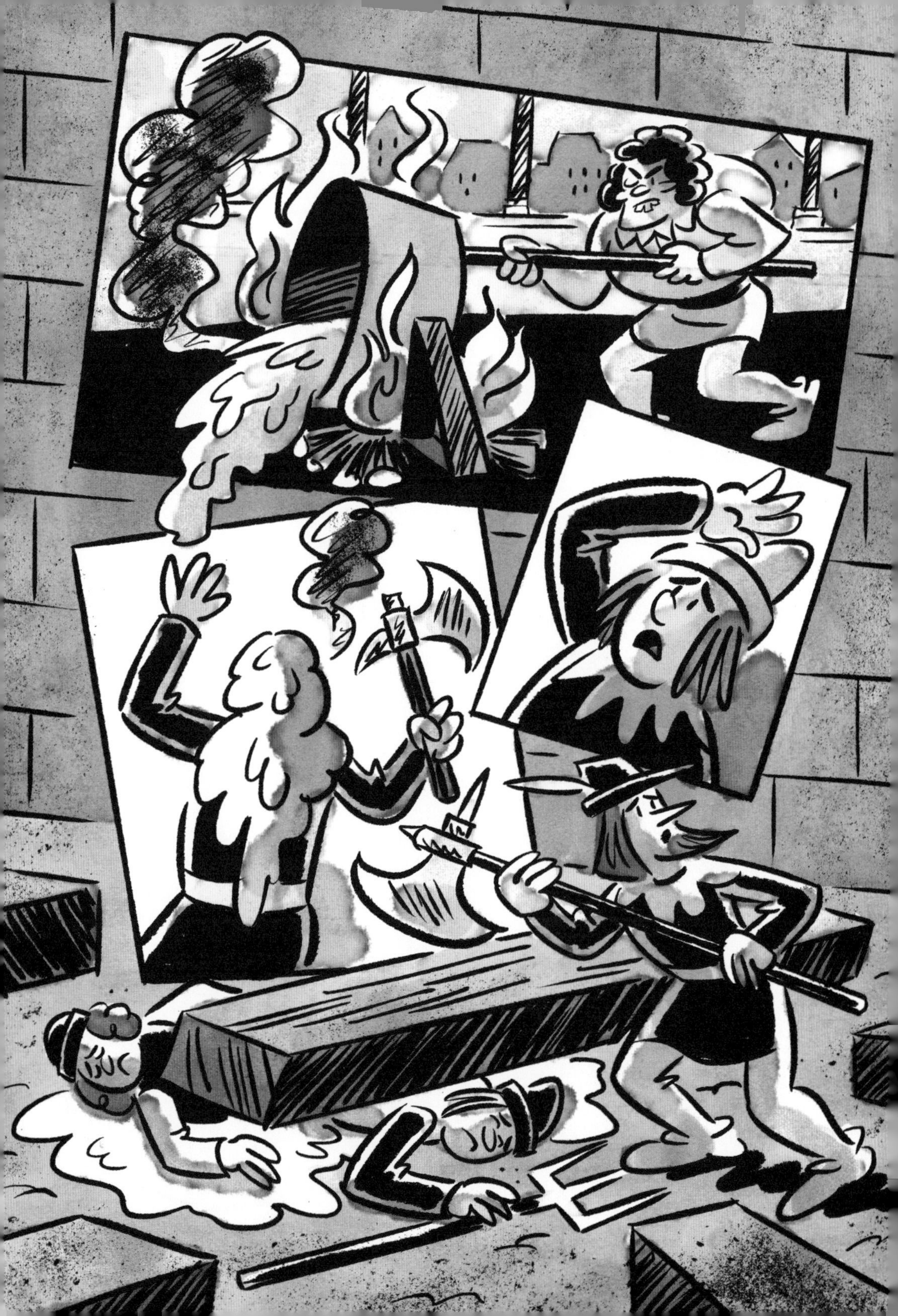

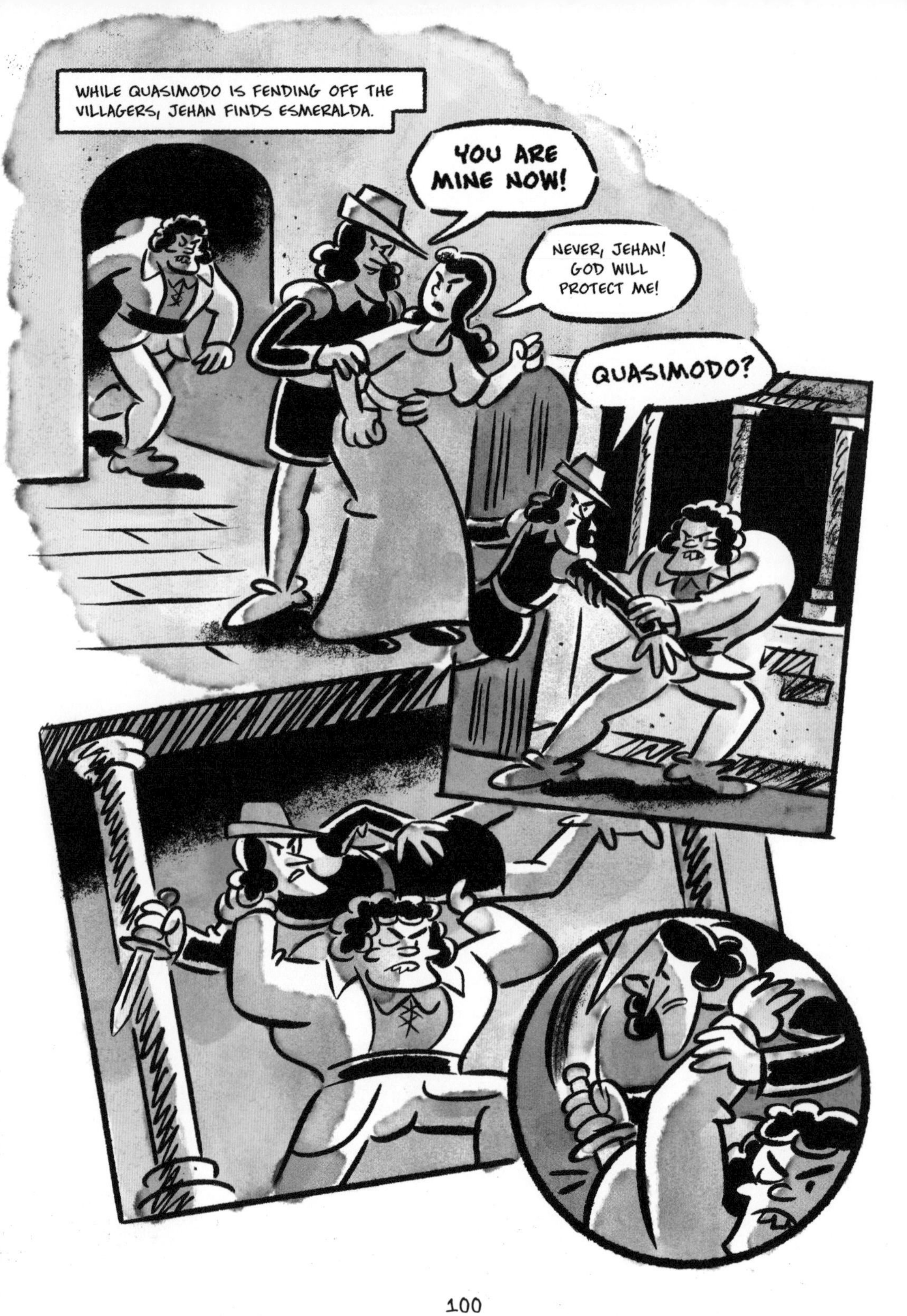
WHILE QUASIMODO IS FENDING OFF THE VILLAGERS, JEHAN FINDS ESMERALDA.
YOU ARE MINE NOW!
NEVER, JEHAN! GOD WILL PROTECT ME!
QUASIMODO?

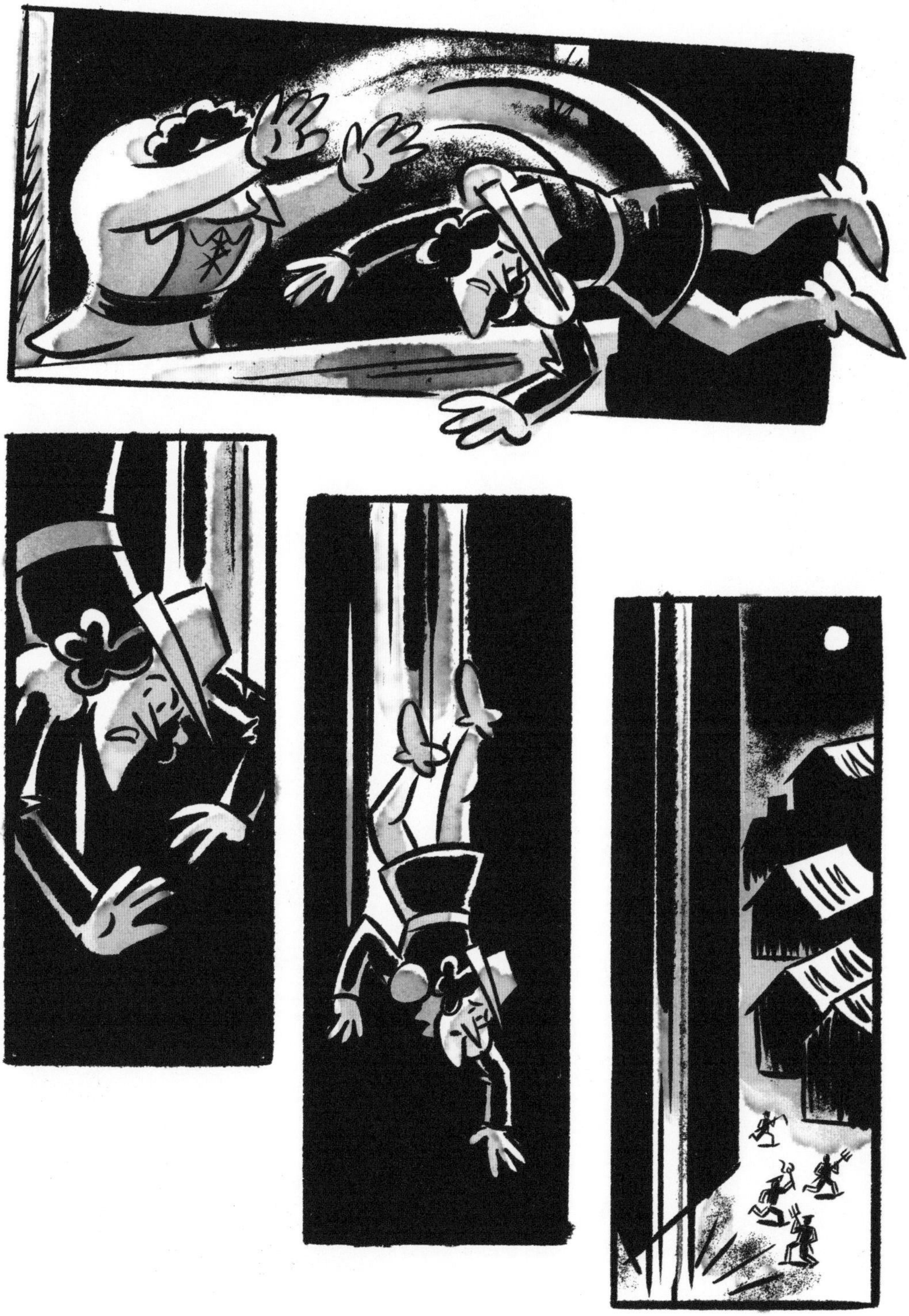

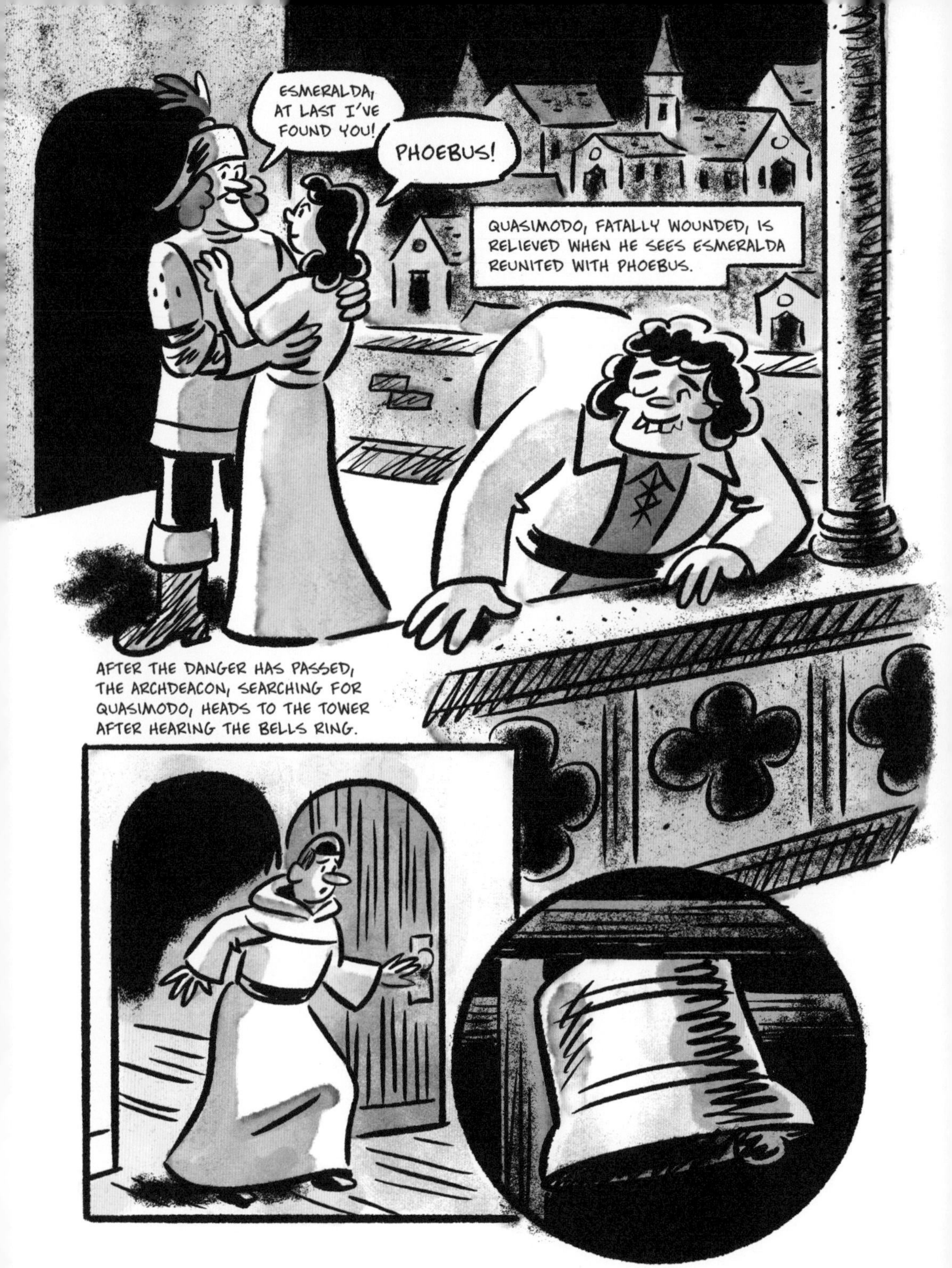
ESMERALDA, AT LAST I'VE FOUND YOU!
PHOEBUS!
QUASIMODO, FATALLY WOUNDED, IS RELIEVED WHEN HE SEES ESMERALDA REUNITED WITH PHOEBUS.
AFTER THE DANGER HAS PASSED, THE ARCHDEACON, SEARCHING FOR QUASIMODO, HEADS TO THE TOWER AFTER HEARING THE BELLS RING.

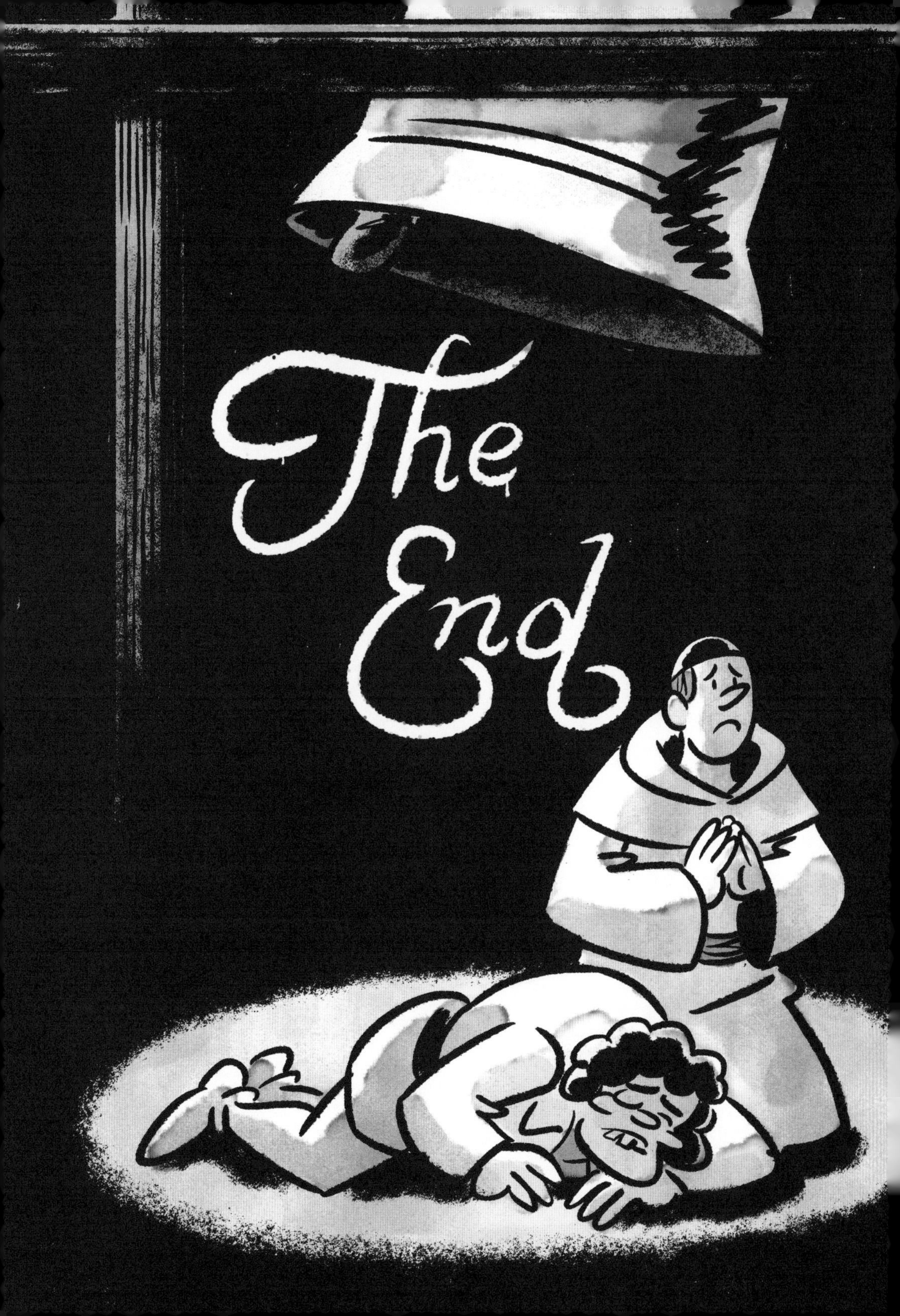
The End

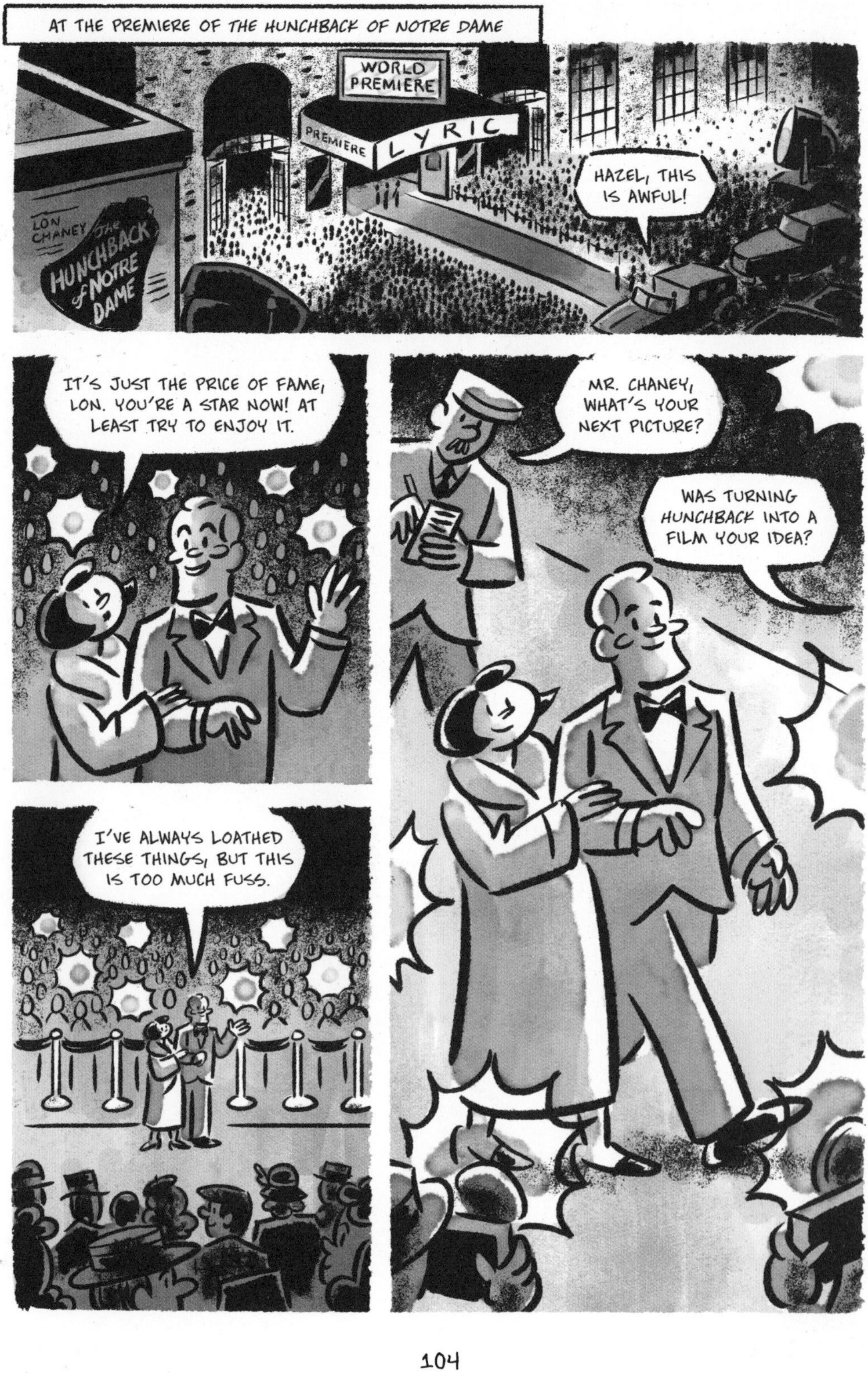
AT THE PREMIERE OF THE HUNCHBACK OF NOTRE DAME
WORLD PREMIERE
PREMIERE
LYRIC
LON CHANEY The HUNCHBACK of NOTRE DAME
HAZEL, THIS IS AWFUL!
IT'S JUST THE PRICE OF FAME, LON. YOU'RE A STAR NOW! AT LEAST TRY TO ENJOY IT.
I'VE ALWAYS LOATHED THESE THINGS, BUT THIS IS TOO MUCH FUSS.
MR. CHANEY, WHAT'S YOUR NEXT PICTURE?
WAS TURNING HUNCHBACK INTO A FILM YOUR IDEA?

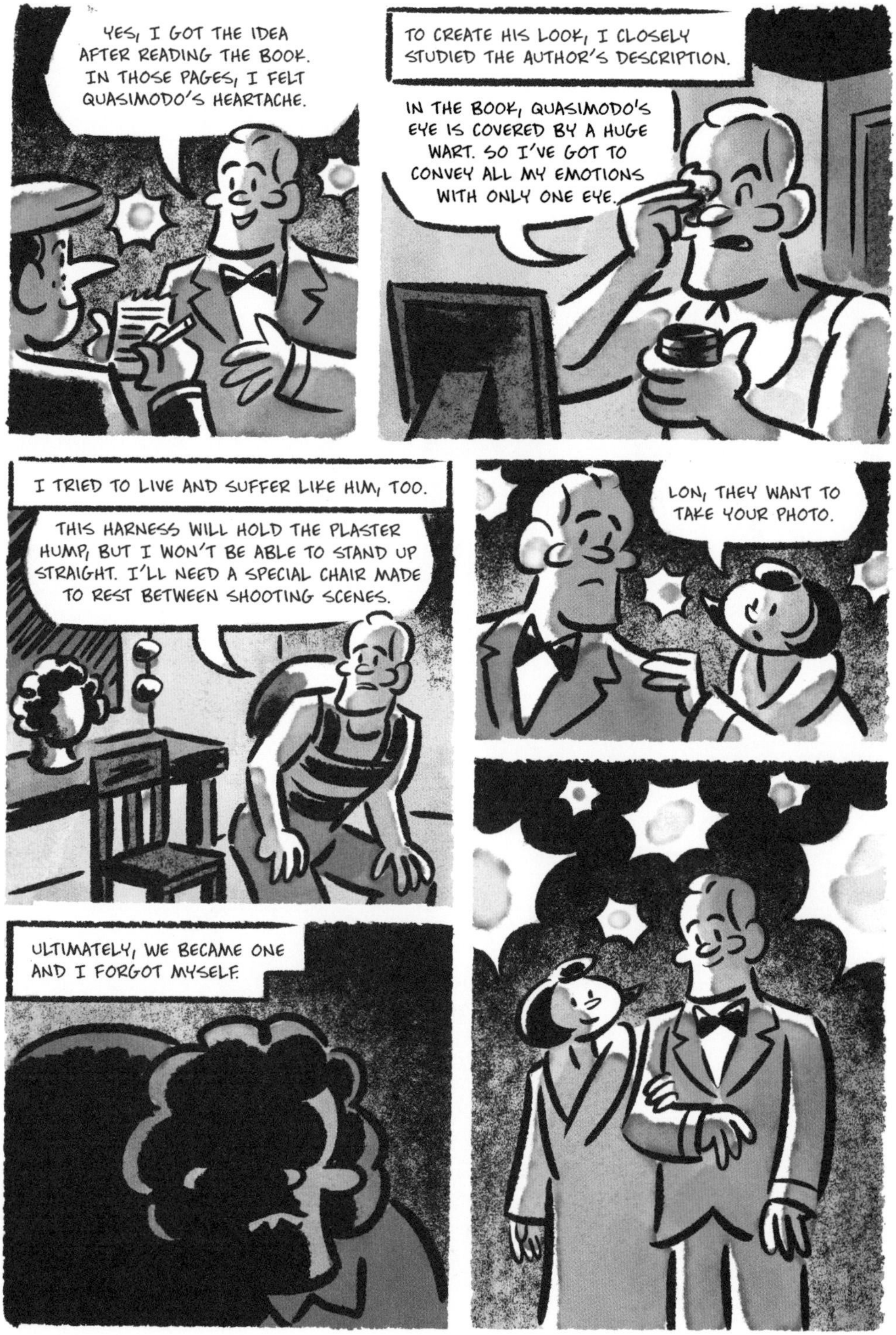

YES, I GOT THE IDEA AFTER READING THE BOOK. IN THOSE PAGES, I FELT QUASIMODO'S HEARTACHE.
TO CREATE HIS LOOK, I CLOSELY STUDIED THE AUTHOR'S DESCRIPTION.
IN THE BOOK, QUASIMODO'S EYE IS COVERED BY A HUGE WART. SO I'VE GOT TO CONVEY ALL MY EMOTIONS WITH ONLY ONE EYE.
I TRIED TO LIVE AND SUFFER LIKE HIM, TOO.
THIS HARNESS WILL HOLD THE PLASTER HUMP, BUT I WON'T BE ABLE TO STAND UP STRAIGHT. I'LL NEED A SPECIAL CHAIR MADE TO REST BETWEEN SHOOTING SCENES.
LON, THEY WANT TO TAKE YOUR PHOTO.
ULTIMATELY, WE BECAME ONE AND I FORGOT MYSELF.

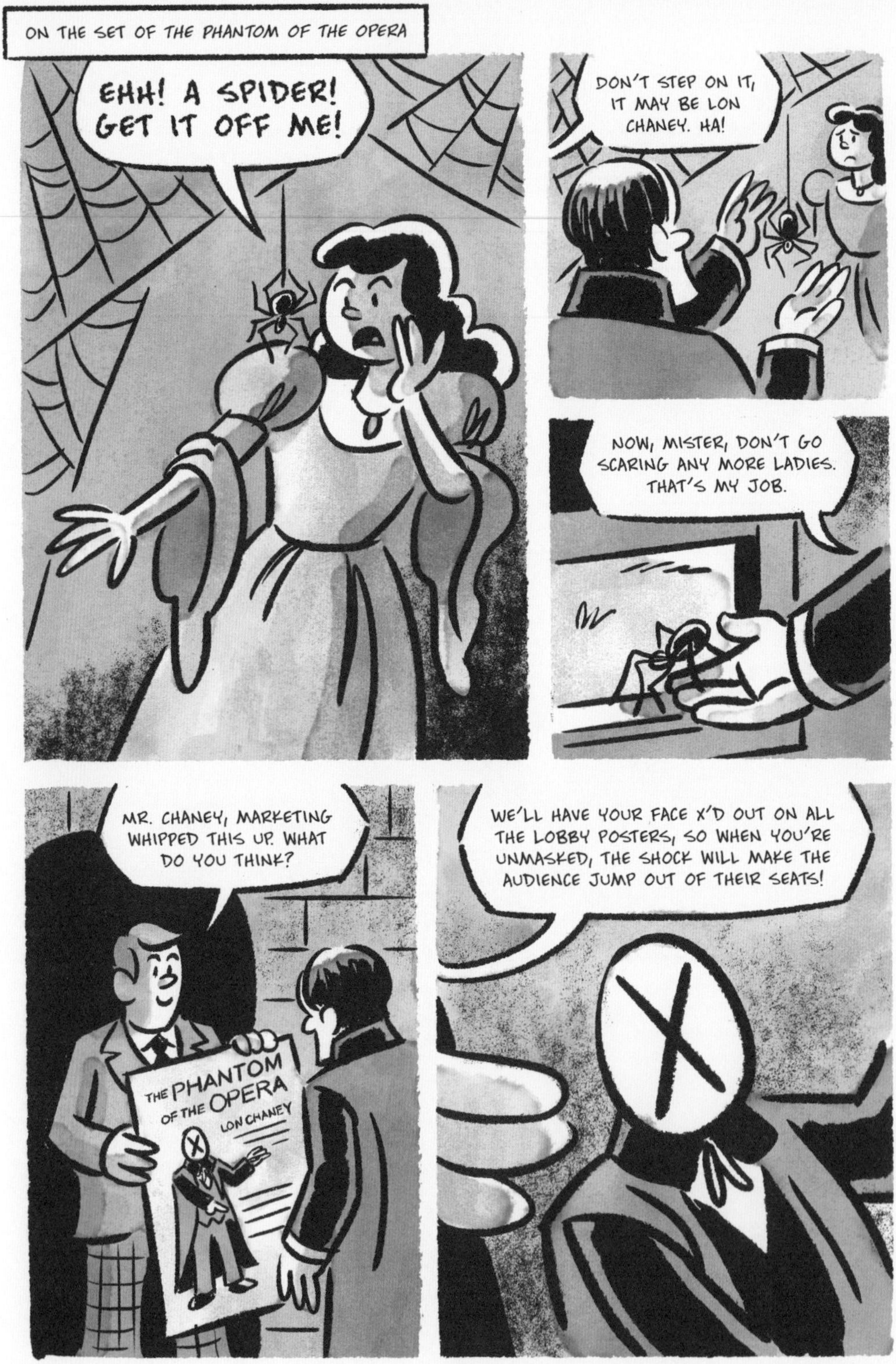
ON THE SET OF THE PHANTOM OF THE OPERA
EHH! A SPIDER! GET IT OFF ME!
DON'T STEP ON IT, IT MAY BE LON CHANEY. HA!
NOW, MISTER, DON'T GO SCARING ANY MORE LADIES. THAT'S MY JOB.
MR. CHANEY, MARKETING WHIPPED THIS UP. WHAT DO YOU THINK?
THE PHANTOM OF THE OPERA
LON CHANEY
WE'LL HAVE YOUR FACE X'D OUT ON ALL THE LOBBY POSTERS, SO WHEN YOU'RE UNMASKED, THE SHOCK WILL MAKE THE AUDIENCE JUMP OUT OF THEIR SEATS!

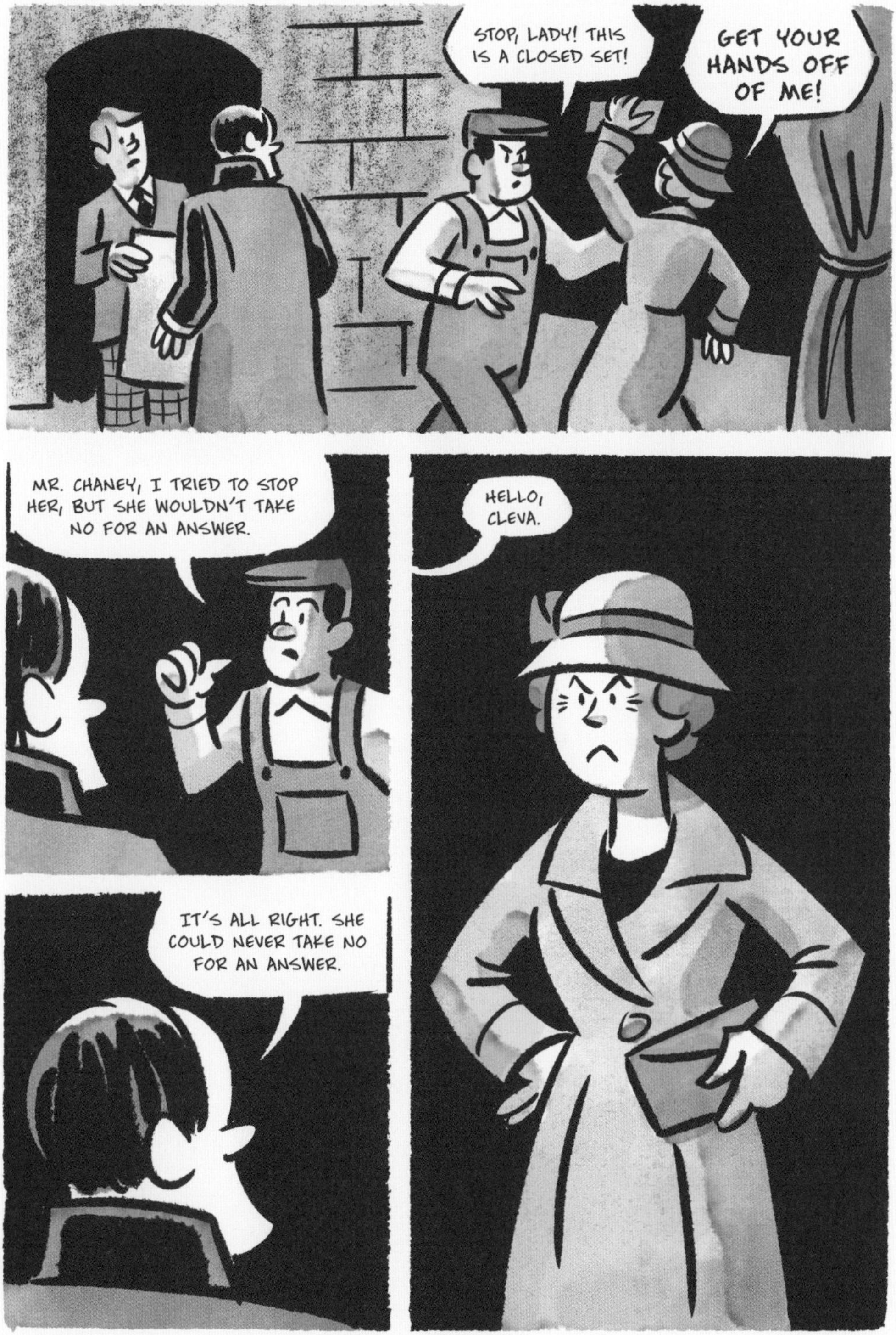
STOP, LADY! THIS IS A CLOSED SET!
GET YOUR HANDS OFF OF ME!
MR. CHANEY, I TRIED TO STOP HER, BUT SHE WOULDN'T TAKE NO FOR AN ANSWER.
HELLO, CLEVA.
IT'S ALL RIGHT. SHE COULD NEVER TAKE NO FOR AN ANSWER.

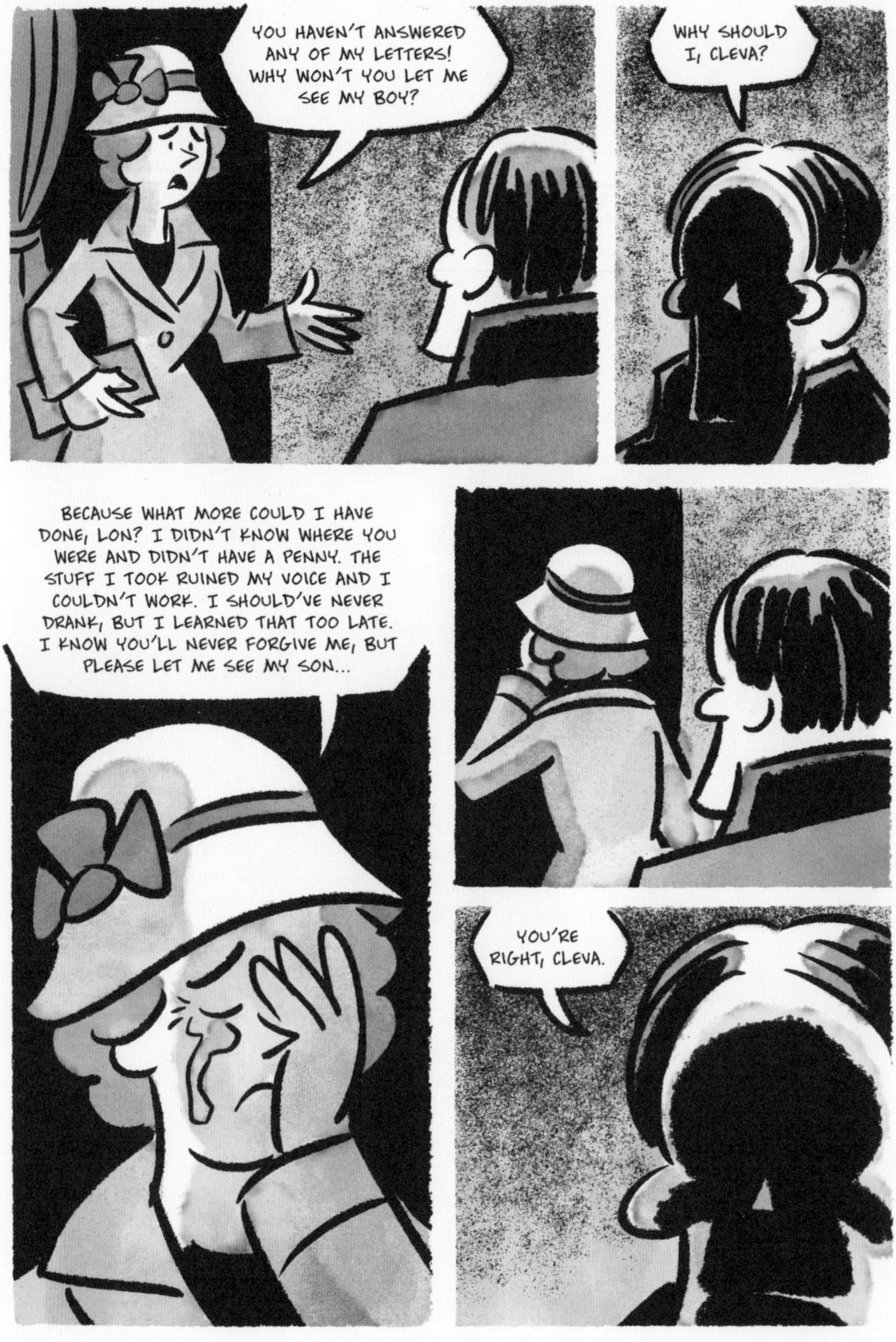
YOU HAVEN'T ANSWERED ANY OF MY LETTERS! WHY WON'T YOU LET ME SEE MY BOY?
WHY SHOULD I, CLEVA?
BECAUSE WHAT MORE COULD I HAVE DONE, LON? I DIDN'T KNOW WHERE YOU WERE AND DIDN'T HAVE A PENNY. THE STUFF I TOOK RUINED MY VOICE AND I COULDN'T WORK. I SHOULD'VE NEVER DRANK, BUT I LEARNED THAT TOO LATE. I KNOW YOU'LL NEVER FORGIVE ME, BUT PLEASE LET ME SEE MY SON...
YOU'RE RIGHT, CLEVA.

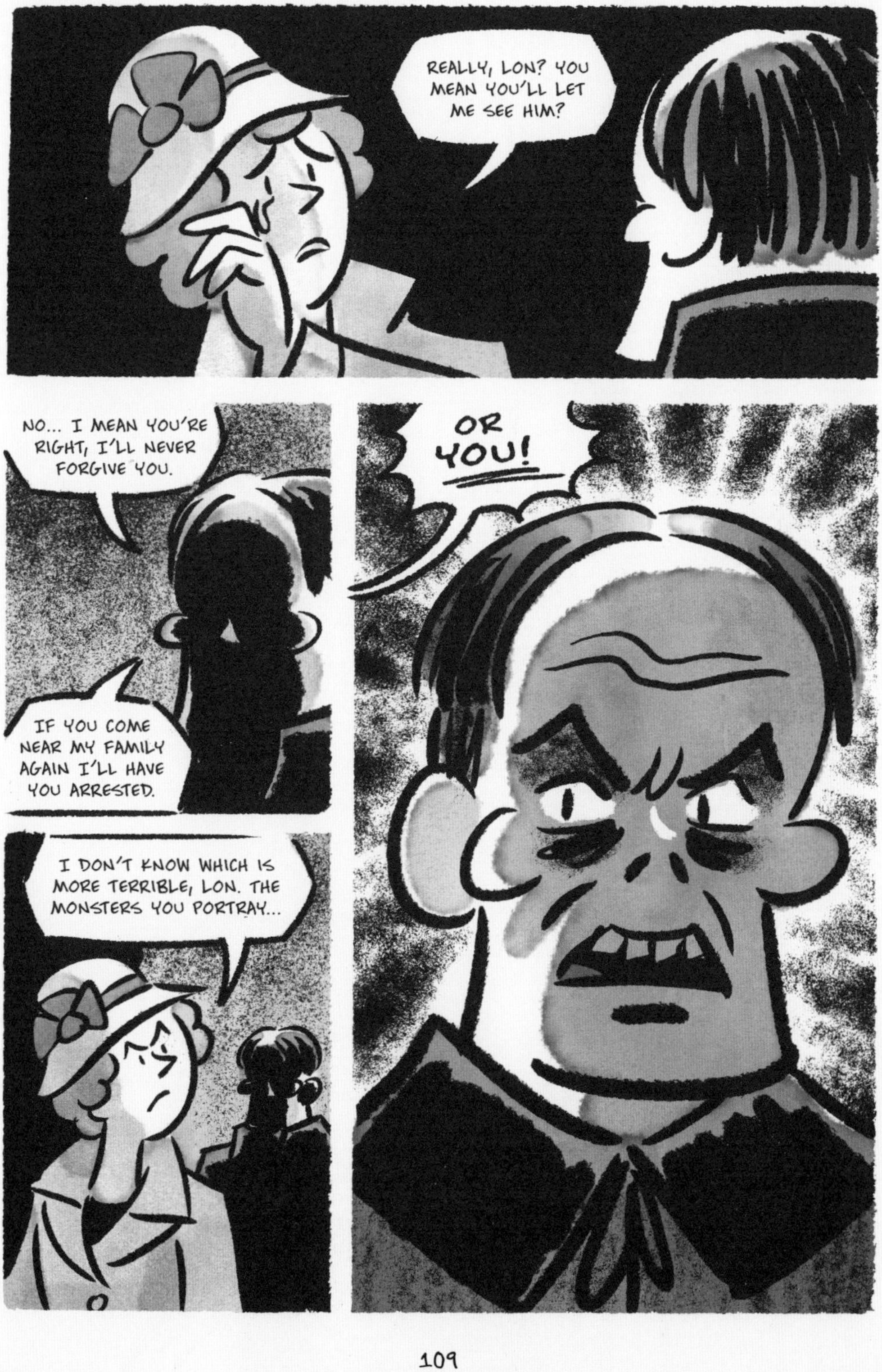
REALLY, LON? YOU MEAN YOU'LL LET ME SEE HIM?
NO... I MEAN YOU'RE RIGHT, I'LL NEVER FORGIVE YOU.
IF YOU COME NEAR MY FAMILY AGAIN I'LL HAVE YOU ARRESTED.
I DON'T KNOW WHICH IS MORE TERRIBLE, LON. THE MONSTERS YOU PORTRAY...
OR YOU!

The Phantom of the Opera

UNIVERSAL PICTURES, 1925

THE NEW MANAGERS OF THE PARIS OPERA HOUSE ARE ENJOYING THEIR BEST SEASON EVER, EVEN THOUGH A MYSTERIOUS PHANTOM (CHANEY) IS HAUNTING THEIR THEATER. AS THE SPIRIT OF MUSIC, THE PHANTOM TUTORS CHRISTINE, A PROMISING SINGER, IN HER DRESSING ROOM. WITH HIS HELP, SHE RISES FROM CHORUS GIRL TO UNDERSTUDY FOR CARLOTTA, THE THEATER'S PRIMA DONNA. RAOUL, CHRISTINE'S LOVER, TRIES TO CONVINCE HER TO GIVE UP HER CAREER AND MARRY HIM, BUT CHRISTINE, OBEYING THE PHANTOM, REFUSES.

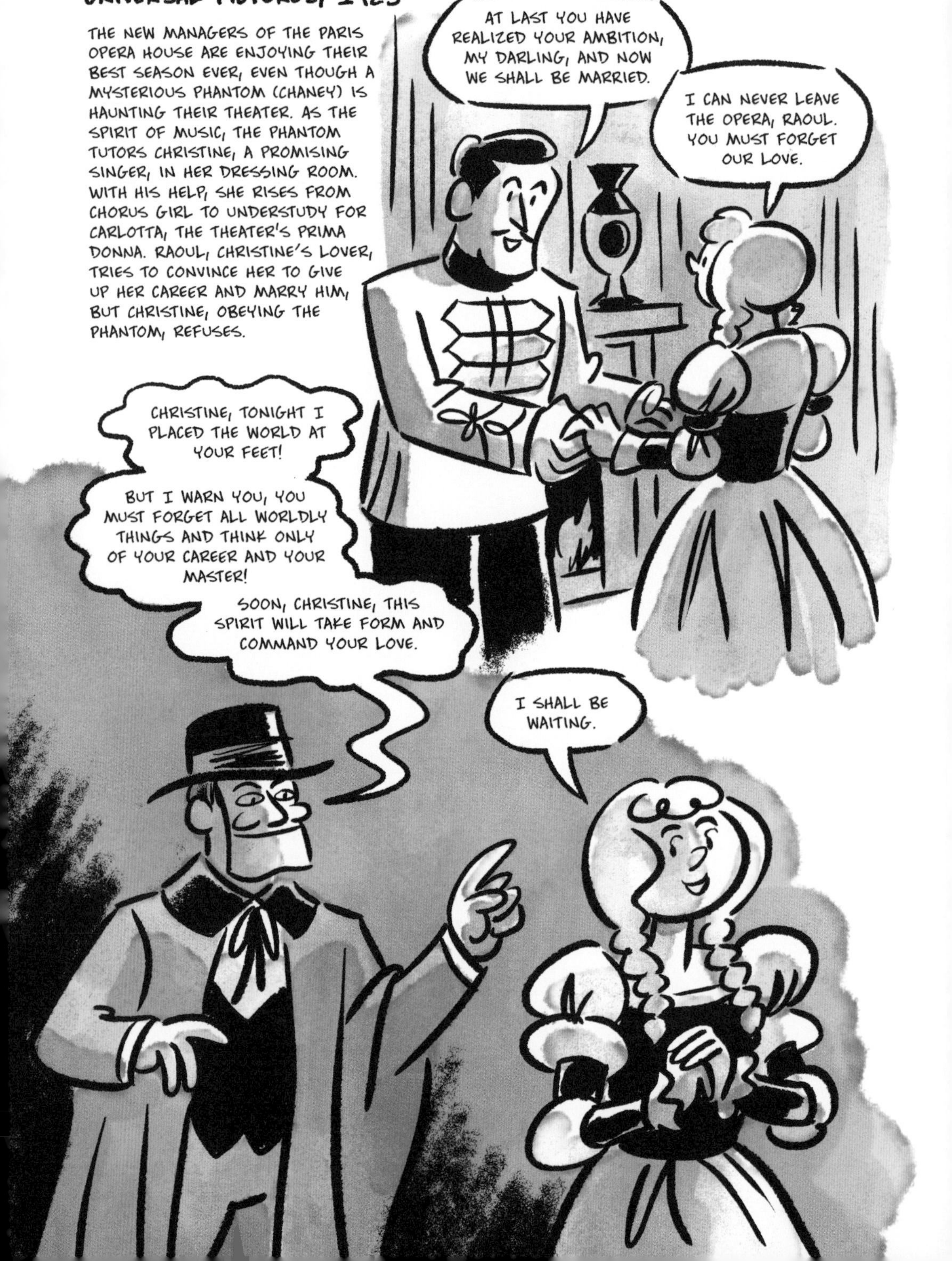
AT LAST YOU HAVE REALIZED YOUR AMBITION, MY DARLING, AND NOW WE SHALL BE MARRIED.
I CAN NEVER LEAVE THE OPERA, RAOUL. YOU MUST FORGET OUR LOVE.
CHRISTINE, TONIGHT I PLACED THE WORLD AT YOUR FEET!
BUT I WARN YOU, YOU MUST FORGET ALL WORLDLY THINGS AND THINK ONLY OF YOUR CAREER AND YOUR MASTER!
SOON, CHRISTINE, THIS SPIRIT WILL TAKE FORM AND COMMAND YOUR LOVE.
I SHALL BE WAITING.

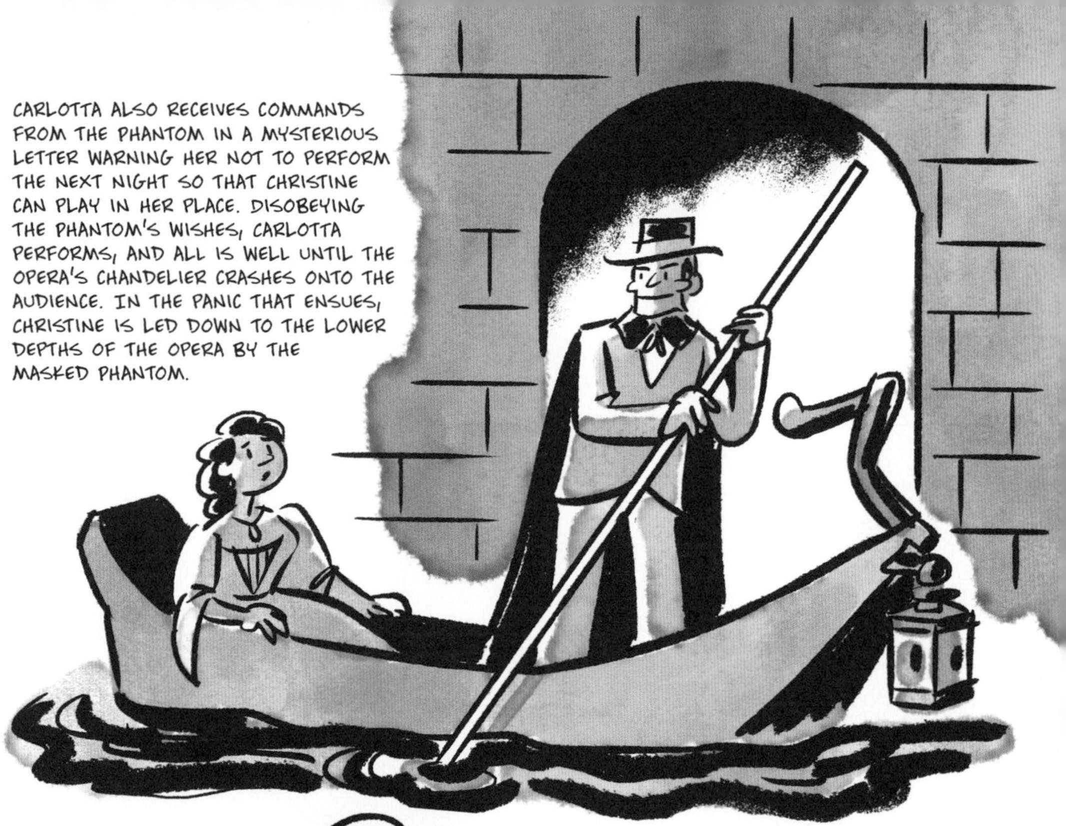
CARLOTTA ALSO RECEIVES COMMANDS FROM THE PHANTOM IN A MYSTERIOUS LETTER WARNING HER NOT TO PERFORM THE NEXT NIGHT SO THAT CHRISTINE CAN PLAY IN HER PLACE. DISOBEYING THE PHANTOM'S WISHES, CARLOTTA PERFORMS, AND ALL IS WELL UNTIL THE OPERA'S CHANDELIER CRASHES ONTO THE AUDIENCE. IN THE PANIC THAT ENSUES, CHRISTINE IS LED DOWN TO THE LOWER DEPTHS OF THE OPERA BY THE MASKED PHANTOM.

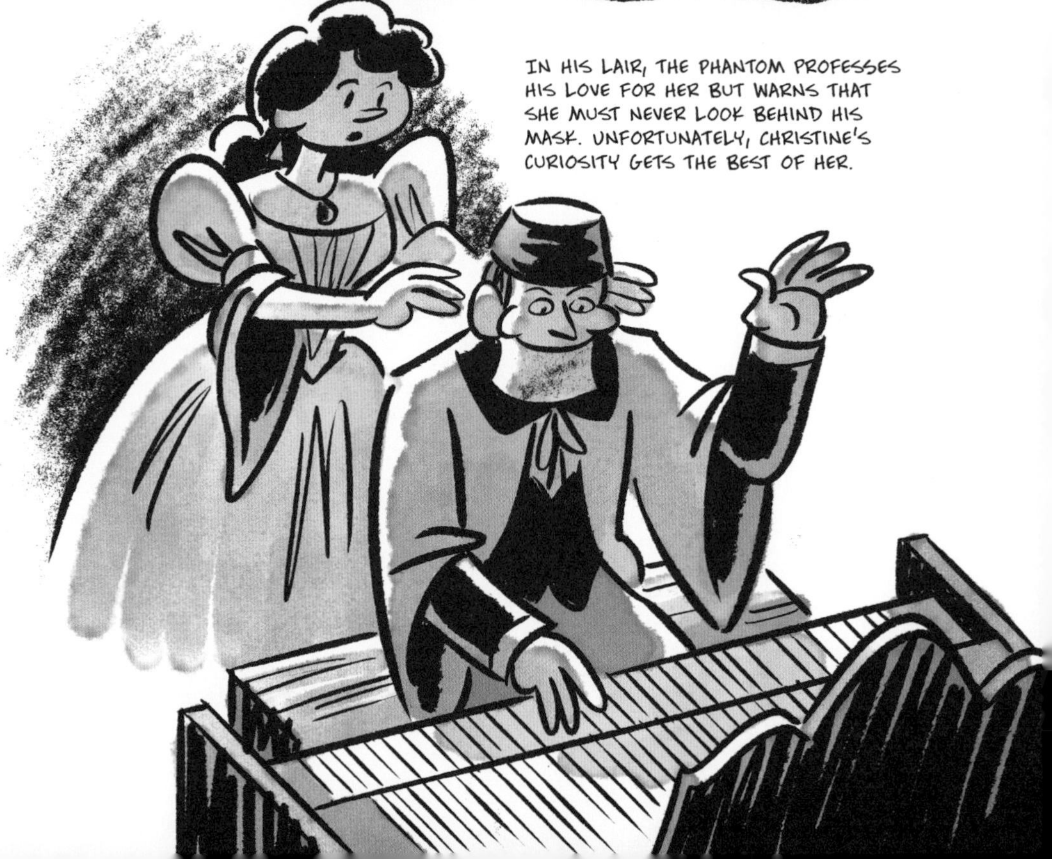
IN HIS LAIR, THE PHANTOM PROFESSES HIS LOVE FOR HER BUT WARNS THAT SHE MUST NEVER LOOK BEHIND HIS MASK. UNFORTUNATELY, CHRISTINE'S CURIOSITY GETS THE BEST OF HER.

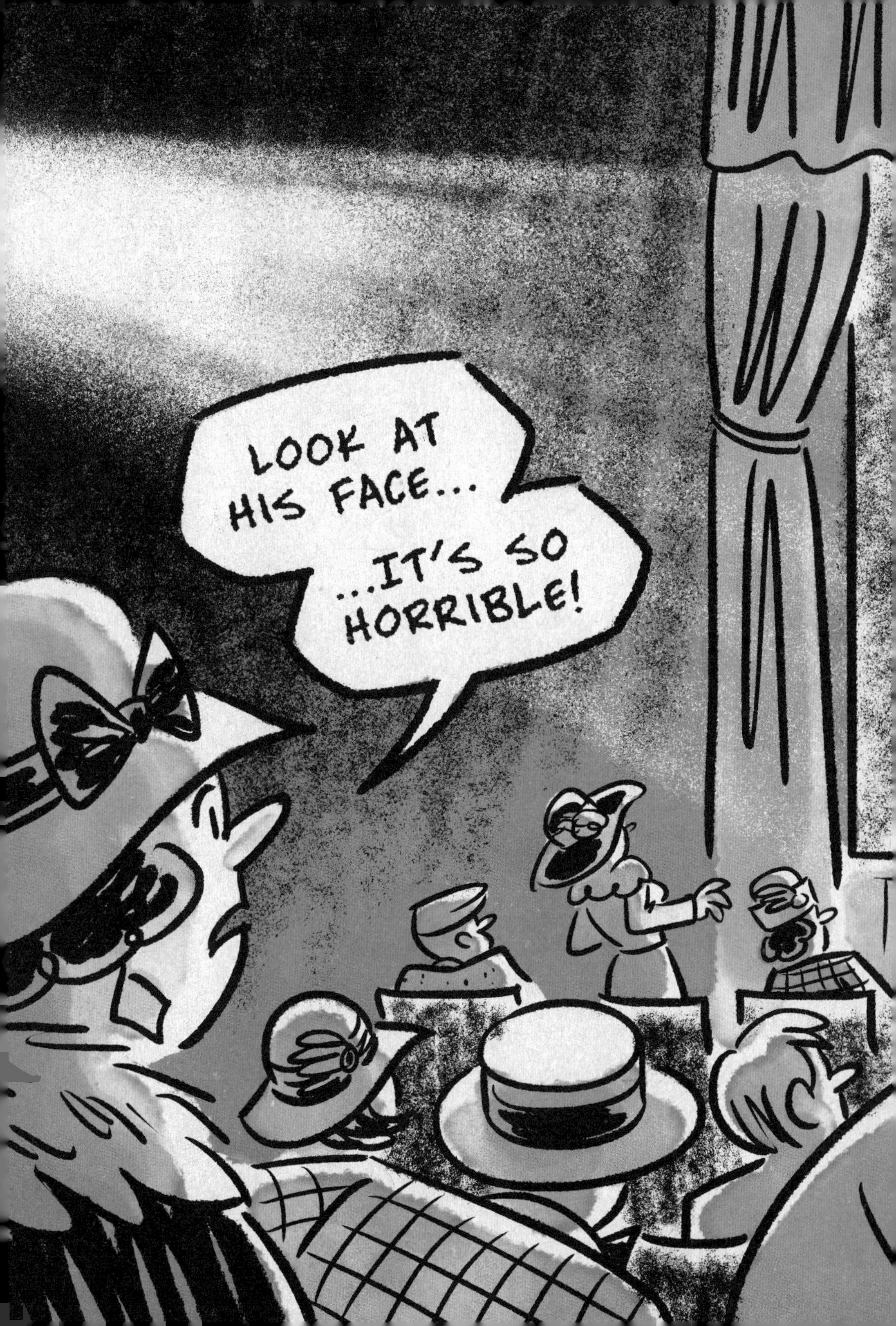
LOOK AT HIS FACE...
...IT'S SO HORRIBLE!

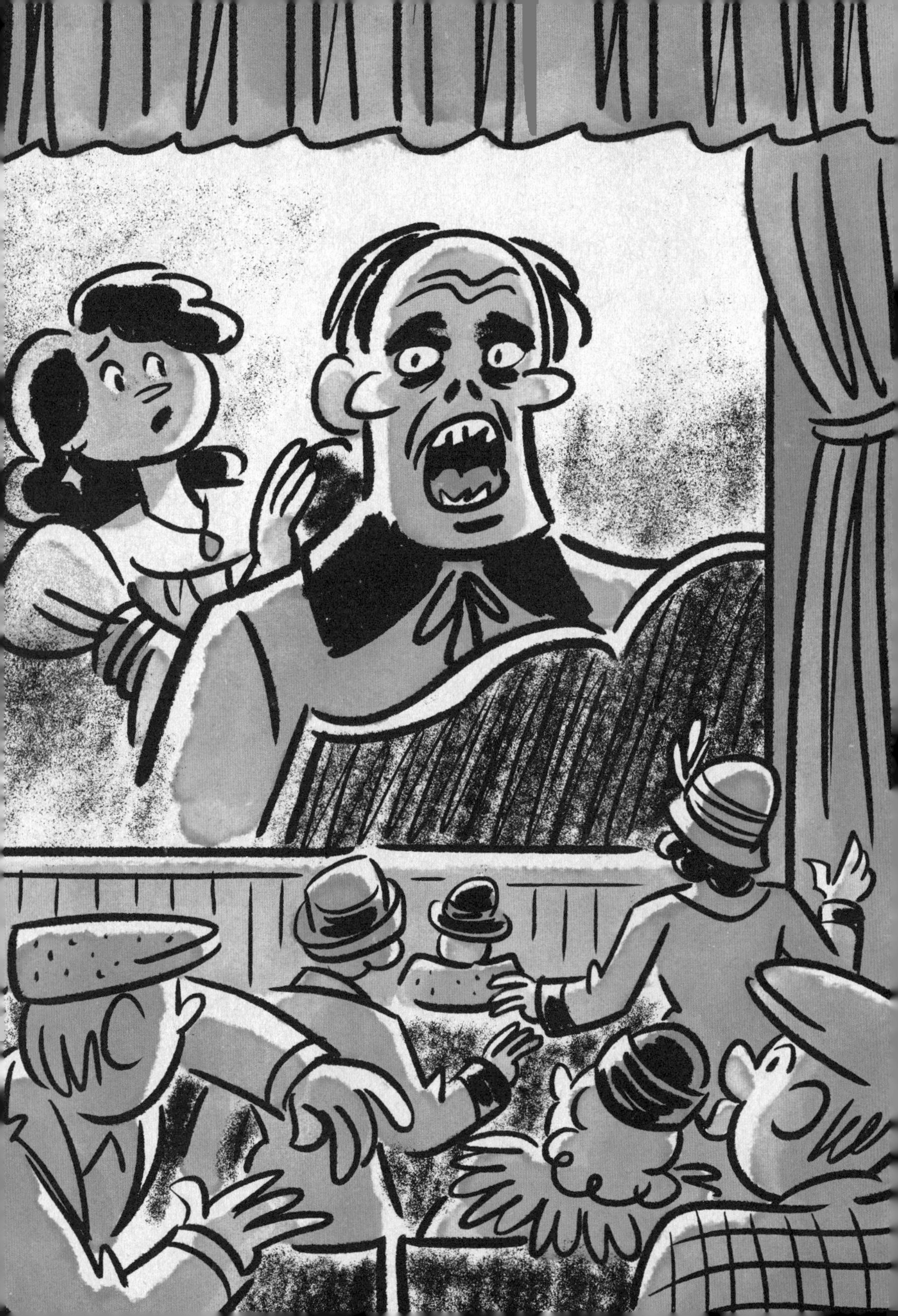

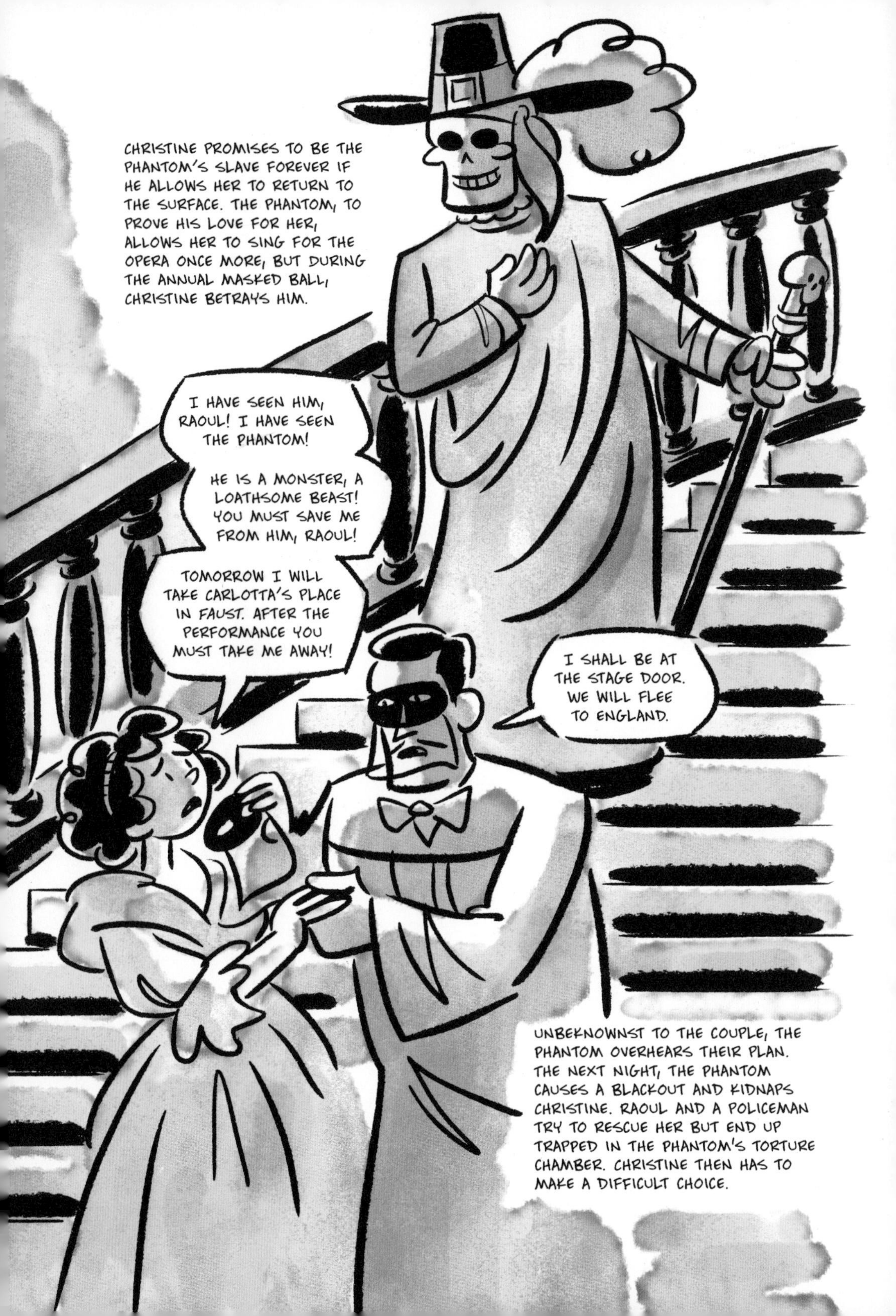
CHRISTINE PROMISES TO BE THE PHANTOM'S SLAVE FOREVER IF HE ALLOWS HER TO RETURN TO THE SURFACE. THE PHANTOM, TO PROVE HIS LOVE FOR HER, ALLOWS HER TO SING FOR THE OPERA ONCE MORE, BUT DURING THE ANNUAL MASKED BALL, CHRISTINE BETRAYS HIM.
I HAVE SEEN HIM, RAOUL! I HAVE SEEN THE PHANTOM!
HE IS A MONSTER, A LOATHSOME BEAST! YOU MUST SAVE ME FROM HIM, RAOUL!
TOMORROW I WILL TAKE CARLOTTA'S PLACE IN FAUST. AFTER THE PERFORMANCE YOU MUST TAKE ME AWAY!
I SHALL BE AT THE STAGE DOOR. WE WILL FLEE TO ENGLAND.
UNBEKNOWNST TO THE COUPLE, THE PHANTOM OVERHEARS THEIR PLAN. THE NEXT NIGHT, THE PHANTOM CAUSES A BLACKOUT AND KIDNAPS CHRISTINE. RAOUL AND A POLICEMAN TRY TO RESCUE HER BUT END UP TRAPPED IN THE PHANTOM'S TORTURE CHAMBER. CHRISTINE THEN HAS TO MAKE A DIFFICULT CHOICE.

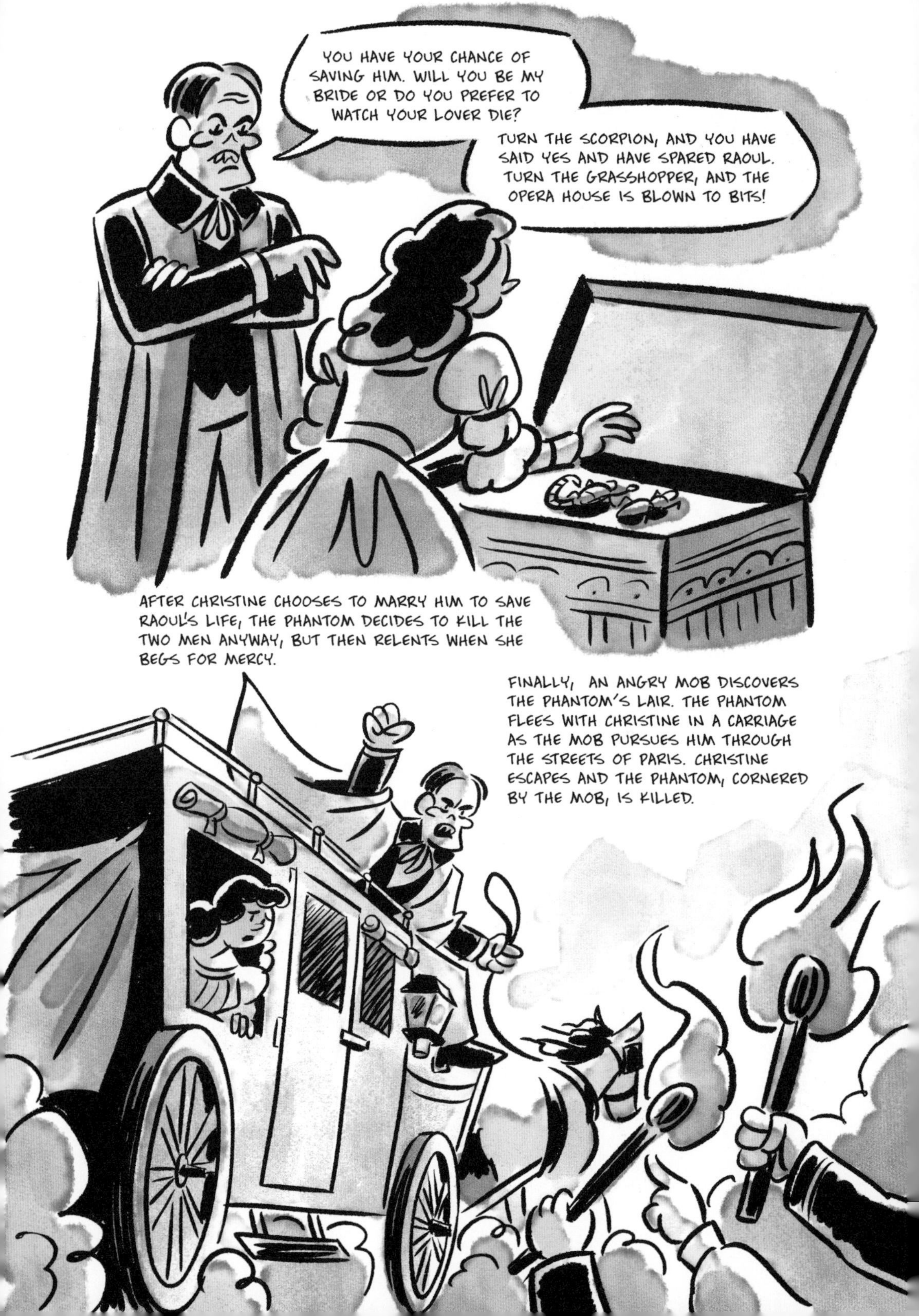
YOU HAVE YOUR CHANCE OF SAVING HIM. WILL YOU BE MY BRIDE OR DO YOU PREFER TO WATCH YOUR LOVER DIE?
TURN THE SCORPION, AND YOU HAVE SAID YES AND HAVE SPARED RAOUL. TURN THE GRASSHOPPER, AND THE OPERA HOUSE IS BLOWN TO BITS!
AFTER CHRISTINE CHOOSES TO MARRY HIM TO SAVE RAOUL'S LIFE, THE PHANTOM DECIDES TO KILL THE TWO MEN ANYWAY, BUT THEN RELENTS WHEN SHE BEGS FOR MERCY.
FINALLY, AN ANGRY MOB DISCOVERS THE PHANTOM'S LAIR. THE PHANTOM FLEES WITH CHRISTINE IN A CARRIAGE AS THE MOB PURSUES HIM THROUGH THE STREETS OF PARIS. CHRISTINE ESCAPES AND THE PHANTOM, CORNERED BY THE MOB, IS KILLED.

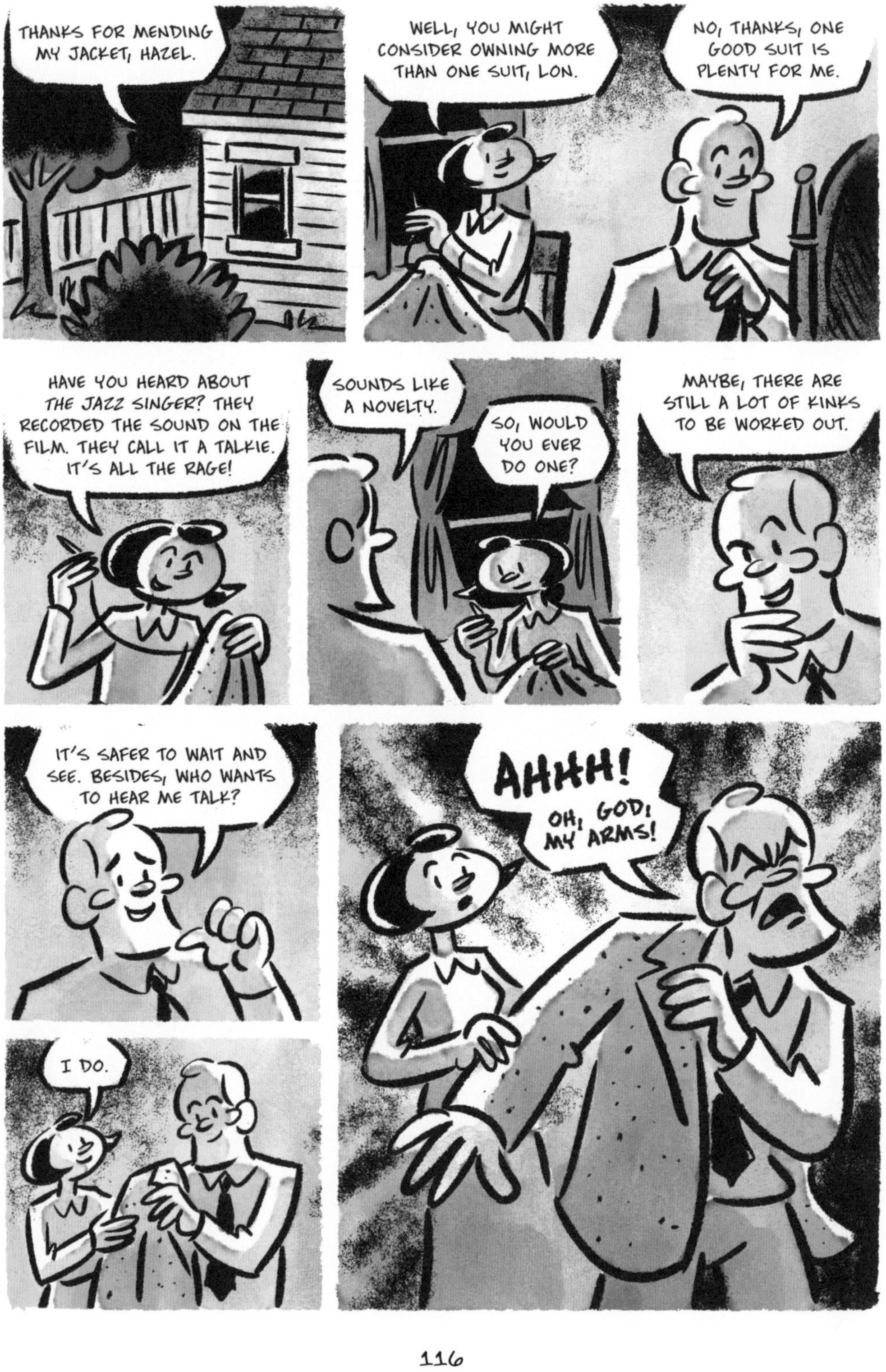
THANKS FOR MENDING MY JACKET, HAZEL.
WELL, YOU MIGHT CONSIDER OWNING MORE THAN ONE SUIT, LON.
NO, THANKS, ONE GOOD SUIT IS PLENTY FOR ME.
HAVE YOU HEARD ABOUT THE JAZZ SINGER? THEY RECORDED THE SOUND ON THE FILM. THEY CALL IT A TALKIE. IT'S ALL THE RAGE!
SOUNDS LIKE A NOVELTY.
SO, WOULD YOU EVER DO ONE?
MAYBE, THERE ARE STILL A LOT OF KINKS TO BE WORKED OUT.
IT'S SAFER TO WAIT AND SEE. BESIDES, WHO WANTS TO HEAR ME TALK?
I DO.
AHHH!
OH, GOD! MY ARMS!

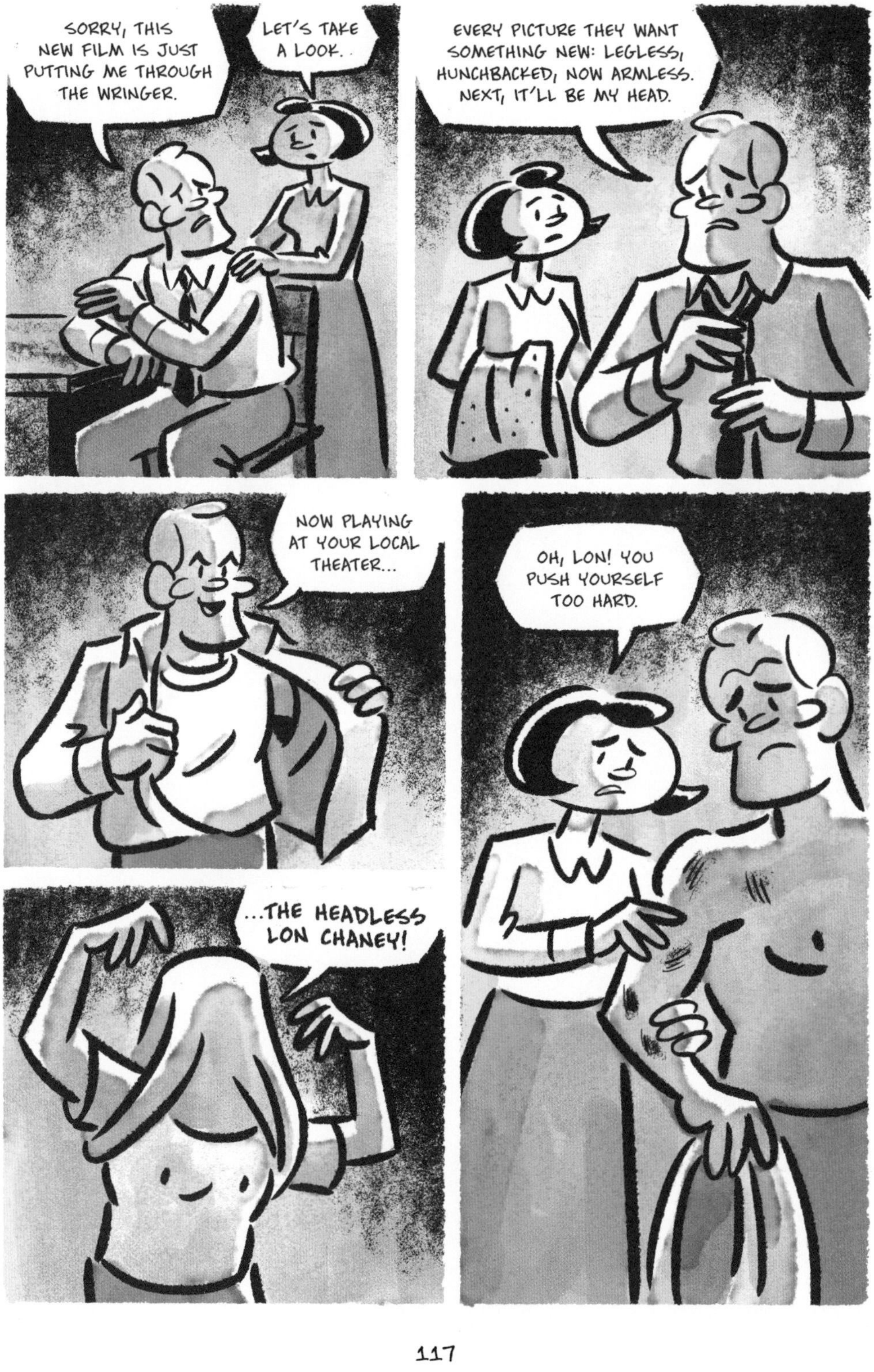
SORRY, THIS NEW FILM IS JUST PUTTING ME THROUGH THE WRINGER.
LET'S TAKE A LOOK.
EVERY PICTURE THEY WANT SOMETHING NEW: LEGLESS, HUNCHBACKED, NOW ARMLESS. NEXT, IT'LL BE MY HEAD.
NOW PLAYING AT YOUR LOCAL THEATER...
...THE HEADLESS LON CHANEY!
OH, LON! YOU PUSH YOURSELF TOO HARD.

THE UNKNOWN

METRO-GOLDWYN-MAYER, 1927

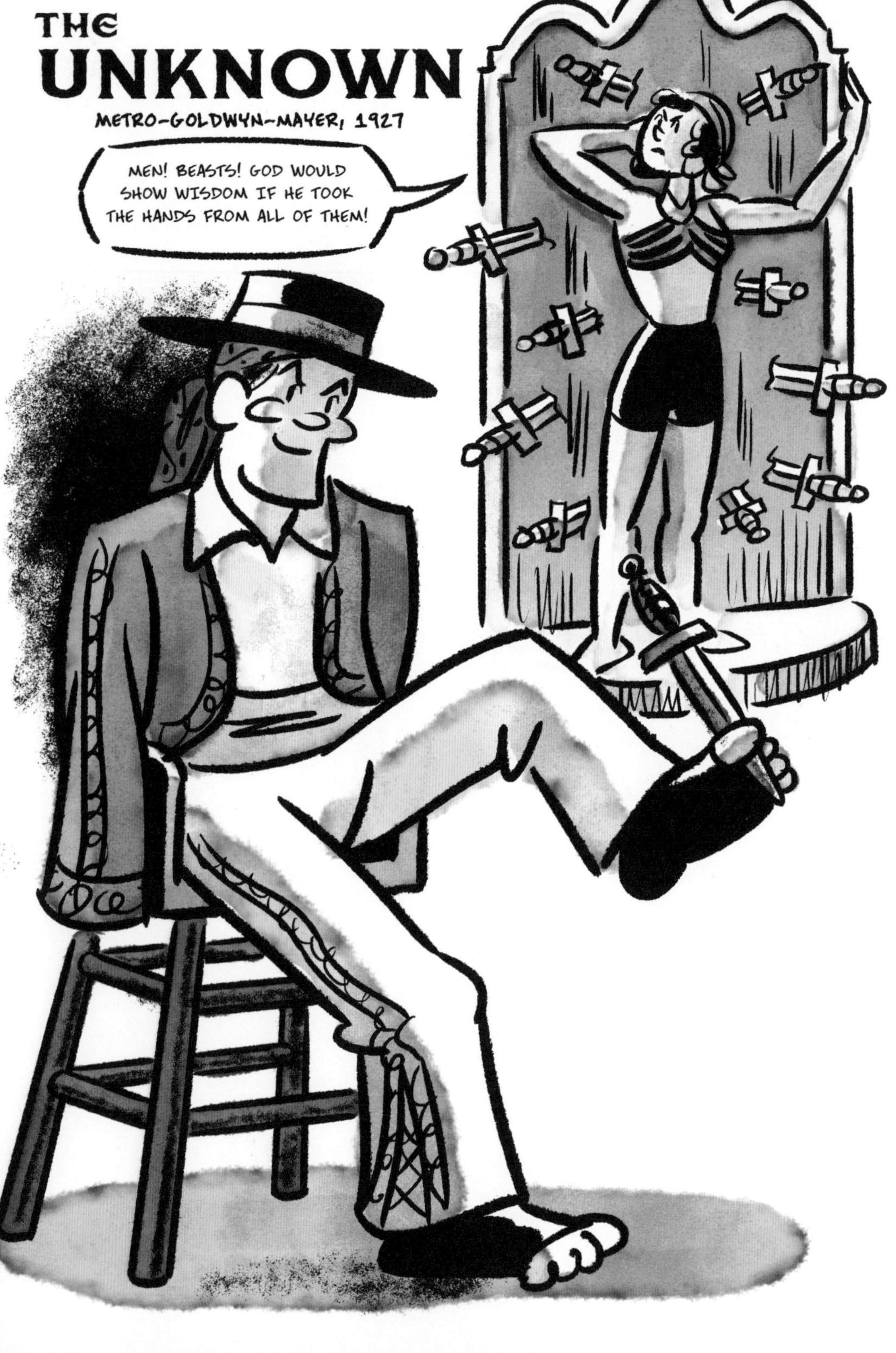
MEN! BEASTS! GOD WOULD SHOW WISDOM IF HE TOOK THE HANDS FROM ALL OF THEM!

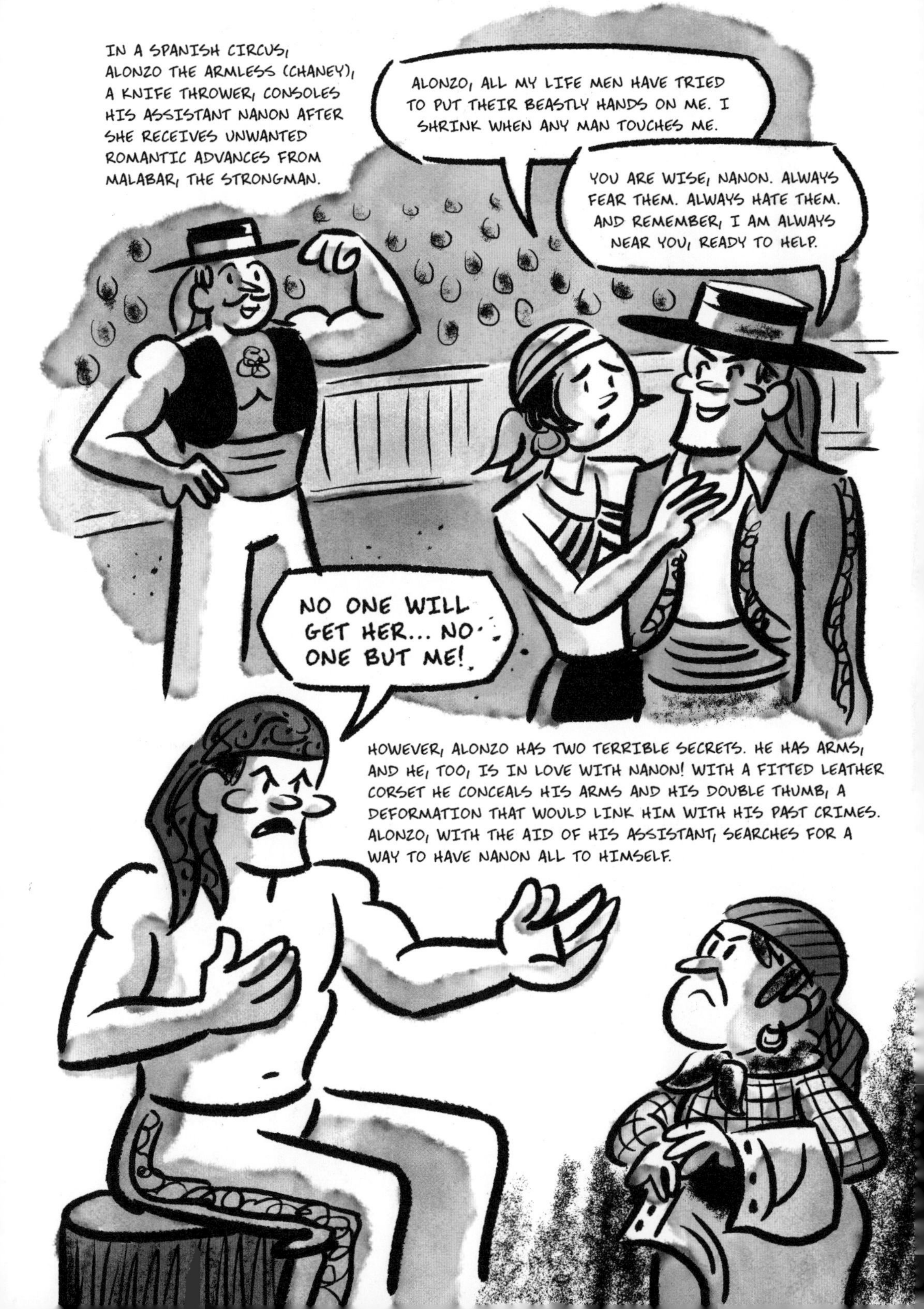
IN A SPANISH CIRCUS, ALONZO THE ARMLESS (CHANEY), A KNIFE THROWER, CONSOLES HIS ASSISTANT NANON AFTER SHE RECEIVES UNWANTED ROMANTIC ADVANCES FROM MALABAR, THE STRONGMAN.
ALONZO, ALL MY LIFE MEN HAVE TRIED TO PUT THEIR BEASTLY HANDS ON ME. I SHRINK WHEN ANY MAN TOUCHES ME.
YOU ARE WISE, NANON. ALWAYS FEAR THEM. ALWAYS HATE THEM. AND REMEMBER, I AM ALWAYS NEAR YOU, READY TO HELP.
NO ONE WILL GET HER... NO ONE BUT ME!
HOWEVER, ALONZO HAS TWO TERRIBLE SECRETS. HE HAS ARMS, AND HE, TOO, IS IN LOVE WITH NANON! WITH A FITTED LEATHER CORSET HE CONCEALS HIS ARMS AND HIS DOUBLE THUMB, A DEFORMATION THAT WOULD LINK HIM WITH HIS PAST CRIMES. ALONZO, WITH THE AID OF HIS ASSISTANT, SEARCHES FOR A WAY TO HAVE NANON ALL TO HIMSELF.

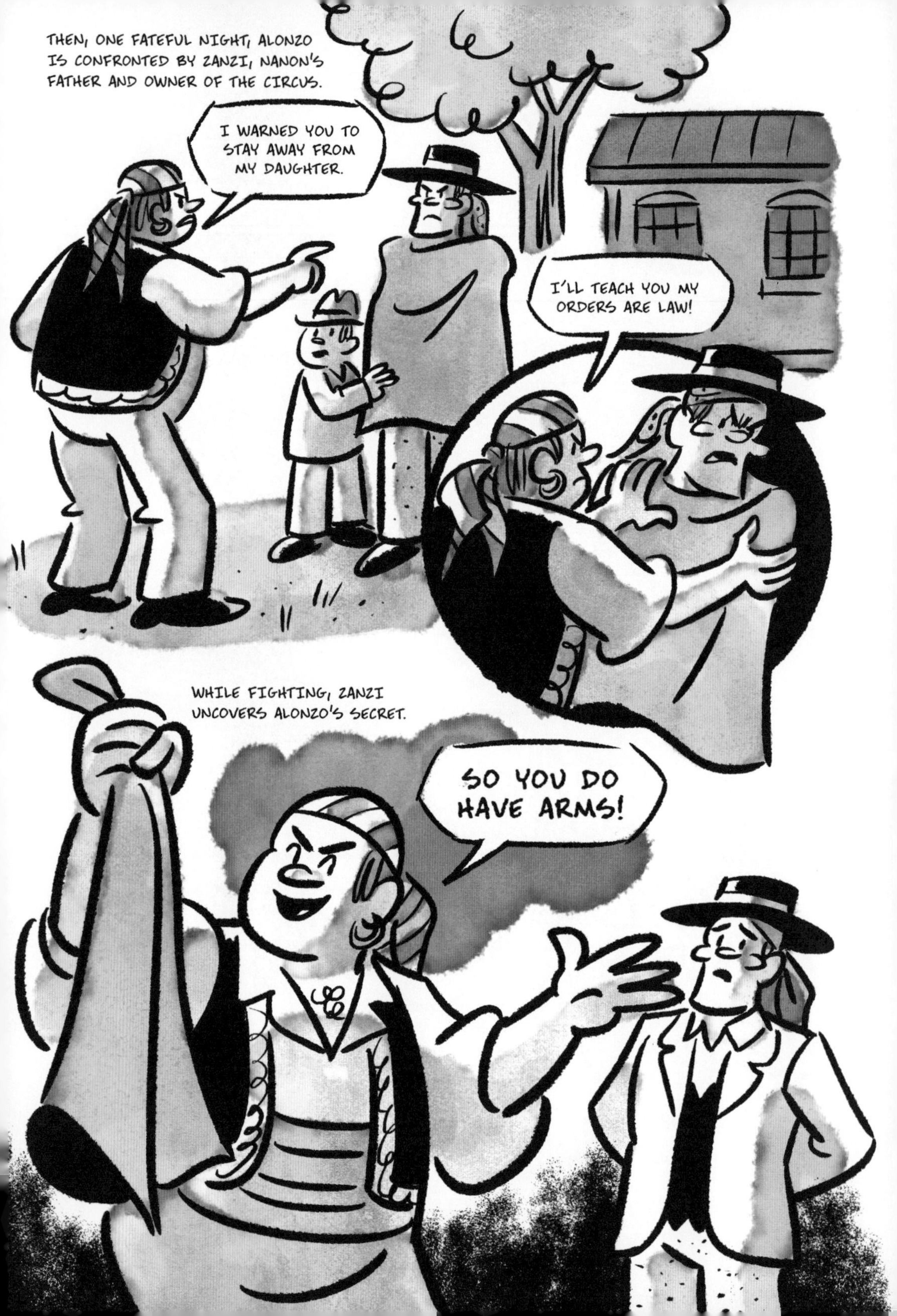
THEN, ONE FATEFUL NIGHT, ALONZO IS CONFRONTED BY ZANZI, NANON'S FATHER AND OWNER OF THE CIRCUS.
I WARNED YOU TO STAY AWAY FROM MY DAUGHTER.
I'LL TEACH YOU MY ORDERS ARE LAW!
WHILE FIGHTING, ZANZI UNCOVERS ALONZO'S SECRET.
SO YOU DO HAVE ARMS!

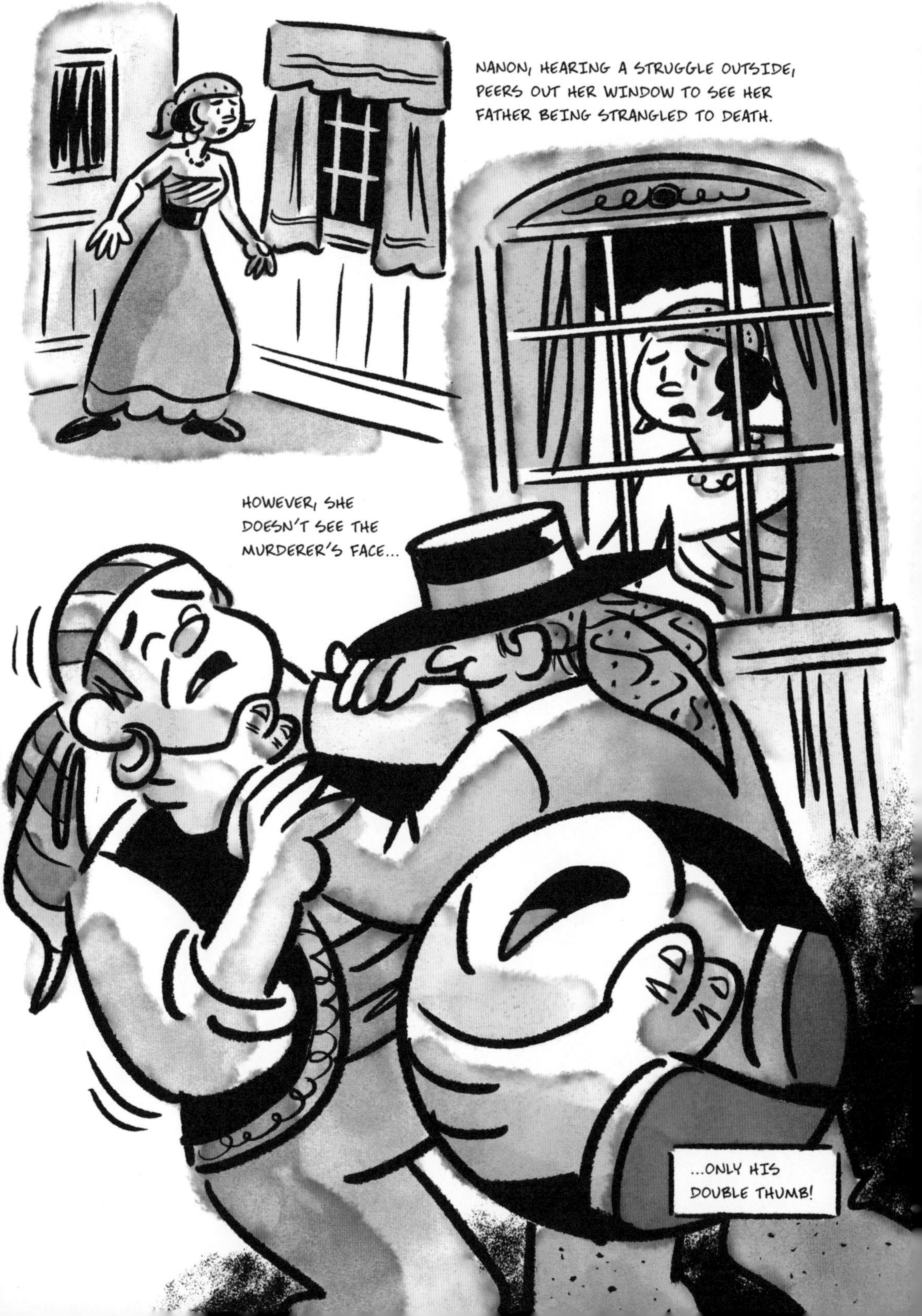
NANON, HEARING A STRUGGLE OUTSIDE, PEERS OUT HER WINDOW TO SEE HER FATHER BEING STRANGLED TO DEATH.
HOWEVER, SHE DOESN'T SEE THE MURDERER'S FACE...
...ONLY HIS DOUBLE THUMB!

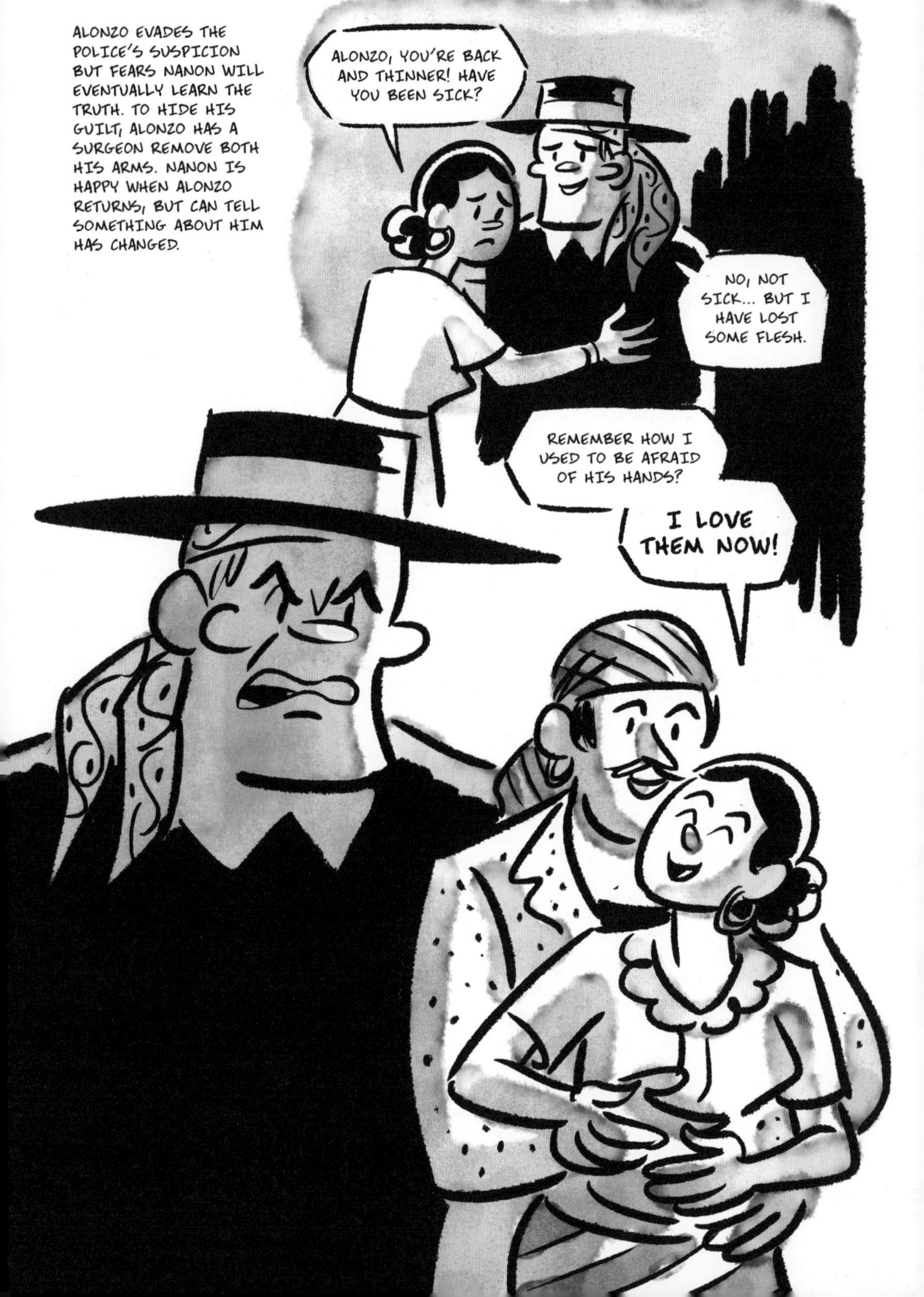
ALONZO EVADES THE POLICE'S SUSPICION BUT FEARS NANON WILL EVENTUALLY LEARN THE TRUTH. TO HIDE HIS GUILT, ALONZO HAS A SURGEON REMOVE BOTH HIS ARMS. NANON IS HAPPY WHEN ALONZO RETURNS, BUT CAN TELL SOMETHING ABOUT HIM HAS CHANGED.
ALONZO, YOU'RE BACK AND THINNER! HAVE YOU BEEN SICK?
NO, NOT SICK... BUT I HAVE LOST SOME FLESH.
REMEMBER HOW I USED TO BE AFRAID OF HIS HANDS?
I LOVE THEM NOW!

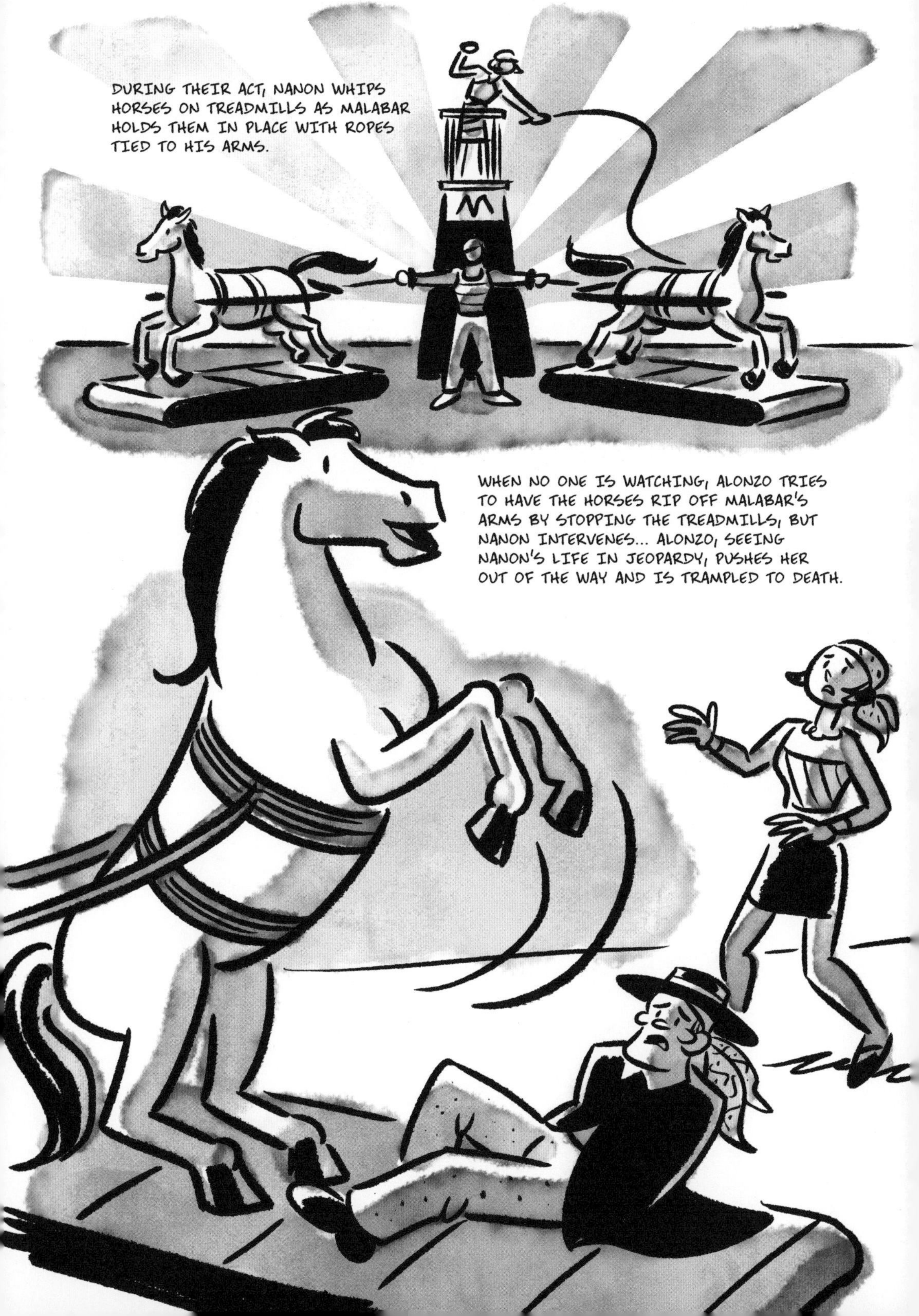
DURING THEIR ACT, NANON WHIPS HORSES ON TREADMILLS AS MALABAR HOLDS THEM IN PLACE WITH ROPES TIED TO HIS ARMS.
WHEN NO ONE IS WATCHING, ALONZO TRIES TO HAVE THE HORSES RIP OFF MALABAR'S ARMS BY STOPPING THE TREADMILLS, BUT NANON INTERVENES... ALONZO, SEEING NANON'S LIFE IN JEOPARDY, PUSHES HER OUT OF THE WAY AND IS TRAMPLED TO DEATH.

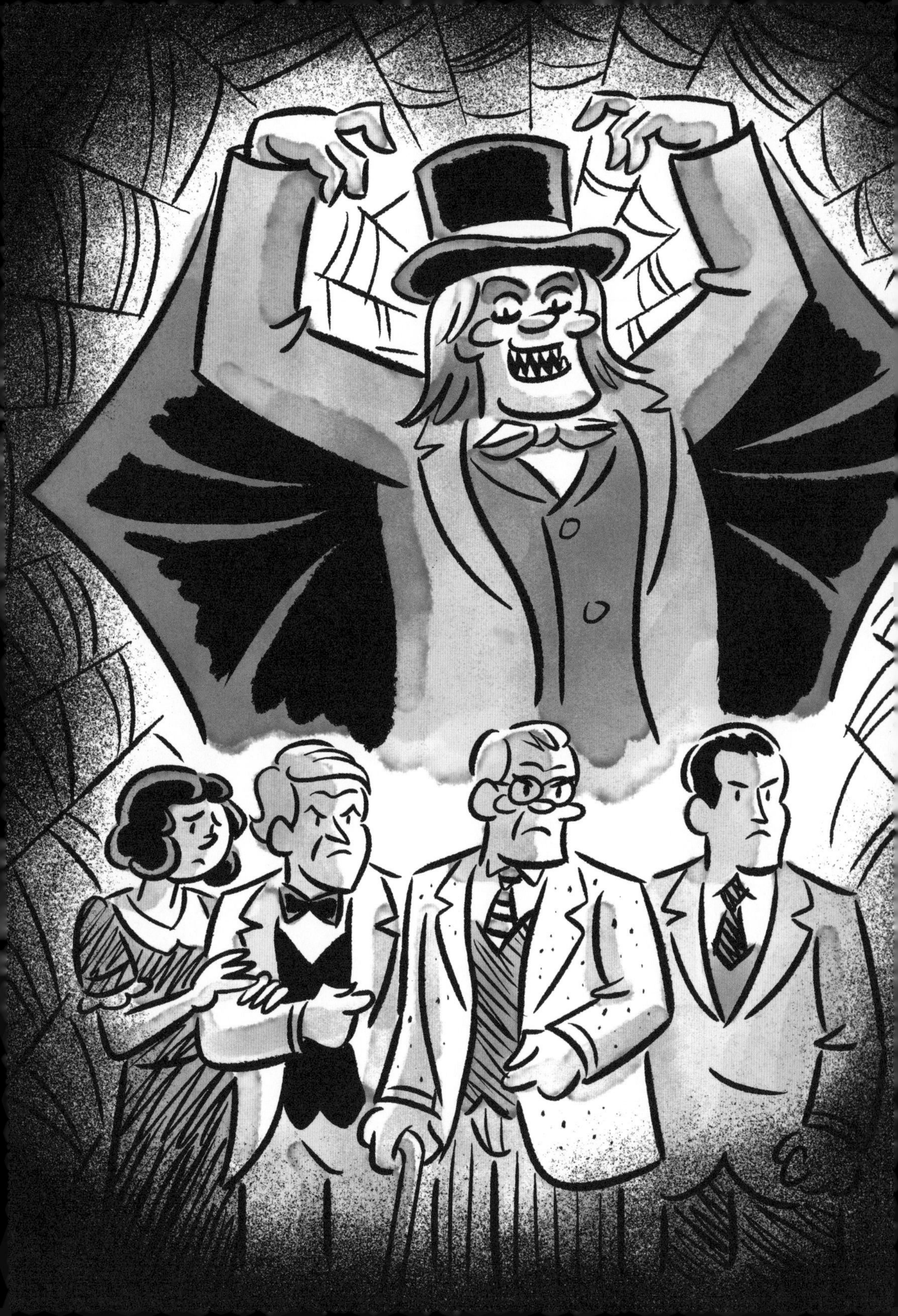

London After Midnight

METRO-GOLDWYN-MAYER, 1927

FIVE YEARS AFTER THE SUICIDE OF ROGER BALFOUR, A VAMPIRE WEARING A BEAVER-SKIN HAT (CHANEY) AND A GHOSTLY PALE WOMAN HAUNT HIS ABANDONED MANOR. THEIR ARRIVAL PROMPTS A NEIGHBOR TO CALL INSPECTOR BURKE (ALSO PLAYED BY CHANEY) TO INVESTIGATE. WHILE THE NEIGHBOR INSISTS THAT BALFOUR IS STILL ALIVE, THE INSPECTOR IS SKEPTICAL. WHEN THEY FIND BALFOUR'S TOMB EMPTY, INSPECTOR BURKE RE-STAGES THE CRIME SCENE WITH THE HELP OF BALFOUR'S DAUGHTER. USING HYPNOSIS, THE INSPECTOR PERSUADES THE MURDERERS TO REVEAL THEMSELVES. THE FILM WAS A COMMERCIAL SUCCESS, ALTHOUGH MANY CRITICS FELT THE STORYLINE WAS INCOHERENT. NO COMPLETE COPY OF THE FILM EXISTS TODAY.

THE FILM ALSO STIRRED UP CONTROVERSY WHEN A LONDON MAN CLAIMED THE FILM DROVE HIM TO COMMIT MURDER.

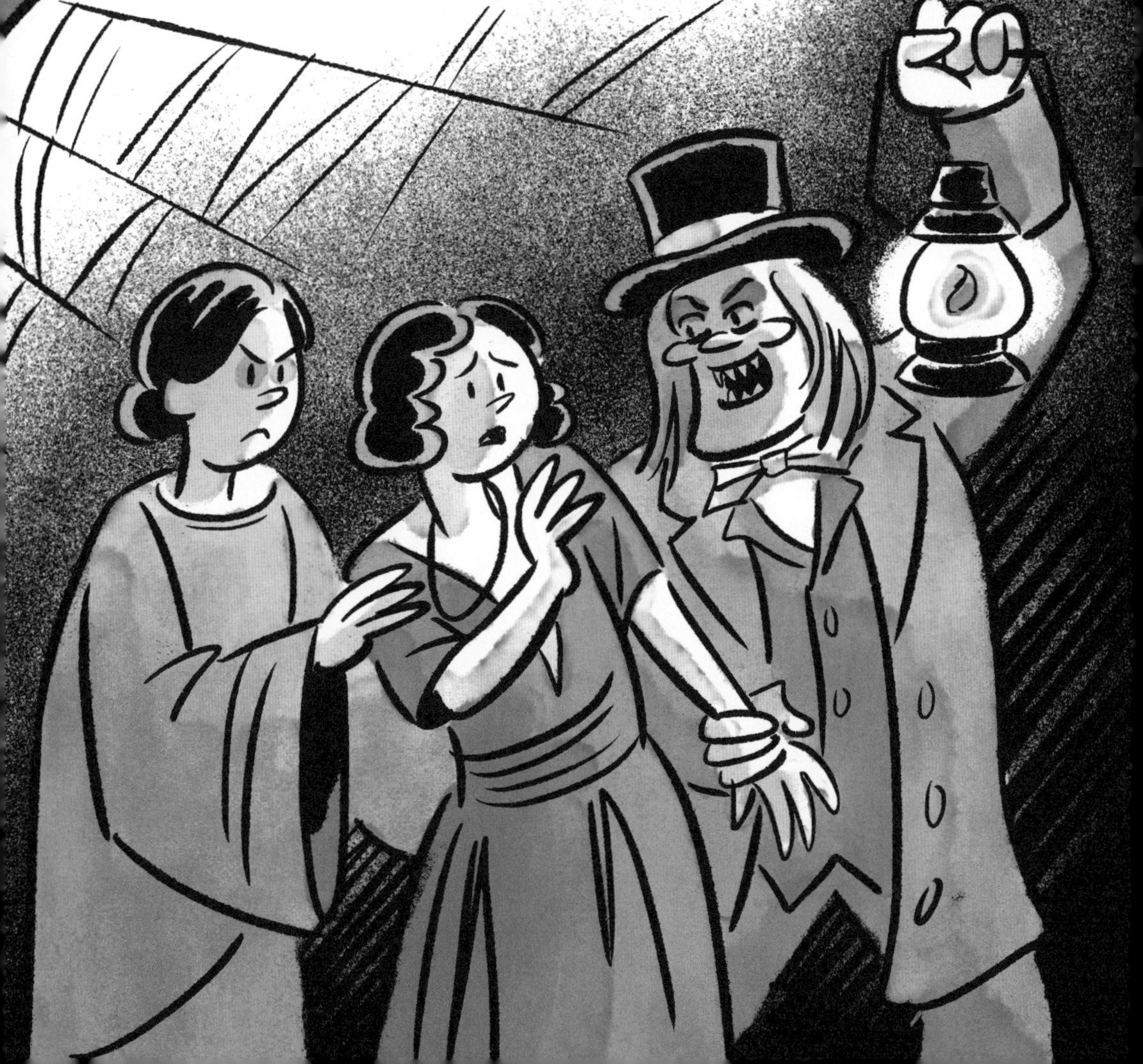

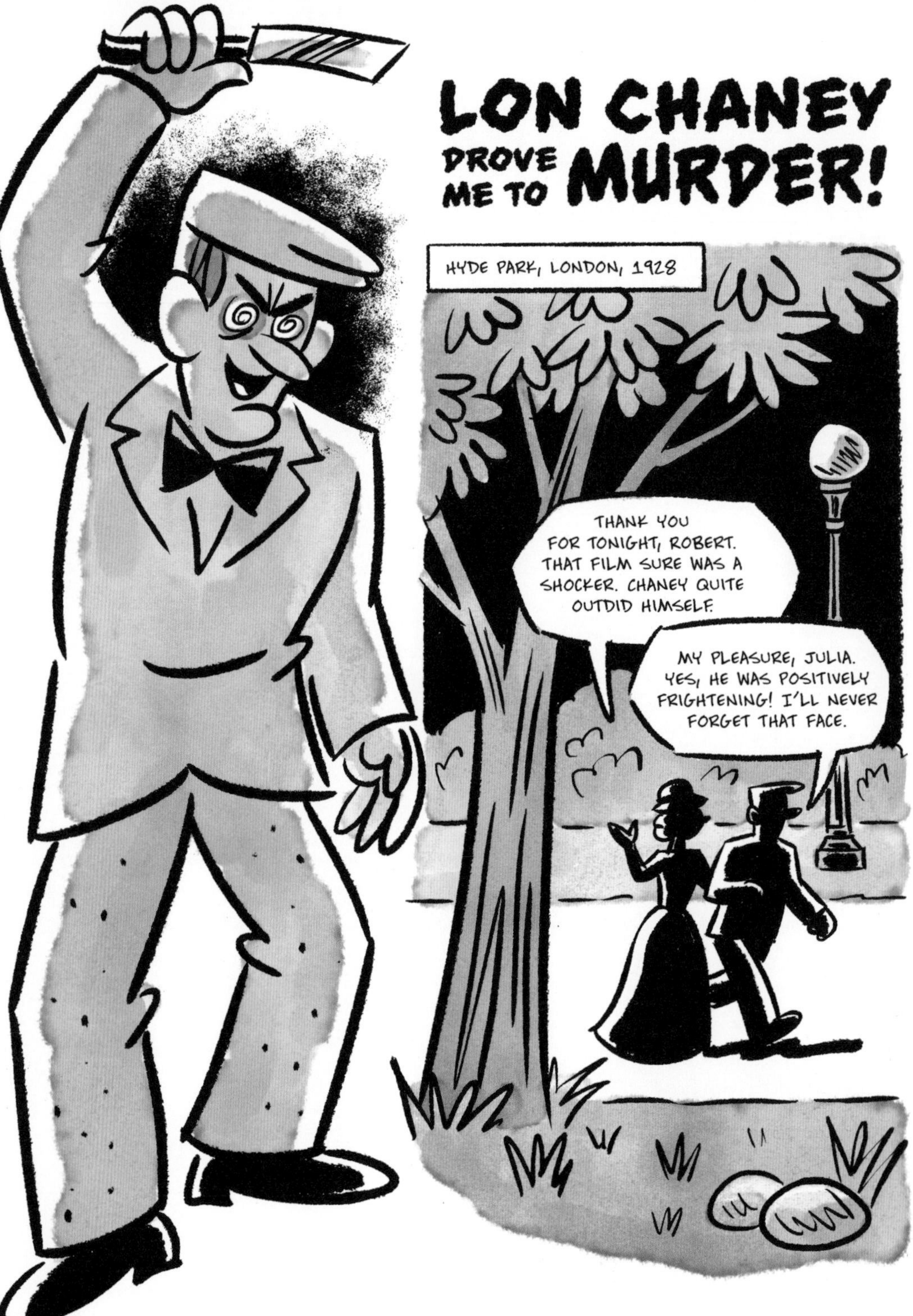
LON CHANEY DROVE ME TO MURDER!
HYDE PARK, LONDON, 1928
THANK YOU FOR TONIGHT, ROBERT. THAT FILM SURE WAS A SHOCKER. CHANEY QUITE OUTDID HIMSELF.
MY PLEASURE, JULIA. YES, HE WAS POSITIVELY FRIGHTENING! I'LL NEVER FORGET THAT FACE.

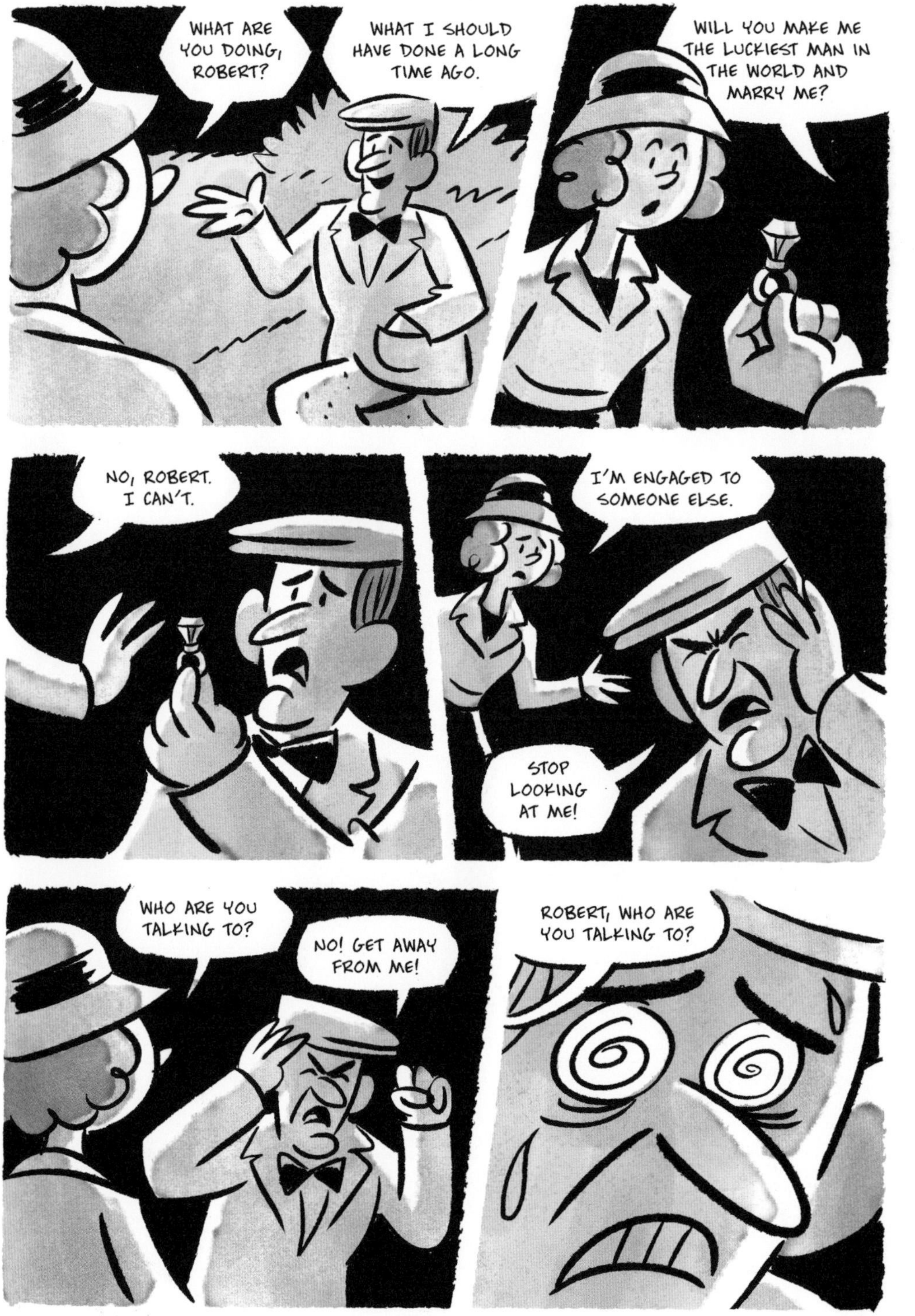

WHAT ARE YOU DOING, ROBERT?
WHAT I SHOULD HAVE DONE A LONG TIME AGO.
WILL YOU MAKE ME THE LUCKIEST MAN IN THE WORLD AND MARRY ME?
NO, ROBERT. I CAN'T.
I'M ENGAGED TO SOMEONE ELSE.
STOP LOOKING AT ME!
WHO ARE YOU TALKING TO?
NO! GET AWAY FROM ME!
ROBERT, WHO ARE YOU TALKING TO?

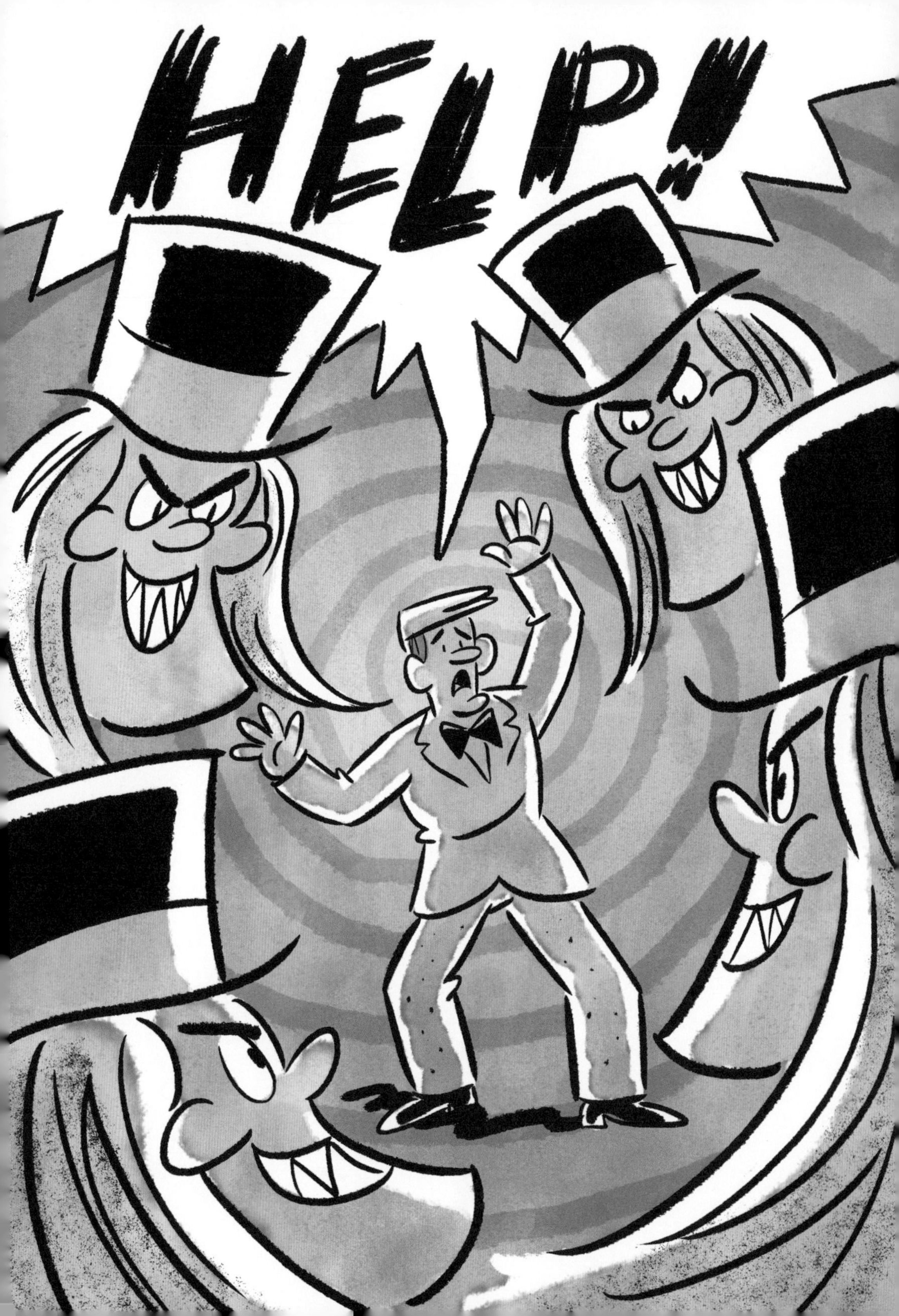
HELP!

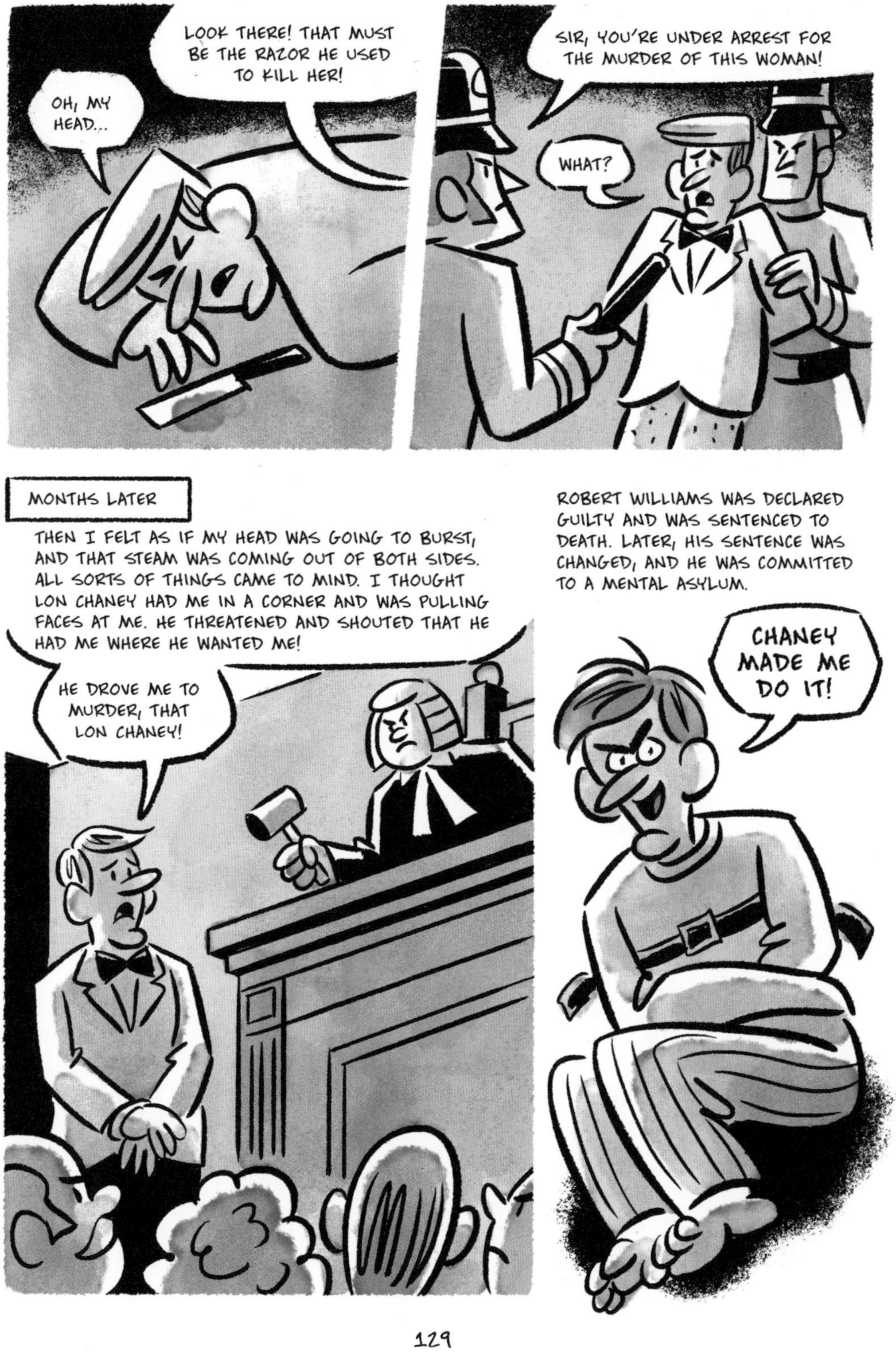
OH, MY HEAD...
LOOK THERE! THAT MUST BE THE RAZOR HE USED TO KILL HER!
SIR, YOU'RE UNDER ARREST FOR THE MURDER OF THIS WOMAN!
WHAT?
MONTHS LATER
THEN I FELT AS IF MY HEAD WAS GOING TO BURST, AND THAT STEAM WAS COMING OUT OF BOTH SIDES. ALL SORTS OF THINGS CAME TO MIND. I THOUGHT LON CHANEY HAD ME IN A CORNER AND WAS PULLING FACES AT ME. HE THREATENED AND SHOUTED THAT HE HAD ME WHERE HE WANTED ME!
HE DROVE ME TO MURDER, THAT LON CHANEY!
ROBERT WILLIAMS WAS DECLARED GUILTY AND WAS SENTENCED TO DEATH. LATER, HIS SENTENCE WAS CHANGED, AND HE WAS COMMITTED TO A MENTAL ASYLUM.
CHANEY MADE ME DO IT!

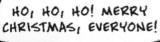
HOLIDAY PARTY AT METRO-GOLDWYN-MAYER

HO, HO, HO! MERRY CHRISTMAS, EVERYONE!

IS THAT LON CHANEY? ALMOST DIDN'T RECOGNIZE HIM WITHOUT HIS HUMP.

WELL, SANTA'S A STRETCH FOR HIM.

SCROOGE'S A BETTER FIT. HA! HA!

YOU GOT CHANEY ALL WRONG, PAL.

REMEMBER TOM, THE STAGEHAND WHO HAD THAT BAD FALL?

YEAH, HE WAS IN THE HOSPITAL FOR MONTHS.

GUESS WHO PAID HIS BILLS? LON!

LON HAS HELPED SO MANY PEOPLE IN NEED WHO DON'T HAVE A CLUE HE WAS RESPONSIBLE.

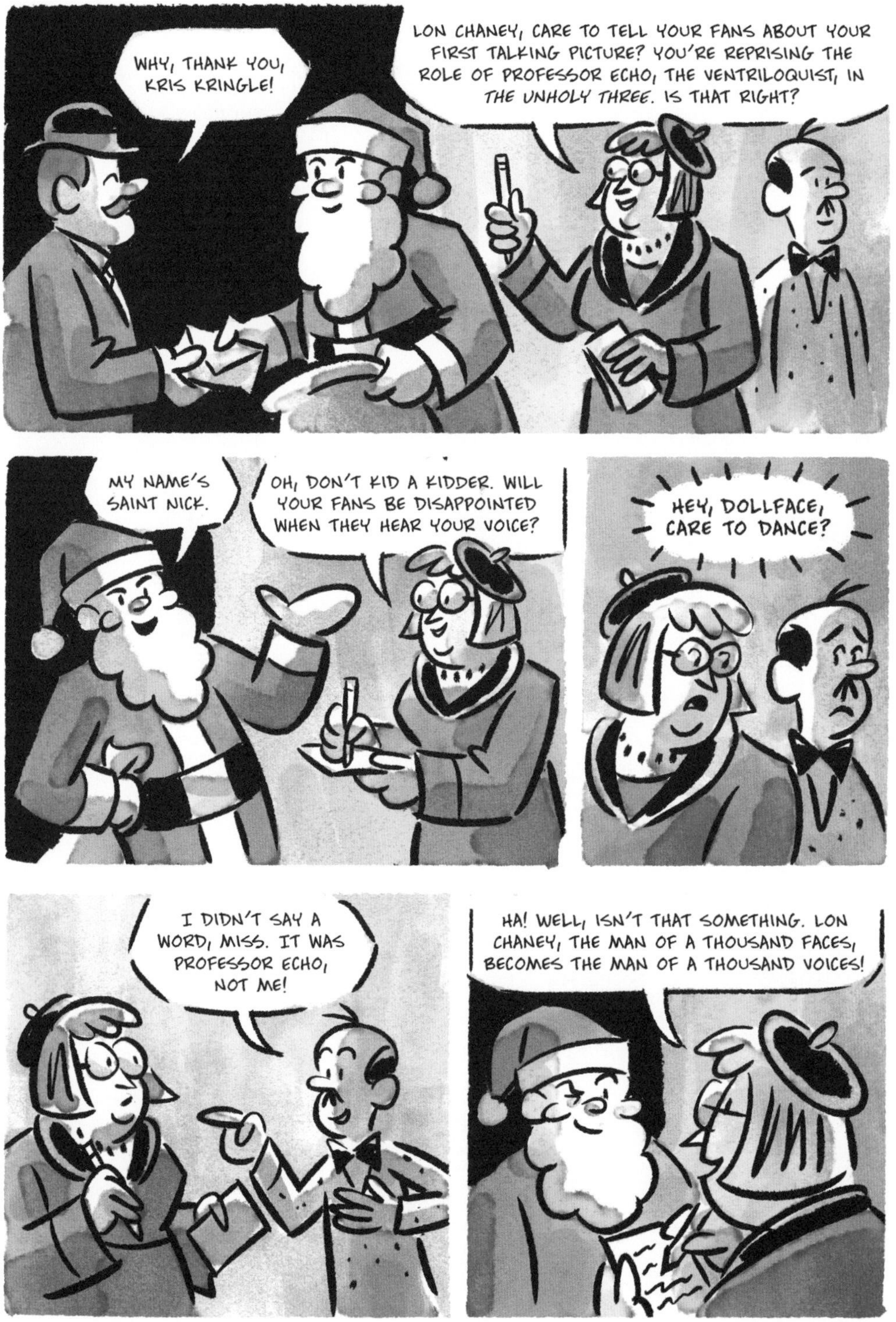

WHY, THANK YOU, KRIS KRINGLE!
LON CHANEY, CARE TO TELL YOUR FANS ABOUT YOUR FIRST TALKING PICTURE? YOU'RE REPRISING THE ROLE OF PROFESSOR ECHO, THE VENTRILOQUIST, IN *THE UNHOLY THREE*. IS THAT RIGHT?
MY NAME'S SAINT NICK.
OH, DON'T KID A KIDDER. WILL YOUR FANS BE DISAPPOINTED WHEN THEY HEAR YOUR VOICE?
HEY, DOLLFACE, CARE TO DANCE?
I DIDN'T SAY A WORD, MISS. IT WAS PROFESSOR ECHO, NOT ME!
HA! WELL, ISN'T THAT SOMETHING. LON CHANEY, THE MAN OF A THOUSAND FACES, BECOMES THE MAN OF A THOUSAND VOICES!

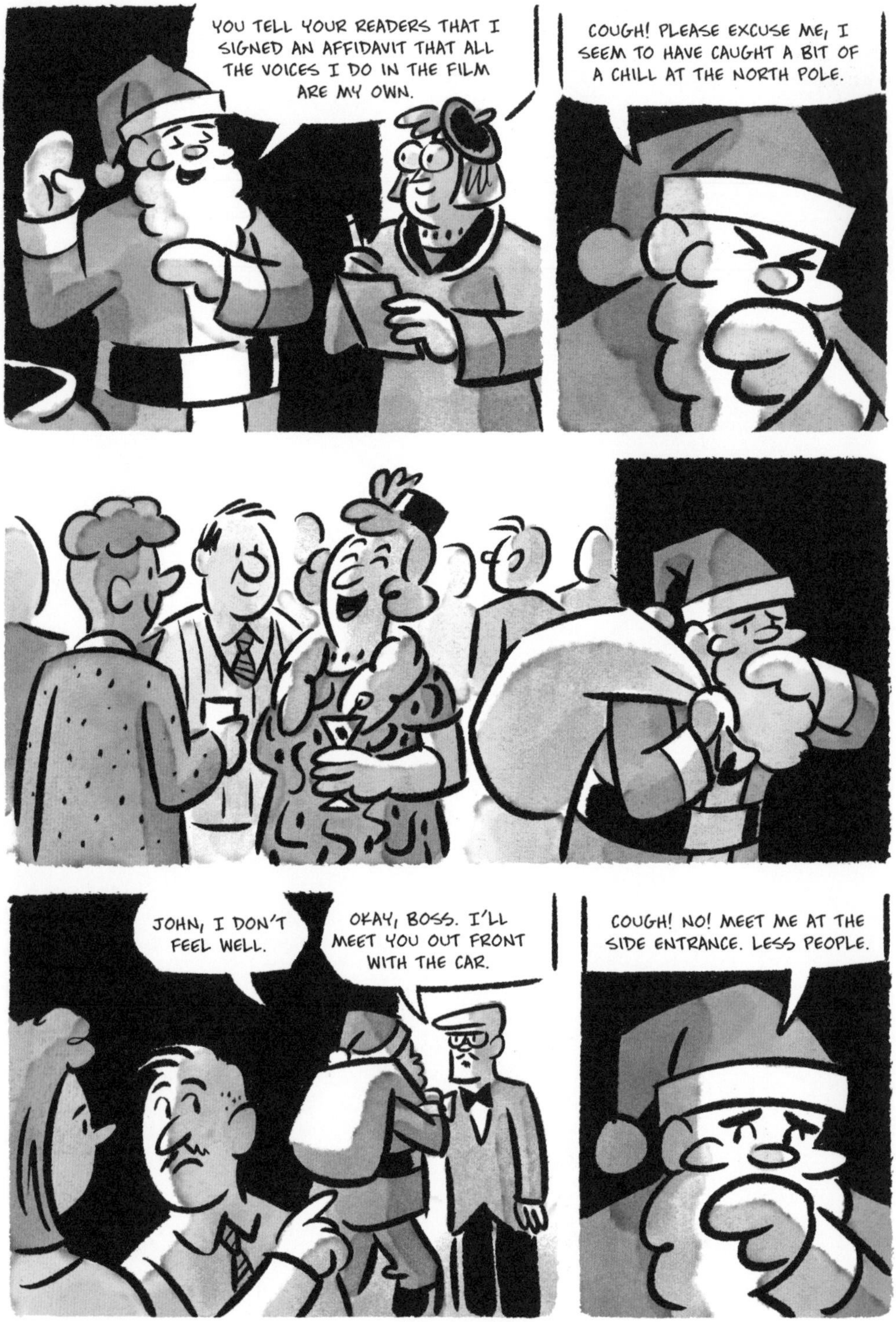
YOU TELL YOUR READERS THAT I SIGNED AN AFFIDAVIT THAT ALL THE VOICES I DO IN THE FILM ARE MY OWN.
COUGH! PLEASE EXCUSE ME, I SEEM TO HAVE CAUGHT A BIT OF A CHILL AT THE NORTH POLE.
JOHN, I DON'T FEEL WELL.
OKAY, BOSS. I'LL MEET YOU OUT FRONT WITH THE CAR.
COUGH! NO! MEET ME AT THE SIDE ENTRANCE. LESS PEOPLE.

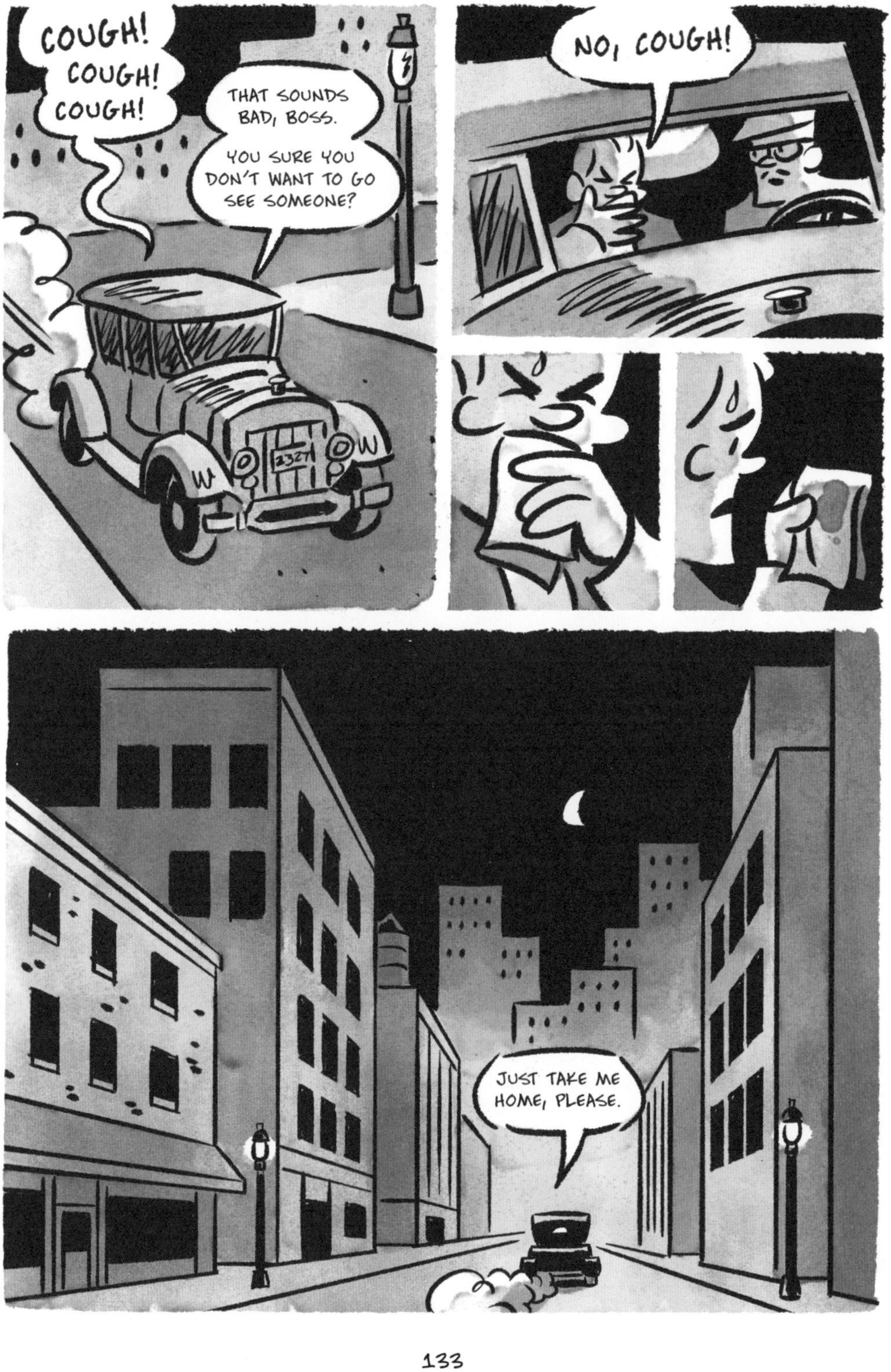
COUGH! COUGH! COUGH!
THAT SOUNDS BAD, BOSS.
YOU SURE YOU DON'T WANT TO GO SEE SOMEONE?
NO, COUGH!
JUST TAKE ME HOME, PLEASE.

THE UNHOLY THREE

METRO-GOLDWYN-MAYER, 1930

METRO-GOLDWYN-MAYER THOUGHT A REMAKE OF THE CRIME-SPREE MELODRAMA *THE UNHOLY THREE* AS A TALKIE WOULD BE A PERFECT VEHICLE TO LAUNCH CHANEY INTO THE WORLD OF SOUND. CHANEY, REPRISING HIS ROLE AS THE VENTRILOQUIST PROFESSOR ECHO, DID SEVERAL DIFFERENT VOICES IN THE FILM, INCLUDING THE OLD LADY AND THE DUMMY. SIGNING AN AFFIDAVIT TO HELP PROMOTE THE FILM, CHANEY SWORE HE WAS SOLELY RESPONSIBLE FOR ALL THE VOICES, AND THERE WAS NO USE OF VOICE DOUBLES. "THE MAN OF A THOUSAND FACES IS NOW THE MAN OF A THOUSAND VOICES" WAS THE SLOGAN THE STUDIO USED TO PROMOTE THE FILM, WHICH OPENS WITH TWEEDLEDEE, A LITTLE PERSON; HERCULES, A STRONGMAN; AND ECHO (CHANEY) PERFORMING AT A CARNIVAL SIDESHOW.

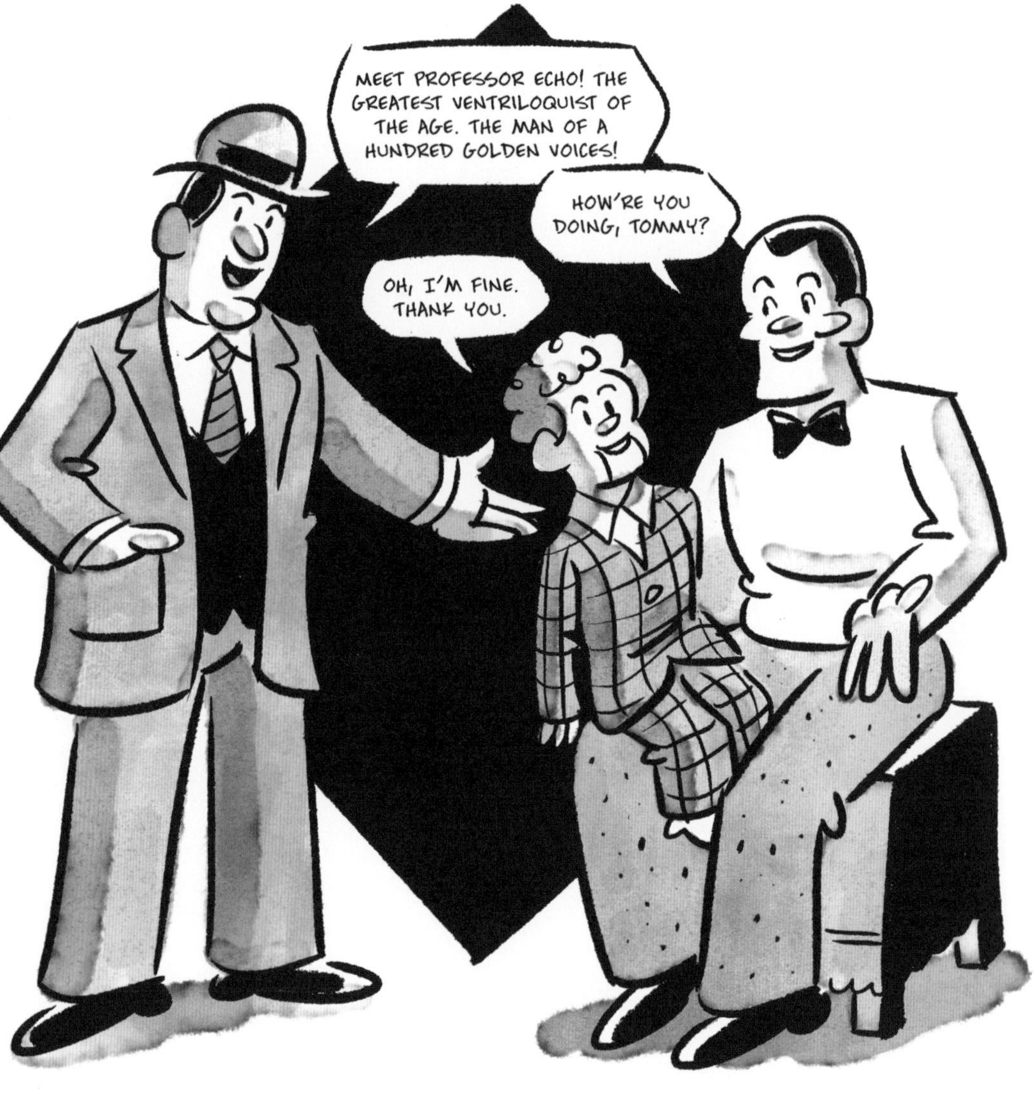
MEET PROFESSOR ECHO! THE GREATEST VENTRILOQUIST OF THE AGE. THE MAN OF A HUNDRED GOLDEN VOICES!
HOW'RE YOU DOING, TOMMY?
OH, I'M FINE. THANK YOU.

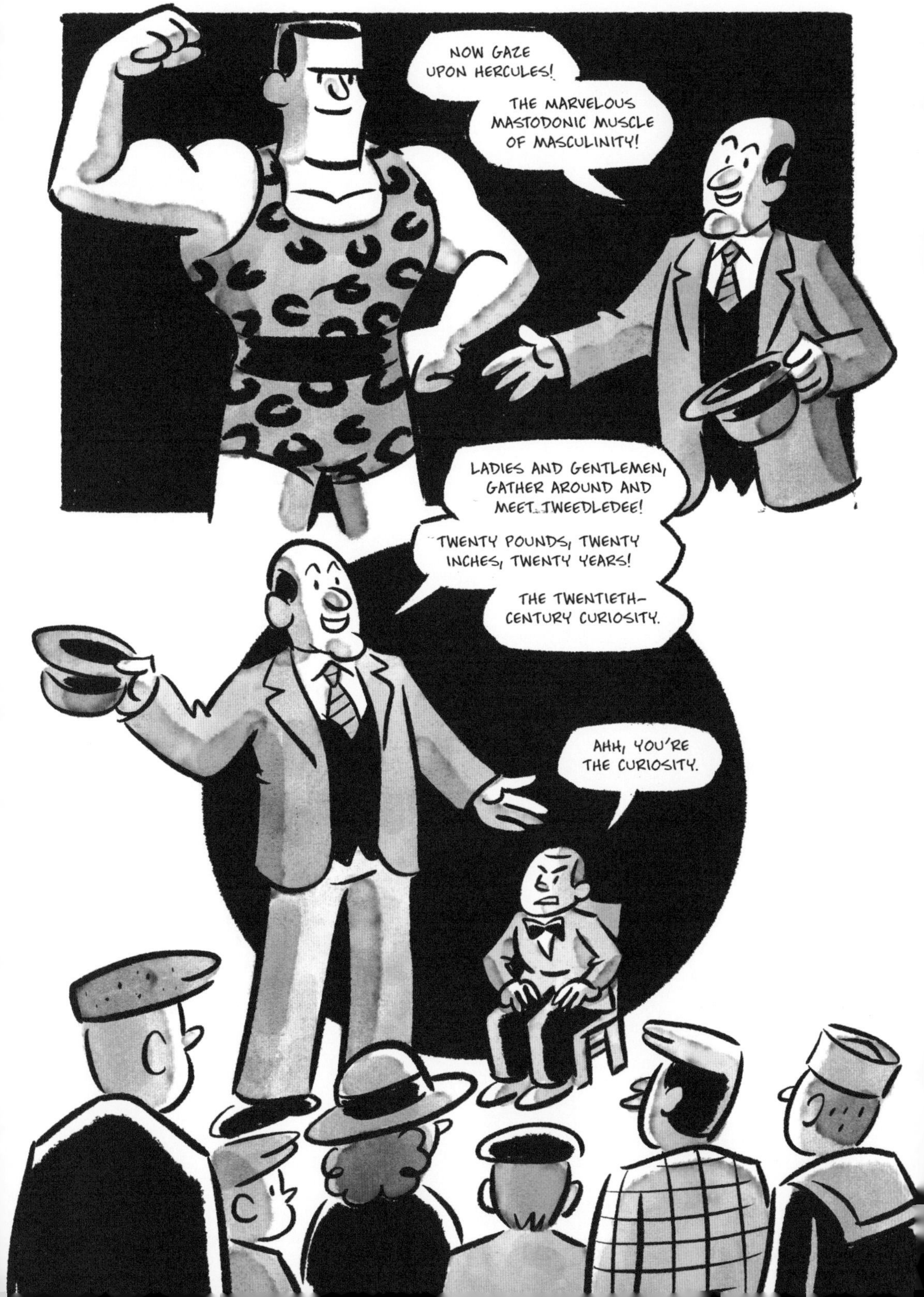

NOW GAZE UPON HERCULES!
THE MARVELOUS MASTODONIC MUSCLE OF MASCULINITY!
LADIES AND GENTLEMEN, GATHER AROUND AND MEET TWEEDLEDEE!
TWENTY POUNDS, TWENTY INCHES, TWENTY YEARS!
THE TWENTIETH-CENTURY CURIOSITY.
AHH, YOU'RE THE CURIOSITY.

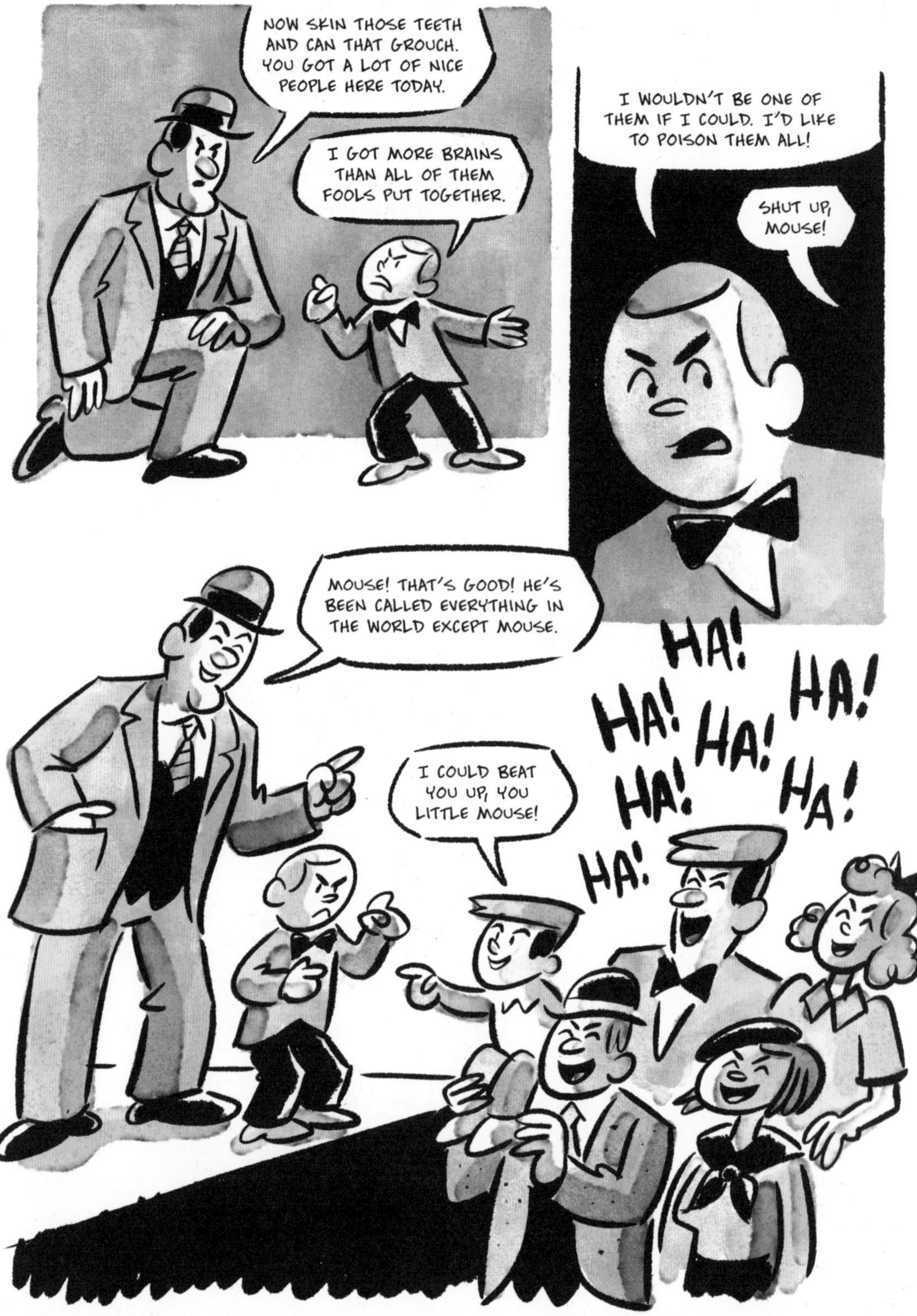
NOW SKIN THOSE TEETH AND CAN THAT GROUCH. YOU GOT A LOT OF NICE PEOPLE HERE TODAY.
I GOT MORE BRAINS THAN ALL OF THEM FOOLS PUT TOGETHER.
I WOULDN'T BE ONE OF THEM IF I COULD. I'D LIKE TO POISON THEM ALL!
SHUT UP, MOUSE!
MOUSE! THAT'S GOOD! HE'S BEEN CALLED EVERYTHING IN THE WORLD EXCEPT MOUSE.
I COULD BEAT YOU UP, YOU LITTLE MOUSE!
HA! HA! HA! HA! HA! HA! HA!

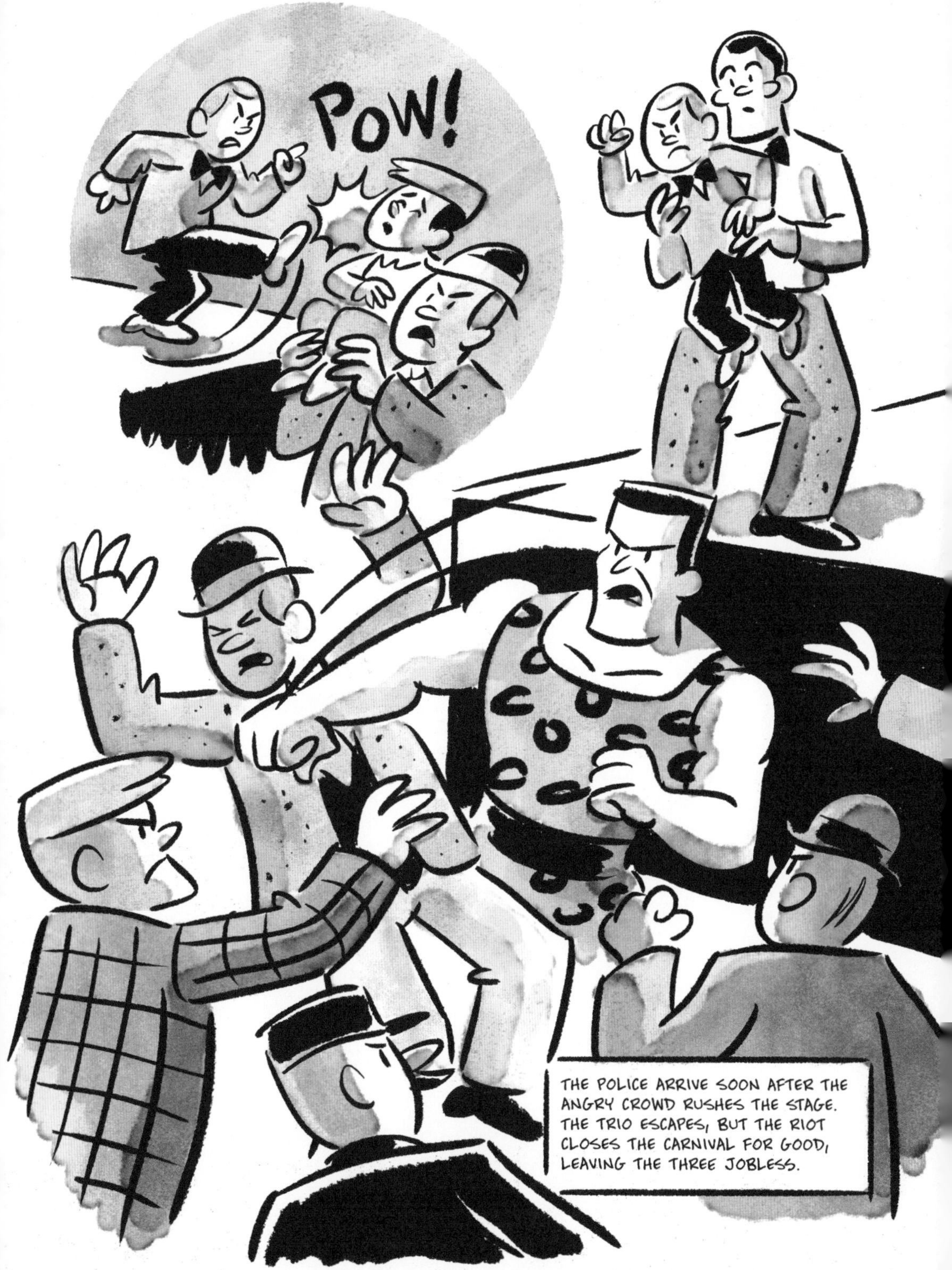
POW!
THE POLICE ARRIVE SOON AFTER THE ANGRY CROWD RUSHES THE STAGE. THE TRIO ESCAPES, BUT THE RIOT CLOSES THE CARNIVAL FOR GOOD, LEAVING THE THREE JOBLESS.

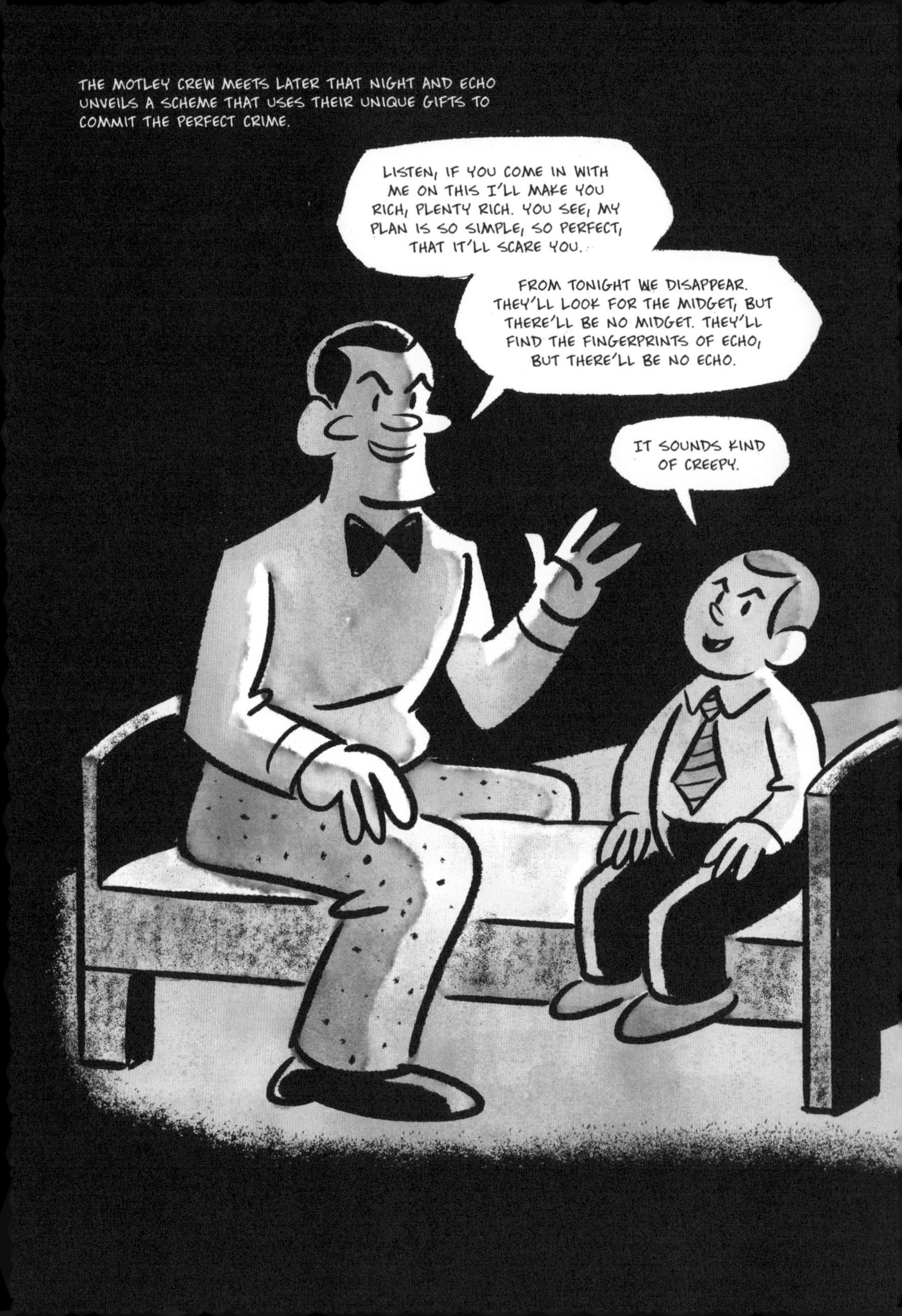
THE MOTLEY CREW MEETS LATER THAT NIGHT AND ECHO UNVEILS A SCHEME THAT USES THEIR UNIQUE GIFTS TO COMMIT THE PERFECT CRIME.
LISTEN, IF YOU COME IN WITH ME ON THIS I'LL MAKE YOU RICH, PLENTY RICH. YOU SEE, MY PLAN IS SO SIMPLE, SO PERFECT, THAT IT'LL SCARE YOU.
FROM TONIGHT WE DISAPPEAR. THEY'LL LOOK FOR THE MIDGET, BUT THERE'LL BE NO MIDGET. THEY'LL FIND THE FINGERPRINTS OF ECHO, BUT THERE'LL BE NO ECHO.
IT SOUNDS KIND OF CREEPY.

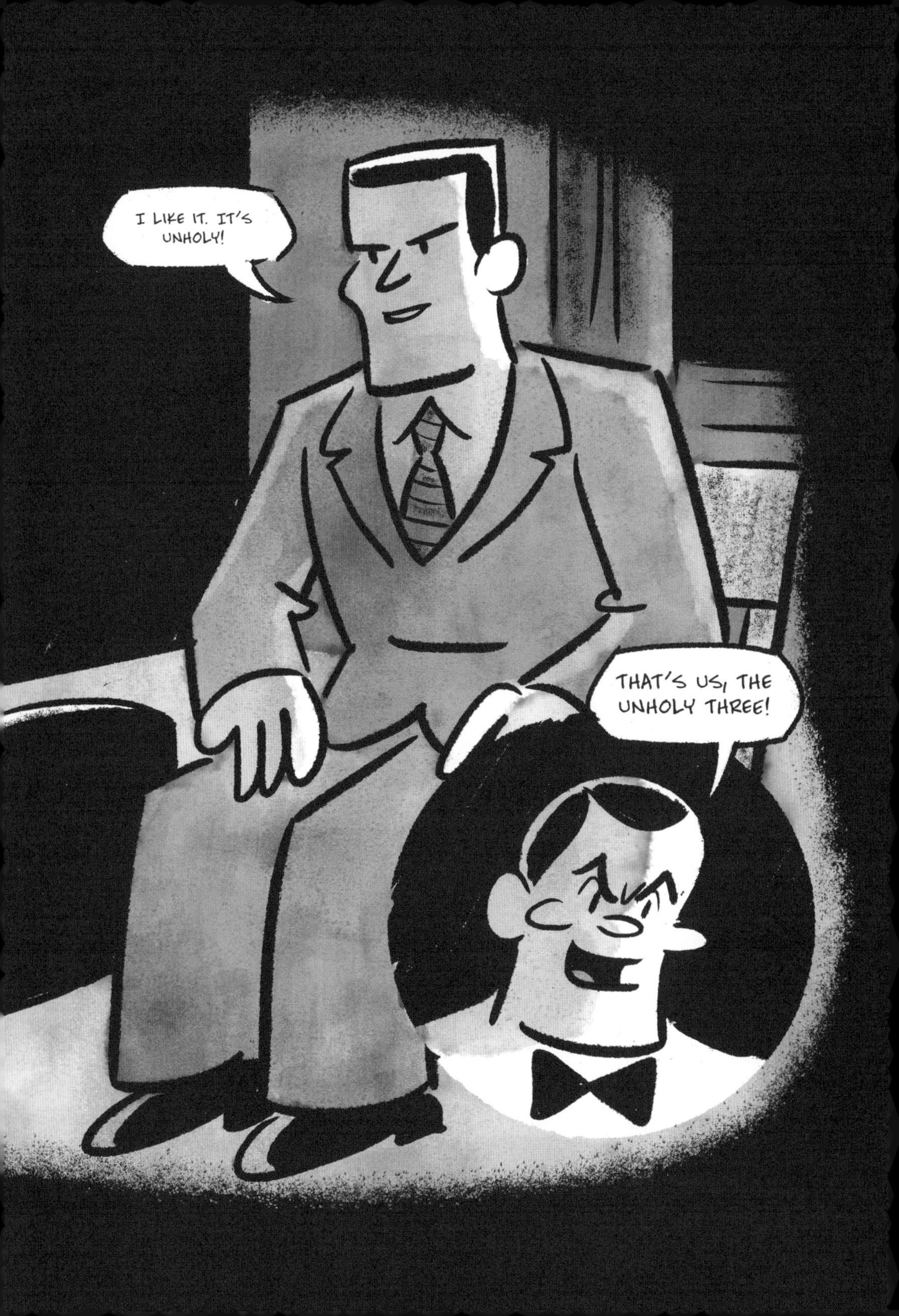
I LIKE IT. IT'S UNHOLY!
THAT'S US, THE UNHOLY THREE!

THE TRIO USES A PET SHOP AS A FRONT FOR THEIR CRIMES. ECHO DISGUISES HIMSELF AS THE KINDLY OLD MRS. O'GRADY, TWEEDLEDEE POSES AS HER INFANT GRANDCHILD, AND HERCULES ACTS AS HER SON-IN-LAW. ROSIE, ECHO'S GIRLFRIEND, POSES AS HIS DAUGHTER AND HELPS RUN THE SHOP WITH HECTOR, AN INNOCENT RUBE WHO IS ENTIRELY UNAWARE OF THEIR SCHEME. USING HIS VENTRILOQUIST'S SKILLS, ECHO SELLS PHONY TALKING PARROTS TO WEALTHY PATRONS.

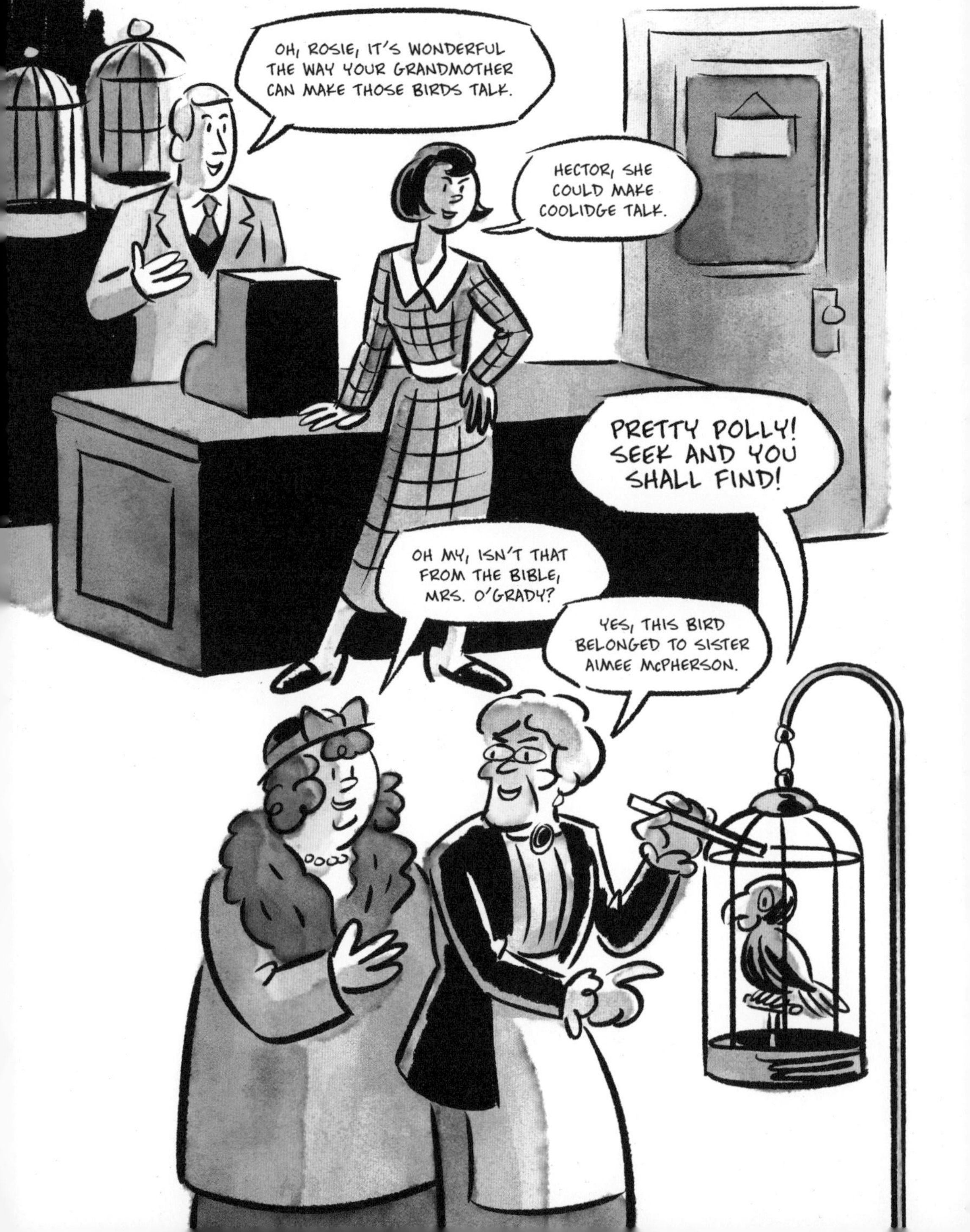
OH, ROSIE, IT'S WONDERFUL THE WAY YOUR GRANDMOTHER CAN MAKE THOSE BIRDS TALK.
HECTOR, SHE COULD MAKE COOLIDGE TALK.
PRETTY POLLY! SEEK AND YOU SHALL FIND!
OH MY, ISN'T THAT FROM THE BIBLE, MRS. O'GRADY?
YES, THIS BIRD BELONGED TO SISTER AIMEE McPHERSON.

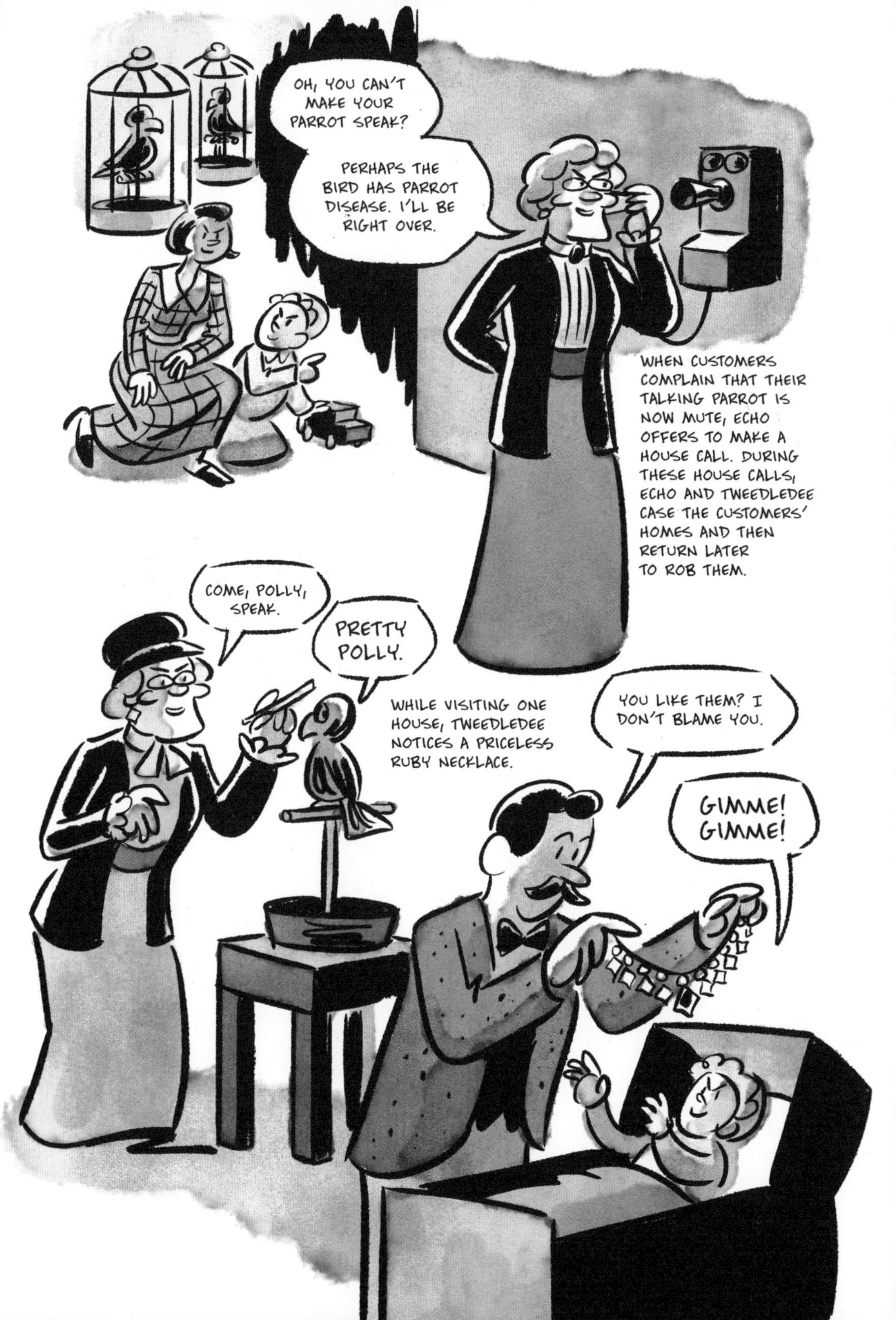
OH, YOU CAN'T MAKE YOUR PARROT SPEAK?
PERHAPS THE BIRD HAS PARROT DISEASE. I'LL BE RIGHT OVER.
WHEN CUSTOMERS COMPLAIN THAT THEIR TALKING PARROT IS NOW MUTE, ECHO OFFERS TO MAKE A HOUSE CALL. DURING THESE HOUSE CALLS, ECHO AND TWEEDLEDEE CASE THE CUSTOMERS' HOMES AND THEN RETURN LATER TO ROB THEM.
COME, POLLY, SPEAK.
PRETTY POLLY.
WHILE VISITING ONE HOUSE, TWEEDLEDEE NOTICES A PRICELESS RUBY NECKLACE.
YOU LIKE THEM? I DON'T BLAME YOU.
GIMME! GIMME!

AS THE TRIO CONTINUES THEIR CRIME SPREE, ECHO BEGINS TO SUSPECT THAT ROSIE IS DEVELOPING FEELINGS FOR HECTOR AND WILL BLOW THE WHISTLE ON THEIR OPERATION.

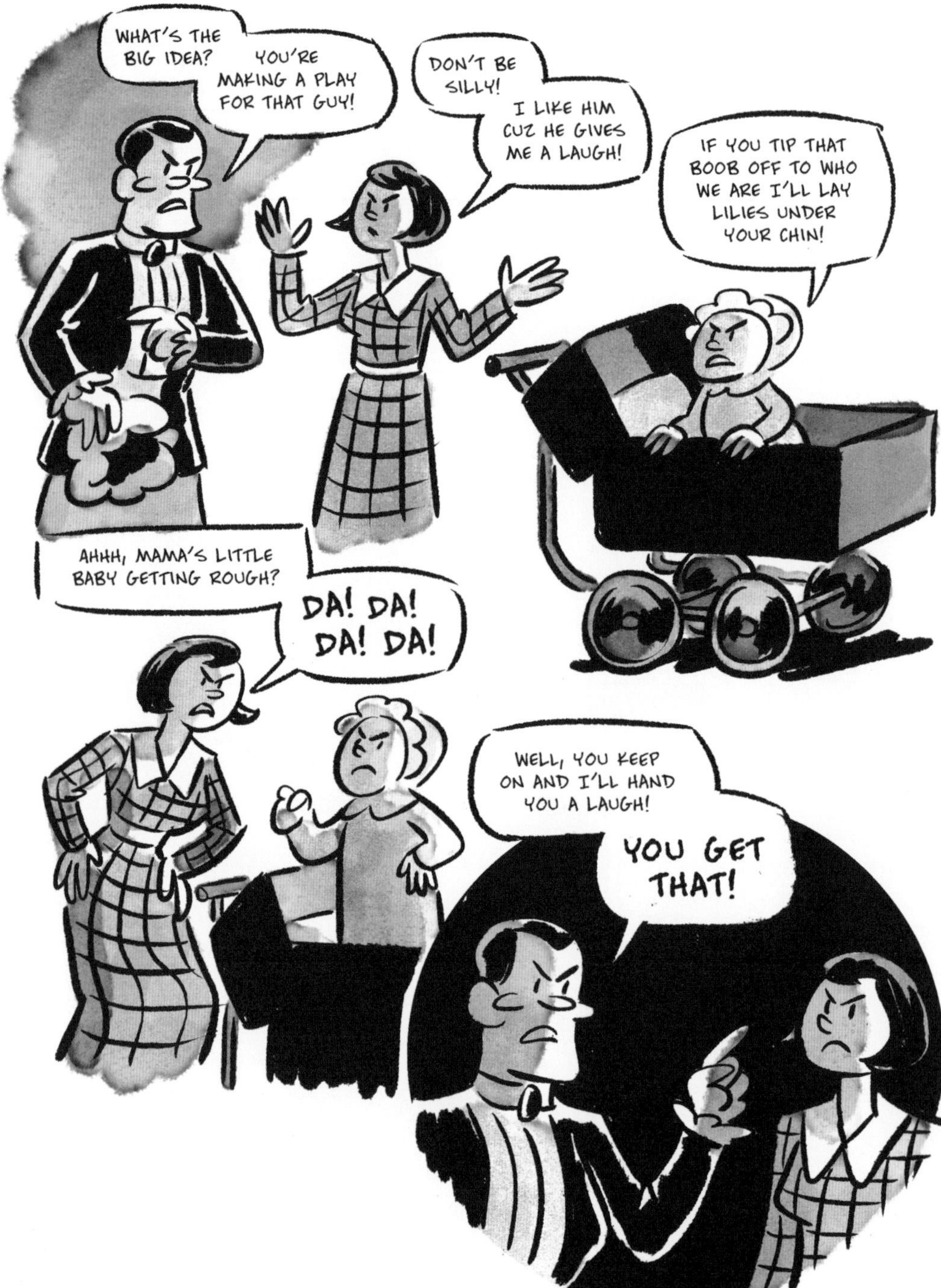
WHAT'S THE BIG IDEA?
YOU'RE MAKING A PLAY FOR THAT GUY!
DON'T BE SILLY!
I LIKE HIM CUZ HE GIVES ME A LAUGH!
IF YOU TIP THAT BOOB OFF TO WHO WE ARE I'LL LAY LILIES UNDER YOUR CHIN!
AHHH, MAMA'S LITTLE BABY GETTING ROUGH?
DA! DA! DA! DA!
WELL, YOU KEEP ON AND I'LL HAND YOU A LAUGH!
YOU GET THAT!

ECHO ALSO BEGINS TO DISTRUST HIS OTHER PARTNERS WHEN HE LEARNS HE'S BEEN CHEATED. HE DECIDES TO USE HIS PET GORILLA TO SCARE THEM STRAIGHT.

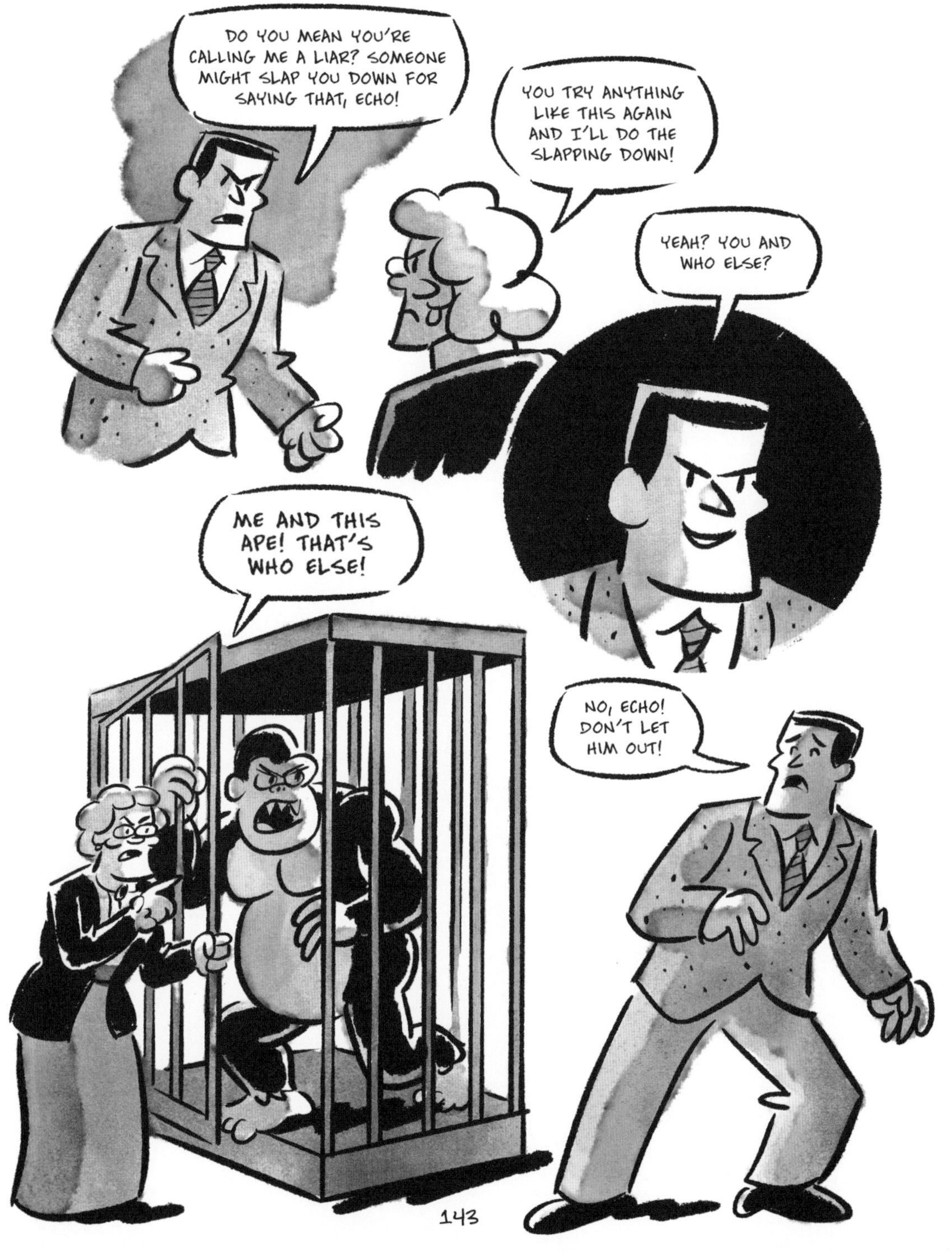

DO YOU MEAN YOU'RE CALLING ME A LIAR? SOMEONE MIGHT SLAP YOU DOWN FOR SAYING THAT, ECHO!
YOU TRY ANYTHING LIKE THIS AGAIN AND I'LL DO THE SLAPPING DOWN!
YEAH? YOU AND WHO ELSE?
ME AND THIS APE! THAT'S WHO ELSE!
NO, ECHO! DON'T LET HIM OUT!

THE POLICE INVESTIGATING THE ROBBERIES START TO CONNECT THE DOTS AND PAY A VISIT TO THE PET SHOP. ECHO THROWS THE POLICE OFF THE TRAIL BY FRAMING HECTOR FOR HIS GANG'S CRIMES. WITH HECTOR ARRESTED AND STANDING TRIAL FOR THEIR SINS, THE UNHOLY THREE LAY LOW IN A SECLUDED CABIN. WHILE HIDING OUT, ROSIE ADMITS TO ECHO THAT SHE CARES FOR HECTOR.

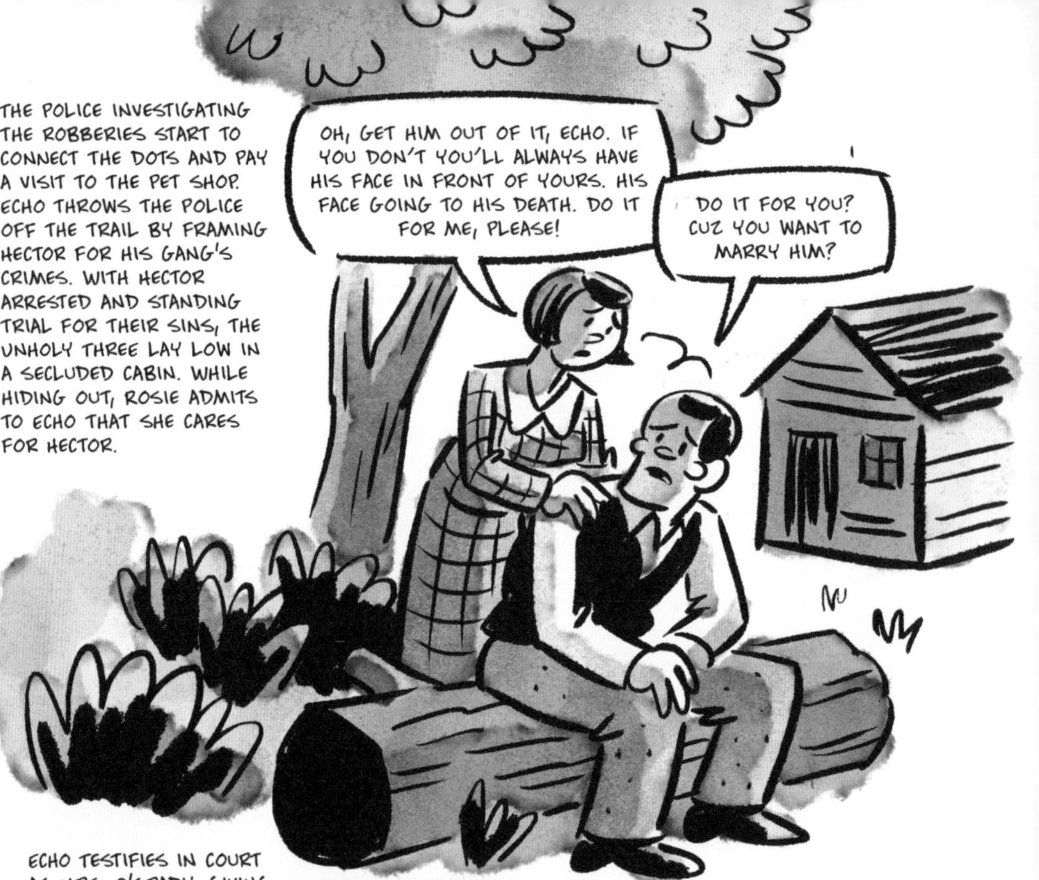
OH, GET HIM OUT OF IT, ECHO. IF YOU DON'T YOU'LL ALWAYS HAVE HIS FACE IN FRONT OF YOURS. HIS FACE GOING TO HIS DEATH. DO IT FOR ME, PLEASE!
DO IT FOR YOU? CUZ YOU WANT TO MARRY HIM?

ECHO TESTIFIES IN COURT AS MRS. O'GRADY, GIVING HECTOR AN ALIBI. WHILE ON THE STAND, ECHO'S SECRET IS REVEALED, SETTING HECTOR FREE AND SENDING ECHO TO PRISON.

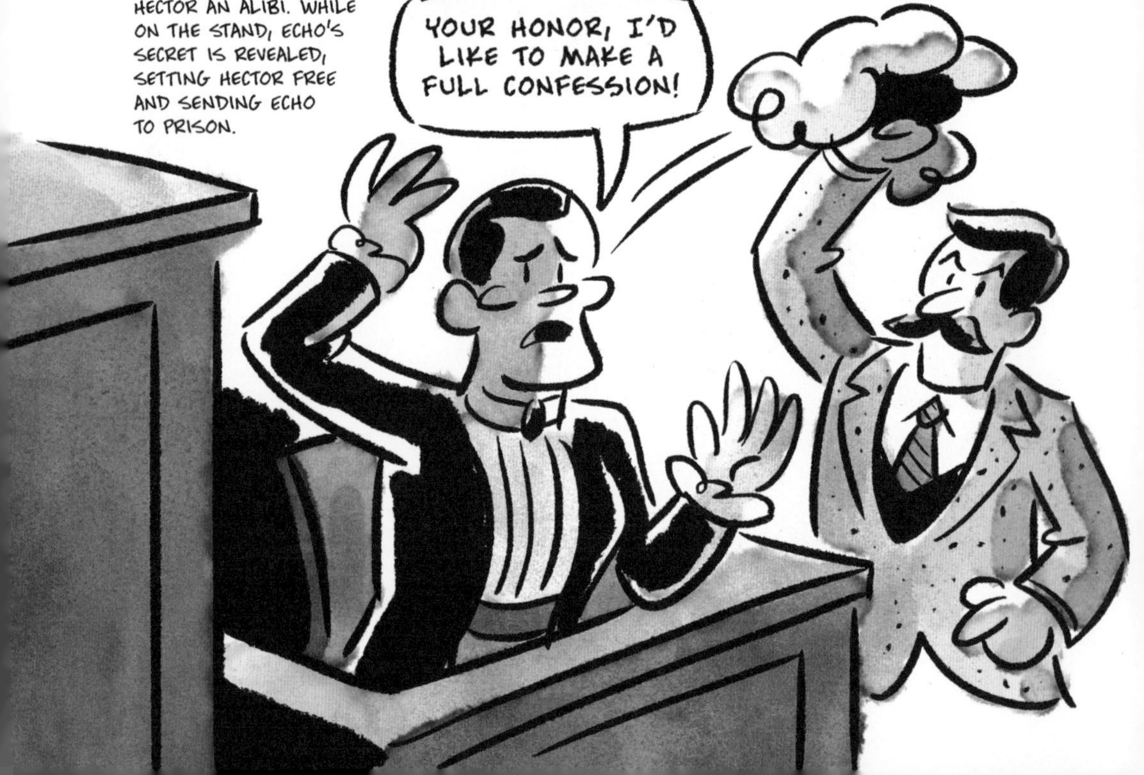
YOUR HONOR, I'D LIKE TO MAKE A FULL CONFESSION!

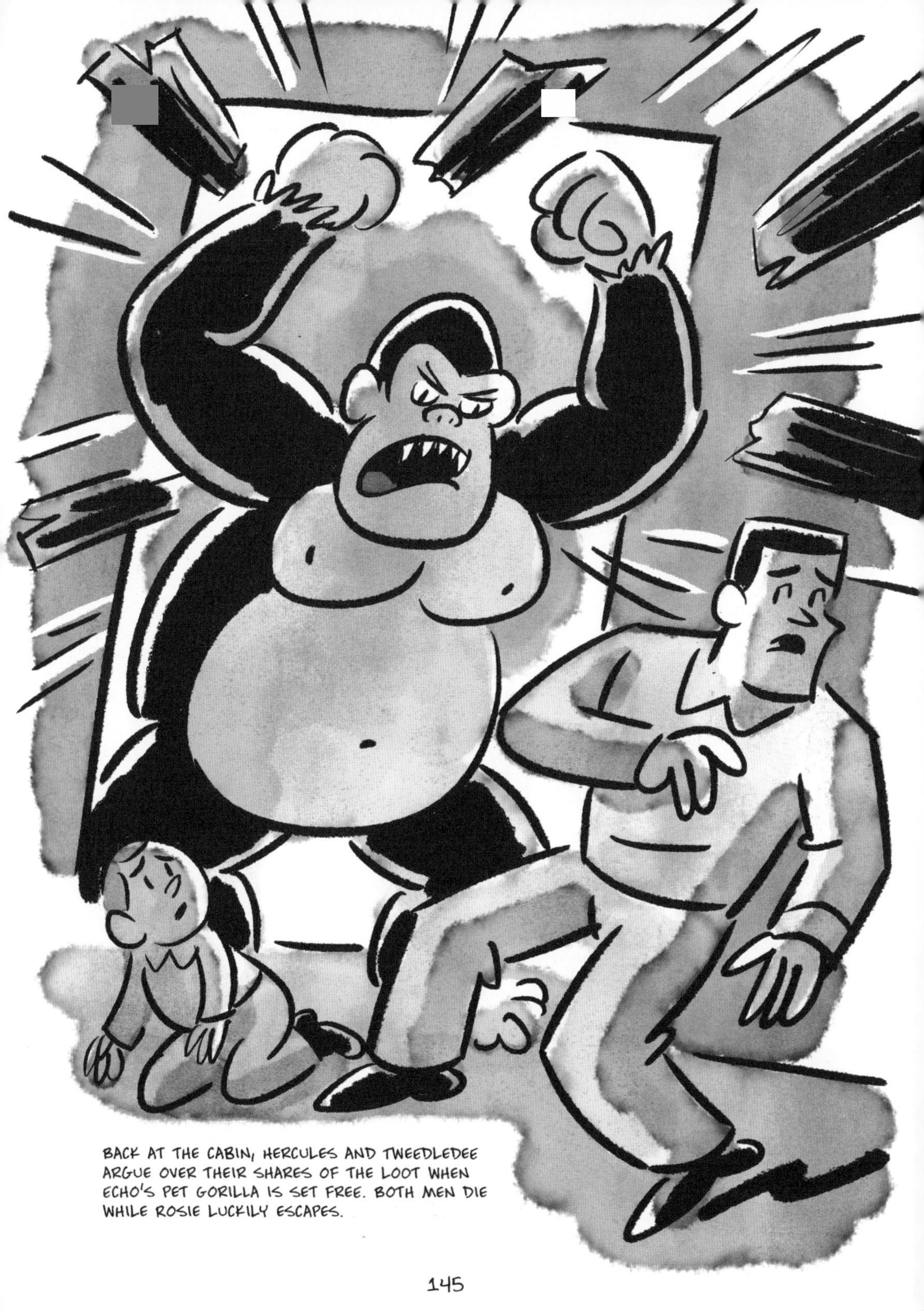
BACK AT THE CABIN, HERCULES AND TWEEDLEDEE ARGUE OVER THEIR SHARES OF THE LOOT WHEN ECHO'S PET GORILLA IS SET FREE. BOTH MEN DIE WHILE ROSIE LUCKILY ESCAPES.

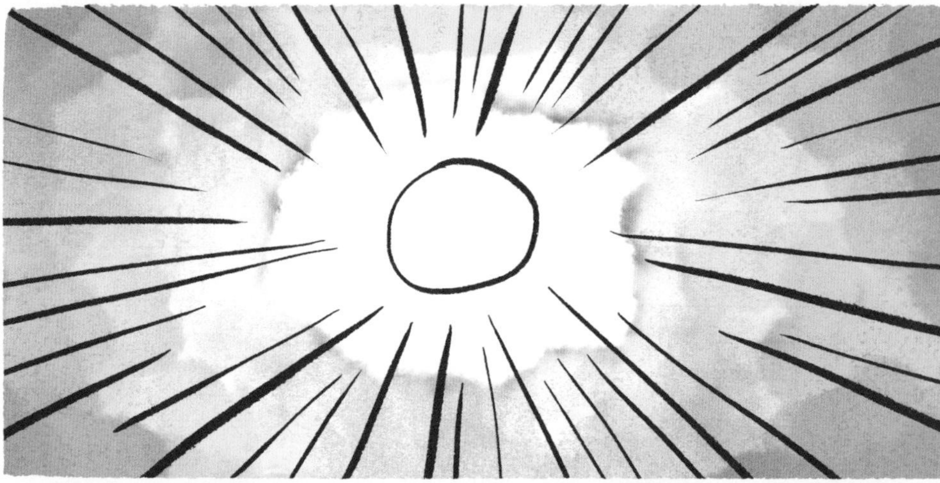

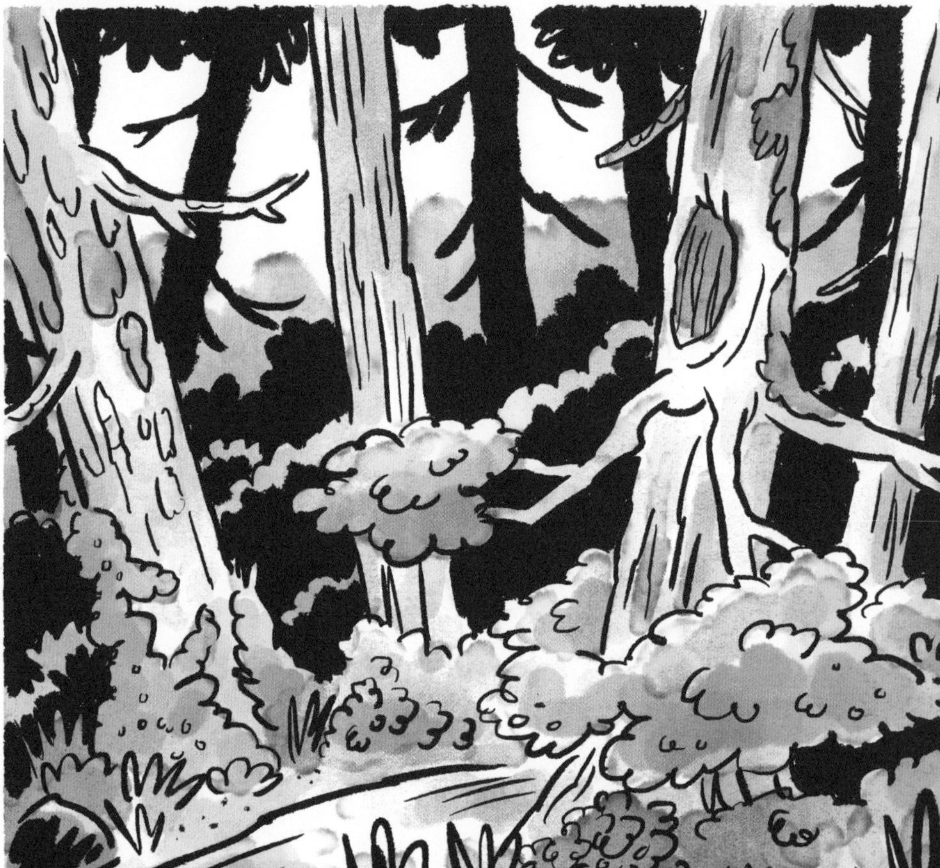

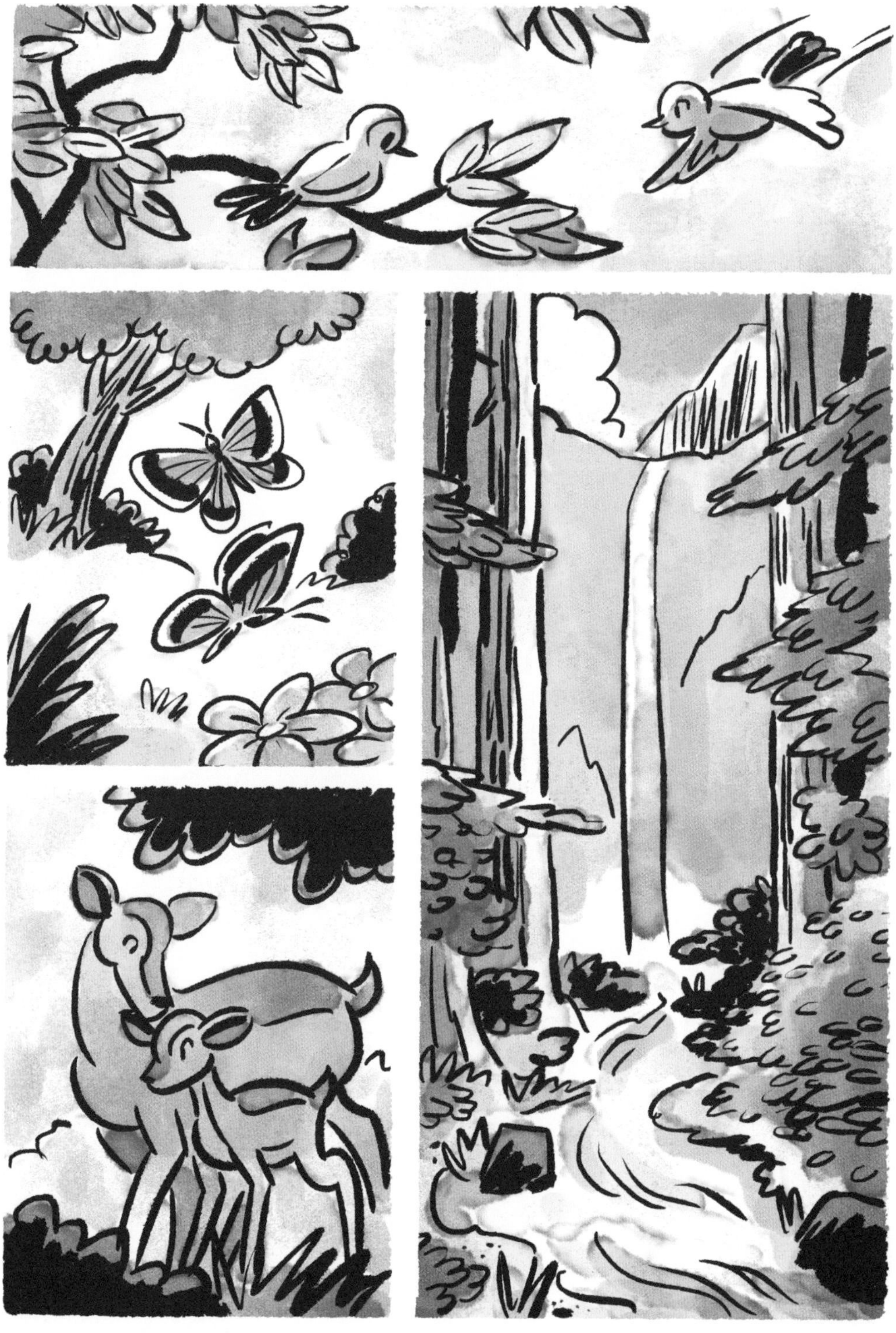

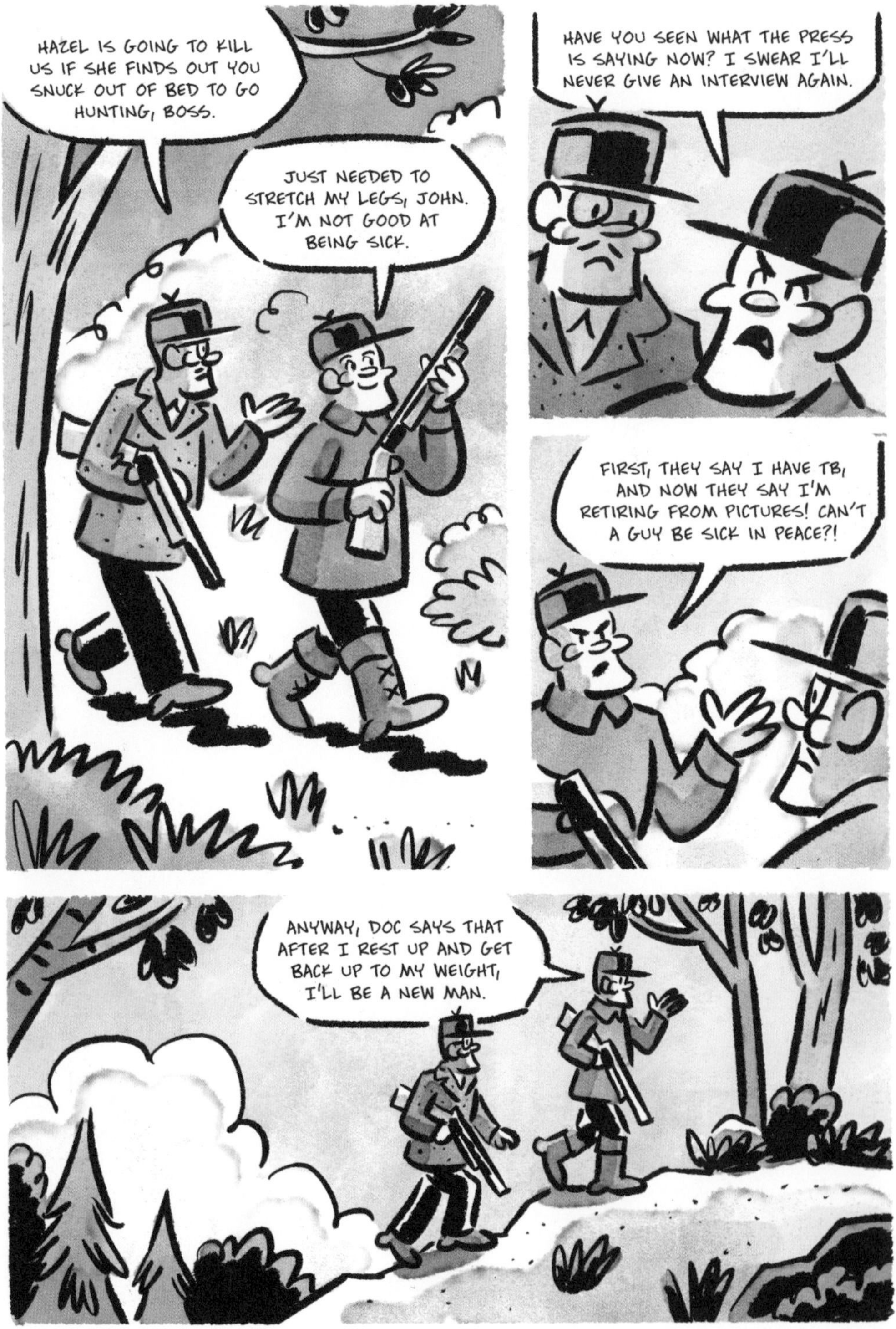
HAZEL IS GOING TO KILL US IF SHE FINDS OUT YOU SNUCK OUT OF BED TO GO HUNTING, BOSS.
JUST NEEDED TO STRETCH MY LEGS, JOHN. I'M NOT GOOD AT BEING SICK.
HAVE YOU SEEN WHAT THE PRESS IS SAYING NOW? I SWEAR I'LL NEVER GIVE AN INTERVIEW AGAIN.
FIRST, THEY SAY I HAVE TB, AND NOW THEY SAY I'M RETIRING FROM PICTURES! CAN'T A GUY BE SICK IN PEACE?!
ANYWAY, DOC SAYS THAT AFTER I REST UP AND GET BACK UP TO MY WEIGHT, I'LL BE A NEW MAN.

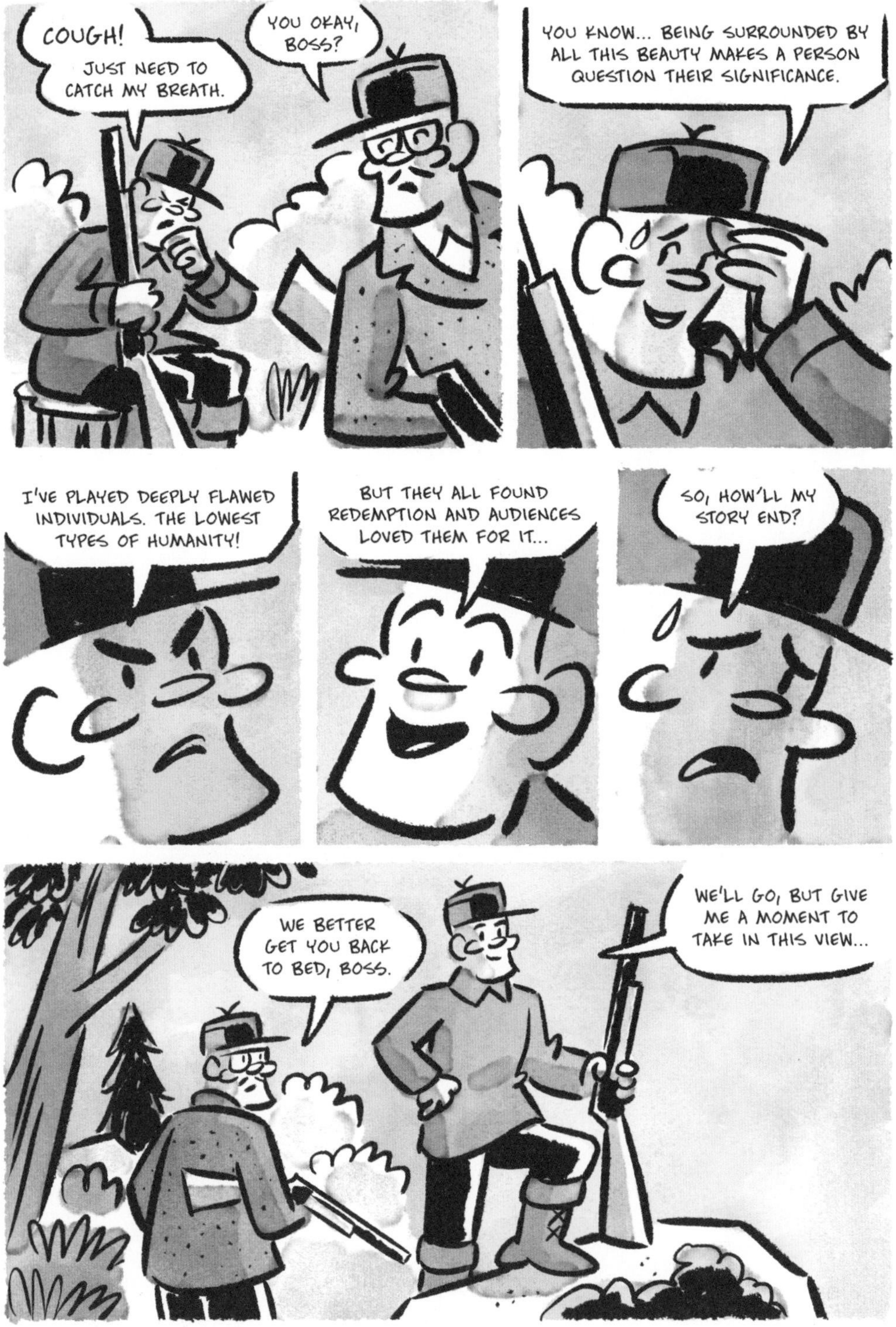
COUGH!
JUST NEED TO CATCH MY BREATH.
YOU OKAY, BOSS?
YOU KNOW... BEING SURROUNDED BY ALL THIS BEAUTY MAKES A PERSON QUESTION THEIR SIGNIFICANCE.
I'VE PLAYED DEEPLY FLAWED INDIVIDUALS. THE LOWEST TYPES OF HUMANITY!
BUT THEY ALL FOUND REDEMPTION AND AUDIENCES LOVED THEM FOR IT...
SO, HOW'LL MY STORY END?
WE BETTER GET YOU BACK TO BED, BOSS.
WE'LL GO, BUT GIVE ME A MOMENT TO TAKE IN THIS VIEW...

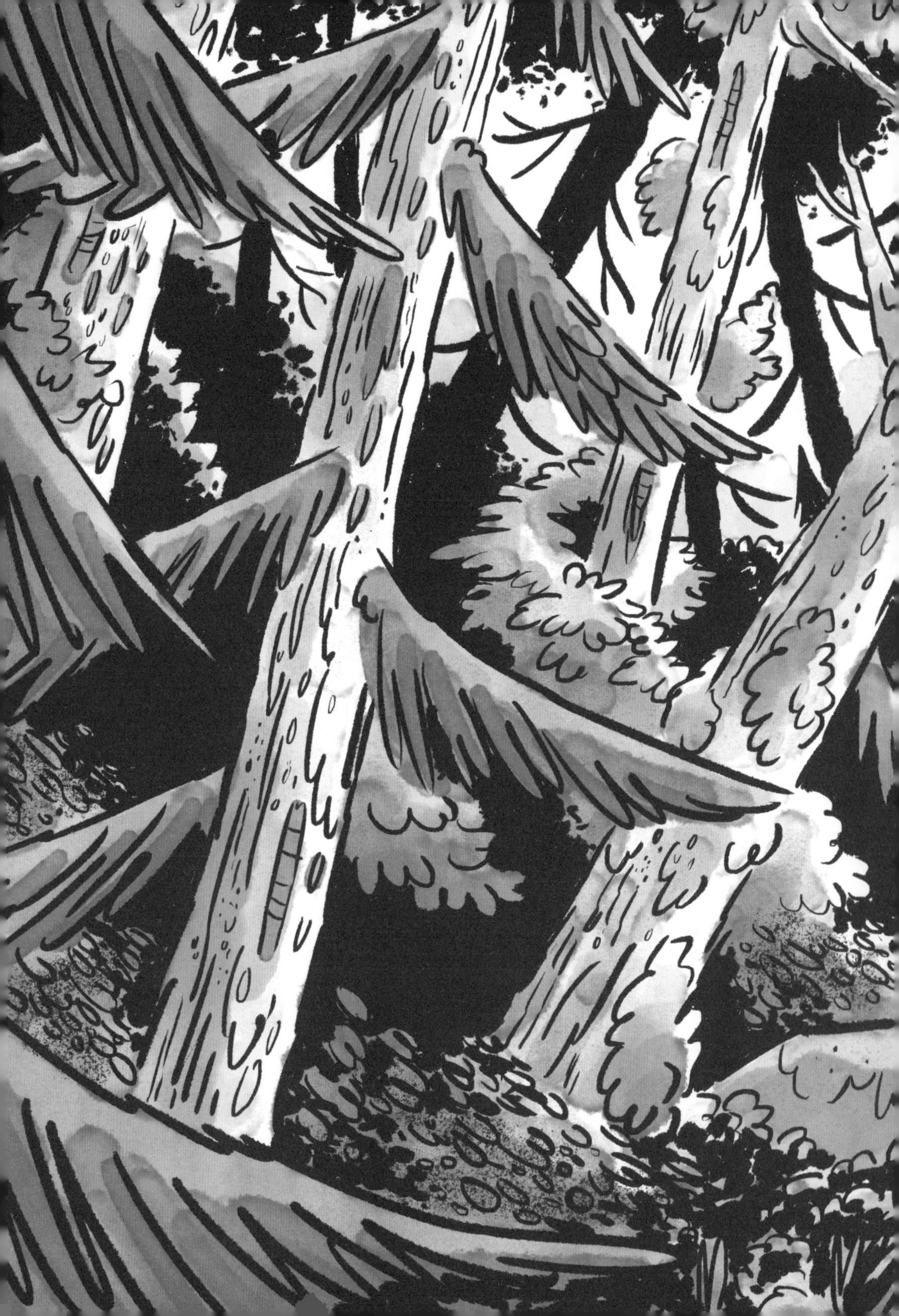

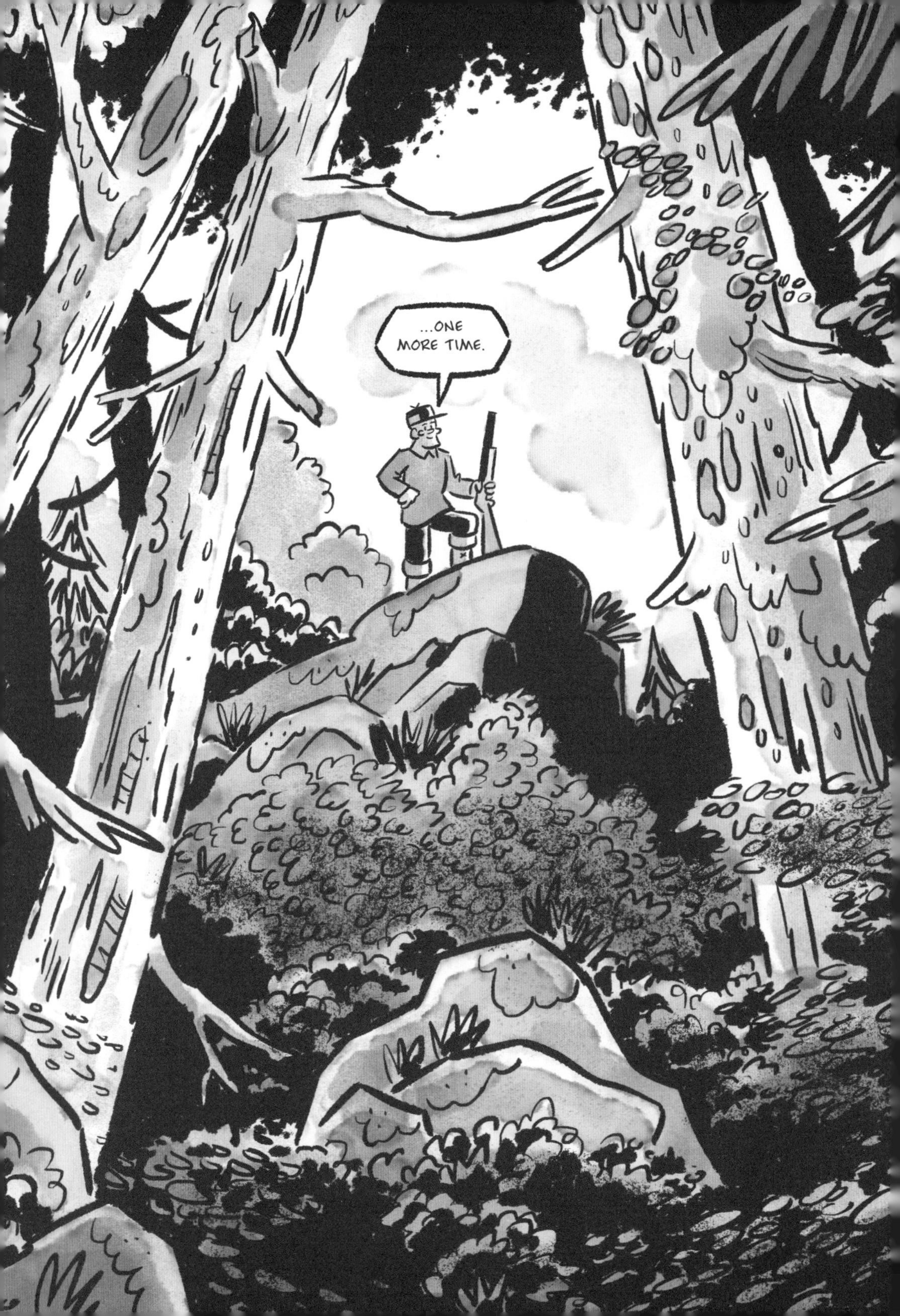
...ONE MORE TIME.

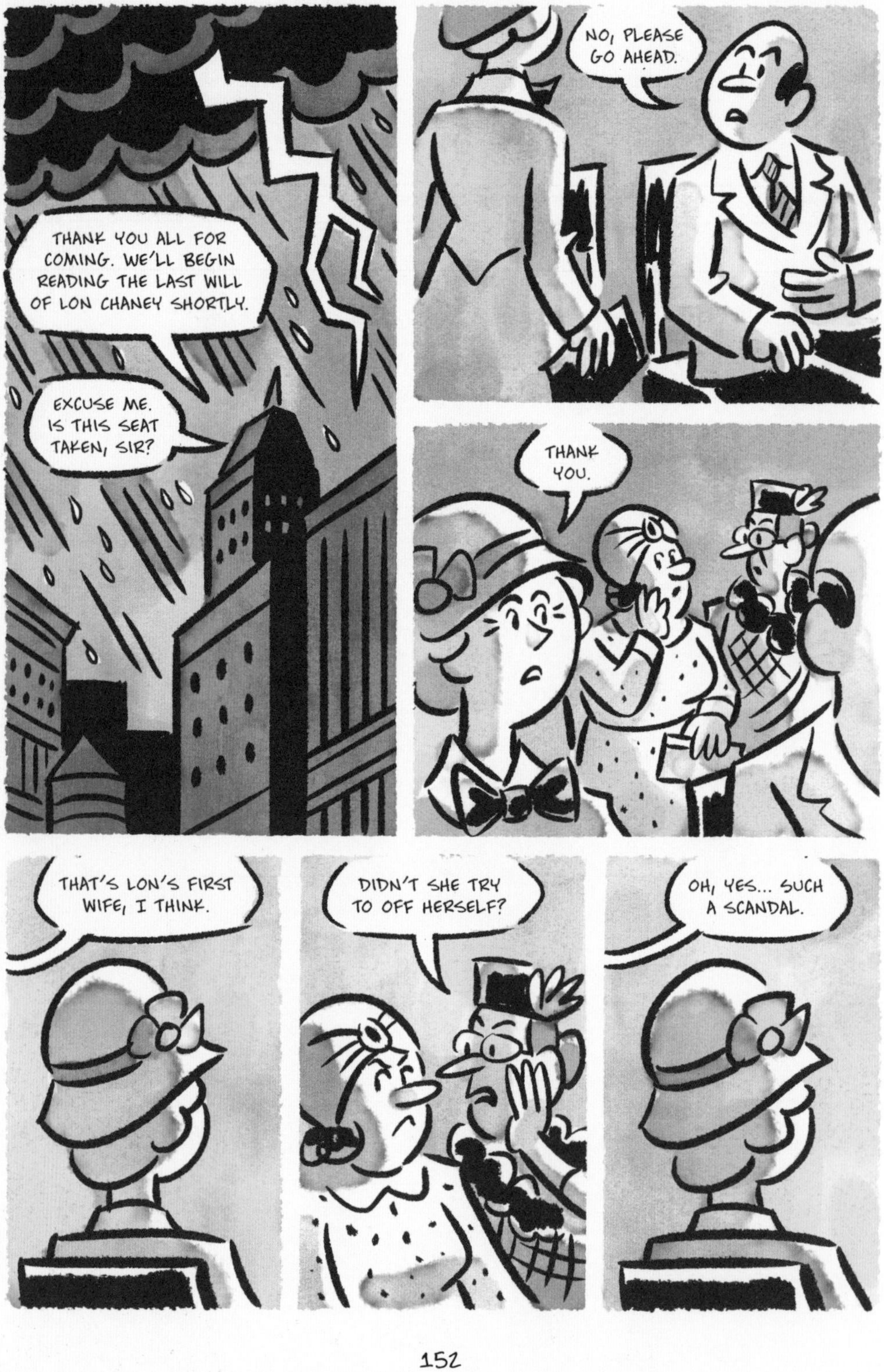
THANK YOU ALL FOR COMING. WE'LL BEGIN READING THE LAST WILL OF LON CHANEY SHORTLY.
EXCUSE ME. IS THIS SEAT TAKEN, SIR?
NO, PLEASE GO AHEAD.
THANK YOU.
THAT'S LON'S FIRST WIFE, I THINK.
DIDN'T SHE TRY TO OFF HERSELF?
OH, YES... SUCH A SCANDAL.

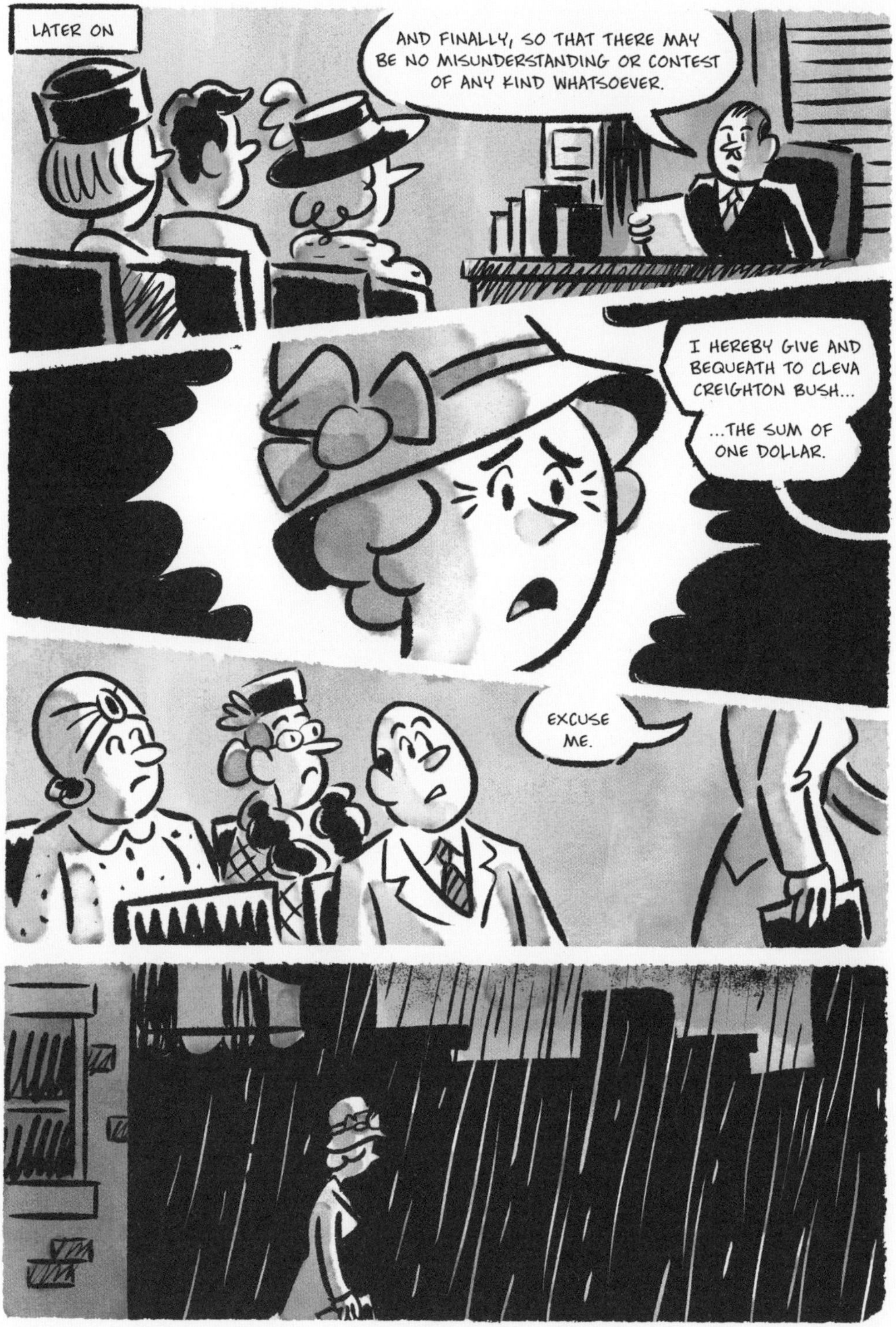
LATER ON
AND FINALLY, SO THAT THERE MAY BE NO MISUNDERSTANDING OR CONTEST OF ANY KIND WHATSOEVER.
I HEREBY GIVE AND BEQUEATH TO CLEVA CREIGHTON BUSH...
...THE SUM OF ONE DOLLAR.
EXCUSE ME.

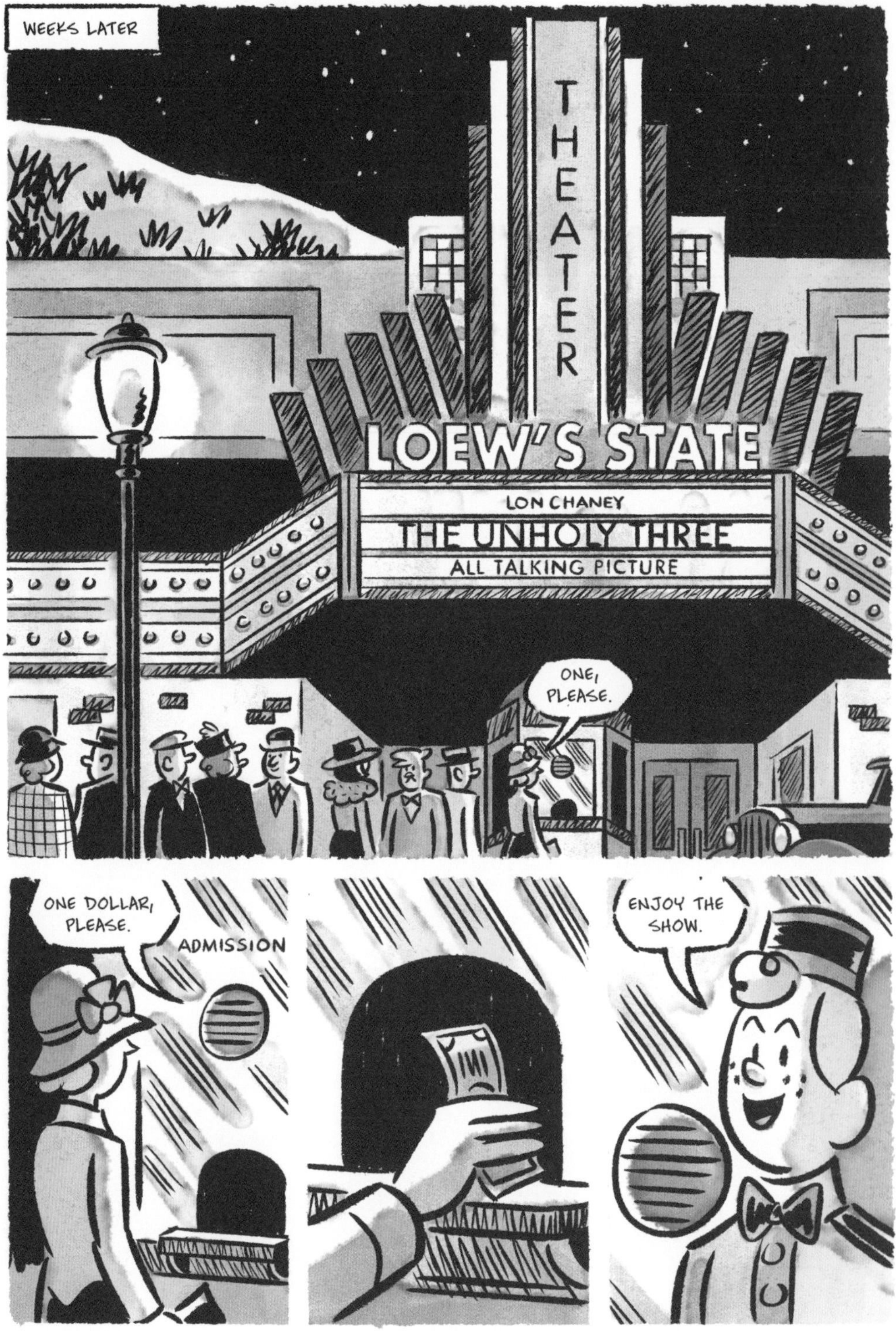
WEEKS LATER
THEATER
LOEW'S STATE
LON CHANEY
THE UNHOLY THREE
ALL TALKING PICTURE
ONE, PLEASE.
ONE DOLLAR, PLEASE.
ADMISSION
ENJOY THE SHOW.

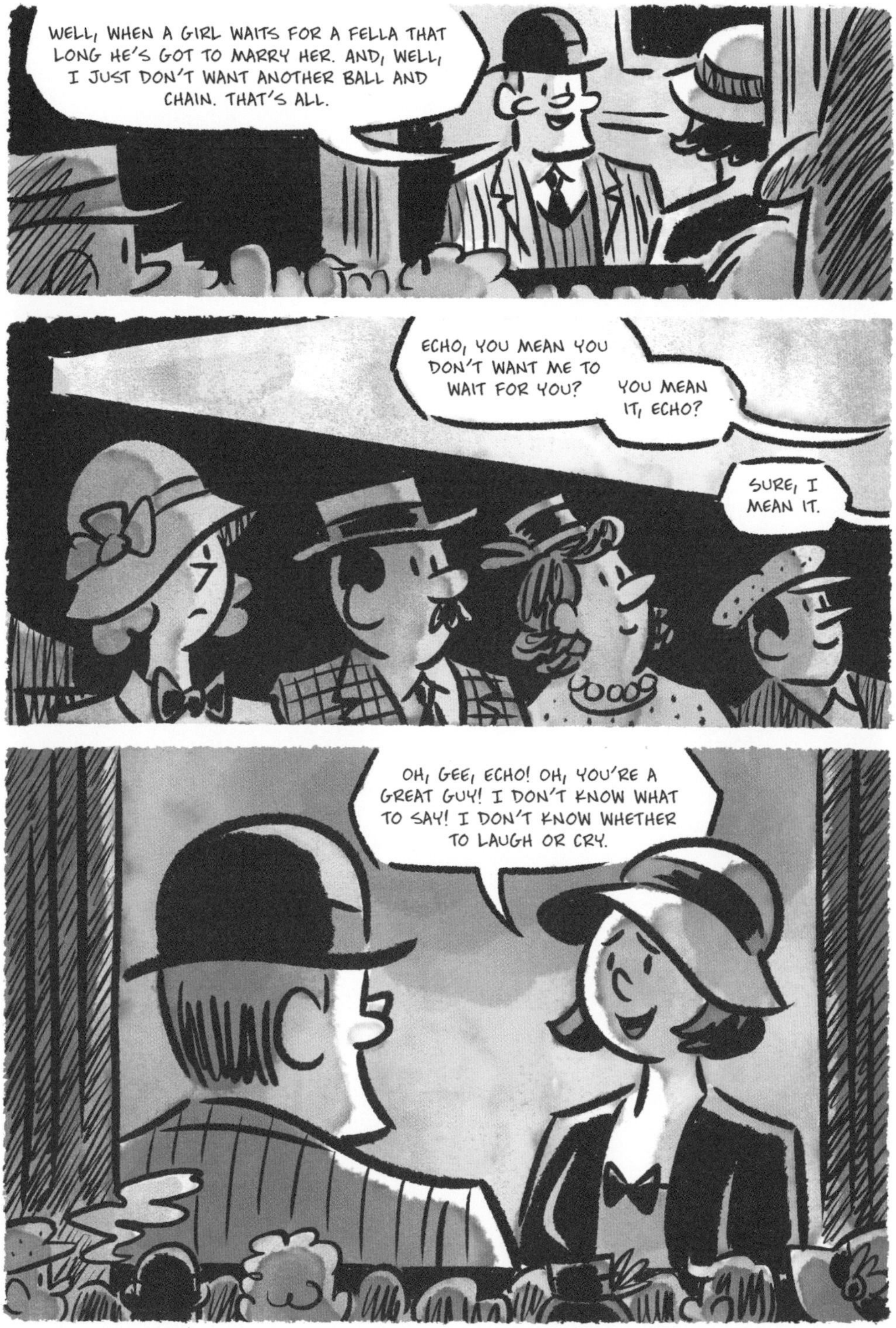
WELL, WHEN A GIRL WAITS FOR A FELLA THAT LONG HE'S GOT TO MARRY HER. AND, WELL, I JUST DON'T WANT ANOTHER BALL AND CHAIN. THAT'S ALL.
ECHO, YOU MEAN YOU DON'T WANT ME TO WAIT FOR YOU?
YOU MEAN IT, ECHO?
SURE, I MEAN IT.
OH, GEE, ECHO! OH, YOU'RE A GREAT GUY! I DON'T KNOW WHAT TO SAY! I DON'T KNOW WHETHER TO LAUGH OR CRY.

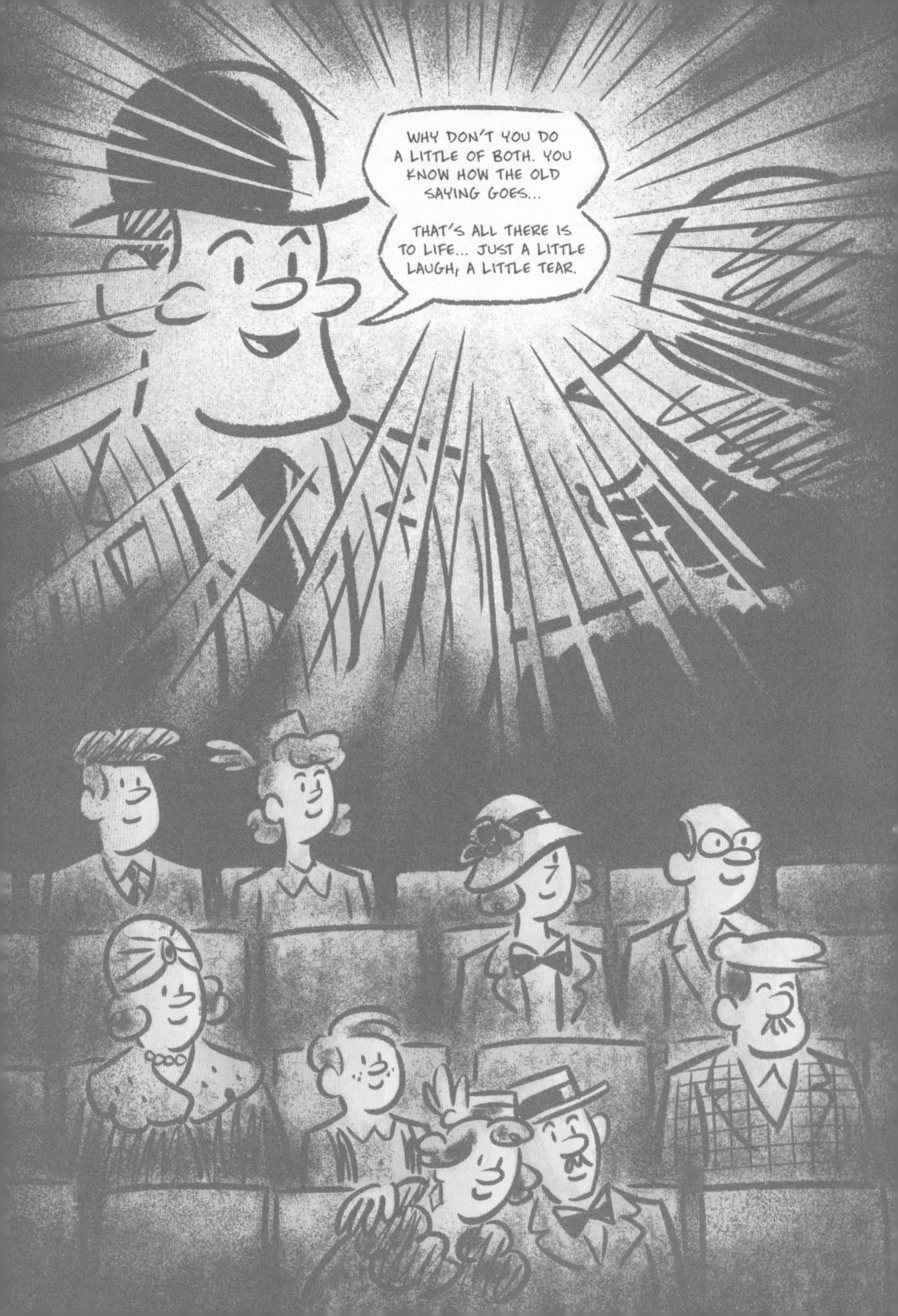
WHY DON'T YOU DO A LITTLE OF BOTH. YOU KNOW HOW THE OLD SAYING GOES...
THAT'S ALL THERE IS TO LIFE... JUST A LITTLE LAUGH, A LITTLE TEAR.

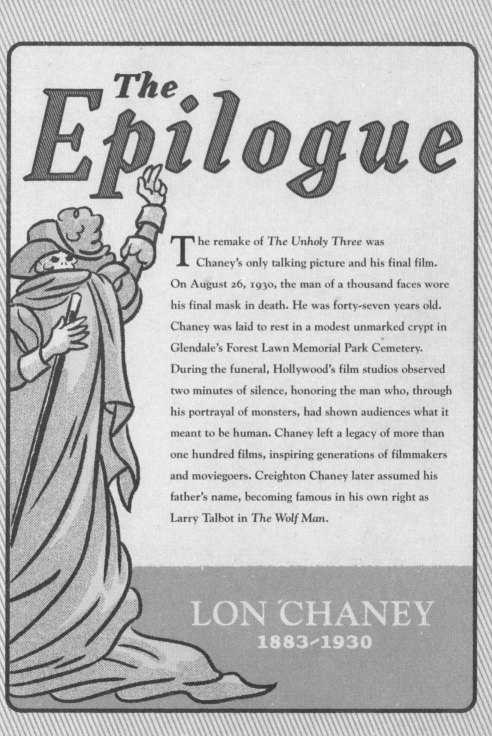

The Epilogue

The remake of *The Unholy Three* was Chaney's only talking picture and his final film. On August 26, 1930, the man of a thousand faces wore his final mask in death. He was forty-seven years old. Chaney was laid to rest in a modest unmarked crypt in Glendale's Forest Lawn Memorial Park Cemetery. During the funeral, Hollywood's film studios observed two minutes of silence, honoring the man who, through his portrayal of monsters, had shown audiences what it meant to be human. Chaney left a legacy of more than one hundred films, inspiring generations of filmmakers and moviegoers. Creighton Chaney later assumed his father's name, becoming famous in his own right as Larry Talbot in *The Wolf Man*.

LON CHANEY
1883–1930

BIBLIOGRAPHY

MICHAEL F. BLAKE,
LON CHANEY: THE MAN
BEHIND THE THOUSAND FACES,
1997, VESTAL PRESS, INC.

MICHAEL F. BLAKE,
A THOUSAND FACES:
LON CHANEY'S UNIQUE
ARTISTRY IN MOTION PICTURES,
1995, VESTAL PRESS, INC.

FORREST J. ACKERMAN,
LON OF 1000 FACES,
2002, JAMES A ROCK
& CO. PUBLISHERS.

ROBERT G. ANDERSON,
FACES, FORMS, FILMS:
THE ARTISTRY OF LON CHANEY,
1971, A. S. BARNES & CO., INC.

JAMES M. FETTERS,
LON CHANEY SCRAPBOOK:
A COLLECTION OF FILM ADS,
NEWSPAPER ARTICLES AND
PHOTOS FROM 1909
THROUGH 1930 AND BEYOND,
2015, JAMES M. FETTERS

ACKNOWLEDGMENTS

THE AUTHOR WOULD LIKE TO THANK MARSHAL
ARISMAN, NICK BERTOZZI, JUSTIN COFFEE, CHRIS
DUFFY, RYAN FLANDERS, SHANE GLINES, CHESTER
GOULD, EDWARD HEMINGWAY, ALTIE KARPER, CHIP
KIDD, BEN MARRA, MARK MINNING, CHARLIE
OLSEN, ERIC RUTLEDGE, OTTO SOGLOW, WILLIAM
STEIG, OSAMU TEZUKA, NICK VERBANIC, JONATHAN
WEBB, VIVIAN WEBB, AND LAUREN WEINSTEIN.

ABOUT THE AUTHOR

PAT DORIAN IS A DESIGNER AND
ANIMATOR WHO TEACHES AT THE
SCHOOL OF VISUAL ARTS AND THE
PRATT INSTITUTE IN NEW YORK.
HIS ILLUSTRATIONS HAVE APPEARED
IN THE NEW YORKER, THE NEW YORK
TIMES, MAD MAGAZINE, AND OTHER
NATIONAL PUBLICATIONS. HE HAS
WORKED ON ANIMATION PROJECTS
FOR THE CARTOON NETWORK AND
COMEDY CENTRAL. HIS MINI-COMIC
ON LON CHANEY WON THE 2016 MOCCA
ARTS FESTIVAL AWARD OF EXCELLENCE
AND EVENTUALLY BECAME THIS BOOK.
THIS IS HIS FIRST GRAPHIC NOVEL.
PLEASE VISIT PATDORIAN.COM FOR
MORE INFORMATION.

ALL RIGHTS RESERVED. PUBLISHED IN THE UNITED STATES BY PANTHEON BOOKS,
A DIVISION OF PENGUIN RANDOM HOUSE LLC, NEW YORK, AND DISTRIBUTED
IN CANADA BY PENGUIN RANDOM HOUSE CANADA LIMITED, TORONTO.

PANTHEON BOOKS AND COLOPHON ARE REGISTERED TRADEMARKS OF PENGUIN RANDOM HOUSE LLC.

LIBRARY OF CONGRESS CATALOGING-IN-PUBLICATION DATA
NAME: DORIAN, PAT, AUTHOR, ARTIST.
TITLE: LON CHANEY SPEAKS / PAT DORIAN.
DESCRIPTION: FIRST EDITION. NEW YORK : PANTHEON BOOKS, 2020.
SERIES: PANTHEON GRAPHIC LIBRARY.
IDENTIFIERS: LCCN 2020000913 (PRINT). LCCN 2020000914 (EBOOK). ISBN 9781524747435
(HARDCOVER). ISBN 9781524747442 (EBOOK).
SUBJECTS: LCSH: CHANEY, LON, 1883-1930—COMIC BOOKS, STRIPS, ETC. MOTION PICTURE ACTORS
AND ACTRESSES—UNITED STATES—BIOGRAPHY—COMIC BOOKS, STRIPS, ETC. GRAPHIC NOVELS.
CLASSIFICATION: LCC PN2287.C48 D67 2020 (PRINT) | LCC PN2287.C48 (EBOOK) | DDC
791.4302/8092 [B]—DC23
LC RECORD AVAILABLE AT LCCN.LOC.GOV/2020000913
LC EBOOK RECORD AVAILABLE AT LCCN.LOC.GOV/2020000914

WWW.PANTHEONBOOKS.COM

PRINTED IN CHINA

FIRST EDITION
9 8 7 6 5 4 3 2 1

Now Playing

LON CHANEY talks~

and NOT in ONE Voice but FIVE!

The mystery star of the silent screen becomes more amazing, more surprising in this gripping All-Talking story of three outcasts who form a partnership of crime.

1 The Voice of the Old Woman
2 The Parrot
3 The Dummy
4 The Girl
5 His Own Voice

... SEE and HEAR...

"The UNHOLY 3"

Metro's All-Talking Triumph

with

Lila Lee Elliott Nugent

Ivan Linow

"I wouldn't be at all surprized to find that *The Unholy Three* becomes the best American motion picture of the year."

—Frederick James Smith in *Motion Picture Classic*

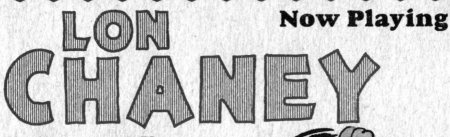

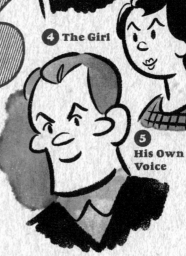

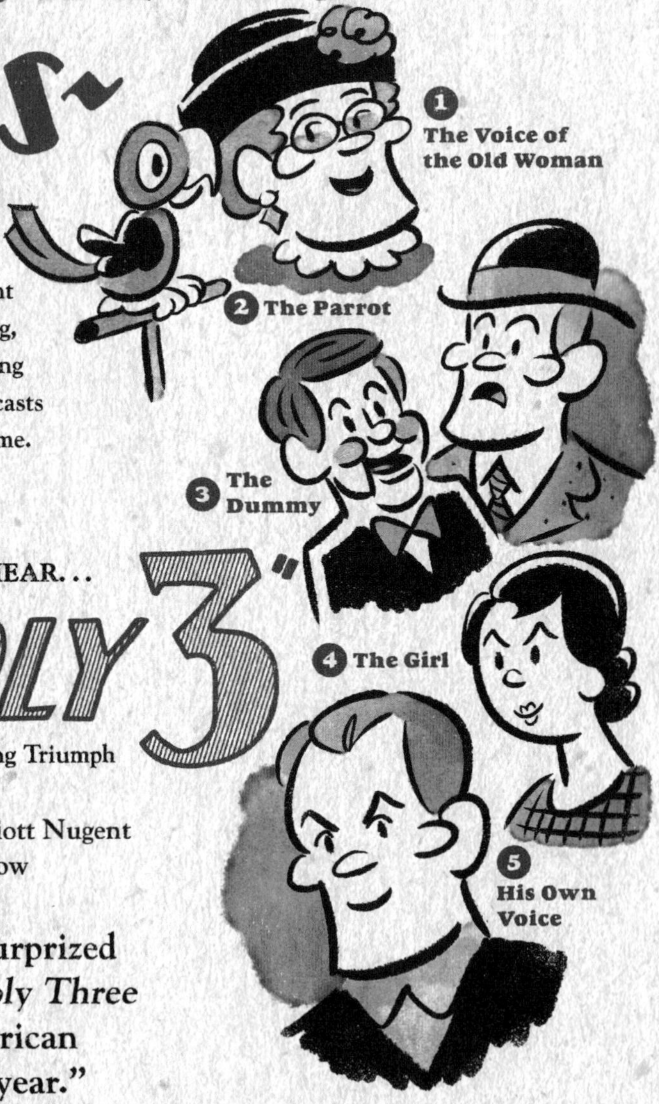

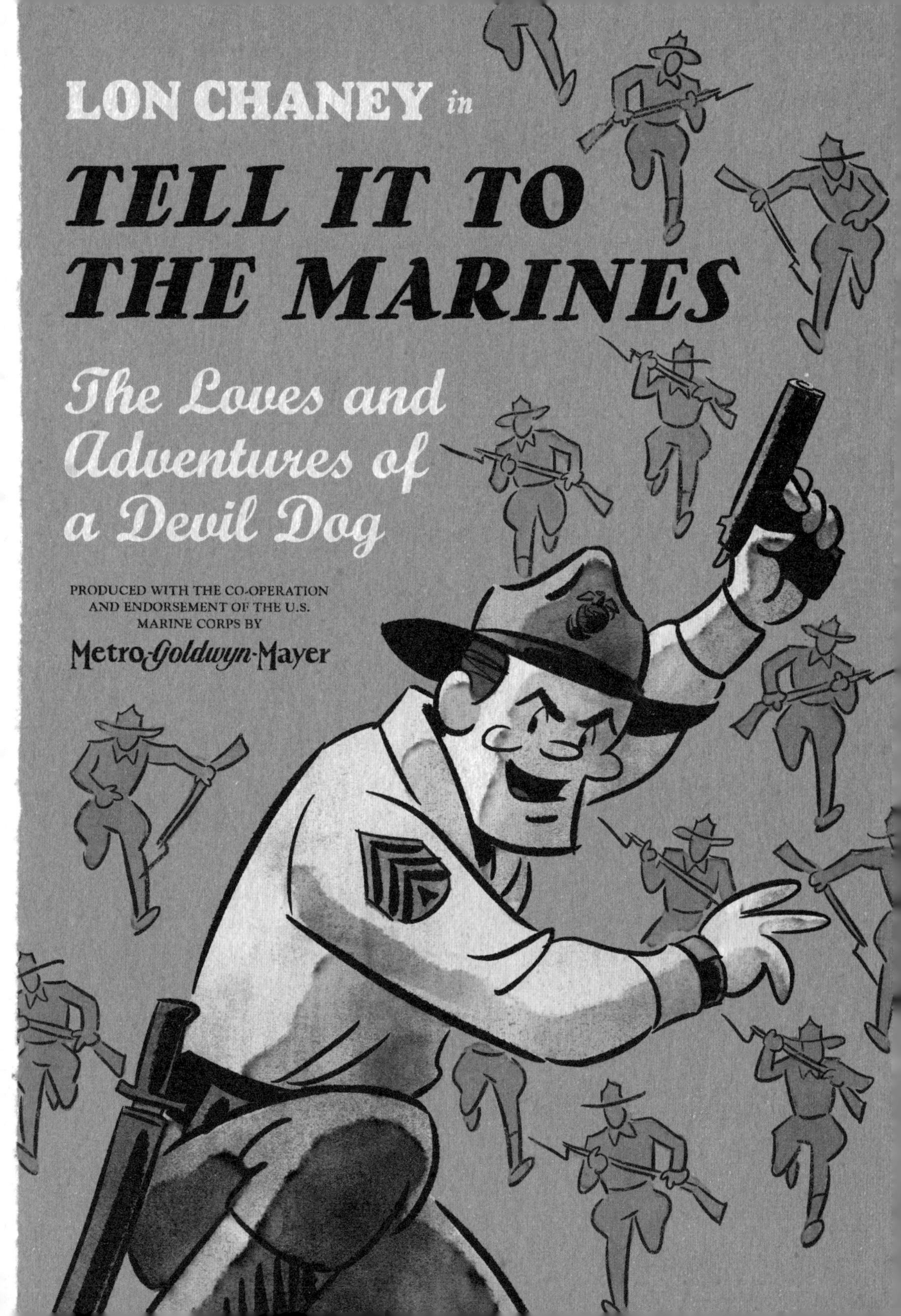
LON CHANEY in
TELL IT TO THE MARINES
The Loves and Adventures of a Devil Dog
PRODUCED WITH THE CO-OPERATION AND ENDORSEMENT OF THE U.S. MARINE CORPS BY
Metro-Goldwyn-Mayer

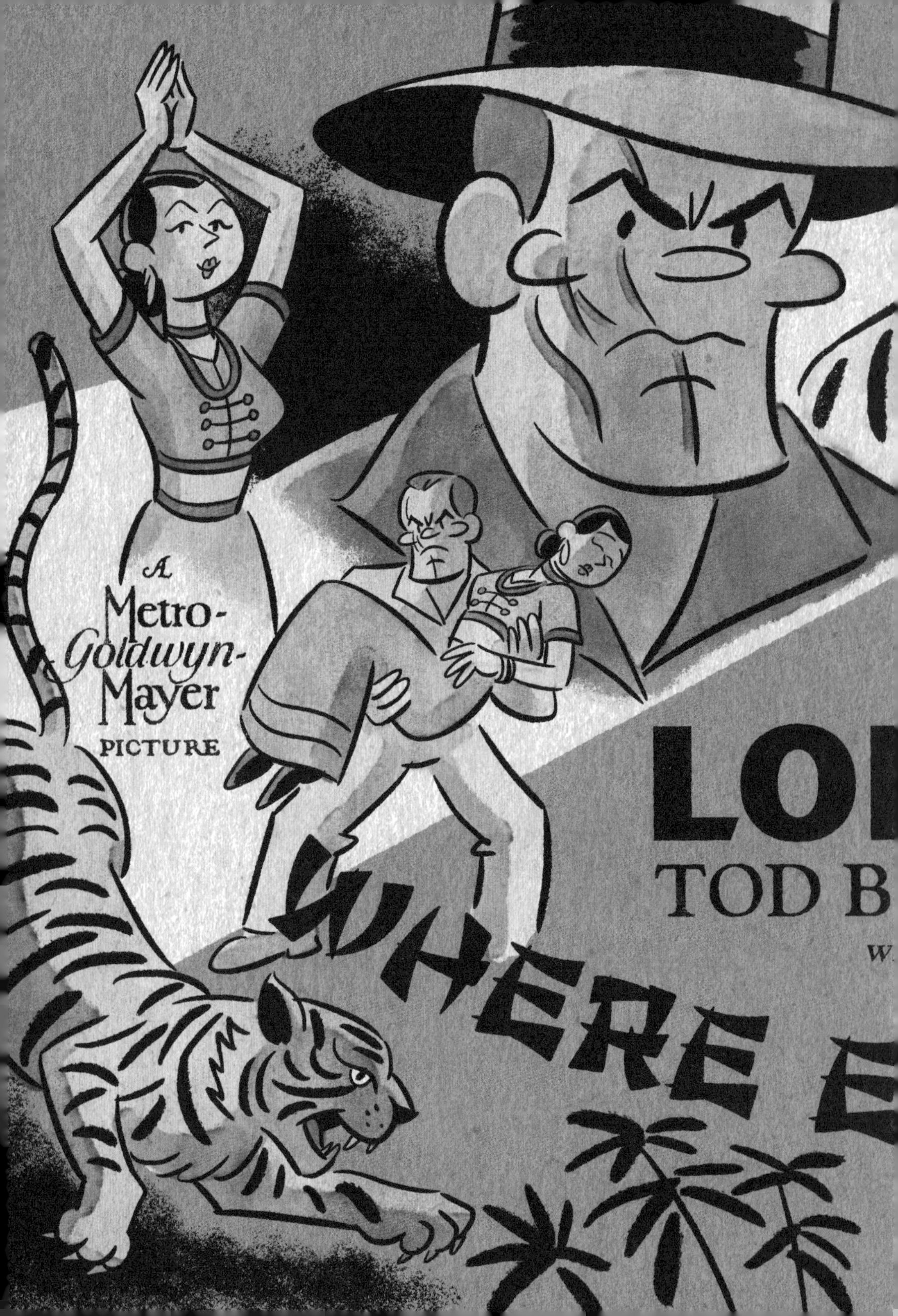
A Metro-Goldwyn-Mayer PICTURE
LO
TOD B
W
HERE E